Great Films and How to Teach Them

Great Films and How to Teach Them

William V. Costanzo
Westchester Community College

National Council of Teachers of English
1111 W. Kenyon Road, Urbana, Illinois 61801-1096

Film photos courtesy of Photofest, 32 East 31st Street, 5th Fl., New York, New York 10016.

Staff Editor: Bonny Graham
Interior Design: Doug Burnett
Cover Design: Pat Mayer

NCTE Stock Number: 39094

Library of Congress Cataloging-in-Publication Data

Costanzo, William V.
    Great films and how to teach them / William V. Costanzo
        p. cm.
    Revision of the author's Reading the movies.
    Includes bibliographical references.
    ISBN 0-8141-3909-4
    1. Motion pictures—Study and teaching. 2. Motion pictures and literature. 3. Motion pictures—Philosophy. 4. Film criticism. I. Costanzo, William V. Reading the movies. II. Title.
    PN1993.7.C59 2004
    791.43'071—dc22

                                        2004013869

To Marlene, with whom I am rewriting the script of my life.

Contents

Preface

*G*reat Films and How to Teach Them is a kind of sequel. Like any movie sequel, it is meant to build on an earlier success. For some time now, the editors at NCTE and other colleagues have been asking me to follow up *Reading the Movies,* published in 1992. They have pointed out the many great films that have appeared during the past ten years as well as significant advances in film studies, film technology, and the film industry itself. Who can disagree? In my own classes, I have noticed many changes. My current students seem much more informed about the movies than their predecessors. They know hundreds of titles, quote entire scenes by heart, and talk about the latest actors and directors as if they were family. Their casual conversation is filled with allusions to the world of cinema. They know all about the business side of motion pictures, watch behind-the-scenes interviews on DVD, and share the hottest movie Web sites. In short, as times have changed, movies have become ever more visible signposts of the times. My teaching, too, has reflected these changes. I find myself including more cultural issues in my classes, addressing questions of representation and ideology, and acknowledging the younger generation's special savvy about film genres, special effects, and box office sales. At times, I even rely on their technical knowledge when the computer fails or the DVD player misbehaves.

To keep abreast of all these changes has required more than a simple updating of material. More than 80 percent of this book is completely new. All of the original chapters in Part I have been carefully revised, and three chapters have been added, on film genres, the business of film, and representation in film. I have added many more great films to Appendix 1, tripled the number of film projects in Appendix 2, and introduced a new appendix on film Web sites. The biggest change, however, is in Part II. Videocassettes were new in 1992, and DVDs had not yet been invented. The fourteen films included in this section are all available on DVD, most with special features. Some of these, like *Casablanca* (1942), are classics; many, like *The Matrix* (1999), have been released within the past few years. As a result, this book is more complete and current than its predecessor. It also contains a glossary of film-related terms, which is new to this edition. Terms highlighted in boldface throughout the text are defined in the glossary at the back of the book.

As any teacher can attest, many students are more familiar with movies than they are with books. They "read" and "re-read" them with an enthusiasm that owes little to teacher prompting. Through film more than books, kids today discover the importance of close viewing, of watching a movie several times in order to understand how it works. For most of us, the magic of motion pictures sweeps us through an imaginary world in a state of voluntary credulity. The first time we watch a film we want to believe that what we see is really happening. Not until the second or third screening is the spell broken. That's when we begin to notice the camera work, appreciate the nuances of acting, or spot the bloopers in the script. In the act of re-reading, we shift gears and engage the critical eye.

There is also something pleasurable in repetition. Children love watching the same movie again and again, just as they enjoy listening to the same bedtime story night after night. A national study conducted at the Annenberg School in Pennsylvania found that 70 percent of children ages two to four watch a video more than once (Yoffe). The ritual is comforting, perhaps because the certainty of knowing what comes next offers assurances not always found in daily life. The finite world of Shrek or Nemo is something a child can master with the rewind button. By watching their favorite video with a remote control, replaying the funny parts or the confusing scenes, kids gain some measure of command over their emotional and cognitive experience. As children grow older, the desire to repeat a film seems to decline somewhat, but it rises again during the teenage years, boosted by new motives. Teenagers enjoy watching movies together, at sleepovers and midnight cult performances. They imitate their favorite actors and anticipate the dialogue in one voice. For young viewers, re-reading the movies is a shared experience, a satisfyingly social activity.

Thanks to advances in technology, all this re-reading is easier to do than it was in 1992. Movies are more available, compact, and portable than ever before. Within months of its theatrical release, we can copy a new film from cable television, buy or rent it for home use, or download it into a computer and watch it on a palm-sized screen. With a remote control or a keyboard, we can analyze great movies as we analyze great books, slowing down selected moments, replaying key scenes, clipping images and sound bytes for close inspection. Meanwhile, as home sales increase, distributors are bringing out the classics in attractive new editions. Many DVDs offer sharper image quality, restored sound tracks, and dozens of "extras," such as production notes, interviews, running commentaries by directors— much like the variorum editions of literary texts.

If movies have become the premier literature of our time, it makes sense to include film study as a regular part of the national curriculum. This is particularly true of English classes, where movies can be read and re-read alongside other forms of storytelling as mirrors of our culture, chronicles of our history, and influential shapers of our daily lives.

Acknowledgments

I wish to acknowledge the dedicated publications staff at NCTE. Pete Feely, former acquisitions editor, got me started on this project. Director of Book Publications Zarina Hock guided me through the composing and production process with her unfailing enthusiasm, gentle wisdom, and abiding support. Bonny Graham, staff editor, reviewed the entire manuscript, tracing my references and sharpening my prose with her incisive eye for detail, clear-sighted judgment, and merciful tact.

For more than thirty years, Westchester Community College has been my academic home. I am grateful to Dr. Joseph N. Hankin, its dedicated president, for sustaining an environment that fosters excellence in teaching while supporting the efforts of faculty to grow through scholarship and publication. The library staff at WCC is first-rate, and I especially wish to thank Chris Kern, Alice DeWaters, Dorothy Freeman, Dale Leifeste, Sandy Schepis, and Una Shih for assisting me with my research. It has been my privilege to work alongside talented colleagues such as Frank Madden, Michael Bobkoff, Greta Cohan, Linda Sledge, and others who continue to inspire. It has been my special pleasure to watch each generation of students pass through our classes, taking with them new views of literature and film and always leaving something precious behind.

Finally, I want to thank three special people in my life. Jonathan Lovell has contributed to my work through his immutable friendship. Eugene Feit offered his expertise in history and his abiding interest in everything I write. Marlene was always at my side, reviewing countless versions of the manuscript, suggesting apt changes, and buoying my efforts with her unwavering belief in me. Without her, this would not be the book it has become.

Introduction

What if all the motion pictures ever made were suddenly to disappear? What would we have lost? There would be no trace of *Star Wars* (1977), *Gone with the Wind* (1939), or *It's a Wonderful Life* (1946). No Little Tramp, no Humphrey Bogart, Bette Davis, Mickey Mouse. If, along with the films themselves, all recollection of them vanished too, we would have no mental images of Gene Kelly singin' in the rain, of King Kong astride the Empire State Building, of Richard Gere climbing the fire escape like a fairy-tale prince to Julia Roberts in *Pretty Woman* (1990). A good portion of our collective visual memory would have disappeared. And since these images are shared around the world, their loss would deeply diminish our global heritage.

More than pictures would be lost. We would probably have to expunge from our vocabulary terms such as *close-up, freeze-frame, reverse angle, fade-out, morphing,* and *out of sync,* along with the perceptual habits they name. Gone with the films would be the countless ways in which they have trained us to observe the world. Without the model of the movies, much of our mental editing, focusing, and filtering would be unthinkable.

Beyond the stories, images, and cinematic methods, there is the industry itself. What if all the people, places, and things associated with the movies were to vanish too? Imagine no more movie theaters, film distributors, studios, or video rental stores. A huge chunk would be gouged out of the national economy. So would a large portion of the working population. Gone would be the screen stars, writers, film directors, camera operators, sound technicians, gaffers, and gofers who populate the movie world. Gone would be their cameras, editing machines, projectors, props—the tools of the trade that make it possible to mass-produce those animated stories for a mass audience.

Beyond the stories, too, are the issues they illuminate. Consider how *I Am a Fugitive from a Chain Gang* (1932) focused national attention on prison reform during the thirties, how the Why We Fight series (1943–1945) contributed to the war effort during the forties, how films like *Rebel without a Cause* (1955) highlighted the problems of alienated youth during the fifties. More recent films have raised contemporary issues to new levels of awareness, among them Steven Spielberg's *Schindler's List* (1993), Spike Lee's *Bamboozled* (2000), Michael Mann's *The Insider* (1999), and Michael Moore's *Bowling for Columbine* (2002). For decades, movies have projected the concerns of every generation onto the nation's screen of consciousness. What would our shared view of world events be like without them?

Then there is the film experience itself, the feeling of being pulled into another world, a place of deferred resistance or suspended disbelief where we can be, for a little while, in someone else's skin, on intimate terms with the unfamiliar, or face-to-face with our own repressed desires. What is this experience that we would lose if it were never possible to have "lost it at the movies"?

The Need to Study Film

Somewhere in this vision of a world without motion pictures are good reasons for studying film. Since their invention well over a century ago, movies have become a significant component of our culture, part of our individual and collective lives. Something of this magnitude demands careful, serious attention, as many teachers, particularly teachers of English, have come to recognize.

"We live in a total-information culture, which is being increasingly dominated by the image," observed John Culkin more than three decades ago. "Intelligent living within such an environment calls for developing habits of perception, analysis, judgment, and selectivity that are capable of processing the relentless input of visual data." Culkin called on the schools to shape these habits. "Schools are where the tribe passes on its values to the young. Schools are where film study should take place" (Schillaci and Culkin 19). In high schools across the country, teachers like Ralph Amelio have taken this challenge to heart. Amelio created a film program at Willowbrook High School in Chicago "to develop in the student the habits of analysis, criticism, understanding, and appreciation of film in a disciplined and creative manner." Amelio linked this goal to the humanistic education of his students, allowing them "to gain insight and aesthetic enjoyment of [their] own experience and of others through film" (7). At the University of Iowa, Dudley Andrew pursued similar objectives within a college setting. To Andrew, "films are cultural objects to be mastered and experiences that continually master us. . . . Education," he believes, "is best served by a dialectic that forces us to interrogate films and then to interrogate ourselves in front of films" ("An Open Approach" 43–44).

The academy has come a long way since the work of these film study pioneers. Their philosophy is now supported by educational organizations such as the National Council of Teachers of English (NCTE) and the International Reading Association (IRA). NCTE and IRA include film study in their *Standards for the English Language Arts,* asserting that "nonprint texts are an essential part of students' reading experience" and encouraging "opportunities to study and create visual texts—including narrative and documentary films, television, advertisements, maps, illustrations, multimedia/CD resources, and other graphic displays." In 1997 NCTE adopted a resolution affirming its position "that media literacy courses meeting the same academic standards of other high school English courses be counted as English credit for admission to universities and colleges" ("On Media Literacy").

Many students already recognize the significance of movies in their daily lives. From a survey that I give my classes every term, I have been astonished to learn that they are now watching an average of twenty films a month. They watch films on broadcast television, cable networks, videocassettes, digital video discs (DVDs), and the Internet, as well as in local theaters. It's not unusual for them to spend an evening with friends watching a double feature in the family entertainment center or to chain-view several movies at the multiplex. Why do they want to study film? Why devote school time to the movies when films are everywhere? My students are fascinated by the pull of motion pictures. "I can forget it's not real sometimes," they say. "I get swept away." They want to understand what lies behind their own attraction to the screen. Many are curious about the creative work that goes into a movie. They want to learn how films are made, how they're "put together," what goes on behind the camera and beyond the screen. More than a few have tried their hand at acting or photography; they are interested in learning more about the people who make films. Nearly all want to be more knowledgeable viewers, to know about the history, the technology, the art, the craft, the principles that drive the films they love to watch.

These are favorable times, then, to bring movies into the mainstream of education, to make film study part of the ongoing curriculum. There has never been a clearer rationale, a more convincing theoretical framework, or a stronger factual foundation on which to build. What's more, recent advances in technology have made the study of film more practical, more practicable than ever before. Anyone with a VCR or DVD player now has access to the same film titles that were available to a few privileged libraries and universities only fifteen years ago. Furthermore, by pressing a few buttons on a standard remote-control device, any teacher or student can perform feats of film analysis that used to require costly, intricate equipment using fragile 16mm film.

The Home Theater Revolution

The **videocassette recorder (VCR), digital video disc (DVD),** and kindred technologies have revolutionized the movies. VCRs and DVD players are much simpler to operate than projectors. Movies in these formats are now easier to carry, less expensive, and more readily available than reels of film. As a result, the technology has changed not only the way we watch and study movies but also the film industry itself.

Movies have become more like books. A digital videodisk can fit into a backpack or be stored on any bookshelf. This means that the film version of *To Kill a Mockingbird* (1962) can sit next to the novel in your literature collection or be carried to class along with the book. Students and their teachers now lend one another copies of Kenneth Branagh's *Hamlet* (1996) or Baz Luhrmann's *Romeo + Juliet* (1996) as readily as they trade copies of the printed plays. My own students often hand in film-study assignments with a cassette already cued to the pertinent scene.

As these formats become more accessible, the number of available films grows. Film titles have proliferated in rental shops, retail stores, and libraries, as well as in supermarkets. People now regularly scan the shelves for a promising film title as they would for a good book. At home, they sometimes watch the video with habits carried over from their reading. They might replay a compelling scene, skip over tedious sections of the story, or save their place at any point. The scan, fast-forward, freeze, and electronic bookmark features of home units give users nearly as much control over their viewing as they have over their reading. With a computer, they can even insert segments of the movie into a multimedia presentation much as they might quote selections from a novel in a research paper.

What does all this mean for the current and future status of film? First, more people are watching more movies. Most homes in the United States now have facilities for showing videos or DVDs. Film sales and rentals for these formats have become multibillion-dollar industries. With many thousands of titles to choose from, Americans have more options than ever before. While not every title is a movie classic, the increasing availability of films has made viewers more conscious of the classics, and it has made the classics easier to see. As people become more experienced viewers, they become curious about the history of film; they want to see earlier examples of their favorite genres and watch other movies featuring their favorite stars or made by the same directors. They are more interested in trying other kinds of movies, including foreign films with subtitles. The more they watch, the more knowledgeable viewers become. The nation is becoming more film literate. And through more widespread exposure to international cinema, it is becoming more globally aware.

This, in turn, creates a larger market for movies. The early fears that home videos would siphon off audiences from the theaters have proved ill founded. In fact, the opposite has happened. Increased revenues from video and DVD sales have enabled film producers to make more movies and rebuild the theater-going audience. This trend has been particularly kind to early films. Film distributors who once were reluctant to bother with old movies now are willing to look for the best available prints and invest in their restoration. On the whole, the movie industry is healthier today than it was just before videocassettes arrived on the scene.

The DVD Experience

In addition to its influence on audience viewing habits and the film industry, digital video is changing the experience of watching films. Part of this experience is technological, part may be perceptual, and part is social and environmental.

Traditional video technology requires that the large-screen image of the theater be shrunk to the proportions of television, thus reducing picture quality. Some of the picture is sacrificed when the rectangular dimensions of the wide screen are clipped to fit the conventional boxlike television screen. Photographic values are also lost. The range of contrast between the brightest and darkest shades of an optical (film) image can be as high as 100 to 1. In a conventional electronic (video) image, the ratio is only 20 to 1. This means that the video version of a movie has only one-fifth as much contrast as the original film (Fantel, "Film to Video" 32). Along with these gradations of detail, much of the rich color and three-dimensional effect of deep-focus photography is diminished in the smaller frame. This is particularly true of those larger-than-life films like *Citizen Kane* (1941) and *Lawrence of Arabia* (1962). Their sense of space and subtlety of tone tend to be eclipsed on video by dialogue and story. Since what survived best is the script, Joseph Mankiewicz and Woody Allen translate better than Orson Welles and David Lean.

Yet this picture is changing with improvements in technology. High-resolution television and wider screens are restoring film aesthetics. **High-definition television (HDTV)** uses more lines to draw a picture on the screen, resulting in clearer images. The new, wider screen dimensions accommodate the full width of most movies instead of cutting off one-third of the picture, as the squarish television screens do. Along with other enhancements, such as Dolby Surround sound, these advances are bringing much of the theatrical quality of movies into the modern home.

But there is more to watching movies than just the images and sounds, however they are produced. There is also the social and environmental context. Compare the experience of sitting in a darkened theater with a group of strangers, concentrating on the screen, to the experience at home, where the surroundings are familiar, the lights are likely to be on, and attention is diverted by innumerable distractions. Going out to the movies makes the act of viewing a more focused event. A larger audience tends to magnify the experience; it multiplies the laughter and the tears. Furthermore, when a movie is projected on the screen, it seems to have its own momentum. Without a remote-control device with which to tinker with the sound or speed, it's easier to be swept along. Nonetheless, advances in digital technology have increased the popularity of videos and their usefulness in the classroom.

VHS and DVD in the Classroom

With so many new technologies competing for the market, a teacher can get lost in the alphabet soup of formats and machinery. The half-inch videocassettes that most of us have used in our VCRs since the 1980s are part of **video home system (VHS)** technology. The VCR records movies on magnetic tape in analog form; that is, the images and sounds are stored as fluctuating signals on the tape. A disadvantage of this format is that the movie quality declines as the recorded signals deteriorate through use. Digital technology records visual and auditory information differently, as binary data, which means that it can be more easily handled by computers and is not degraded by constant use. Digital data are encoded as tiny pits arranged in layered spirals, which makes it possible to compress a whole movie onto a 120mm disc.

The first commercial DVDs were introduced in 1997. Since DVD technology can store a full-length movie on a disc the size of a compact disc (CD), it has proved ideal for film. In 2001, consumers spent $4.6 billion on DVDs, more than twice as much as the year before, the first time that DVD sales exceeded video sales. DVD offers many advantages over VHS. The quality of picture and sound is far superior. Because so much information can fit onto a single disc, a DVD lets viewers screen a movie in several versions. They can watch it in letterboxed or wide-screen formats, listen to the dialogue in different languages, or hear a running commentary by the director. DVDs also have certain interactive features, enabling viewers to jump directly to preselected scenes or "chapters." Even more important for film study are the many "extras" that are routinely packaged with the main feature. The five-disc boxed set of *The Godfather* trilogy (2001) includes production stills, storyboards, theatrical trailers, unused footage, interviews with the filmmakers, and a behind-the-scenes documentary. The "special extended edition" of *The Lord of The Rings: The Fellowship of the Ring* (2002) devotes an entire disc to the process of adapting the book into a screenplay and planning for the film. It also features a longer version of the movie and quantities of material related to production itself. These special DVDs are comparable to the variorum editions of printed texts.

All this may seem both bewitching and bewildering to teachers of English who are concerned about preparation, curricular priorities, and time. Their uneasiness can be heard in the faculty lounge: "I'm an English teacher, not a media specialist. I know that movies have this power, but I have no special training to teach them. Most of my students know more than I do about films"; "My main business is with reading, writing, listening, and speaking; I just don't have much time for showing movies"; "Yes, I know that many of my kids prefer to watch the movie than to read the book, but what can I do about it?"; "Actually, I feel a little guilty if we're having fun."

This book is partly a response to voices such as these. It will not answer all the arguments or allay all the anxieties, but for those who recognize the importance of film in their students' lives and want to acknowledge this importance in their classrooms—actively, productively, significantly—*Great Films and How to Teach Them* is offered as a resource and a guide.

Organization of the Book

I have divided the book into two parts. Each chapter in Part I takes up an area of film study that has been productively explored by scholars and offers rewarding opportunities for further exploration by students and teachers. Chapter 1 adopts an aesthetic view. It considers filmmaking as an art, especially an art of storytelling, comparing literary narratives to cinematic narratives, as well as film's relationship to the other arts. Chapter 2 traces the codes and conventions that enable us to understand a film. Drawing on research in semiotics and viewer response, this chapter considers the degree to which watching movies is a natural or a learned behavior and the degree to which cinema constitutes a language or symbol system. In so doing, it clarifies the place of film study among the language arts. The technical side of film production—the machinery behind the movies and the people behind the machines—is discussed in Chapter 3, while Chapter 4 gives a concise chronology of film from its beginnings to the present, identifying major trends and variations. Chapter 5 looks at film as a business, tracing the industry's growth from Edison's Kinetoscope to the studio system and today's media conglomerates. Chapter 6 is a survey of film theory. It introduces some of the most influential and illuminating thoughts on the nature of cinema and its place in our culture and our private lives. This is followed by chapters on film genres and representation. Chapter 7 asks why genres come and go, exploring the nature of genres as diverse as Westerns, science fiction, horror, screwball comedy, and film noir. Chapter 8 asks how movies represent the diversity of American identities. It follows the changing images of African Americans, Latinos, Asians, Jews, gays, and other groups throughout the history of American cinema. Concluding the first section is Chapter 9, which provides an overview of film study in the profession, including pedagogical trends, various approaches, classroom methods, activities, assignments, and issues of censorship and copyright.

Part II focuses on fourteen films that have proved successful in the classroom. For each film, I have included screen credits, cast listings, background information, discussion questions, topics for further study, and suggested films and readings. In selecting these films, I found it difficult to be fully representative. The list does span a range of periods and styles (from *Casablanca* to *The Matrix*), genres (gangster, combat, comedy), and themes (growing up, society and individuality, the American dream), but there are inevitable omissions and some uneasy proportions. There are no silent films, for example, or documentaries; there are only a few international films, three films directed by women, and none directed by an African American. For the most part, I have chosen mainstream American feature films—all screened in class with favorable results—under the assumption that readers will make their own selections and supplement these films to suit their students and objectives.

Let me explain my choices. I emphasize feature films because they are closer to the content of most English courses than are documentaries or experimental films. Because they tell a story, feature films can be read as literature. I emphasize American films because they are more readily available and easier to read than foreign films, both culturally and literally. Students who have seen few foreign-language films often are distracted by the subtitles, especially on a small screen. That doesn't mean our students ought to go through life as cinematic xenophobes; a judicious introduction to films from other countries can open their eyes to worlds beyond the American screen.

Initially, my students are as resistant to black-and-white photography as they are to literary classics, but they often thank me for introducing them to Humphrey Bogart, Katharine Hepburn, Clark Gable, and other "old-time greats." Once they get used to the idea of watching movies made before 1990, once past the barrier of unfamiliarity, they even seek more classics on their own. Yet a course based entirely on the traditional film canon would have disadvantages. There is the issue of value, for example. What makes a movie great? Who decides when a film becomes a classic? By including recent films that have not yet stood the test of time, we give students the chance to evaluate movies before telling them they have been watching an acknowledged masterpiece or a fleeting fad. Then there are issues of authorship and representation. The sexual and racial history of Hollywood and of the nation has included few women or minority directors. With a few exceptions, it is only in the last decade or so that filmmakers like Mira Nair, Gurinder Chadha, and Niki Caro have had access to the means of film production for a large audience. I have selected films like *Mississippi Masala, Bend It Like Beckham, Glory, Run Lola Run*, and *The Matrix*—all made within the last fifteen years—partly to restore some balance to the classical canon. But I have also included them because, with my students, I believe them to be well-made films about important subjects. Fortunately, videocassettes and DVDs have reduced the span between a film's appearance and its availability for study. No longer do schools have to wait ten years to buy a 16mm print, then keep it for another twenty to justify the cost. Our film libraries need not smell like mausoleums.

My list of fourteen great films, then, is only one of many possibilities. The list of "More Great Films" (Appendix 1) offers some alternatives, while Appendix 2 suggests some specific projects, and Appendix 3 provides an annotated list of film-related Web sites. Your readings, your students, and your film experiences will give you still more options. And that is what I've aimed for. If this book encourages you to create your own film course, or to introduce films in your classes with greater confidence, awareness, and success, it will have served its purpose.

Note

Throughout the book, I have included a release date for each film the first time it is mentioned. Since this date can vary from source to source, I have checked my dates against the three most reliable sources I know: Bruce Kawin and Gerald Mast's *A Short History of the Movies, Leonard Maltin's Movie & Video Guide*, and the Internet Movie Database (IMDb) at www.imdb.com. In instances when these sources disagree, I follow Kawin, Maltin, and IMDb in that order. Occasionally, when a film was made and released in different years, I give both dates if it seems relevant.

I Reading the Movies

1 The Art of Fiction Film

Why see the movie if you've read the book? Why read the book if you've already seen the movie? One reason such questions keep coming up lies in the extraordinary number of movies that are based on literature. John Harrington estimated that one-third of all films ever made are derived from novels (*"Film and/as Literature* 117). Dudley Andrew put the figure closer to 50 percent ("Adaptation" 29). If we add other literary forms, such as drama and short stories, the estimates increase. We know that movies such as *A Passage to India* (1984) and *Mrs. Dalloway* (1998) can reach a greater audience in a few weeks than the books have enjoyed since they were published. We also know that a successful movie adaptation can catapult a book high up on the bestseller list.

Beyond questions of numbers, the practice of comparing literature and film raises deeper issues about literacy, contrasting media, and the purposes of art. Consider these statements made by students in a first-year literature class that includes the study of both literature and film:

> In high school, when I read *To Kill a Mockingbird,* I kept getting distracted. I couldn't get the full meaning of the book. Then I borrowed the videotape and watched it with some friends. That's when I really enjoyed and understood the story.

> Film lets you see pictures of what's going on. I got more out of watching *Julius Caesar* than out of reading just the words.

> Literature provides more stimulation than movies. In a film, it's all provided for you. When I saw *Lord of the Flies,* I was disappointed in the characters.

> Film can use things like lighting and sound to create effects that are not really possible in literature. It was hard for me to follow the scene changes when I read *Death of a Salesman,* but I could see [them] clearly in the movie.

> Film can distort the story in translating it to the screen. Young children may never learn to read if we show movies instead of giving them books.

> Film is another form of storytelling. Film should be taught as film.

> Film and literature should go hand in hand.

Teachers of English will recognize the seeds of a debate here, the first steps of an inquiry into the nature of narrative and our universal need for stories. What do we look for in a story? What do literary texts and fiction films deliver? What are the common elements and the differences in their delivery? What does it mean to be "faithful to the book"? How have literature and film influenced each other? How are they related to music, architecture, dance, and the other arts?

The Art of Storytelling

We are dealing here with films and books that narrate stories. Scholars like Seymour Chatman use the term *narratology* to emphasize the shared features of storytelling, no matter what the medium may be: a speech, a written text, a movie, or a dance. In the history of narrative, film is a latecomer. Homer's epics date back to about 800 BC, the novel is generally said to have begun in the eighteenth century, the short story in the early nineteenth century, but movies have been around only since the 1890s. Yet we know that each new narrative form derives from earlier traditions. The *Odyssey* and *Beowulf* can be traced to stories developed and preserved through earlier oral forms. The novel has its origins in the Renaissance novella, the medieval romance, and even works of classical antiquity such as *The Satyricon.* The short story form reaches back to folklore, myth, fable, and parables. So it should not surprise us that film, too, draws on earlier strategies and structures of narration.

Chatman distinguishes between story and **discourse,** the "what" and the "how" of narrative. He identifies story with plot, character, setting, and the other elements that critics have traditionally ascribed to a story's "content." He identifies discourse with the means by which a story is communicated. From this point of view, a novel and a film might share the same story, say of Anna Karenina, but they may vary widely in their literary or cinematic forms of discourse. The novel represents the character of Anna in printed words, through dialogue, description, interior monologue, and the author's comments. The 1935 film represents Anna in sound and moving images: the gestures, face, and voice of Greta Garbo complemented by the conventions of music, sound effects, costumes, sets, camera work, and a supporting cast.

Our perceptions of Anna depend partly on our understanding of literary, cinematic, and socially constructed codes. As viewers, we know that Anna is in love with Vronsky by the light in Garbo's eyes and the warmth in her voice. We also know this from the camera's lingering close-ups and the music swelling through the sound track. We have learned to read these signs by watching people and from watching films. As readers, in a sense we have less work to do because Tolstoy interprets Anna's face for us. His description makes us see the flash in her eyes, the brimming smile. At one point, he simply tells us she's in love.

Our understanding of character also depends on another element of narrative: point of view. A novel or short story can be related from varying perspectives, ranging from omniscient to restricted, objective to subjective, and authoritative to unreliable. As readers, we learn to weigh information according to its source, so we look for clues about the story's point of view. We look for contradictions between the author and the authorial voice, between dialogue and monologue, between speech and action. In John Cheever's story "The Swimmer," bits of overheard conversation and references to changing seasons hint that the story is being told from the protagonist's subjective and increasingly questionable perspective, that the events take place over a period of years, not in a single day. The movie version (1968) follows the same unreliable point of view, but viewers tend to take each event as an objective fact because the discourse of film is more literal-minded. So strong is the illusion of reality in movies that filmmakers have developed a set of codes to indicate subjective points of view. Ingmar Bergman uses a distorting lens to represent Professor Borg's dreams in *Wild Strawberries* (1957). Tony Richardson uses freeze-frames in *The Loneliness of the Long Distance Runner* (1962) to show flashes of the runner's past. Robert Enrico uses slow motion and special sound effects in *An Occurrence at Owl Creek Bridge* (1962) as clues that we are witnessing events in Farquhar's imagination, not reality. Similar distinctions can be made about the use of setting, symbolism, plot, or tone. These elements are common to both written and filmed fiction, but they are developed quite differently within the discourse of each medium.

The Elements of Film Discourse

In some ways, cinematic discourse may seem richer than literary discourse. Films appeal more directly to the eye and ear. True, written language has a visual form and can be read aloud, but the foundering of a ship and the howling of the wind must be evoked by words in the reader's imagination, whereas they can be recreated in light and sound for the film audience. To verbal language, film adds the languages of color, movement, music, and natural and artificial sounds. To the linguistic conventions of diction and syntax, film adds principles of framing, lighting, editing, visual transitions, and montage. This is not to say that film is somehow superior to literature; on the contrary, it is often argued that literary codes are far more precise and elaborately developed than those of film. The point is simply that film covers a wider range of direct sensory experience. Consider just a few of the filmmaker's tools:

Lighting. Etymologists like to remind us that the word *photography* means "writing with light." The language of lighting has its own vocabulary, which viewers learn partly by attending to the visual texts of films. As Bernard Dick observes, "lighting can express subtleties of character, plot, and setting" (7). High-key lighting, in which most of the scene is brightly lit, produces a buoyant mood, as in the party scene of *Citizen Kane* (1941). Low-key lighting, in which less illumination produces deep contrasts, lends an eerie, ominous feeling to moments like Kane's deathbed scene. Front lighting softens a face, giving it the look of innocence. Bottom lighting makes a face look sinister by casting shadows on the upper lip and hollowing the eyes. Such effects control the connotations of a scene, creating fine shades of emotional meaning. Lighting can be symbolic, too. When the reporter in *Citizen Kane* speaks of searching for the meaning of Rosebud, his face is obscured in shadow. Literally and figuratively, he is in the dark.

Color. Filmmakers use the social codes of color to develop character and mood. In *The Graduate* (1967), the seductive Mrs. Robinson appears in stark shades of red or black, while her ingenuous daughter dresses in soft pinks. The whites and ice-blue tones of Ben's suburban home reaffirm the cold sterility of his parents' world. In *Rebel without a Cause* (1955), Jim's red jacket and Judy's red coat link them to each other and isolate them from the adults who fail to heed their cries for help. My students have little trouble noticing these cues once they recognize the signficance of color in our lives, but they sometimes ask how deliberately a filmmaker selects the colors for a set. They are often intrigued to learn that Michelangelo Antonioni repainted the bedroom set of *Red Desert* (1964) so that it changed from white to red after the lovemaking scene, and that he spray-painted an entire marsh a certain shade of grey in order to reflect the mood of his characters in that scene.

Framing. The four edges of the movie screen frame the camera's field of vision, our window on the events of any cinematic story. We see only what the camera lets us see, through whatever lens is used, from whatever angle is selected. As viewers, our interpretation of setting, character, and action often depends on deliberate placements of the camera. As an example, take the Colorado sequence in *Citizen Kane*. It opens with a long shot of a boy playing in the snow. Then the camera pulls back, revealing that we have been watching him through a window from his mother's point of view. She is inside a cabin, her figure to the left side of the window, calling, "Be careful, Charles. Pull your muffler 'round your neck." Next we hear a man's voice, which becomes more distinct as the camera pulls back even farther into the cabin to show the figure of a well-dressed gentleman on the right.

Figure 1. Understanding personal relationships through framing: young Kane meets Mr. Thatcher.

Charles's mother says, "I'll sign those papers now, Mr. Thatcher," and moves to the center of the frame, obscuring our view of the window and her son. Now a third figure appears in the cabin, squeezed against the left side of the frame. He says, "You people seem to forget that I'm the boy's father." When the camera finally comes to rest, all four figures are in view: Mrs. Kane and Mr. Thatcher seated at a table in the foreground, the legal papers spread before them; the husband standing on the left, in the middle ground, partly off screen; the boy, a tiny figure in the background, glimpsed through the window in the center of the frame. Even without the dialogue, we would understand these personal relationships from the framing. Later, outside the cabin, when Charles learns that he is being sent away, the configuration changes (see Figure 1). Charles and Mrs. Kane dominate the front and center of the frame, Mr. Thatcher looms large but half-obscured by the left edge of the screen, and the father wavers in the background. Now the main interest is between mother and son; the banker's threat and the father's insignificance are represented by these characters' positions in the frame.

Motion. Tolstoy was fascinated by this feature of the movies. "The cinema has divined the mystery of motion," he said, "and that is its greatness. It is closer to life" (qtd. in Harrington, *Film and/as Literature* 211). Cinema has produced a language of motion that often speaks louder and more precisely than words. It is Marlon Brando's gestures, not his speech, that reveal most about the character of Terry Malloy in *On the Waterfront* (1954). A quick jerk of the head or a tugging at his nose tell all we need to know about his history as a boxer or his embarrassed sensitivity to Edie Doyle.

Film's movements can be broad as well as slight. When the camera sweeps slowly over Kane's accumulated wealth at the end of *Citizen Kane,* we recognize the emptiness of his career. In another scene, when the camera climbs up to the roof of Susan Alexander's nightclub and swoops down through the skylight to reveal her figure slumped over a table, we feel it as an intrusion into one of the world's small, broken lives.

Sound. Films reproduce sounds where books can only describe them. Music, dialogue, voice-over (words that are not synchronous with the actors' lips), and natural sounds (sound effects) can contribute not only to a movie's realism but also to the story's plot, characterization, or symbolism. The sirens that begin and end *Rebel without a Cause* are part of the story line—the police are on the way—and also part of the film's symbolic structure, a metaphor for an anguished cry for help. In *The Birds* (1963), Hitchcock makes similar use of bird sounds. When Melanie crosses the street to the pet store, someone gives a bird whistle. In the store, she asks for a talking bird. Later on, the screech of gulls and the whirring of their wings take on ominous significance. These sounds are genuinely chilling, and they seem all the more threatening when we do not see the birds themselves. But most terrifying is the absence of sound, when we can neither see nor hear the threat.

Transitions. The simplest transition from one shot to another is the cut, produced by splicing together two pieces of film. Filmmakers soon learned to use special effects—fade-outs, **iris** shots, dissolves—to move more deliberately between shots or scenes. To some extent, these optical transitions have come to represent predictable relationships. A dissolve may signify a shift in time or place; a fade may close the shade on a suggestive scene. Cinematic transitions have not become as standardized as punctuation marks, but they do represent a kind of code. Bordwell and Thompson have cataloged some of Welles's ingenious uses of transitions in *Citizen Kane* (8–23). To contrast the happiness of Kane's Colorado childhood with the dreary circumstances of his adolescence in New York, Welles dissolves from the image of Kane's sled, left behind in the snow, to another sled, a gift from his legal guardian. The white wrapping paper looks like a poor substitute for snow, especially in his new surroundings, a cramped Manhattan apartment where the boy is flanked by solemn servants who intone, "Happy Birthday, Charles." Welles bridges another gap in time, between Kane's first meeting with Susan Alexander and his political career, with a transition of sound. The applause Kane gives to Susan for her singing turns into the ovation for his campaign speech, a campaign that will end abruptly when his affair with Susan is disclosed. Bordwell and Thompson note that the slow dissolves that link the shots of Kane's estate suggest stagnation and decay. They point out that the transitions joining each scene in the breakfast montage of Kane's first marriage are swish pans, swift camera movements that lead from one scene to the next. The blur of each transition matches the tempo of a waltz theme on the sound track, which grows more dissonant as the marriage breaks down. As viewers, we learn to read such transitional devices as clues, even statements, about relationships within the film.

Acting. While we may think of actors as autonomous performers, their performances are often strongly directed, even dictated by forces beyond their own interpretations of character. Some directors like to control the acting as they would any other element of filmmaking. Alfred Hitchcock, for example, kept Cary Grant and Eva Marie Saint closely tethered to the shooting script in *North by Northwest* (1959). Other directors give their actors more artistic freedom. Many of the best moments in *The Godfather* (1972) emerged from sessions in which Coppola let Marlon Brando improvise on the set. Beyond the director, a small army of specialists—makeup artists, costume designers, voice coaches, and combat choreographers—can help ease actors into their roles. An actor might spend weeks or months preparing. In researching her part in *The Hours* (2002), Nicole Kidman reportedly read all the works of Virginia Woolf, learned to mimic Woolf's handwriting, and practiced rolling her own cigarettes as Woolf used to do. Meryl Streep prepared for her role as Clarissa in the film by listening to the kind of music Clarissa liked. In film after film, it is often an actor's attention to such details of personality that brings a character to life. Michael Cunningham, the author of *The Hours*, once defined the difference between the film and the book in terms of such details:

> When I saw the finished movie, I understood that what you lose in turning fiction into film—the ability to enter your characters' minds, and to scan their pasts for keys to their futures—can be compensated for by actors. You lose interiority. You gain Ms. Streep's ability to separate an egg with a furious precision that communicates more about Clarissa's history and present state of mind than several pages of prose might do. (22)

Adaptation: Questions of Fidelity

Alain Resnais once compared cinematic adaptations to a reheated meal (Beja 79). Why rehash the book when you can serve up original films about original stories? Aside from aesthetic reasons, there are clear economic motives for producing **adaptations**. First, a book offers a ready-made plot. There's no need to develop an untested script. Second, since published books already have an audience, much of the publicity comes free. Third, for all the critical complaints that "the book was better," three out of four Academy Awards for Best Picture have gone to adaptations. And the majority of top-grossing films are adaptations (Beja 78). In recent years, the Oscar for Best Adapted Screenplay has gone to a steady succession of successful features, including *Dances with Wolves* (1990), *The Silence of the Lambs* (1991), *Schindler's List* (1993), *Forrest Gump* (1994), *Sense and Sensibility* (1995), *Sling Blade* (1996), *American Beauty* (1999), *Traffic* (2000), and *A Beautiful Mind* (2001). No wonder that most bestselling novels are turned into films. But what about the artistic side? What should we expect of cinematic adaptations? What does it mean to be faithful to the book?

George Bluestone was one of the first to study in depth the phenomenon of adaptations and is still one of the most illuminating writers on the subject. Bluestone sees the filmmaker as an independent artist, "not a translator for an established author, but a new author in his own right" (62). He points out that many film adapters never read the book, but get their stories from summaries. What they adapt is a kind of paraphrase, "characters and incidents that have detached themselves from language" (63). Bluestone reminds us that some stories are better suited to one medium than another because "what is peculiarly filmic and what is peculiarly novelistic cannot be converted without destroying an integral part of each" (63). Joyce and Proust, he concludes, would seem as pointless on screen as Chaplin would in print.

Bluestone would agree with the French director Rene Clair, who once said, "a faithful translation is often a betrayal of the original" (qtd. in Harrington, *Film and/as Literature* 3). Clair believed that a filmmaker must refashion the substance of the story—its plot, characters, settings, themes—using the tools of cinema, not merely copying the finished artifact produced by the writer's tools. A literal translation would be as foolish as constructing log cabins out of concrete cylinders.

A good example of translating the spirit rather than the letter of a book is Tony Richardson's adaptation of *Tom Jones* (1963). The film opens with a parody of silent movies. The old-fashioned harpsichord music, subtitles, iris shots, and overstated style of acting help to set a comic tone. The sequence also does the job of condensing an expository section of the narrative into a few hilarious minutes of action. What is most ingenious, though, is Richardson's use of cinematic counterparts to Fielding's literary methods. The film parodies old movies much as the novel parodies early literary forms. Another clever parallel is the celebrated dining scene between Tom and Mrs. Waters. Where Fielding extends for several pages a ludicrous metaphor of sexual battle, Richardson shows the couple devouring the meal while they devour each other with their eyes. The film replicates in moving images the novel's verbal tour de force.

There are other fine examples. Stuart McDougal has analyzed Jack Clayton's film *The Innocents* (1961) to demonstrate how it duplicates in cinematic terms the verbal ambiguities of Henry James's novel *The Turn of the Screw* (146–52). Where James uses a first-person narrator of questionable reliability, Clayton uses sound to underscore the subjectivity of our experience as viewers. Where James frames the governess's narrative with a testimony of her character, Clayton frames the body of the film with an interview. Thus Clayton balances the objective nature of photography against the film's codes of subjectivity in order to reenact in cinematic terms the duplicities of James's point of view. *The Grapes of Wrath* (1940) presents another kind of challenge to the art of adaptation. John Steinbeck's novel is full of generalizations about politics and history that would be difficult to show on screen. McDougal shows how John Ford's film repeatedly converts abstractions to specifics by representing the displaced masses as a single family (31–35). Steinbeck's long discussion of corporate takeovers in Chapter 5 becomes a bulldozer that levels the Joads' home. An anonymous old woman sorting through her possessions in Chapter 9 becomes a poignantly silent scene of Ma Joad and her hope chest on the eve of her departure. It almost isn't necessary when Ma says at the film's finale, "We'll go on forever, Pa. We're the people."

We should not forget, however, that many of the differences between literature and films are due not to artistic limitations of the media but to matters of business. As Bluestone puts it, "The Hollywood producer is governed less by the laws of aesthetics than by the laws of the marketplace" (38). Whereas a novel can make a profit with twenty thousand copies, a movie must reach millions. And movies cost more to produce. Movies, then, must be mass-produced for a mass audience. This means that no film is wholly the product of a single author; it bears the signatures of many hands and countless social forces. It also means that filmmakers tend to be more responsive to a general audience and therefore to a more restricted range of tastes; they can't appeal to special interests in the audience if this means losing the main group.

This book offers many opportunities to compare movies to their literary origins. Most of the films discussed in Part II are adaptations. In the background for these films, I have sought to highlight the process of moving from page to screen. Students will have a chance to see how a fortuitous confluence of great screenwriting, acting, and cinematography transformed "one of the world's worst plays"—*Everybody Comes to Rick's*—into one of the top movies of all times—*Casablanca*. They will come to understand why Harper Lee, the author of *To Kill a Mockingbird*, believed that Horton Foote's screenplay of the book "should be studied as a classic." They will learn how Francis Ford Coppola prepared to direct *The Godfather* by annotating Mario Puzo's popular novel page by page and how Frank Darabont turned a little-known novella by Stephen King into *The Shawshank Redemption* (1994). They will also be able to study films based on historical sources (*Glory, Schindler's List*), Shakespeare (*Romeo and Juliet*), and video games (*Run Lola Run*).

Long after the publication of Bluestone's landmark book, adaptation continues to be a focus of serious academic study and debate. A sampling of recent books on the subject reveals a wide diversity of methods and attitudes. In *The Classic Novel from Page to Screen*, Robert Giddings and Erica Sheen assemble essays based on works from the English literary canon, offering close readings of classics, such as *The Old Curiosity Shop* (1935), *Pride and Prejudice* (1995) (the BBC production), *A Passage to India* (1984), and *The Age of Innocence* (1993), in the now old tradition of New Criticism. *Vision/Re-vision: Adapting Contemporary American Fiction by Women to Film*, edited by Barbara Lupack, brings together ten essays on popular film adaptations—including *Ordinary People* (1980), *The Joy Luck Club* (1993), and *Fried Green Tomatoes* (1991)—all with an emphasis on feminist messages. *Jane Austen in Hollywood* is a collection of essays on the remarkable Austen adaptations of the 1990s, edited by Linda Troost and Sayre Greenfield. In *Adaptations as Imitations*, James Griffith takes a different tack, arguing that a film is faithful by imitating a book's form and technique, not by copying the experience of its materials. Griffith applies this approach to *The Natural* (1984), *Deliverance* (1972), *To Kill a Mockingbird* (1962), and *2001: A Space Odyssey* (1968). Finally, in *Film Adaptation*, James Naremore selects a set of essays meant to counter the usual discussions about fidelity and contrasting media with some new directions. "The problem with most writing about adaptation as translation," says Naremore, "is that it tends to valorize the literary canon and essentialize the nature of cinema" (8). The lead essays by Dudley Andrew and Robert Stam take a postmodern view, claiming that every feature film is a kind of adaptation, translating into cinematic terms some other system of signs, whether it be a literary work, a historical event, or the multilayered text of life itself. Andrew proposes "a sociology of adaptation" that examines the roles of adaptations at different times in history. Stam suggests "a dialogics of adaptation," acknowledging the endless intertextuality of movies, literature, and other texts "with no clear point of origin" (Naremore 66).

The Influence on Other Media

The relationship between literature and film goes well beyond questions of adaptation. Literature has influenced the course of film and vice versa. Film directors like Robert Bresson, D. W. Griffith, and Ingmar Bergman owe immense debts to their readings of the classics. Writers like John Dos Passos, Lawrence Durrell, and Thomas Pynchon have openly borrowed film techniques. Then there are those writers whose methods could be said to be, in some ways, cinematic, among them James Joyce, Charles Dickens, Gustave Flaubert, and Laurence Sterne. Here it is not a matter of influence but of aesthetic affinity, artists working out ideas in one medium that would eventually find full expression in another.

Sergei Eisenstein, the Soviet film pioneer, credited Dickens with creating effects in his novels that parallel an extraordinary number of film techniques later used by directors like Griffith, including close-ups, dissolves, crosscutting, montage construction, and certain sound effects (*Film Form* 195–255). Eisenstein took this as a sign of Dickens's keen visual sense and his ability to think in plastic forms. Further, he considered it good evidence that literature is, to a great extent, an art of seeing.

William Faulkner offers an even more intriguing case of correspondences between literature and film. Bruce Kawin has called Faulkner "the most cinematic of novelists" (*Faulkner and Film* 5). Kawin has written the definitive study of Faulkner's work in Hollywood (*Faulkner and Film*) as well as editing the hitherto unpublished screenplays Faulkner wrote for MGM (*Faulkner's MGM Screenplays*). Faulkner's experience with cinema ran the gamut. He collaborated on other people's films (*To Have and Have Not*, 1944; *The Southerner*, 1945; *The Big Sleep*, 1946), and he worked on adaptations of his own works, some of which made it to the screen (*Intruder in the Dust*, 1949), some of which did not ("Barn Burning"). There are also film versions of his novels that he had no part in adapting, like *Sanctuary* (1961) and *The Reivers* (1969), and finally, there are those novels that Kawin considers cinematic in themselves, such as *The Sound and the Fury*. To study the interplay between Faulkner's achievement as a novelist and his accomplishments in Hollywood is to explore the lively conversation between art forms that takes place within a great artist's work.

The exchange between literature and film has been explored more broadly by Keith Cohen. Cohen traces many of the innovations of the modern novel to cinema, arguing that "the contours of modern narrative would not be what they are without the precedents set by the movies" (10). While not insisting on direct influence, Cohen pursues a number of correspondences to arrive at some intriguing insights. He compares, for example, the modern novelist's preoccupation with shifting points of view to the filmmaker's placement of a camera. The need in film to combine shots taken from different camera angles encourages a relativistic approach to storytelling. Cohen is suggesting that the mechanical requirements of cinema coincide with the thematic interests of writers like Joyce and Proust. Another coincidence is the way human and nonhuman figures appear on the screen. Motion pictures represent objects and people on the same level of existence, a phenomenon exploited for comic effect by Charlie Chaplin and Buster Keaton and, more seriously, by Franz Kafka and Samuel Beckett. Like other scholars, Cohen observes that cinema has also influenced literature by taking over some of its traditional roles. Just as photography displaced the representational function of painting, film nudged written fiction away from realism toward the task of depicting the inner life.

Film and the Other Arts

So far, we have been comparing film to narrative forms of literature, primarily the novel and short story. It's worth remembering, however, that silent movies were called "photoplays" and that many films today are still classified as dramas. In fact, much of the early cinema was modeled on the theater. The first "art films," in particular, depended on the stage for their subjects, performers, and techniques, yet most critics agree that film is most like film when it is free of the proscenium arch. Kawin contrasts the "unshifting presence" of the stage, where all motion is inscribed within a continuum of space and time, to the movie frame, which can transport us instantly to other times and places (*How* 394). Furthermore, the frame can redefine our point of view, bringing us closer to the action or letting us watch it from below. In contrast, the stage requires us to shift or focus our attention on our own. As Beja notes, "at a film more is done to and for us, and less by us, than at a play" (67). Then, because dramatic performances are live, we make different psychological connections to the action. Cohen expresses it this way: "While in the theatre the spectator is basically a witness, in the cinema he is more of a voyeur" (74).

Film has been compared to poetry, music, dance, and even architecture. This is especially true of non-narrative, experimental forms, which are less concerned with telling stories than with conveying moods and ideas. It's worth considering how a movie can be like, or unlike, a dance number or a musical composition. Some movies do include dances, poetry, or music, of course, but there is a difference between a filmed dance and a dance film. There is an even greater difference between the art of dance and the art of film. How do films handle the elements of rhythm or plastic form? How does a filmed experience compare to a live performance or the experience of walking through a cathedral?

Viewed from these perspectives, a movie adaptation is not so much an illustrated copy of a book but a new rendering of the story, to be appreciated on its own terms. The narrative terrain, with its significant settings, characters, and actions, is redrawn onto a different kind of map by a different sort of cartographer. For students of English, studying adaptations means learning about the possibilities and limitations of literary mapmaking. By paying close attention to what is unique about each medium (What exactly do we get from a work of literature or film? What is added to or missing from the experience?), students become more aware of what it means to represent reality through fiction. By attending to the similarities between a movie and a book, they can come to recognize what is universal in all narratives, the motives and rewards of storytelling that transcend all media. If the movie makes them want to read the book, or vice versa, they may well conclude that one is better than the other. At least they will be in a better position to explain why.

2 The Languages of Film

I t was Christian Metz who said, "A film is difficult to explain because it's so easy to understand" (qtd. in Monaco 127). Metz, who spent a good deal of time trying to explain how movies work, was fascinated by their ostensible simplicity. Motion pictures seem so easy to produce (just point the camera and shoot) and to interpret (just sit back and watch) that we tend to think of them as natural phenomena. We forget that at the heart of film there is a language—actually several languages—that must be learned.

Making Sense of Movies

Consider how we come to understand what movies mean. How do we learn that when the image of an eye fills the screen, it means we're watching a close-up rather than a giant eyeball? How do we learn that when the screen gradually grows black, a scene has ended? When do we learn that when a row of houses glides across the screen, what is really moving is the camera, not the houses? Most of us learned by watching lots of motion pictures. We grasped the significance of close-ups, fade-outs, and panorama shots while viewing them in otherwise familiar contexts, long before anyone taught us their technical names.

The fact that understanding movies is not automatic is illustrated many times in the early history of film. In the United States, during the days of silent movies, viewers were at first confused by flashbacks, crosscutting, and reaction shots, techniques understood by even the youngest filmgoers today. When Robert Flaherty showed film clips of *Nanook of the North* to his Inuit friends in 1922, they failed to recognize themselves in the movie. Having had no previous experience with photography, they did not realize that the play of light and shadow on the screen was meant to represent their likenesses.

Similar misunderstandings have been duplicated elsewhere in the world whenever film has not been seen before. In Russia, audiences thought that the close-ups in Eisenstein's *Potemkin* (1925) were photographs of severed limbs and heads. In Iran, a group of villagers being shown a health department film gasped in horror when they saw a close-up of some insects: "Thank Allah we don't have such large mosquitoes!" In a West African country, when each scene of a film ended in a fade-out, the spectators kept turning around to see what was wrong with the projector (Forsdale 612). These audiences had not yet learned the technical conventions of the cinema and its codes.

Although we often learn a language through exposure and practice just by living in the language environment, a more formal study of the language can make us more aware of how it works. English grammar offers a systematic way of understanding English. Similarly, we can appreciate the behavior of motion pictures systematically by studying the "grammar" of film. Film is not a language in exactly the same way that English is a language. There is nothing in a movie that corresponds precisely to a word, for instance, or a question mark, nor is the order of events in a movie as strictly regulated as the order of words in a grammatical sentence. For the moment, though, it will be helpful to look at film from a linguistic point of view.

Cinematic Grammar

The key to understanding any grammar is to understand the language as a system. Think of film as a system of images and sounds. The images may represent real objects, imaginary events, even ideas. The sounds may include music, sound effects, or speech. Filmmakers arrange these images and sounds systematically. The arrangement is meaningful to us because we understand the system. Let's take a short film sequence as an example. First, we see the image of a man standing on a bridge, a rope around his neck. Next, we see a close-up of his face. Beads of sweat form on his forehead. As he shuts his eyes, we hear the first strains of banjo music. Then we see the image of a woman, elegantly dressed and smiling, seated on a garden swing and swaying gently to the music. Her motion is exceptionally slow. What does this sequence mean? How do we interpret it? We may guess that the man is about to be hanged. The rope and sweat are clues to his predicament. But what do the music and the woman have to do with him? Maybe there is someone on the bridge with a banjo. Maybe this woman is watching the event. More likely, though, the music and the woman represent his thoughts. We know that slow motion and special music in a movie often signal a flashback, a quick visit to the past. The fact that this slow-motion image follows a close-up of the man's face suggests that his mind is focused on the past. So we read the sequence as a subjective event: the man is thinking of his loved one at the moment of his death. What enables us to make sense of a film like this is our understanding of the systems of images and sounds, close-ups, and flashbacks through which filmmakers communicate meaning.

Photography can be regarded as a signifying system because photographs, like words, refer to things beyond themselves. A snapshot of a cat is not a cat, or else we couldn't slip it into our wallet. Yet photographs are more like the things they represent than words are. Photographs are likenesses; they bear a visual resemblance to some material original. Words usually are arbitrary sounds; the sounds represented by the letters *c-a-t* have no obvious similarity to the animal. That's why a non-native speaker is more likely to understand the picture than the word.

Signs and Referents: How Do Movies Signify?

Those who study signifying systems—semioticians or semiologists, as they are sometimes called—make a crucial distinction between a signifier and what it signifies. The sound and the image of the word *cat* (its pronunciation and its spelling on the page) are **signifiers.** What speakers think of when using the word *cat* is the **signified.** The signified is not the animal itself, but a conception. Most likely, that conception involves mental images and personal associations formed through years of contact with furry, feline creatures. Semioticians use the term **sign** for the relationship between a signifier and the signified. A verbal sign is the relation between a sound-image and a concept. The actual animal—the thing to which the sign refers (its referent)—is something else again. We'll leave that part to the zoologists.

What then is a photographic sign? Like a verbal sign, a photographic sign is a relation between the signifier and the signified. In this case, the signifier is the photographic image—patterns of shade and color on the screen—and the signified is the mental image—what those patterns evoke in our imagination. Because motion pictures are so lifelike, it's easy to forget that the signifier (what is projected on the screen) is not the signified (what we project in our imagination), or that the sign (a relation between the perceptual image and our conceptual response to it) is not the referent (what was in front of the lens when the camera was turned on). It's as if images of the world are transferred directly to the film stock, to the movie screen, and then to the inner screens of people in the audience, with very little effort or translation. This may help to explain why movies seem so real and why we rarely give much credit to the viewers for the mental work involved.

Yet it is important to remember that watching movies is an interpretative act. Despite the remarkable realism of photography, a photograph is still a sign, and signs must be read. Some images are more abstract than others. When Picasso represents a cat with a few circles and some squiggly lines, his drawing may be more challenging to read than, say, a painting by Mary Cassatt, especially for someone unfamiliar with the ways of abstract art. Similarly, Cassatt's painting or a Japanese woodblock print may be harder to read than a modern documentary film on cars. We can imagine a spectrum of signs ranging from the most abstract to the most specific. Words are more abstract than images, and drawings generally are more abstract than photographs. While the word *car* may represent any year or make of automobile, a pencil sketch begins to look more like a sports car or a sedan, and a photograph is more specific still.

The specificity of film creates special problems of interpretation. Writers can use words like *vehicle, automobile, station wagon,* or *Volvo* to indicate different levels of abstraction, but how do we know the intention of a filmmaker when what we see on the screen are 1985 Jaguars or 1990 Coupes de Ville? It seems that the language of speech is better equipped than the language of pictures for making direct statements. When I say, "This car is old" or "That car is fast," I'm making an assertion. But when I film a certain car, I'm not so sure how it will appear to viewers. I can manipulate the image to emphasize the car's age or speed, but essentially the image is a presentation rather than a statement. In this sense, visual and verbal texts require complementary forms of interpretation. Images evoke assertions; words evoke images. The audience completes the message by supplying mental words or pictures.

In addition to being more abstract and arbitrary, verbal language tends to be more analytic than film language. To describe a scene in English, we have to break down what we see into parts that can be represented word by word. An earthquake, for example, may take place in an instant, but the discrete nature of words forces speakers and writers to analyze the experience into linguistic bits: the rumble, a swaying chandelier, the sounds of falling bricks and shattered glass, the panic. Or take a simpler, more typical event: "The girl kicked the ball." The rules of English syntax compel us to distinguish among the action (kicked), an agent (the girl), and an object (the ball), even though it is difficult to picture the act of kicking without someone doing it or something being kicked. In this way, the language of film is more holistic. The photographic sign gives a less fragmented replication of experience. The whole quake can be pictured instantaneously. The kicker, the kicked, and the kickee can be represented as one event.

The fact that movies include sounds as well as photographs compounds the issue. The sound effects, background music, and dialogue of films can be studied as signifying systems in themselves. Sound effects, like photographs, resemble what they represent. The sound effect of horses' hooves bears an auditory likeness to the actual tramp of horses over cobblestone, although it may have been produced by coconut shells on a studio table. Music, on the other hand, tends to be more abstract. The swelling sound of violins may be more important for its evocation of emotion than for its reference to instruments. What the music usually signifies is pride or romance, not the presence of violins. Yet, in some scenes, the musicians are clearly visible on screen, and what their music signifies may be primarily their role as musicians.

To understand such varieties of signification, it is helpful to borrow three terms from the American philosopher Charles Sanders Peirce. Peirce described three kinds of signs: icons, indexes, and symbols. An icon bears some similarity to what it represents. Photographs and sound effects are icons since they look or sound like their referents. An index has a physical bond with what it represents. Smoke indicates fire; a sundial indicates the time of day. Yet there is no clear resemblance between smoke and fire or between a sundial and the passage of time: one signifies the other by virtue of a physical relationship. Fire produces smoke; the sun's movement over time produces a moving shadow on the sundial. A symbol is an arbitrary sign. It depends on an agreement between users to interpret it a certain way. Thus a flag becomes a symbol of a nation by common consent (Peirce 48–119).

Peter Wollen and other semiologists often emphasize that verbal language is primarily symbolic, while cinema is primarily iconic and indexical (143). For the most part, words are arbitrary. Their meanings are established by agreement among native speakers. The signs of cinema, by contrast, depend heavily on visual and acoustic similarity. The screen image of a cat or the pitch of its meow on a sound track are iconic because they resemble what they represent. These images and sounds are also indexical insofar as they depend on a physical connection to their referents. The photographic image was produced by light reflected from a real animal. The sound track was produced by recording actual noises.

Films bear the imprint of reality in ways that books do not. This is not to say that words are never icons. Onomatopoeic language—words like *buzz* and *rat-a-tat-tat*—works by virtue of auditory correspondences that may be recognized even by non-native speakers. Nor is cinema always indexical and iconic. When the clumping of hollow coconuts signifies the sound of horses or when violin music signifies romance, the relationship between sign and referent is neither simple nor direct. Motion pictures and their sound tracks often function symbolically. The villain's mustache, the iris shot, and the symphonic crescendo are symbols whose meanings are established by convention. We learn to interpret them by mastering the code.

Cinematic Codes: Syntagms and Paradigms

Semioticians study two orders of code, called syntagms and paradigms. These are often represented as two axes. The syntagmatic axis runs horizontally, unfolding in time. The order of words in an English sentence is governed by a syntagmatic code, the rules of syntax. "The cat bit the boy" has one meaning; "The boy bit the cat" has another. "Cat boy bit the" is virtually meaningless. The paradigmatic axis runs vertically. If you replaced the verb "bit" in the first sentence with another verb, say "kicked" or "kissed," you'd be exchanging elements from the same paradigm. Simply stated, **syntagm** refers to the order of words, and **paradigm** refers to the choice of words.

But what corresponds to words in a movie? What is a film's basic element of signification? John Harrington identifies the **frame** as a film's "smallest discernible unit" (*Rhetoric* 8). If you examine a reel of film, you'll see that it's composed of many individual still photographs, called frames, printed end to end on a translucent **celluloid** strip. An average feature-length movie contains about 130,000 of these stills. During projection, the frames are flashed onto the screen one at a time, but so rapidly that the mind connects them into a seamless moving picture. The frame is more of a technological division than an artistic one, however, because filmmakers think not in terms of frames, but of shots. A shot consists of the frames produced by one continuous operation of the camera. Since any shot can be removed or rearranged during the editing stage of filmmaking, Harrington considers the shot to be the smallest functional unit of film, comparable to the word in spoken or written language (*Rhetoric* 10). Shots, like words, can be taken out of context and recombined into new contexts to form new meanings, but, as Harrington admits, shots differ from words in several respects. The high density of information in a single photograph can require hundreds of words to represent it verbally. In this sense, a shot is more like a sentence or a paragraph. It has its own internal structure.

Filmmakers have long understood, by training or instinct, that a framed space embodies certain principles of composition. Even the "empty" area of a blank screen has a kind of invisible terrain that we can explore by moving a shape within its borders. Rudolf Arnheim has shown how a disk within a square is subject to hidden lines of force. A single disk appears unstable when it is located slightly off center, but a second disk restores the balance when it is properly placed (*Art* 11). An object in motion also seems to follow unseen forces. When it moves from left to right, it appears to be flowing with the current; when it moves from right to left, it encounters an intangible but noticeable resistance. Such psychological relationships between an object and its surrounding space, between figure and ground, have been studied carefully by scholars of film and other visual arts, who emphasize how much of viewing is interpretive (Wead and Lellis 70–73).

Visual and verbal signs differ in another way. The words of a spoken language already exist before the speaker chooses them; the English lexicon is finite. For the filmmaker, the visible world already exists, but each new image must, in a sense, be invented. No two shots, even of the same event, will be exactly alike. Because of changes in lighting, framing, movement, color, and the other variables involved in photographing an image, the filmmaker's lexicon, the paradigmatic range, is infinite. This open-endedness of photography, together with the fact that every image presents an indefinite amount of information to the viewer, is a major reason why film is not always regarded as a language. Yet, as film studies continue to point out, cinematic equivalents can be found for nearly every variety of speech, from metonymy to metaphor, from pun to cliché (Monaco 130–42; McDougal 242–86; Bluestone 20–31).

Questions about units of meaning, visual composition, and cinematic lexicons are essentially paradigmatic. They concern the choices available to filmmakers and viewers within a movie frame: the quality of lighting, camera angle, speed of action, acting style, or dress. The choices concerning how these frames are organized—the order of shots within a scene or scenes within a sequence—are syntagmatic. To study film syntax is to observe how shots are edited into a meaningful arrangement. Take a simple target-practice scene. It might begin with a long shot of someone with a raised rifle, followed by a medium shot of the target, then a close-up of a squinting eye, a close-up of a finger on the trigger, a close-up of the smoking barrel, a close-up of the target with a hole in it, and finally a medium shot of the person's smiling face. No surprises there. Most viewers would assume a bull's-eye.

Knowing what they know about the operation of firearms, the significance of smiles, and the order of events in films, viewers would connect these individual shots into a coherent story. If the smile were replaced by a scowl, or the target by another person (both paradigmatic changes), the story would be different. If the same shots were presented in a different sequence (a syntagmatic change), it might also be a different story. How would we interpret the scene if the close-up of the bullet hole preceded the close-up of the smoking barrel?

Christian Metz has proposed one of the most ambitious schemes for understanding film syntax. His *grande syntagmatique* identifies eight distinct patterns by which cinema transforms the world into discourse. In his words, the scheme "gives us a better outline of the *deep structure* of the choices that confront the filmmaker for each one of the 'sequences' of [the] film" (*Film* 123, emphasis in original). One pattern is the *bracket syntagma*, a series of brief scenes representing a common idea, as a familiar vignette of lovers running through a field, gathering flowers, and riding a Ferris wheel might represent romance. Another pattern is *parallel montage*, which cuts back and forth between two simultaneous events, like the alternating shots of a heroine tied to the railroad track, a galloping hero, and an approaching train in an old silent movie. Metz recognizes that his "cinematographic grammar" is not a real grammar in the usual sense, but simply "a body of partially codified semantic implications" (*Film* 223). Yet the scheme is useful for comparing the structures of film narrative to spoken and written forms of storytelling. Writers often use bracket syntagms to illustrate abstract ideas and parallel montage to contrast and compare events.

One benefit of paying close attention to syntagms is the recognition of how people organize the signs by which they represent reality into meaningful compositions. Whether their stories are embedded in the rules of written language or in the encoded sounds and images of film, these compositions reflect the deeper structures of the mind. A sustained comparison often begins by stressing similarities and ends by emphasizing differences. The history of film semiotics has followed such a course. Early theorists made bold claims for the analogy of cinema and language partly to validate film as an art, bolstering its status as an academic subject. Later on, as some of the more obvious analogies wore thin and semiotics called for greater sophistication, theorists became more interested in pointing out divergences between cinema and other languages, underscoring their uniqueness. Even the most ambitious semioticians, such as Metz, have found the effort to be scientifically precise and complete about the codes of film and its correspondences to language something of a dead end.

What, then, are the lessons to be learned from this inquiry? First, as Robert Scholes has noted, semiotics reminds us that "much of what we take to be natural is in fact cultural" (127). Cinema and spoken discourse are based on systems that are learned. We can study codes of dress or manners as languages because we have forgotten that we have learned these things. The discipline of semiotics is, in Scholes's précis, "a continual process of defamiliarization; the exposing of conventions, the discovering of codes that have become so ingrained we do not notice them but believe ourselves to behold through their transparency the real itself" (127). Second, semiotics helps to shift attention from the author's intentions to the audience's expectations. It reminds us that meaning resides in both our manner of constructing messages and our manner of construing them within certain cognitive and cultural conventions. By recognizing that our students are interpreting the codes of cinema, we give them credit for what they know while engaging them in the process of investigating *how* they know. Finally, by looking for the structures—and the structuring abilities —that transcend a single medium, we move toward a broader understanding of thinking and communicating. This is not to say that we should reduce all filmmaking and writing to common terms; nor is the significance of any statement only a matter of paradigms and syntagms. When we think of meaning in cinema as a matter of experience—felt experience, shared experience, the life of the mind—we begin to connect film to everything that counts.

3 The Technology of Film

F ilm is an art, but it is also a technology. While any writer can produce a novel with some paper and a pen, movies require cameras, film stock, sound equipment, editing machines, and more. Furthermore, technology demands technicians. A feature film might call for hundreds of specialists in lighting, cinematography, sound technology, makeup, costumes, set design, and special effects.

Students often want to know more about the machinery behind the movies and the individuals behind the machines. Where did King Kong's voice come from? Who trained all those birds in Hitchcock's thriller? How did they get Keanu Reeves to fly in *The Matrix* (1999)? What tricks do Foley artists use to create those striking sound effects?

This chapter is for those who are curious about the technical side of motion pictures. It explains some basic principles on which movies are based. It describes some of the instruments behind the art of film. It traces the steps of film production, highlighting the people and the tools that make it happen. But this is not a story of technology alone. In the history of film, technology goes hand in hand with art. Technological advances bring fresh, creative possibilities; new artistic practices inspire scientific innovation. The cycle continues, like a revolving reel.

Tools of the Trade

Most people enjoy driving without knowing much about the engine, but knowing how a car works can increase both their mastery and appreciation of the vehicle. Knowing more about the instruments of cinema can bring similar benefits. It can often make the difference between simply viewing and truly seeing a film.

The Film. Photography is a chemical process. A photograph is formed when celluoid film coated with light-sensitive chemicals is exposed to light. The portions of this coating that receive the most light turn darkest, forming a negative image of the visual event. This **negative** makes it possible to reproduce the image, for when light is directed through the negative onto another piece of film, a positive print is the result. Sensitivity to light varies with **film stock.** A fast film stock, being more sensitive, is best for filming at night or whenever light is scarce. The problem is that fast film stock produces a grainier, less distinct image than slow film stock. Some filmmakers exploit this technical feature for artistic reasons. They use a faster stock to lend an unpolished, documentary look to a realistic scene. More recently, the chemical basis of photography is being challenged by the new technology of **digital photography**, which records images in electronic form. *Star Wars Episode II: Attack of the Clones* (2002) was the first big budget movie to be shot entirely in digital video, although most theaters projected it in the traditional 35mm format. The innovations of digital filmmaking are described later in this chapter.

Lenses. The camera's lens acts as a glass eye to focus rays of incoming light onto a strip of film. Lenses are classified by **focal length**, the distance from the plane of the film to the optical center of the lens when the lens is set to infinity. For a 35mm camera, a focal length of roughly 35 to 55mm produces something close to what we see with the human eye. This is the focal length of a normal lens, which gives the least distortion. A **wide-angle lens** (also called a *short-focus lens*), because it's shorter, takes in a wider field of view so that objects seem farther away. This also increases the illusion of depth and distorts linear perspective. A face filmed with a wide-angle lens looks rounder, with a longer nose and pinned-back ears. Camera operators have used this fact to exact revenge against the vanity of actors. By contrast, a **telephoto lens** (or *long-focus lens*), because it's longer, takes in a narrow field of view. The image looks closer. Since a telephoto lens compresses depth, objects moving toward or away from the camera appear to move more slowly. The famous shot of Dustin Hoffman running to the church in *The Graduate* (1967) was taken with a long lens to exaggerate the slowness of his progress. A long lens also has a shallower depth of field; there is a shorter range within which an image will appear in focus. This fact is useful when a filmmaker wants to isolate one face in a crowd or a lion in a field of grass. The features of normal, long, and wide-angle lenses are combined in the **zoom lens,** which allows the filmmaker to change the focal length during shooting. The camera can zoom in for a close-up or zoom out to a long shot while the action continues.

Shutter Speed. By itself, the lens would produce not a moving picture but a blur. Something is needed between the lens and the film to stop the light just long enough so that the image frozen on a single frame of film can be moved out of position and a new frame moved into its place. This is done by a revolving plate called the **shutter.** The shutter in a movie camera usually revolves 24 times per second, the normal shutter speed for a sound film. With each revolution, a new frame is photographed, so that twenty-four successive frames of film will be projected later as one second of motion picture film. We see motion, instead of individual frames, because the human eye is slower than the machine. The retina retains the image for an instant longer than the image is presented, just enough time for a new frame to replace it on the screen. This phenomenon, called **persistence of vision**, accounts for the illusion of smooth motion. In reality, we're watching a succession of still photographs. When film is shot at higher speeds, say 240 frames per second, the projected result is seen as slow motion. In this case, one second of filmed motion will be stretched out to ten. **Slow motion** is produced by *overcranking* the camera, a term left over from the days when film was cranked by hand. **Undercranking** produces **fast motion.** An action filmed at only 12 frames per second will be speeded up to twice its normal rate on the screen, a familiar trick in comic chase scenes.

The Screen. The audience's window on the world is defined by the four edges of the screen. The relationship between the horizontal and vertical dimensions of the screen is called its **aspect ratio.** A ratio of 1.33:1 (the **Academy ratio**) used to be standard, but times and standards change. In the early 1950s, **widescreen** ratios were introduced, standardized in Europe as 1.66:1 and in the United States as 1.85:1. Since then, screens have been stretched into Panavision, **CinemaScope, Todd-AO,** and other imaginative shapes, all of which require special screens or lenses to adjust the image. There are clear commercial motives behind these tinkerings with the image size, but there are artistic motives too. While the Academy ratio was long regarded as the best shape for most spatial compositions, it does not necessarily support the most interesting views. Think of what would be lost if the Super Panavision of *2001: A Space Odyssey* (1968) were confined to standard proportions. In fact, some distributors of widescreen films on video have done just that. In a process called **pan and scan**, they modify what viewers see by leaving out parts of the image that don't fit the boxy dimensions of a televison screen. This means that the person who is panning and scanning ends up with creative control over the film's director and editor. An alternative to pan and scan is **letterboxing** (also called widescreen), which places blank bars above and below the full frame so that its orginal aspect ratio is preserved.

Technology has also tried to add a third dimension to the screen. **Three-dimensional (3-D) photography** uses two lenses spaced 2 1/2 inches apart to record a scene as if it were being viewed by a pair of human eyes. During 3-D projection, the two views are filtered by special glasses worn by all spectators so that the image recorded by each lens is seen only by the corresponding eye. Kawin demonstrates how Hitchcock used this process effectively in *Dial M for Murder* (1954), but for the most part, 3-D movies have been little more than box office gimmicks (Kawin, *How* 167).

Shots and Angles. As noted earlier, a **shot** is a single length of film produced by a continuous running of the camera. Many filmmakers consider it the basic unit of film editing, although a great deal can happen in one shot. The elements within a shot—the action, dialogue, camera movements, choice of lenses, and so forth—are known collectively as mise-en-scène. **Mise-en-scène** refers to what happens on the set (literally, what is put into the scene), in contrast to the editing (**montage**) that happens after shooting.

Shots are conventionally defined by the size of the subject within the film frame. A **close-up** might show an actor's head or hand. A **medium shot** might show his body from the knees up. A **long shot** might show her entire figure running through a field. The definitions of these terms are not precise, and additional terms are often used for special cases, such as *extreme close-up* or *medium long shot.* The subject's size may even vary within a single shot. The camera might, for example, zoom in from a long shot of a mob to a close-up of the leader's face.

Most scenes are filmed from a normal height, at the subject's eye level. The camera angle may vary, however, for particular effects. A **low-angle shot** is taken from below the subject. A **high-angle shot** is taken from above. Welles changes the angle of his camera in *Citizen Kane* (1941) to signal shifting points of view. Kane's campaign speech is seen from several perspectives. We see Kane loom larger than life from the angle of an appreciative audience, and then we see him from the extreme high angle of a balcony, where Kane's enemy is preparing to bring him to his knees. Elsewhere in the film, the camera angle gives a telling slant to individual shots. (See Figures 2 and 3.)

Movement. The earliest cameras were fixed, but today the camera moves. It can **pan** a subject horizontally by pivoting left or right. It can **tilt** up or down by pivoting along a vertical axis. The camera can also move through space. When it moves horizontally—with, toward, or away from the subject—the result is called a **tracking shot.** Some cameras actually move on tracks; others move on wheeled platforms called dollies. For this reason, the horizontal camera movement is also called a **dolly shot.** When the camera moves vertically through space, sometimes lifted by a boom or crane, the result is called a **boom shot** or a **crane shot**. Today, many filmmakers use a **Steadicam** to get smooth camera movements. By combining the fluidity of a dolly with the freedom of handheld filming, this stabilization device gives a new range of flexibility to the artist behind the camera.

Viewers sometimes confuse tracking shots with zooms. In a tracking shot, the camera moves. In a **zoom shot**, only the lens moves. A zoom lens is really a variable lens that can be moved toward the wide-angle po-

Figure 2. A low-angle shot of Mr. and Mrs. Kane at breakfast.

sition (for a long shot) or the telephoto position (for a close-up). Since the camera remains fixed in a zoom shot, the relative distances between objects remain constant, even though the objects may appear to grow or shrink in size. Contrast this with a tracking shot, which propels the viewer through space; objects near the frame's edge grow larger more quickly than objects near the center, creating a dynamic effect.

Lighting. Because movies are essentially recorded light, special attention is given to the technology of lighting. Cinematographers use several standard lighting styles, or "keys." The chief light illuminating the subject to be filmed is called the **key light**. In **high-key lighting**, the scene is flooded with bright illumination, giving it a cheerful, buoyant tone. In **low-key lighting**, illumination is low and soaked with shadows, creating an ominous or melancholy mood. Visitors to a movie set are often impressed by the number and variety of lights. **Spotlights** cast intense beams on the subject. **Floodlights** wash the scene with a less focused form of illumination. Sometimes a translucent shade, or **scrim**, is placed between the subject to soften the key light. **Fill light** provides a weaker, broader glow and is used to fill in shadows. An **eyelight** might be placed near the camera to add sparkle to the subject's eyes. A strong light from behind (**backlighting**) separates the

Figure 3. A high-angle shot of Kane and Leland outside the office of the *Inquirer.*

subject from the background. Backlighting also creates a silhouette effect when the subject is not illuminated from the front. **Front lighting** generally softens a face, flattening the features and sometimes hiding facial marks. **Sidelight** adds solidity and depth, accentuating features that give a face its character. Each lighting angle gives the filmmaker another tool for sculpting the subject.

Color. Although color films were not used widely until the late 1930s, filmmakers experimented with color from the start. Edwin Porter had individual frames painted by hand in *The Great Train Robbery* (1903). D. W. Griffith tinted certain scenes of *The Birth of a Nation* (1915) by dipping filmstock into colored dyes. He used blue tints for night scenes and red for the burning of Atlanta. Some of the best-known effects were used in *Gone with the Wind* (1939) and *The Wizard of Oz* (1939), both of which were filmed in **Technicolor**, a process in which the primary colors of an image are recorded on separate strips of film and recombined in the lab.

The Sound Track. Whereas our eyes focus selectively, fixing on one thing at a time, our ears are locked in place and register many sounds at once.

This fact is reflected in the systems that record sounds for movies. Directors often use several microphones while shooting, some to capture the actors' voices, others to record background noises. A standard practice is to record **ambient sound** before or after the shoot. This sampling of a location's auditory identity—the spectrum of rustling leaves, crickets, or other natural sounds that might be heard without the actors present—later serves as a baseline for the sound track. Without ambient sound, the film would seem artificial and lacking in depth.

Robert Bresson liked to say, "The eye is superficial, the ear profound" (qtd. in Geuens 198). To deepen our sensory engagement, filmmakers may use dozens of separate sound recordings to create a layered sound experience. Essentially, though, there are four basic kinds of sound in movies: dialogue, sound effects, music, and voice-over. **Dialogue** and **sound effects (SFX)** are usually synchronous; we see lips moving or cars colliding as we hear the words or clash of metal. Music and **voice-over** are usually not in sync with the picture. The music may come from an unseen orchestra; the voice-over may belong to someone not on screen, such as the story's narrator.

All sounds eventually are transferred to a **sound track.** In a single-system format, the most common, the sound track runs vertically alongside the picture on a strip of film. The sound track is usually magnetic or optical. A magnetic sound track is similar to audiotape. Sound is encoded on a stripe of magnetized particles that can be read by the magnetic head on a projector and converted back into sound. An optical sound track represents sound as a stripe of light bands, varying in density, which are read by a photoelectric cell in the projector and converted into sound. Unlike the images in a film, which stop and go through the projection system like individual slides, the sound track must pass the sound head of the projector in a continuous movement. That is why the sound corresponding to a given image is not next to the matching frame. In 16mm film, the sound is twenty-six frames ahead of the picture.

Like images, sounds can be edited creatively. A sharp shift from one sound to another is called a **sound cut.** A gradual transition between sounds, the auditory equivalent of a dissolve, is called a **segue.** Sometimes the sound from one scene precedes the picture. Mike Nichols uses this technique quite often in *The Graduate*. At one point, for example, Ben is in bed with Mrs. Robinson and we hear his father's voice, "What are you doing here?" The scene then shifts to Ben, who is lying on a raft in the backyard pool, squinting at his father's figure. The voice belongs to the pool scene, not the bedroom, but a significant connection has been made more strikingly through sound. In *The Godfather* (1972), when Michael Corleone is about to commit his first murder in a restaurant, we hear a sharp, metallic screech before we learn that it belongs to a passing elevated train. This off-screen sound grounds the moment in a particular location and puts everyone on edge.

Special Effects. Increasingly more of the action in today's films is a matter of special effects. Nuns fly, giant marshmallows stalk the earth, live actors dance with cartoon rabbits. Contemporary audiences are not only amused by these improbable feats, but they're fascinated by the technological wizardry behind them. Documentaries on the making of *Star Wars* (1977) or *The Matrix* (1999) are nearly as captivating as the feature films themselves.

At the heart of many special effects is the principle of **stop-motion photography.** In stop motion, shooting is interrupted at intervals while the scene is rearranged. **Animation** is created when a drawing or clay object is changed slightly every time the camera stops. When the film is projected at normal speed, the drawing or the object seems to move with a life of its own. **Pixilation** follows the same procedure, only with live people as the subject. An actor standing on one foot moves an inch forward. The camera shoots one frame. The actor inches forward in the same position again, and another frame is filmed. When the film is projected, the actor seems to glide across the screen on the same foot. Animation and pixilation can be tedious work. It takes about 14,400 frames to produce a ten-minute film (Monaco 106). Thanks to computers, though, the process is becoming easier to manage.

Ingenious special effects have been devised in the interests of time, money, safety, and imagination. When gorillas scale apartment buildings and moths devour Cleveland in old movies, the effect was usually achieved with miniatures or model shots. A small-scale model was filmed to look full size. The camera had to be overcranked (run at faster speeds) to slow down the action of the model so that it approximated normal motion. Today these small models can be big business. Steven Spielberg employed a colony of model makers and millions of dollars in equipment to supply the settings for his Indiana Jones and science fiction films. George Lucas's **Industrial Light & Magic (ILM)**, founded in 1975 to create the special effects for *Star Wars,* has refined the art of model building and propelled it into the digital age. ILM continues to win awards with its groundbreaking effects in movies like *The Perfect Storm* (2000), *A.I.: Artificial Intelligence* (2001), and *Star Wars Episode II: Attack of the Clones* (2002).

When live actors interact with fictitious settings, the effect is often achieved with glass or matte shots. A **glass shot** uses scenery painted on transparent glass. The camera photographs the action through the glass so that the painted portions seem to be continuous with the action. The scenes of Xanadu in *Citizen Kane* were shot this way, with the hill and castle painted on glass. In a variation of this method called **rear projection**, the action is filmed in front of a screen while another action is projected on the screen from behind. This is how those shots of moving trains and taxis used to be filmed. The actors sat in a stationary vehicle while a movie of the landscape rolled past the "windows." A **matte shot** uses an opaque screen or matte to obscure certain portions of the frame. The film is exposed twice, first with one matte and then with a second matte that covers the area obscured by the first. When projected, the two separately filmed sections of the frame appear as a single image. This is how a cast of thousands stormed through medieval Paris in *The Hunchback of Notre Dame* (1939). First the action of the crowd was shot while a matte covered the outline of the city. Then the film was exposed again; this time a miniature model of old Paris appeared in place of the first matte while a second matte blocked out the crowd. The mattes were so carefully aligned that the combined images seem part of one continuous scene.

A great leap forward was made with the invention of the **blue screen process**, pioneered in the 1950s and popularized in the 1970s. The process usually begins by filming an actor in front of a blue (or sometimes green or red) screen. When the film is processsed, the blue area becomes transparent so that a background image can be filmed and inserted, seamlessly matched to the action. All of Peter Pan's flying in *Hook* (1991) was filmed this way. So were many of the special effects in *The Lord of the Rings: The Fellowship of the Ring* (2001).

How Movies Are Made

Any major movie goes through four distinct stages: development, preproduction, production, and postproduction.

Development. A film starts with an idea. It may come from a book, an actual event, another film, or someone's raw imagination, but soon thereafter it goes through many transformations. Somebody may sketch out the main idea in a brief **synopsis** or story outline. Later this may be expanded into a **treatment**, a fuller version of the narrative that might contain scenes, character development, and some dialogue, much like a short story, but without detailed descriptions of the set or camera setups. Further along, a scenario or **screenplay** fleshes out the action, dialogue, and perhaps some directions for the camera. The most complete version before production is the **shooting script**, which usually provides a shot-by-shot blueprint of the film. Any of these versions of a story may be revised by other writers or studio personnel. Authorship is typically a collaborative enterprise.

In addition to script development, several key decisions are made before a film is given the green light. In large studios, specialists estimate expenses, investigate the market, and consider legal issues. Relatively few ideas make it past the development stage to preproduction.

Preproduction. Preproduction begins with the approval of a film project and ends just before the actual shooting. This stage includes a great deal of planning that few viewers ever think about. Screen tests are taken. The actors are cast. Locations are scouted. Background research is conducted. Sets are designed and decorated, props made, costumes fashioned and fitted. On a large production, these activities are carried out by a small army of specialists, including a casting director, production designer, art director, makeup artists, researchers, illustrators, draftspeople, set builders, propmakers, a set dresser, even a greens handler to take care of any flora used on the set. Eventually, the producer and assistants arrive at a final shooting schedule and production budget. Times and costs for filming each shot are worked out in detail. The film is ready for production.

Production. The main job of the director is to turn the screenplay into a film. Whereas the **producer** bears the ultimate responsibility for the final product, the **director** is responsible for directing the actors, supervising the technicians, and managing all action on the set. Some directors prefer to spend more time on preproduction than others. Most of Alfred Hitchcock's creativity went into scripting, casting, costumes, and art direction. For him, the task of shooting was mostly a matter of filling in the script. Other directors, like Federico Fellini, pay little attention to the script; their best ideas happen on the set. Still others, like Sergei Eisenstein, achieve their greatest effects after shooting, during the editing stage. On the whole, however, we think of directors as rulers of the movie set, perched on a canvas throne, giving the commands for "lights, camera, action."

Helping the director is a small crew of lieutenants. There may be one or more **assistant directors** to handle delegated tasks like planning the day's shooting, managing the extras, or keeping interlopers off the set. The **script supervisor** keeps track of the script, noting which shots are filmed, ever on the lookout for variant readings and visual discontinuities, like a change in lighting or the length of a lit cigarette. A **cuer** and a **dialogue director** may help keep track of dialogue and coach the actors with their lines. In a big production, there is simply too much for one director to coordinate.

Among the most important technicians on the set is the **cinematographer**, or director of photography, responsible for the camera work and related operations. While the director specifies the effect desired from each shot, this highly skilled individual usually selects the camera setup, lenses, film stock, and whatever else is needed to achieve that effect. In large crews, a **camera operator** will actually run the camera, while an assistant or two will **follow focus**, or adjust the lens when the actors or the camera moves. Other crew members take care of lighting, sound, special effects, and so on. A **production mixer** decides how to set up the sound equipment for the best sound. Usually there are separate sound tracks for recording dialogue, ambient sound, and live sound effects. If many shots must be taken of a single continuous action, like a dance, the action may be filmed to fit a prerecorded sound track, the **playback.** Later, the shots will be edited to match the music. Finally, no major set is complete without the gaffer, grips, and gofers. The **gaffer** is the chief electrician, responsible for lighting the set as directed by the cinematographer. The **grips** take care of equipment, sets, and props. The **gofers** run errands for everybody else, who order them to "go for this" and "go for that."

Apart from these technicians and assistants stand the **actors**, almost like a separate breed. Whether we think of them primarily as artists, celebrities, or human props depends partly on their status in the movie world, partly on their role within the film, partly on the director. Alfred Hitchcock was notorious for treating them like cattle, prodding them into roles fixed by the shooting script. Elia Kazan, on the other hand, gave his actors freedom to interpret character. Some of the best moments in Kazan's *On the Waterfront* (1954) were unplanned, impromptu lines and gestures that Marlon Brando discovered during the course of shooting.

A distinction is often made between two kinds of acting: method and technique. In **method acting**, performers try to get in character by identifying with the role. They may make an emotional connection between their character's plight and events in their own lives, drawing on genuine feeling rather than relying on external acting techniques. The principles of method acting were developed by Soviet stage director Konstantin Stanislavsky and popularized in the United States by people like Elia Kazan and Lee Strasberg. Marlon Brando is a method actor. His strength as a performer lies in his ability to live his parts. **Technique acting** is more traditional. A technique actor like Bette Davis tries to convey character by imitating visible behavior. She might roll her eyes in disbelief, for example, or pout her lips in anger. Each gesture is a technique, a sign deliberately adopted to represent a given mood. Bruce Kawin neatly summarizes the difference between these acting styles in a brief story:

> When Dustin Hoffman (a method actor) got himself into his role for John Schlesinger's *Marathon Man* (1976) by staying up for days on end, breaking himself down so that he could fully realize the behavior of the tortured, bedraggled hero, Olivier [a technique ac-

tor] is said to have come up to him and asked, "But Dustin—wouldn't it be easier to *act*?" (*How* 368).

On the set, the actor's life is not very glamorous. Instead of facing a live audience, he or she is usually eye to eye with an unblinking lens, speaking lines into a microphone instead of to another human being. The most intimate love scene must be played amid a crowd of technicians and machines. And since shooting schedules are arranged for budgetary reasons rather than dramatic continuity, actors learn to perform scenes out of order. This makes it difficult to steep oneself in a role or build a sense of character development. Screen actors must continually remind themselves who they are, what they want, and where they're going for each shot, and they must learn to do this on demand, repeatedly, since the director may request many **takes** (repeats) of the same shot.

A standard method for filming a scene begins with the **master shot**, a continuous long shot covering the entire action. Then portions of the action are filmed again, from different distances and angles. Later, the best shots will be selected and edited for continuity, using the master shot as a general guide. To ensure continuity of action, the scene is **blocked**, usually by the director, by walking the actors through each movement before shooting. Critical points on the set are marked by tape or chalk so that the performers will always be in camera range. They quickly learn to hit their marks to avoid another take.

There is time for one more take. The actors are poised for action, sweating a little under the heavy lights. A makeup artist dabs the beads away. Wires and booms surround the set, just off camera. The gaffer adjusts a spotlight; the production mixer checks the needles on the sound equipment. Several grips stand by the dolly, ready to wheel the camera through the set. Standing near the director's chair, the script supervisor consults the script once more and nods. The director calls out, "Camera!" The camera operator turns on the camera and waits until the motor revs up to 24 frames per second before responding, "Speed." An assistant says, "Mark!" and snaps the clapsticks together smartly. Now the director calls, "Action!" Scene 5, Take 8 begins and continues until the director says "Cut!" The words everybody wants to hear are "Cut and print!" That means the take has been successful. Good takes (there may be several for any given scene) are printed overnight and viewed as **dailies** or **rushes** the next day by the director and the editor. The best takes are chosen, and if necessary botched scenes are reshot.

Postproduction. With the set struck (dismantled) and the good takes in the can (safely stored on a reel in its container), the editor takes over. Usually with the guidance of the director, the editor assembles the raw footage into a continuous sequence, marking the places where **optical effects** (fades, dissolves, and so on) are to be inserted by the photographic lab and assembling all the different sound tracks. Eventually the fine cut and all the tracks are sent to a sound lab, where music, dialogue, and sound effects are mixed to match the picture. The photographic lab then produces several generations of prints that result in the final release print that will be distributed to theaters nationwide.

Editing, or *cutting*, is the process of compiling a film from its constituent parts. The best shot is selected from the takes. Shots are arranged into scenes, scenes into sequences. A **scene** is usually composed of several shots of the same general action, time, and location, like the scene of Charlie's Colorado childhood in *Citizen Kane*. A **sequence** covers a broader range but is unified by some thematic concern, like the marriage sequence in *Citizen Kane*, which is composed of five breakfast scenes spanning years of a relationship.

Traditionally, the process starts by cutting a roll of film into separate shots. Each shot might be labeled and hung over a cutting bin for easy access. Then the picture is matched with its corresponding sound, now recorded on **mag stock**, a length of magnetic sound tape. The editor synchronizes sound and image with the aid of a coupling machine, such as the old upright Moviola or the flatbed Steenbeck. The usual trick is to locate the frame before each take in which the clapsticks meet and align it with the matching sound, a distinct bang on the mag stock. Once aligned, both picture (film) and sound (mag stock) are cut together. The editor's next task is to create an **assembly cut** (or *editor's cut*), usually by trimming the best shots and splicing them end to end into a tentative order. The splices are made temporarily with tape or, more permanently, with cement. The rough cut may be twice as long as the final film in order to leave room for artistic experimentation. Later on, the director and others may help to create the **director's cut**, a tighter version that may include some sound and be screened for the executives. Once final changes are approved, a **fine cut** is forwarded to the sound mixers and photographic laboratory for final processing.

The creative side of editing calls for a sense of rhythm, continuity, and the conventions of film narration. The editor might start a scene with an **establishing shot** to orient the viewer, like the shot of Manhattan's skyline that begins *King Kong* (1976). In an action scene, she or he might add an **insert**, like the close-up of the villain's missing finger in *The 39 Steps* (1935). The editor might insert a **cutaway**, like the shot of a single crow that Melanie Daniels sees when she is sitting in the schoolyard in *The Birds* (1963).

A dialogue might require several alternating **reverse-angle shots**, each speaker filmed from the other's point of view. Or it might call for a **reaction shot**, showing a character's reaction to some important action. When a single action is covered by two shots, most editors would make a **match cut** so that the second shot begins precisely when the first shot ends. Further, they would achieve **matching action** by cutting at a visual turning point, like a boxer's jab to the chin or the moment of a torpedo's impact. Sometimes, though, editors create deliberate discontinuity with a **jump cut**, omitting part of the action between shots. Jean-Luc Godard uses this technique to jar the viewer into a higher level of awareness, much like Bertolt Brecht's alienation effect. Two simultaneous actions are often shown in alternating shots through the technique of **crosscutting**, or **parallel montage**. The old silent melodramas used this technique to alternate between the victim on the railroad tracks, the oncoming train, and the hero riding to the rescue. Cutting from one action to another heightened the suspense. In *The Godfather*, Coppola used parallel montage for thematic reasons, crosscutting between the peaceful baptism of Michael's son and the brutal acts of murder being carried out elsewhere at the same time under Michael's orders.

Some of the most striking visual effects are created in the lab. **Transitions** between shots, such as fades, dissolves, and wipes, are usually produced on an **optical printer**, a machine for filming film. The optical printer can rephotograph any frame and manipulate it visually. **Fades** are a common visual effect. *Fade-outs* are created by darkening each successive frame. *Fade-outs* are created in a reverse manner. **Dissolves** are made by superimposing a fade-out over a fade-in, so that one shot seems to blend into the next. In a **wipe**, one image seems to wipe another off the screen. Images can also be reduced, enlarged (blowups), repeated (**freeze-frames**), skipped (fast motion), or combined one over the other (**superimposition**).

Postproduction sound techniques involving music, dialogue, and sound effects have become highly sophisticated in recent years. It is not uncommon for a film to use a dozen separate sound tracks—sometimes hundreds—all blended into one. The music track (or tracks) might be created in a **scoring session**, during which the studio orchestra plays music specially composed or arranged for the scene. A **musical conductor** leads the orchestra while the film is being screened. The conductor may also have access to a **click track**, which measures each scene in frames per musical beat, or clicks. Click tracks are usually prepared by the **music editor**, whose main task is to coordinate the visuals with music written by the **composer** or arranger. The dialogue track, recorded during shooting, may actually be several tracks, one for each actor, so that the voices can be adjusted in relation to one another. Sometimes the voices are **dubbed** or postsynchronized, rerecorded in the studio in a process called **automated dialogue replacement**, or **ADR.** This is done when there is too much noise on the set, or when a movie filmed in one language is recorded into another, or when the script is altered after shooting. According to one account, Welles was forced to change one of the butler's lines in *Citizen Kane* after the film was shot. Raymond's appraisal of Kane, "He was a little gone in the head" was dubbed over in the studio: "He acted kind of funny sometimes" (Carringer 113).

In addition to music and dialogue, most sound effects (abbreviated SFX) are added in the studio. These sounds may be selected from a library of standard sound effects or created on the spot. King Kong's voice, for example, was created by slowing down the recorded roar of a caged lion. The sound-effects editor may replace live sound effects with synchronized substitutes in a process called **Foley editing.** Foley artists are experts in finding equivalents to sound effects that might be lost in a crowded sound track. They know that the noises made when walking on corn starch sound more like snow than walking on snow itself. They also know that striking a watermelon will produce a more effective sound for fight scenes than striking someone's jaw—with a lot less damage to the actor. When all separate sound tracks are ready, they are blended in a process known as **mixing.** The tracks are combined into a single channel by means of a mixing console. The **sound mixer** controls the volume and quality of each track, adjusting an echo, making the music swell above the dialogue, letting the pounding waves segue or fade into a heartbeat. The resulting **composite master**, the final product of the mix, is sent to the photographic lab for synchronization with the negative print. Titles, credits, and optical effects will be added before producing the **release prints** for distribution and projection.

Computers and Film

As in all areas of modern life, computers have had a major impact on the world of motion pictures, transforming the way films are made and watched. The early Star Wars movies (1977–1983) used computers to control the cameras, enabling technicians to shoot model spaceships so that their movements were more complex and realistic than ever before. *Jurassic Park* (1993) used computers to synchronize the movements of digital dinosaurs with live actors. By the midnineties, entire feature films (*Toy Story,* 1995; *A Bug's Life,* 1998) were being generated and animated in three dimensions using **computer-generated imagery (CGI).**

The most impressive advances are being made with special effects. Ordinary physical effects can be both dangerous and expensive. In *The Fugitive* (1993), a single scene—the train wreck—cost $1.5 million to shoot because a real train was used. The wreck in *Back to the Future III* (1990) cost less because it used a quarter-scale miniature train. Spielberg saved millions in *Saving Private Ryan* (1998) by using CGI to create many of the ships in the background of the Normandy Beach invasion scene. In addition to creating and moving images in intricate ways, computers also integrate images through **digital compositing.** Unlike the blue screen process, which places the actor in front of or behind the background, digital compositing allows actors (or imaginary figures) to interact with the environment and with one another. That's how Tom Hanks gets to meet Elvis and Nixon in *Forrest Gump* (1994). And it enables a computer-generated Gollum to fight with a live Frodo in *The Lord of the Rings: The Two Towers* (2002).

More and more, **digital nonlinear editing** is replacing Moviolas and Steenbecks in the editing room. The old mechanical tools were linear, requiring editors to line up their shots and work with them sequentially. If an editor wanted to move something in the sequence, it was necessary to locate the correct frames on a reel, cut them out, and reattach them somewhere else. With digital editing, the film is in electronic form—stored as coded bits of information on a disc, not as chemicals on a celluloid strip. With a computer, editors can jump to any section of the film on disc and move, delete, or change it, much as writers play with text on a word processor. Since digital information doesn't fade, there is no loss of image quality with this kind of editing. The overall quality of digital film, however, is still not considered good enough for theatrical release, so the usual practice for big budget movies is to shoot film in 35mm and make a digital copy for editing. This way, the copy can be edited on a computer, and later the original 35mm film can be cut to match the edited version. Still, many independent filmmakers are finding it expedient to work entirely with digital film from start to finish. The time may not be far off when Hollywood will follow suit. As this book is being written, digital technology already dominates home entertainment systems with innovations like DVD players and surround sound. Dolby Digital sound systems are standard features of the multiplex, and enterprising businesses have begun to experiment with digital distribution, transmitting movies by satellite to theaters equipped with high-definition projectors. The next hundred years of film technology is likely to follow the lead of this digital revolution.

Resources

For readers whose curiosity extends beyond the scope of this chapter, some excellent resources are available. One of the most popular treatments of film technology is Louis Giannetti's *Understanding Movies* (2002), currently in its eighth edition. Giannetti includes chapters on photography, mise-en-scène, movement, editing, sound, and acting. Richard Peacock offers another approach in *The Art of Moviemaking: Script to Screen* (2001). Peacock's book is a kind of illustrated glossary covering hundreds of film terms and organized along the lines of the production process, with expansive sections on scripting, casting, directing, cinematography, editing, sound design, marketing, and distribution. For an instructive description of modern filmmaking by some of the practitioners themselves, read *From Script to Screen* by Linda Seger and Edward Whetmore. Seger and Whetmore have compiled accounts by dozens of artists and technicians, who illustrate their work with examples from well-known movies. For a more theoretical perspective, see Jean-Pierre Geuens's *Film Production Theory,* which applies the insights of philosophers like Heidegger and Derrida to filmmakers like Godard, Bresson, and Altman in a fascinating fusion of practice and ideas. In a class by itself is *The Conversations: Walter Murch and the Art of Editing Film* by Michael Ondaatje. Ondaatje became acquainted with Murch when the talented sound and film editor was working on the movie of Ondaatje's novel *The English Patient.* As a novelist and documentary filmmaker, Ondaatje was fascinated by Murch's work, which ranges from *The Godfather* movies (1972–1990) and *Apocalypse Now* (1979) to *Crumb* (1994) and *The Talented Mr. Ripley* (1999). With rare intelligence and insight, the two men explore the creative decision-making process that takes place behind closed doors in the editing room.

Bruce Kawin's textbook *How Movies Work* still has one of the best treatments I know of the technology of film. Instead of relying on second-hand knowledge, Kawin has gone into the studios, labs, and archives of Hollywood to compile an accurate account of many misunderstood and misrepresented facts about film production. Kawin's explanations—always technically precise, astute, and delivered in a lively style—are regularly updated in successive editions of *A Short History of the Movies* (Kawin and Mast). Many of the examples and much of the information in this chapter are borrowed from Kawin's books.

Don't overlook the many videos that show what books cannot. One of the best is *Visions of Light,* a ninety-minute documentary on the history and craft of cinematography. Directed by Arnold Glassman, it features interviews with some of the industry's great camera artists, including Allen Daviau (*E.T.*) Gordon Wills (*The Godfather*), and Vittorio Storaro (*Apocalypse Now*).

Film Production and the Classroom

What's the best way for students to learn about the process of producing films? One method is to make a film, or part of it. This is the most direct, most challenging, and most fun. Students work in production teams, taking charge of the film's script, shooting, sets, sound effects, or editing. As members of a team, they learn about group dynamics and individual responsibility, as well as film technology. Some guidelines for this option are given in Chapter 9 and Appendix 2.

Another method is to analyze part of a film very closely, taking note of the decisions that went into its production. Students select a scene and study its component shots, observing the action, camera work, lighting, effects, and sounds for each shot, as well as the transitions between shots. This option is described in Appendix 2 as the Shot-by-Shot Analysis.

A third method is to research a particular phase of filmmaking, such as acting or set design. Students choose some aspect of a favorite film—the choreography in *Singin' in the Rain,* Marlon Brando's role in *On the Waterfront*—find out more about it, and report on their findings. This option is described in Appendix 2 as Behind the Scenes.

4 A Brief History of Film

The dream of capturing the flow of life and projecting it again as motion pictures is probably as old as dreams themselves. For centuries, people have known that if you make a pinhole in the wall of a darkened box, light from outside will shine through the hole and cast a moving image on the opposite wall. As early as the Renaissance, Italians called such a box a **camera obscura,** or dark room, and wondered how to fix the image to the wall. It was not until the nineteenth century that inventors discovered how to make lasting copies of the image. In the 1820s, an Englishman named William Talbot experimented with images on paper negatives, trying to "write with light" through the marvel of photography. By 1839 the French chemist Louis Daguerre had perfected a process for reproducing sharp, permanent images on treated metal plates called **daguerreotypes.** Meanwhile, various inventors had been tinkering with a phenomenon known as "persistence of vision." This is what happens when the retina retains an image of any object for a fraction of a second in the dark. Because our view of the object persists, a succession of still images can appear to move as one if they are properly presented to the eye. The inventors gave their ingenious toys sophisticated Greek names—the thaumatrope, the zoetrope, the phenakistascope—but they were little more than curiosities. Not until the principles of the camera obscura, persistence of vision, and the daguerrotype were combined were motion pictures as we know them born.

Exactly when this happened is a matter of debate among film historians. Some give credit to Louis Le Prince, a Frenchman who produced several strips of film in Britain as early as 1888. Little is known of Le Prince, however, because he and his equipment vanished in 1890, after boarding a train for Paris. Other scholars cite the work of Thomas Edison's assistant, William K. L. Dickson, who used a roll of celluloid film (a medium perfected by George Eastman) to record sequential photographs in his **Kinetograph** of 1891. Perforations in the film allowed it to be lifted into place behind a shutter and exposed to flashes of light, frame by frame. Later, when the pictures on these frames were viewed through Dickson's Kinetoscope, a peep-show device, persistence of vision created the illusion of a fluid motion. But a peep show is not a movie screen, and so some historians credit the first real motion picture to two Frenchmen, August and Louis Lumière, who used their own invention, the **cinematographe,** to record and project motion pictures for a theater audience in 1895.

Soon the Lumière brothers had another rival, a French magician named Georges Méliès. Whereas the Lumières were serious inventors interested in capturing reality on film, Méliès was fascinated by the new medium's capacity for trickery and spectacle. According to his own account, he was filming the traffic in Paris when the mechanism jammed. Méliès got it to run again, but when the film was later projected, he made a curious discovery: a taxi that had been passing when the camera stopped seemed to turn into a hearse. With further experimenting, Méliès learned to use stop-motion photography to make actors disappear, and soon his bag of special effects included fades, dissolves, and superimposition. So while the Lumière brothers filmed trains entering a station or workers leaving a factory, Méliès was making movies like *A Trip to the Moon* (1902) and *The Palace of Arabian Nights* (1905). As early as the turn of the century, cinema had already taken the forked paths of reality and fantasy.

It is difficult to say precisely who invented each new film technique. Perhaps it doesn't matter very much. What seems most important is that the earliest practitioners extended the language of film, deliberately or through trial and error, while trying to tell their stories. Edwin S. Porter learned how to build sequences from individual shots while recounting *Life of an American Fireman* (1903). For *The Great Train Robbery* (1903), he cut between indoor and outdoor scenes without playing each scene to its dramatic conclusion. While that would be unthinkable in a stage play, it seemed a logical way to shoot a film. Another American movie pioneer, D. W. Griffith, discovered innovative uses for close-ups, long shots, traveling shots, pans, and crosscutting in the course of his remarkable career, from one-reel melodramas like *The Adventures of Dollie* (1908) to large-scale epics like *Intolerance* (1916). Film by film, the medium of motion pictures was growing away from its dependence on staged action to become an independent art form.

The Rise of a New Art Form

To be sure, most run-of-the-mill film productions leaned heavily on theatrical models and inexpensive formulas. They were still considered cheap entertainment for the masses well into the years of World War I. Then, as new studios began turning out full-length features, movies became more widely acceptable, middle-class fare. The Hollywood moguls got their start during this period, among them Carl Laemmle, Adolph Zukor, Jesse Lasky, Samuel Goldwyn, Louis B. Mayer, and Jack Warner. Their shrewd business deals formed the large studios such as Universal, Paramount, MGM, and Warner Brothers, which in turn ruled the American movie industry for the next three decades.

In the early silent features we already find many of the roles and genres that characterize so much of American cinema. Theda Bara (her name was said to be an anagram for "Arab Death") played the exotic vamp, while "Little Mary" Pickford played the Virgin in Perpetual Peril. William S. Hart became the rugged Western hero who prefers his horse before his girl, while Douglas Fairbanks became the prototype for all urban, urbane idols. Meanwhile, D. W. Griffith's artful melodramas and Mack Sennett's wacky comedies laid the cornerstones for screen tragedy and comedy on which other directors (Cecil B. DeMille, King Vidor, Henry King, Erich von Stroheim, Ernst Lubitsch, Charlie Chaplin) and actors (Clara Bow, Pola Negri, Gloria Swanson, Greta Garbo, John Barrymore, Ronald Colman, Lon Chaney, Harold Lloyd, Harry Langdon, Buster Keaton) were soon to build.

The 1920s witnessed other trends in other countries. In Germany, a strong current of expressionism produced haunting films like *The Cabinet of Dr. Caligari* (1920), *Nosferatu* (1922), and *Metropolis* (1926). Unlike the entertaining dreams of Hollywood, these German films explored subjective images of horror interlaced with psychological and social themes. Robert Wiene's Caligari is a stylized portrait of insanity; Fritz Lang's *Metropolis* is an allegorical study of the class system and its monumental inhumanity. It is hard to imagine such pictures, with their focus on ideas rather than on performance, emanating from the studios of Paramount or MGM.

In the Soviet Union, directors were anxious to capture the spirit of their new revolution on film. Lacking the film stock for producing movies, they concentrated first on editing techniques. Lev Kuleshov, Dziga Vertov, Vsevolod Pudovkin, and then Sergei Eisenstein learned the power of manipulating images. Working with Hegelian notions of thesis and antithesis, Eisenstein fashioned an elaborate theory of montage to show how individual shots of film can be joined in a creative synthesis of ideas and ideology. While Eisenstein owes much to his studies of Griffith, the movies he produced during these times, such as *Strike* (1925) and *Potemkin* (1925), deliberately replaced the Hollywood story line with a documentary-style chronicle of events and substituted a new kind of mass hero for the individual star. So German and Soviet cinemas, each in its own way, moved away from Hollywood's example along different national paths.

By the 1930s, the motion picture industry was at its peak. In 1938, for instance, 80 million Americans were going to the movies every week. That was 65 percent of the population. More than 500 features had been produced by Hollywood the previous year. Compare these figures to those for 1968, when only 20 million (10 percent) attended movies weekly, or to those for 1969, when no more than 175 features were made (Mast, *Short History* 225). There were several reasons for this surge in film production. The introduction of sound in the late 1920s and its artistic exploitation in the 1930s enlarged the range of motion pictures and broadened their appeal. The Great Depression put millions out of work and created a huge market for inexpensive entertainment offering escape from the troubles of the day. Hollywood's studios were willing to provide this entertainment in abundance, using mass production methods that would be the envy of Henry Ford.

The genres of the 1930s typically reflected the times or deflected attention toward some glittering dream. A succession of gangster movies (*Little Caesar*, 1930; *The Public Enemy*, 1931; *Scarface*, 1932) captured the grittiness of big city life, as did tough-talking stories about news reporters (*The Front Page*, 1931; *Front Page Woman*, 1935). At the other extreme, a wave of musicals (*Flying Down to Rio*, 1933; *Top Hat*, 1935; *Gold Diggers of 1933*, 1933, and sequels in 1935 and 1936) and screwball comedies (*It Happened One Night*, 1934; *Bringing Up Baby*, 1938) stressed the bright side of things. Theda Bara and Mary Pickford were replaced by Mae West, Marlene Dietrich, Carole Lombard, and Claudette Colbert. William S. Hart and Douglas Fairbanks were succeeded by a galaxy of stars, including Clark Gable, Jimmy Stewart, Errol Flynn, and Charles Boyer. Some actors, like Jimmy Cagney and Paul Muni, created a new type of Depression hero whose toughness and unabashed ethnicity appealed to those for whom the American Dream had recently turned sour.

As the major studios gained power, they became associated with certain kinds of films. Paramount specialized in witty, sophisticated, "European" dramas; MGM appealed to the American middle class; Warner Brothers produced movies with the feel of social documentaries; RKO made sophisticated musicals and comedies; and Universal specialized in low-budget genres, especially Westerns and horror films. It was a little like the assembly plants of Detroit specializing in Cadillacs or Buicks, with each studio hiring directors to carry out its own production goals. The films of Paramount's Josef von Sternberg, MGM's Victor Fleming, Warner's Michael Curtiz, and Universal's Tod Browning all bore the stamps of studio policy as often as these men put their individual imprints on the films they made.

The 1930s were particularly good years for French cinema. While Germany mobilized for war with films like *Triumph of the Will* (1935), and Russia prepared for its defense with films like *Alexander Nevsky* (1938), France enjoyed a golden age of screen diversity. René Clair entered the sound era with two popular musicals and a cautionary tale about industrialization (*À nous la liberté*, 1931) that prefigures Charlie Chaplin's *Modern Times* (1936). Jean Cocteau continued his **avant-garde** experiments; Jean Vigo produced two masterpieces of **poetic realism** (*Zéro de conduite*, 1933; *L'Atalante*, 1934), a tradition carried on by Jacques Feyder and Marcel Carné. But the most influential director of this period was Jean Renoir, who created such enduring works as *Grand Illusion* (1937) and *The Rules of the Game* (1939).

Cynicism and Postwar Decline

For the United States, the Great Depression ended with the entry into World War II. With it, the genres of the 1930s took on a darker cast. The formula for screwball comedy acquired a strong dose of cynicism (*His Girl Friday,* 1940; *Meet John Doe,* 1941) and reflexivity (*Sullivan's Travels,* 1941). The romance of the thirties' gangster movies shaded into the hard-boiled pessimism of film noir (*The Maltese Falcon,* 1941; *The Big Sleep,* 1946). Some directors of the thirties, such as Frank Capra, John Ford, and Howard Hawks, adopted a more skeptical tone. New directors, like Orson Welles, arrived with their skepticism full-blown. Welles's masterpiece, *Citizen Kane* (1941), is probably on more ten-best lists than any other movie. Although it owes much to German expressionist imagery and French poetic realism, its self-conscious innovations in photography and editing made it a landmark in American cinema and a highly influential film for years to come. It is probably the most thoroughly studied movie ever made.

The war left European moviemaking in a shambles. Facilities in Germany, France, and Russia were virtually destroyed. In Italy, however, where an early surrender left the industry more or less intact, filmmakers were able to begin the movement that became widely known as **neorealism.** It began with Luchino Visconti's *Ossessione* (1942) and reached the world with Roberto Rossellini's *Open City* (1945), films which take the camera out of the studio and into the streets. Vittorio De Sica's *The Bicycle Thief* (1948), probably the most popular neorealist film today, illustrates the emotional power that can be achieved by shooting an unformulaic story with nonactors and without sets on grainy film stock—the complete antithesis of Hollywood studio productions.

The taste for serious, realistic movies was probably only a small factor in Hollywood's postwar decline. True, the "social consciousness film" enjoyed a vogue with American audiences. Elia Kazan turned to serious subjects like anti-Semitism in *Gentleman's Agreement* (1947) and racism in *Pinky* (1949). In 1949, directors were tackling themes like southern demagoguery (Robert Rossen's *All the King's Men*), juvenile delinquency (Nicholas Ray's *Knock on Any Door*), and corruption in sports (Robert Wise's *The Set-Up*). But some old genres, notably musicals (*Singin' in the Rain,* 1952; *South Pacific,* 1958) and comedy (*Scared Stiff,* 1953; *The Seven Year Itch,* 1955) survived into the 1950s. And others, like science fiction and the Western, emerged as the most popular film forms of the next two decades. While the West and outer space were hardly new to motion pictures, they became central concerns in movies like Robert Wise's *The Day the Earth Stood Still* (1951), Fred M. Wilcox's *Forbidden Planet* (1956), Fred Zinnemann's *High Noon* (1952), and John Ford's *The Searchers* (1956). The United States was looking back with nostalgia and forward with anticipation to expanding frontiers.

Meanwhile, the giant studios were breaking up. Financial problems, political threats, and the arrival of television were beginning to take their toll. Hollywood fought back with a round of gimmicks and inventions. In an effort to regain its audiences, it sought to entice them with highly publicized campaigns for Technicolor, **Cinerama,** CinemaScope, 3-D, and blockbuster films (*Ben-Hur*, 1959; *Spartacus*, 1960; *Exodus*, 1960), but the studio system's power weakened year by year. It was time for new initiatives.

The Sixties Generation and Its Progeny

The American audience was changing with the times. By the mid-1960s, it had become a younger, better-educated, more affluent group. It had also become smaller. While older viewers generally stayed home with the family television set, the younger audience went out to see a new, sophisticated brand of film, typified by *Bonnie and Clyde* (Arthur Penn, 1967), *2001: A Space Odyssey* (Stanley Kubrick, 1968), and *The Wild Bunch* (Sam Peckinpah, 1969). Films like Haskell Wexler's *Medium Cool* and Dennis Hopper's *Easy Rider* (both made in 1969) introduced a new level of violence and social protest, reflecting the counterculture that developed in response to Vietnam.

In the 1970s, as the country moved from the upheavals of an unpopular war to the economic uncertainties of inflation, the industry experimented with a series of disaster films (*Airport*, 1970, and sequels in 1974 and 1977), gangster films (*The Godfather*, 1972, and the first sequel in 1974), horror films (*The Exorcist*, 1973, and the first sequel in 1977), and space films (*Star Wars*, 1977), among others. Meanwhile, individuals such as Woody Allen and Robert Altman were producing films like clockwork. Allen directed ten films in as many years; Altman directed fifteen. Many of the new directors, unlike their learn-on-the-job predecessors, were graduates of film schools: Francis Ford Coppola and Paul Schrader (UCLA), George Lucas and John Milius (USC), Martin Scorsese and Brian De Palma (NYU). Not surprisingly, their productions sometimes showed the mark of academic study, but more often they succeeded in creating vigorously original images and stories for yet another generation.

Sometimes the children of rebels rebel by turning to tradition. The Reagan era, 1980–1992, was marked by reactionary politics and movies. Ronald Reagan brought his 1940s screen persona to the White House, the same image of rugged individualism that had characterized his roles in

Westerns and war movies. The optimistic spirit he announced in his presidential campaign, "It's morning in America," caught on in Hollywood, which spawned a series of upbeat nostalgic films like *Cocoon* (1985), *Back to the Future* (1985 and sequels in 1989 and 1990), and *Field of Dreams* (1989). Reaganite movie themes were conventionally mythic rather than overtly or subversively political. Heroes tended to be simply drawn, like figures in a comic strip. The popularity of Arnold Schwarzenegger and Sylvester Stallone reflected a growing confidence in hard bodies and uncomplicated motives, demonstrated in the Rocky and Rambo films. Just as audiences once cheered Reagan's "Gipper" character in the football movie *Knute Rockne, All American* (1940), now they identified with Stallone's do-or-die efforts in the boxing ring (*Rocky I*, 1976; *Rocky II*, 1979; *Rocky III*, 1982; *Rocky IV*, 1985; *Rocky V*, 1990) and on the battlefield. Ever the underdog, Stallone achieved successes in Cambodia (*Rambo: First Blood Part II*, 1985) and Afghanistan (*Rambo III*, 1988) denied to an earlier generation in Vietnam. He got to win one for the Gipper. Meanwhile, the Gipper-turned-president launched a blockbuster defense program, which became known as Star Wars. It was getting difficult to distinguish film fantasy from government policy.

Although many 1980s movies echoed Reagan's conservative agenda, some filmmakers spoke out against the trend. Oliver Stone refocused attention on the horrors of Vietnam in *Platoon* (1986) and *Born on the Fourth of July* (1989). David Lynch exposed the dark side of small-town middle America in *Blue Velvet* (1986). The Coen brothers (*Blood Simple*, 1984) and Quentin Tarantino (*Reservoir Dogs*, 1992) unsettled audiences with strange, disturbing images of domestic life. These young directors brought a quirky imagination, an ironic wit, and a taste for bizarre violence to their work. They also brought an intimate familiarity with classic film genres and pop culture, from which they borrowed self-consciously in a manner that is considered characteristic of **postmodernism,** which fuses elements of high and low culture into an entertaining cinematic pastiche.

In the 1990s, the film school generation matured and diversified. Spielberg, who had once created mythic spectacles like *Close Encounters of the Third Kind* (1977) and *E.T. the Extra-Terrestrial* (1982), turned to more realistic, adult subjects with *Saving Private Ryan* (1998) and *Schindler's List* (1993). Scorsese continued to re-create the gritty, urban tensions of *Mean Streets* (1973) and *Raging Bull* (1980) in *Goodfellas* (1990) and *Gangs of New York* (2002) but proved that he could also make kinder, gentler period films like *The Age of Innocence* (1993) and *Kundun* (1997). Male actors grew gentler too. Kevin Costner was appreciated for his sensitive performance in *Dances with Wolves* (1990). Tom Hanks was valued for his vulnerability in *Sleepless in Seattle* (1993). Schwarzenegger graduated from *Terminator* (1984) to *Kindergarten Cop* (1990). But while some heroes became more tender and compassionate, the whole idea of heroes was deconstructed in other films. Clint Eastwood's *Unforgiven* (1992) squeezed all glory from the image of the Western gunfighter. Robert Redford's *Quiz Show* (1994) took the concept of media celebrity to task. Robert Zemeckis's *Forrest Gump* (1994) exposed the hero as an empty signifier, a blank slate on which devoted fans project their standards and ideals.

Filmmaking in the nineties was marked by the unprecedented rise of independent-minded filmmakers whose individual statements and styles offered alternatives to Hollywood. Among these talented indies were John Sayles, who continued to raise the nation's social consciousness with *Lone Star* (1996) and *Men with Guns* (1997), and Oliver Stone, who continued to rouse supporters and opponents with his outspoken politics (*JFK,* 1991) and biting satire (*Natural Born Killers,* 1994). Audiences also got a richer dose of Jim Jarmusch's minimalist sensibility (*Night on Earth,* 1991; *Ghost Dog,* 1999), David Lynch's sense of bizarre paradox (*Lost Highway,* 1996; *Mulholland Dr.,* 2001), and John Waters's sly affinity for bad taste (*Cry-Baby,* 1990; *Serial Mom,* 1994).

Many of the younger filmmakers, raised on videos and armed with inexpensive new technologies, found that they could refashion the imagery and plots of their favorite movies into savvy, innovative forms. Quentin Tarantino, whose film school was the video store in which he worked as a clerk, captured the imagination of his generation with the audaciously innovative *Pulp Ficton* (1994), a film with more technique than content. The Coen brothers turned out a succession of ingenious genre parodies, including *Fargo* (1996), *The Big Lebowski* (1998), *O Brother, Where Art Thou?* (2000), and *The Man Who Wasn't There* (2001).

This postmodern trend of self-conscious borrowing found its way to Hollywood, which issued an unprecedented number of remakes and genre films. The 1990s saw three sequels to *Lethal Weapon,* four sequels to *Batman,* and four sequels to *Star Trek.* The same period produced a crowded crop of revisionist Westerns, neo-noirs, rethreaded screwball comedies, and parody horror films. Of course, Hollywood has always relied on spin-offs to duplicate the returns of box office hits. It institutionalized the genre system so audiences would know what they were getting for their money. But more than one critic has complained about the death of the story or the loss of moral backbone to special effects. In *Film Genre 2000,* Wheeler Dixon laments the drift toward "facelessness" that subsumes modern movies into the larger framework of genre cinema, movies without individual identities, concerned more with style and effects than having something original to say (1–2). But others are more positive. In "The New Hollywood," Thomas Schatz identifies a "purposeful incoherence" in the trend of postmodern films that opens them up to various readers and readings (25). Schatz notes a shift from narrative integrity to intertextuality, commenting that the integration of popular culture today (movies linked to rock songs, comic books, TV, video games, and the Internet) means that young audiences experience characters and stories in a variety of media (35). Jim Collins warns against applying old standards to new forms. He argues that the "hyperconscious eclecticism" of hybrid films like *Batman* (1989) and *Thelma & Louise* (1991) are not signs of creative failure or intellectual decline, but a feature of new cinema in which style is a function of narrative and classic genres serve new ideological agendas (254).

Meanwhile, African Americans, Latinos, Asians, women, and other groups that had been underrepresented or misrepresented in mainstream cinema are starting to emerge, not only in more balanced images on the screen but also as directors, scriptwriters, editors, and other shapers of those images. Their progress is chronicled in Chapter 8.

New Waves Abroad

Since the 1950s, wave after wave of filmmaking activity has swelled, crested, and spread its influence around the world. The first new wave began in France. After World War II, filmmakers like Robert Bresson, Jacques Tati, and Max Ophüls originated highly personal directorial styles. Critics used the term *auteur* to emphasize that such directors were the authors of their films, more like the authors of books than most earlier directors hired to oversee the collaborative efforts of large studios. Some of the critics who proposed this **auteur theory** tried their own hand at directing, contributing to a "new wave" (*nouvelle vague*) in French cinema. While their films were individual creations, they shared certain characteristics—the use of handheld cameras, natural lighting, shooting on location, improvised plots, and deliberately disruptive editing techniques—which gave them the look of **cinéma vérité,** movies that seemed more true to life because they lacked the polish of professional films. The new wave reached a peak in 1959 with Alain Resnais's *Hiroshima, mon amour* and François Truffaut's *The Four Hundred Blows,* and then settled into a kind of steady momentum as fresh talent like Louis Malle, Eric Rohmer, and Agnès Varda contributed their creative energies. Through the seventies, eighties, nineties, and beyond, the currents of French cinema have remained vigorous and varied, with directors like Claude Berri, Bertrand Tavernier, Robert Bresson, Leos Carax, Olivier Assayas, André Téchiné, Chantal Ackerman, and Claire Denis bobbing up and down.

The French new wave was highly influential abroad, particularly in Britain, where the English studios, built up in the 1930s by Alexander Korda and Michael Balcon, had been languishing. The new impulse from the continent helped to stimulate a British "New Cinema," advanced in the 1950s by the work of Karel Reisz, Tony Richardson, and Lindsay Anderson, and continued throughout the 1960s and 1970s by John Schlesinger, Bryan Forbes, Joseph Losey, Richard Lester, and Ken Russell.The British cinema has produced a steady stream of high-quality movies ever since, surfacing most recently in the working-class pictures of Mike Leigh, Ken Loach, and Derek Jarman.

In Italy, those who learned their craft from the neorealists developed distinctive styles during the 1960s and 1970s. Federico Fellini and Michelangelo Antonioni won international recognition for their films, as did, to a lesser extent, Pier Paolo Pasolini, Ermanno Olmi, Bernardo Bertolucci, and Lina Wertmüller. Italy still exports some of the world's most popular movies, exemplified by *Cinema Paradiso* (1989), *Il Postino* (1995), and *Life Is Beautiful* (1997).

In Germany, a movement called ***das neue Kino*** ("the new cinema") grew out of a meeting of ambitious young filmmakers in Oberhausen. Their manifesto, published in 1962, became the impetus for a radical shift in German cinema, from postwar "rubble films" to the bold, sensuous, richly ambiguous films of Volker Schlöndorff, Margarethe von Trotta, Rainer Werner Fassbinder, Werner Herzog, and Wim Wenders. Tom Tykwer's *Run Lola Run* (1998) has quickened the pace of German filmmaking today.

Meanwhile, on the other side of the globe, Japan gradually emerged from its cinematic isolation of the prewar years. The first to break through to international audiences was Akira Kurosawa, with *Rashômon* (1950), an intriguing tale of rape and murder told from multiple points of view. Kurosawa's films bore strong marks of Western influence, but they cleared a path between Western filmgoers and more traditional Japanese directors, such as Kenji Mizoguchi and Yasujiro Ozu in the 1950s and Masahiro Shinoda and Nagisa Oshima in the 1960s. Japan's film industry got another boost with the economic boom of the 1970s and 1980s, giving the world a taste of Juzo Itami, Shohei Imamura, Takeshi Kitano, and **anime.**

Renaissance in Eastern Europe

The 1960s witnessed an extraordinary burst of filmmaking activity in another corner of the world, in eastern Europe. In the countries most dominated by Soviet policies since Stalin, film had long been recognized as an important social and political force. In Poland, Yugoslavia, Czechoslovakia, and Hungary—all nations of the Soviet bloc—the motion picture industries revolved around state-governed film schools that controlled the means of production, the professional training, and the kinds of films being made. From the 1940s to the 1960s, these schools concentrated chiefly on local political and economic issues, their films being heralds of the state. Then, as policies became more liberal, they began producing movies that appealed to larger audiences. In Poland, directors like Andrzej Wajda, Jerzy Skolimowski, and Roman Polanski became international figures. In Czechoslovakia, there were Jiří Trnka, Ján Kadár, Jiří Menzel, and Milos Forman. There was Miklós Jancsó in Hungary, Dušan Makavejev in Yugoslavia, and Gueorgui Stoyanov in Bulgaria. When Soviet pressure put a stop to the eastern European renaissance, some of these directors fled to the West. Polanski and Forman, for example, have been making movies in English. Unfortunately, the renaissance did not survive the cold war. Except for a few names like Poland's Krzysztof Kieslowski (*Three Colors* Trilogy, 1993–1994; *Dekalog*, 1988) or Serbia's Emir Kusterica (*Underground*, 1997), few post-communism filmmakers from eastern Europe are known in the West. Perhaps censorship is a greater incentive for creativity than free enterprise. Even in the former Soviet Union, the collapse of the Iron Curtain has not produced a new cinematic wave, although more and more movies have made their way to theaters in the West. Today, Americans are becoming familiar with directors whose work was formerly suppressed, such as Andrei Tarkovsky (*Andrei Roublev*, 1966; *Solaris*, 1972); those who now feel free to express anti-Stalinist sentiments, such as Nikita Mikhalkov (*Burnt by the Sun*, 1994); and those whose originality has flourished in a new political environment, such as Alexsandr Sokurov (*Mother and Son*, 1997; *Russian Ark*, 2002).

Fresh Currents in the Nineties

Some of the most celebrated art films of the 1990s originated in unlikely places: communist China, Islamic Iran, and straightlaced Denmark. During Mao's Cultural Revolution, Beijing's only film school was closed for a decade. When it reopened in 1978, a new group of directors, the "**Fifth Generation**," began making up for lost time. Led by Zhang Yimou and Chen Kaige, these filmmakers had a distinctive visual style and something important to say. *Yellow Earth* (1984) and *Red Sorghum* (1987), which caused a sensation at world film festivals, were followed by *Ju Dou* (1990), *Raise the Red Lantern* (1992), *Farewell My Concubine* (1993), and a succession of beautifully photographed, deeply affecting historcal films. By the early 2000s, Zhang and Chen were still making popular movies, though with more contemporary settings, such as *Happy Times* (2001) and *Together* (2002). Iranian cinema achieved a similar breakthrough with Jafar Panahi's *The*

White Balloon (1995), the story of a young girl's journey through the streets of Tehran. To avoid governmnent censorship, Iranian directors like Mohsen Makhmalbaf (*Gabbeh*, 1996) and Majid Majidi (*The Children of Heaven*,1999) used deceptively simple parables, often about children, to convey their messages. Only recently, with Panahi's *The Circle* (2000) and Majidi's *Baran* (2001), have they begun to address their subjects more directly. The Danes took another approach, launching the **Dogme** movement in 1995. In a widely publicized "Dogme Manifesto," Lars von Trier and Thomas Vinterberg deliberately adopted a policy of artistic self-discipline in reaction to a film culture they considered to be too unrestrained and superficial. The results can be seen in films like *The Idiots* (1998), *The Celebration* (1998), and *Italian for Beginners* (2001).

A New Internationalism

Some countries are represented in the world's eyes mainly by a single, often singular directing talent. Sweden has its Ingmar Bergman, India its Satyajit Ray. This does not mean that Sweden or India has not produced other good filmmakers, nor does it mean that other countries have not produced good films. Developing nations, for example, have been especially active in recent years. In Africa, Ousmane Sembene has achieved international status for his films about life in Senegal. In South America, the Brazilian director Gláuber Rocha led a movement, called *cinema novo* ("new cinema"), which spread throughout the continent during the 1960s. *The Hour of the Furnaces,* by the Argentine directors Fernando E. Solanas and Octavio Getino (1968); *Lucía*, by Cuba's Humberto Solás (1969); and *Blood of the Condor* (1969), by Bolivia's Jorge Sanjinés, were among the first of many in this militant new wave of Portuguese- and Spanish-speaking films. The flow of Latin American films continues today with talented directors like Brazil's Walter Salles (*Central Station*, 1998), Mexico's Alejandros González Iñárritu (*Amores perros*, 2002), and Argentina's Fabián Bielinsky (*Nine Queens*, 2000).

As cinema enters its second hundredth year, filmmakers have begun to cut across national boundaries toward a new internationalism. In the 1980s, movies like Roland Joffé's *The Mission* (1986), Nikita Mikhalkov's *Dark Eyes* (1987), Bertolucci's *The Last Emperor* (1987), and Wim Wenders's *Wings of Desire* (1988) were made in several countries, in several languages, with casts and crews of several nationalities. The 1990s witnessed an even greater number of global co-productions. A good example is *The Red Violin* (1998). To secure financing for the film, director François Girard spent two years forming alliances with companies in Italy, Austria, England, and Japan before turning to the United States and his native Canada. The film's story follows the odyssey of a violin across five countries and four centuries, with each episode filmed in a different language and visual style. When it was shown to a worldwide audience, *The Red Violin* was in many ways a demonstration of its theme: the power of music (and, by analogy, film) to transcend national boundaries and human limitations.

The reasons for such international collaborations are economic and political as well as aesthetic. Filmmakers can avoid local restrictions, draw on a wider range of resources, and reach a wider audience. For directors who cannot depend for financing on government subsidies or audiences who speak their mother tongue, multinational contracts and world-class stars can be crucial factors in getting a film made. Sometimes filmmakers such as Jafar Panahi or Zhang Yimou can use the prestige of an international festival or the promise of foreign currency as leverage to make movies that would be banned in their own countries. And there are the growing ranks of moviemakers who choose to live in other countries. Ang Lee, born in Taiwan, has made most of his film in the United States. His enormously successful *Crouching Tiger, Hidden Dragon* (2000) was produced by companies in Taiwan, Hong Kong, mainland China, and the United States.

It may still be too soon to appraise the 1990s or speculate about the new millennium. After years of general decline, the industry seems to be flourishing again throughout the world, aided by advances in technology and the favorable market trends of multiplex cinemas, cable television, computers, and DVDs. But technical and monetary progress do not guarantee artistic achievement. We've come a long way from the dark ages of the camera obscura. Whether we will realize the full, bright potential of the camera lucida remains to be seen.

In this chapter, I have left out a great deal. I haven't mentioned Alfred Hitchcock, Howard Hawks, or George Cukor, for example. Nor have I said much about Australian, Indian, or Canadian film. This is not so much a matter of oversight as of spatial constraint. To be brief, I have had to exclude a number of important names, countries, and entire histories of film. A more complete view would include documentaries and independent films. It would include the names of cinematographers, performers, and set designers, as well as individual directors. In Chapters 5 and 8 respectively, I have sketched a brief economic history of film and a modest history of representation. A technological history would trace the development of inventions, as well as artists, examining the impact of cameras, color, sound, and screens on the state of the art. A social history would stress the changing audience, reflecting changes in the times. Many of these histories are available in other books, and I have listed some of these as references. Still other histories of film are waiting to be written.

5 The Business of Film

Garson Kanin, writer, actor, and director, once said, "The problem with film as an art is that it's a business, and the problem with film as a business is that it's an art." This uneasy partnership of aesthetic and financial interests has driven much of the history of movies in the United States, pitting talent against money like twins who can't live with or without each other. For most of that time, the story has been told from the artists' point of view. After all, books about Hollywood are more likely to be written by screenwriters (often unemployed) rather than by busy film producers. More recently, however, scholars and popular authors have given more attention to the commercial side of filmmaking. Book-length studies by David Bordwell, Thomas Schatz, Neal Gabler, Bruce Kawin, and others have shown not only that industrial forces shape the movies as we know them, but also that these forces are a fascinating subject to investigate.

The motion picture industry has come a long way since the modest **nickelodeons** of 1910, when 26 million Americans paid a nickel a week to see a program of vaudeville acts and silent movies. Times have also changed since the golden age of Hollywood, from 1929 to 1948, when six mighty studios ruled the industry and 80 to 90 million people—nearly everyone in the country from six to sixty years of age—attended the grand movie palaces and neighborhood theaters of that era every week (Belton 3). When the studio system collapsed after World War II, theatrical attendance suffered too. The numbers fell to 60 million in 1950, plummeted to 15.8 million in 1971, and slowly rose to about 20 million in the 1990s (Belton 257).

During the last sixty years, the nature of moviegoing has changed dramatically. Exhibitors introduced a succession of new ways to watch films, including drive-in theaters, Cinerama, CinemaScope, 3-D, and Todd-AO. New technologies enabled movies to be seen at home on television, cable, video, laserdisc, DVD, and the Internet. Today, movies are as portable as books. We can stop the motion, scan forward or back at will, and revisit our favorite scenes in ways that were once only possible with printed stories. And as movie studios are absorbed by large corporate conglomerates, it is no accident that the boundaries between movies and other media are blurred. Movies begin to look like videos; books begin to read like films. It's often hard to tell a motion picture from an ad. Our movies, books, commercials, magazines, toys, fashions, and theme parks seem to blend into one continuous stream of tie-ins. The story of how this situation came to be is largely a matter of dynamic economic forces at work behind the screen. It is a story worth listening to.

The story begins with Thomas Edison. Edison may not have invented movies, but he was film's first great businessman. His patented Kinetoscope camera made it possible to record motion pictures and mass-produce them for a paying audience. Edison's original idea was to show his motion pictures in Kinetoscope parlors on individual machines. This method, launched in 1894, enabled viewers to watch short films for five cents each by looking into a peephole and cranking a handle. The Kinetoscope was a clever way to maximum sales (in principle, a kind of forerunner of the modern videocassette player), but it was soon outstripped by a more popular form of exhibition, the movie theater. Modeled on the vaudeville playhouse, these theaters projected motion pictures onto a screen for a large audience. By 1905 the age of the nickelodeon had begun. The low cost of admission opened the doors to working-class viewers, particularly the increasing number of immigrants who streamed into U.S. cities from abroad. They came in droves to enjoy a "cinema of attractions," a mixture of novelty films, live acts, and "actualities" about famous people and places that stressed showing more than telling. Some historians see the nickelodeons as instruments of assimilation. The early movies appealed to both working- and middle-class customers, to both newly arrived immigrants and established Americans, helping to stir the melting pot into a homogeneous mass market. At the same time, movies became a powerful force in American culture, defining what it meant to be American.

Nobody understood this better than the men who created Hollywood. As immigrants or sons of immigrants themselves, they understood the American dream. They worked hard, and their aspirations were high. Seeing that the usual roads to riches were controlled by entrenched captains of industry, they founded what Neal Gabler calls "an empire of their own." They moved the center of filmmaking from New York to Southern California, where the climate was well suited for a young industry that needed sunlight, picturesque locations, and room to grow. One by one, between 1912 and 1928, the major studios established themselves on the West Coast—Paramount, MGM, Warner Bros., Twentieth Century Fox, and RKO—followed by the three "minors": Columbia Pictures, Universal, and United Artists. These film studios were modeled on the principles of mass production pioneered by Henry Ford. They produced movies as efficiently as Ford's factories turned out automobiles.

The **studio system** was a masterpiece of American technology and enterprise. All the elements required to make movies were concentrated on the studio lot. Each studio had an ever-ready pool of writers, costume designers, and carpenters on the premises. A story department sifted through news items and pulp fiction, generating and evaluating new ideas for scripts. A "stable" of screenwriters did the writing, often in teams, patching and revising the emerging script in response to suggestions from the directors, actors, and marketers. Special departments handled casting, budget, sound recording, editing, and set design. The sets themselves were constructed on huge indoor stages or outdoors on back lots and were planned for repeated use in different films. A typical back lot might have a haunted house for horror movies, a city street for gangster films, a saloon for Westerns, and so on. This high degree of specialization was the equivalent of Ford's standardized labor and interchangeable parts, enabling studios to assemble movies piece by piece.

Studio production was controlled by a hierarchy. At the top was a head of production or studio chief like Adolph Zukor (Paramount), Louis B. Mayer (MGM), or Harry Cohn (Columbia). Below this movie mogul, unit producers supervised the actual production process. They selected the story, found a director, and managed the film's development from preproduction to postproduction, taking a particular interest in matters of cost. In this arrangement, directors worked for studios like any other employee. They were hired to direct a project in keeping with the studio's distinctive style and marketing goals. With few exceptions, the studios were not compatible with auteurs who had an individual voice and something original to say. Actors, too, were cogs in the great wheel. They were considered commodities, part of a studio's inventory. The studios offered high salaries and glamour to their stars, but at a cost. An actor's seven-year contract was iron clad, requiring him or her to work long hours and six-day weeks playing assigned roles.

There was a kind of genius to the system, as several film historians have noted (Schatz, *Genius*). Movies present special challenges to manufacturers. Unlike cereal or mattresses, movies are intangible, one-of-a-kind goods. Films last only a few hours, and no two are exactly alike. This makes movies trickier to mass-produce. It also makes them difficult to market, since consumers must be willing to pay for an unknown product. The assembly-line methods of the studio system proved efficient and economically sound. With a reliable pool of resources readily at hand and a streamlined method for producing films, the studios turned out large quantities of successful products during the golden age of Hollywood, from the late 1920s well into the 1940s. If many of these films seemed much alike, that was deliberate. Hollywood favored genre films—romantic comedies, gangster movies, Westerns, and the like—because they required less time and expense for creativity and because they offered audiences familiar merchan-

dise. Together with the star system, which reduced the customer's guess-
work at the box office by offering brand-name performers, Hollywood's
reliance on genres, sequels, and remakes made movies more like cereal or
cars—predictable products that promised a reliable experience with a few
new variations every year. It was a triumph of business over the costly
vagaries of art.

The studio system became even more profitable through an arrangement known as **vertical integration.** This enabled a single studio to control the three sectors of production, distribution, and exhibition. A vertically integrated company can make its own films, distribute them through
its own channels, and exhibit them in its own theaters. Edison's old Motion Picture Patents Company had done this during the nickelodeon era,
controlling the patents for movie technology as well. Independent exhibitors and distributors, such as William Fox and Carl Laemmle, challenged
Edison and won a landmark antitrust case in 1915. Before long, however,
Fox (a founder of Twentieth Century Fox) and Laemmle (later head of
Universal Studios) had established their own integrated companies, each
of which controlled the entire course of its films from production to exhibition. Elaborate systems were devised to ensure markets even for bad films.
The major studios all owned theater chains, which were divided into **zones.**
First-run theaters in each zone had exclusive rights to a new film, requiring customers to pay higher prices if they wanted to see the film before it
was released for general distribution. In a practice known as **block booking**, theaters were forced to rent films in bundles. If they wanted one, they
had to rent all the others, even if the others were duds. In **blind bidding**,
theaters had to sign contracts for films even before they were made. Later
these practices were ruled illegal because they prevented independent theaters from entering the marketplace, but while they lasted the five major
Hollywood studios dominated the industry.

Collectively, the studios fashioned a certain way of telling stories and
a certain look, the **classical Hollywood style** recognized by filmgoers
around the world (Bordwell, Staiger, and Thompson). The character-centered narrative machinery of these films follows a standard pattern similar
to the plots of ancient Greek plays: a conflict upsets a stable environment,
leads through moments of rising action and emotional intensity to a crisis
or climax, and returns to the status quo when the conflict is resolved. Some
scripts trace the rise and fall of a central character; some follow the hero on
a quest; others describe a circular path, returning to the point of origin
(Belton 27–39). From a business point of view, the Hollywood narrative is
motivated by economy. It is an efficient way of telling stories to audiences
that like to hear them again and again. The Hollywood style developed for

similar reasons. With its principles of seamless editing, mood music, and focus on the stars, it never draws attention to its own construction. Instead, it draws its viewers into the story and the characters' lives, fostering the illusion that they are witnessing reality. We go to these movies for entertainment and escape, to lose ourselves.

Despite their broad similarities, however, the old studios developed distinctive styles of their own, which helped to individualize their products. MGM specialized in big pictures with glossy photography and glamorous stars supporting middle-class family values. Warner Bros., the workingman's studio, featured low-budget sets and action genres like gangster films. Paramount appealed to a more educated class with its European stylishness and wit. These studio styles have been analyzed in fascinating detail by Ethan Mordden in *The Hollywood Studios: House Style in the Golden Age of Movies.*

By the 1950s, the Hollywood system was unraveling. An antitrust suit, the Paramount Case, ended in 1948 with a judgment against the studios, which were ordered to separate production and distribution from exhibition. In the new era of prosperity following World War II, Americans spread into the suburbs, where new forms of entertainment competed with the old neighborhood theaters. Most important, television evolved into a robust competitor, keeping families at home. The studios tried to lure people back to the movies with widescreen innovations like Cinerama and CinemaScope. They opened outdoor theaters where families could bring their kids and watch from the comfort of their cars. They experimented with better sound, 3-D glasses, and even smell-o-vision, but box office attendance kept falling. By the early 1970s, 60 million homes had television sets, and moviegoing was at its lowest ebb.

Film producers needed to think out of the box, as we would say today. More accurately, they had to rethink their relationship *to* the box. When they began to see television as a new market rather than the enemy, things began to change. The studios started selling movies to the networks. They began producing made-for-television films. More broadly, they began to realize that they were in the entertainment business rather than the movie business, a paradigm shift that paved the way for corporate conglomerates, the modern successors to the old studio system.

The movement actually began in the 1960s when MCA bought Universal Studios and Gulf & Western purchased Paramount. Soon United Artists had become part of Transamerica, and Warner Bros. became a subsidiary of Kinney. Big fish were eating the little fish, turning the pond into a hunting ground for profit-hungry predators. In 1985, Twentieth Century Fox became a property of Rupert Murdoch's News Corporation, the Australian firm that launched the Fox television network. In 1989, Time Warner combined Time Inc. (a publishing house with lucrative recording studios and HBO) with Warner Bros., adding Turner Broadcasting in 1996 and AOL in 2000. In 1994, Viacom (with its many cable systems and MTV) joined Blockbuster (video and music stores) to buy Paramount Communications (which already included publishers, television holdings, movie theaters, and theme parks, as well as the Paramount Pictures movie studio). In 1996, Disney acquired Capital Cities/ABC, leaving the originators of Mickey Mouse with six film production and distribution companies, three record companies, theme parks in three countries, and more than a hundred magazines, as well as book publishers, cable networks, a cruise line, and a hockey team. The ocean proved no barrier to such mergers. Japan's Matsushita Electric (owner of video and DVD equipment) bought MCA (the parent company of Universal) to furnish movies for their hardware. For similar reasons, Sony Corp. merged with Columbia Pictures. And the trend continues.

What do these new alliances mean for the business and the art of film? First, the emphasis on corporate activity places a high priority on economic interests. As Bruce Kawin and Gerald Mast observe, "Throughout the 1980s and 1990s, the American film industry was more interested in making deals than in making movies" (556). Decisions made at the highest level of the corporate hierarchy set agendas, influencing what kinds of films are made as well as how to make, publicize, and distribute them. At the management level, a new breed of young executives trained in marketing and finance is now running the industry. These people lack hands-on studio experience, and they possess little knowledge of film history or the visual arts. Instead, their focus is on marketing research, a tool that favors remakes and sequels rather than new ideas.

In this new economic climate, it may look as though the old studio system is back with a vengeance. The movie moguls are now media moguls presiding over vast global empires of entertainment. The studio oligopoly of the 1930s was tiny by comparison. Vertical integration has given way to a more comprehensive form of ownership that combines all sectors of a multibillion-dollar industry, what Mark Crispin Miller calls "the media cartel."

The studios themselves are no longer self-contained cities housing everyone involved in the production process. They have sold off large inventories of props to private collectors and museums. They have shifted to the new corporate practice of outsourcing, hiring freelance talent to work on special projects. Would-be filmmakers still pitch their ideas to studio executives, but more often the pitchers are agents, and what they're pitching are "packages" rather than stories. A package includes the film wrapped in a bundle of accessories: advertising concepts, marketing plans, and tie-in products, all designed to make the movie more financially attractive. Today's studios are large, multilayered companies with complex hierarchies, organized by departments (Wilson 40). The acquisition department scouts new film projects and acquires distribution rights. The production department is in charge of making the film, with production executives buying the screenplays and signing directors, stars, and other talent. The distribution department selects release dates, creates trailers, and books theaters. The marketing department organizes campaigns to create a demand, targets audiences, tests previews, and works with advertisers to promote the film through posters, billboards, print, and other media. The publicity department handles the press, creates profiles, and feeds information to talk shows. The aftermarket department attends to television sales, cable markets, home video, and foreign distribution.

The people who perform these tasks are many, as anyone knows who has stayed to the end of the credits for a major film, and the length of the credits has increased with the complexity of the business. The number of producers alone may be confusing. In addition to the producers who bear the nuts-and-bolts responsibilities of making the film, there may be executive producers (to provide the financing), line producers (to manage the crew), and associate or assistant producers (to help the producers with various managerial tasks). Then there are the directors, who direct the shooting and often have a hand in the script and editing. These days, independent directors generally have more power than studio directors did in earlier times. Finally there are the casting directors, art directors, makeup artists, cinematographers, camera operators, actors, agents, and dozens of specialists, from animal wrangler to best boy. *Behind the Screen*, put together by the American Museum of the Moving Image, describes more than 120 of these jobs (Draigh).

With all these jobs and new technologies, costs have risen dramatically. Since *Jaws* broke all box office records in 1975, the industry has relied heavily on blockbusters with large budgets and expensive marketing campaigns. During the 1980s, expenses rose from $11 million to $20 million per film on average. By the early 1990s, the average **negative cost** (what it takes to produce the film negative, or first complete version of a film) had reached $30 million, a figure that nearly doubled by the end of the decade. For many films, an equal amount is needed for marketing and distribution. This means that a studio has to make three times its production costs just to break even. More and more, studios depend on the revenues from **subsidiary rights:** foreign markets, cable and network TV, video and DVD, books, television series, clothing, toys, and "product placements": cameo appearances of brand-name products in the film itself. These revenues can be stagger-ing. *Star Wars* is estimated to have sold some $3 to 4 billion in merchandise worldwide (Wilson 64).

As of this writing, a quick survey of the nation's main production companies shows that most of the five major and three minor studios of the classical Hollywood era are still around, although conglomerates own all of them. Paramount is part of Viacom, MGM and United Artists belong to Matsushita, Warner Bros. to AOL Time Warner, Twentieth Century Fox to News Corporation, Universal to Vivendi, and Columbia to Sony. In ad-dition, there are also Walt Disney Studios, with several film subsidiaries, and DreamWorks SKG, founded by Steven Spielberg, David Geffen, and Jeffrey Katzenberg in 1994.

Beyond these large companies are the independents, producers and directors who work outside the studio system. In the 1990s, a growing number of such filmmakers were able to make film after film without Hollywood's pressures on their artistic or political integrity. Directors such as Robert Altman, John Sayles, Henry Jaglom, Jim Jarmusch, Susan Seidelman, Spike Lee, Julie Dash, Wayne Wang, Gus Van Sant, Allison Anders, and John Waters are among the best known of this group. Some young filmmakers, who began as independents with small budgets and big ideas, were invited to Hollywood after their first breakthrough success. Robert Rodriguez made *El Mariachi* (1992) at home for a reported $7,000. His Hollywood budget for *Spy Kids 2* (2002) was $68 million, more than half of that for advertising and publicity. After making a few small movies as struggling unknowns, the Coen brothers (*Blood Simple*, 1984; *Barton Fink*, 1991; *Fargo*, 1996; *The Big Lebowski*, 1998; *O Brother, Where Art Thou?*, 2000) have been turning out big movies almost every year.

While Hollywood has looked to the independents for fresh talent, it has also looked abroad. Overseas markets have always been important in the film business. The Vitagraph Company, located in New York, was pro-ducing movies for export as early as 1907. By 1930, the United States was supplying 65 percent of the world's films. By 1994, American cinema was taking in more money from foreign markets than from consumers at home (T. Miller 371). More and more, the movies themselves are produced over-seas as **runaway productions,** which rely on foreign labor and facilities. *The Lord of the Rings* trilogy (2001–2003) is a good example. All three mov-ies based on J. R. R. Tolkien's classic fantasy were filmed in the striking land-scape of New Zealand. Meanwhile, foreign firms continue to invest in Hollywood. More than half the budget for *The Lord of the Rings* was raised outside the United States. As the world becomes a global village, U.S. busi-nesses have become more involved in joint productions that cross national barriers. Film financing and marketing are the healthy offspring of these global partnerships.

All this boundary crossing has important cultural implications. For years, critics have complained that American movies are destroying local cultures abroad. Young Germans, Russians, and Koreans have come to embrace James Bond and E.T. at the expense of their own traditional forms of storytelling and entertainment. But influence can work both ways. India, for instance, has enjoyed a strong film industry for years. Whereas Hollywood releases about 250 commercial films annually, India turns out more than 800 a year, many of them musical extravaganzas with exuberant dancing and improbably romantic plots. Now "Bollywood," the movie industry based in Bombay, has begun to have an impact on Hollywood. *Monsoon Wedding* (2001) was directed by Mira Nair, an independent filmmaker born in India and educated at Harvard. The film, about a Punjabi wedding, was shot in India with Indian actors. But while it has a recognizable Bollywood style, it treats issues of character and morality with a realism more characteristic of Western films. Universal Studios picked up *Monsoon Wedding* and distributed it with subtitles in Europe and the United States, where it was a box office hit. Nair's film is a good example of the new alliance of Hollywood muscle, independent talent, and multiculturalism in today's global economy.

The next chapter in this story of the business of film is hard to predict. By the time today's students are old enough to be running the world, technology and historical events will have changed the movies into something different yet again. One thing is certain, though. We will always need good stories, and the hands that sculpt our economic institutions will continue to shape the forms our stories take.

6 Theories of Film

Sooner or later, most teachers begin to look at any subject they are teaching as a whole. If you've been introducing films into your classes now and then, it's natural to make connections between films, to link your individual insights into a coherent pattern that is larger than any single film. What may have started as an occasional diversion becomes, with further thought and systematic study, a deeper understanding of the principles that underlie the magic of the movies. It is this search for underlying principles that leads us to theories of film.

Like theories of literature or composition, theories of film attempt to answer fundamental questions of identity, process, and effect. How is cinema different from the other arts? How does it work? What are the sources of its aesthetic, social, psychological, and ideological power? As in other fields of study, certain film theories have had their camps, their champions, their moments of ascendancy and decline. The realists have stressed the recording properties of film, its special ability to capture slabs of life on celluloid. The formalists have focused on film's expressive and manipulative powers, emphasizing the medium's capacity to transform the visible world into private or collaborative visions of reality. Advocates of auteur theory have seen movies primarily as works of individual artists; they view directors as the authors of their films. Other theorists believe that movies are best seen as products of an entire society, reflecting values so ingrained that even those who make and view the films are unaware of them. This is the premise of cultural studies.

My approach in this chapter is to introduce some of the major film theorists and theories chronologically. This is not a comprehensive view, and it necessarily reflects my individual inclinations. I offer it for those who want a sampling of the most influential thoughts and thinkers on the nature of cinema.

Film as Art

Back in the days when motion pictures were still called "photoplays," some notable writers sought to make a case for film as art. In *The Art of the Moving Picture* (1915), Vachel Lindsay explored the basic differences between stage and screen. He noticed the importance in movies of action over words, of setting over acting, of splendor and speed over passion and character. Lindsay's observations were intuitive rather than methodic, the insights of a poet, but his ideas anticipated much of the work carried out by more systematic theorists such as Sergei Eisenstein, Siegfried Kracauer, and Marshall McLuhan.

Film as a Reflection of the Mind

A year after Lindsay's book appeared, a German psychologist named Hugo Münsterberg published *The Film: A Psychological Study* (1916/1970). Münsterberg was fascinated by relationships between the public images of photoplays and the imagery of mental life. He regarded the close-up, for example, as analogous to the mental act of attention, a perceptual technique that "has furnished art with a means which far transcends the power of any theater stage" (38). Similarly, he saw the flashback as "an objectification of our memory function" (41). Münsterberg's analysis made serious claims for film's artistic and psychological powers, stressing a point that later critics would elaborate in great detail: watching movies is not a matter of passive spectatorship, but a mentally engaging act of interpretation.

Marxism and Russian Formalism

The first comprehensive efforts to develop a theory of film took place not in the United States or Germany, but in Russia, the home of **Marxism** in the twentieth century. Soon after the revolution of 1917, the Soviets recognized the power of motion pictures to move the masses. As few cameras were available, the State Film School in Moscow concentrated on the art of editing. Experimenting with existing film footage, Lev Kuleshov showed his students how new meanings result from new arrangements of the same images. In one famous experiment, he interspliced close-ups of the actor Ivan Mozzhukhin with shots of a coffin, a bowl of soup, and a little girl. At first the students marveled at Mozzhukhin's ability to emote grief, hunger, and compassion. Then they realized that these feelings were not in his face; they were in the viewer's consciousness, influenced by Kuleshov's arrangement of the shots. Vsevolod Pudovkin was among those who learned this lesson well. In *Film Technique* (1926) and *Film Acting* (1935), Pudovkin methodically applied the concept of "relational editing" to show how the sequence of shots can guide the spectator's thinking. Another student of the State Film School, Sergei Eisenstein, took the concept further. In *The Film Sense* (trans. 1947) and *Film Form* (trans. 1949), Eisenstein developed a more dynamic view of editing, what he called "montage." To Eisenstein, the essence of montage was conflict, a dialectic in which A collides with B to form something entirely new. Drawing on sources as diverse as Chinese ideograms and Hegelian philosophy, Eisenstein fashioned an elaborate system to explain the dynamics of audience response and to guide future filmmakers toward a creative new frontier.

Some Marxists, like the Hungarian theorist Béla Balázs, have also focused on the formal elements of film. In his *Theory of the Film* (1952/1970), Balázs astutely analyzed the close-up, the camera angle, framing, and sound for their emotional impact on the viewer. He also recognized, with remarkable clarity, the social and economic significance of film. Other Marxists have followed other paths. George Lukács, another Hungarian, was less interested in manipulations of form than in objective reproduction. A realist, he believed that "the artist must honestly record, without fear or favor, everything he sees around him" (qtd. in Giannetti 1990, 391). One of the most influential Marxist critics, Walter Benjamin, proposed a provocatively historical view of film. In "The Work of Art in the Age of Mechanical Reproduction," Benjamin argued that motion pictures are the first form of pictorial art to be consumed as products by the masses. Since movies are mechanically reproduced, they satisfy a desire to bring things closer to large audiences for mass consumption. Benjamin explored the political implications of this phenomenon, which he saw as unique in the history of art (Mast and Cohen 675–94).

Whatever their differences, however, most Marxists view art as an instrument for social change. Films, for them, are always ideological; they embody the value structures in which they are produced. In *Ideology and the Image*, Bill Nichols defines ideology as "the image a society gives of itself in order to perpetuate itself" (1). Because movies are photographic, so like life, they usually obscure the fact that they themselves are constructs and that the values embedded in their images are also constructs. A major function of the Marxist critic, then, is to "demystify" the image, to expose the artifice in cinematic art and remind us that what seems natural and necessary may be only a matter of historical arrangements and therefore can be changed.

Bazin and the Mise-en-Scène Approach

Eisenstein's emphasis on montage editing is often contrasted with the emphasis placed on mise-en-scène by the French critic André Bazin. Mise-en-scène, literally translated as "put into the scene," refers to all the elements in a single shot of film: the action, costumes, framing, camera placement, and so on. Whereas montage essentially is an arrangement of time, mise-en-scène is an arrangement of space. Bazin was especially interested in deep-focus photography because it offers a richer space and more closely mirrors the real world. In contrast to rapid montage, it allows the viewer to become more deeply engaged in the film image, to explore its textures and ambiguities. Bazin's essays, collected in *What Is Cinema?*, are concerned with the ability of film to stop the flow of time and hold it in abeyance, in an eternal present tense. For him, "photography does not create eternity, as art does, it embalms time, rescuing it simply from its proper corruption" (14). Cinema—photography in motion—preserves not only the image of things but also the sense of their duration.

German Realists and Antirealists

This ability of film to salvage time is a central issue for Siegfried Kracauer, whose *Theory of Film* offers a comprehensive analysis of **realism** in cinema. Like other realists, Kracauer argues that film, because it reproduces reality so well, has an obligation to record it, to reveal it, to "redeem" it. His work is partly a response to the German tradition of **expressionism,** which he regards as dangerously divorced from the concrete world. In place of a sterile "art for art's sake," he proposes an aesthetically fruitful return to nature.

Rudolf Arnheim's *Film as Art* represents an opposing, antirealist view. For Arnheim, the power of film is related to its limitations. The goal is not to achieve a more complete picture of reality but to exploit the very qualities of film that prevent it from being a perfect imitation of life. The fact that motion pictures are two-dimensional, that they are fixed within a rectangular frame, and that they are cut off from the flow of action and edited as shots and scenes are what gives filmmakers the tools they need to make cinema an art.

Structuralism and Semiotics

Increasingly, in recent years, film theorists have paid more attention to the arbitrary nature of the moving image, and they have sought to do so in a more systematic fashion. The movement known as **structuralism** is often allied with semiotics in an effort to study film with a rigor usually reserved for the sciences. **Semiotics** is the study of signs and codes. It views cinema, literature, and even clothing as systems of signs that derive their meaning from the conventional structures, or codes, which members of a given society share with other members of that society. The underlying principles of semiotics usually are traced back to the Swiss linguist Ferdinand de Saussure. Saussure regarded the sign as a unit of relation between a signifier and what it signifies. When we say, "A goat ate my hat," the word *goat* is the signifier, while the idea of a goat is the signified. The sign here is neither the spoken nor the written word itself, nor the idea behind the word, but a relationship between the two. (See also the discussion in Chapter 2 in the section Signs and Referents: How Do Movies Signify?) Semiotics, then, proposes a relational view of language—language as a system of structural affinities. Saussure emphasized that the signifier bears no necessary relation to the signified. Words are arbitrary, artificial, even meaningless. There is no natural reason why the sound represented by the letters g-o-a-t should make us think of a four-footed, hairy creature with a beard; it is just an agreement among English-speaking people—a convention, a code—as is the order of words in a sentence. "A goat ate my hat" is meaningful, while "Ate goat hat my a" is not, because the word order does or does not follow the code of English syntax. Saussure's ideas and development of semiotics are explained more thoroughly in several useful introductions to the subject, among them Terence Hawkes's *Structuralism & Semiotics* and Robert Scholes's *Semiotics and Interpretation*.

One of the first to apply these principles to motion pictures was Christian Metz, whose *Film Language* is a standard text of film semiotics. His analysis of film "language" is more sophisticated than most, though he concludes that the analogy to language can be applied only with great caution. For one thing, notes Metz, film lacks the arbitrariness of natural languages. The signifiers of film—like the photographic image of a goat or the recorded bellow on a sound track—bear a likeness to the signified, which words do not. Second, while the order of shots in a film sequence may make a difference in their meaning, the codes for editing are far from being as precise as the codes for syntax. As Metz observes, "film is a rich message with a poor code" (69). (His effort to formulate this code in a grand syntagm —a universal syntax of film—is described in Chapter 2.) While semioticians have helped to clarify a good many questions of film theory, their efforts to produce a rigorous framework for understanding films have done little to illuminate the films themselves.

Lacan and the Psychoanalytic Approach

Metz himself has turned to other methodologies. In *The Imaginary Signifier*, he looks to psychoanalysis for help in understanding the power of film to hold its audience. Specifically, he draws on the work of French psychoanalyst Jacques Lacan. According to Lacan, the child begins to form a separate identity during the "mirror stage" of its development. Looking in the mirror, the child identifies with its likeness as something other than the image of its mother. It perceives its mirror image as a coherent whole, but always as "over there," as elsewhere. Metz sees the cinema screen as yet another mirror, but one in which the spectator never sees his or her own reflection. With what, then, does the spectator identify? Metz answers: With the pure act of perception. This line of analysis leads deep into post-Freudian territory, linking film spectatorship with voyeurism, exhibitionism, fetishism, and castration anxiety.

For film theory, the special interest in Lacan lies primarily in his emphasis on perception (and misperception) during key moments in the growth of the psyche. Lacan links the infant's scopic drive (its visual curiosity) to pleasure and to early assumptions about its own identity. According to Lacanian film critics, much of the pleasure of watching films can be traced to a childhood desire to peer into forbidden worlds. In the darkness of the theater, the spectator observes people on the screen, but these people can't see the spectator. Spectatorship is thus a form of voyeurism, tinged with erotic longing for the visual object: the movie star becomes a sex object. But the screen is also a reflective medium, as when the spectator identifies with a film performer.

Feminist Approaches

The socializing process—more specifically, the male bias in this process—is of special interest to feminists and **feminist theory.** In her essay "Recent Developments in Feminist Criticism," Christine Gledhill begins with the idea that "women as women" are not represented in the cinema. It's not that movies have no female roles, but that these roles too frequently are stereotypes, that they are presented from a male point of view as an object for men's eyes, for "the male gaze." In Claire Johnston's words, "within a sexist ideology and a male-dominated cinema, woman is presented as what she represents for man" (qtd. in Gledhill 818). Feminist criticism has drawn from several sources for theoretical support. Semiotics offers a way to look beyond the female stereotypes to the way film texts are composed. It helps show how what is often taken to be natural, a slice of life, is actually constructed. Like the Marxists, feminists are apt to look for signs of a dominant ideology embedded in the cinematic text. By recognizing patriarchal structures in a film, some feminists believe, the educated viewer can resist being taken in.

Laura Mulvey's essay on "Visual Pleasure and Narrative Cinema" (803) uses psychoanalytic theory as a political weapon, examining the language of patriarchy with its own tools. She argues that the female figure on the screen is fashioned for men's visual pleasure, that the way she is to be looked at is built into the spectacle itself, and that the audience is unwittingly stitched into the fiction. The glamorized actress, isolated on the screen, is a sexual icon on display for the male protagonist and the male spectator. She is the bearer, not the maker, of meaning. But Mulvey finds a contradiction in the play of voyeurism, fetishism, and castration fears within this cinematic structure. Her study of Alfred Hitchcock and Josef von Sternberg is a classic, setting a tone and level of complexity for more than a decade of feminist thought.

As feminist thinking has evolved, the branches of thought have multiplied and diversified. Scholars no longer speak of the feminist view, but of views. Anthologies such as *Multiple Voices in Feminist Film Criticism* (Carson, Dittmar, and Welsch 1994), *Feminist Film Theory: A Reader* (Thornham), and a special edition of *Women's Studies Quarterly* (Kolmar) continue to harvest voices as robust and distinct as Judith Mayne, Tania Modleski, bell hooks, Janet Staiger, Janell Hobson, Linda Williams, Poonam Arora, and Esther Yau. Moreover, single-sex perspectives have been subsumed under the more comprehensive umbrella of gender studies, which includes male perceptions of movies as well as a growing body of thought known as queer theory.

Spectatorship and Reception Theory

In recent years, feminists, Freudians, Marxists, and nearly all other film theorists have given more attention to the complex nature of spectatorship. In contrast to auterism, which focuses on the intentions of a film's creators, or to textual analysis, which looks for meaning in the film itself, theories of **spectatorship** emphasize the roles played by viewers in determining what a movie means. The sounds emanating from a projector and the play of light on a movie screen are meaningless until people in the audience make sense of them. How do spectators interpret what they see and hear? What cultural and private filters color their perceptions? What makes them accept a film's illusions as reality or resist its ideological messages? Such questions have led to fascinating answers and debates between a wide range of film theorists.

Much of the earliest audience research was alarmist. Published reports such as *Our Movie Made Children* (1933) and *Movies and Conduct* (1933) regarded movies as a social problem, warning that films were harmful to youth and the future of society (Hill and Gibson 203). Such campaigns to protect the public by censoring movies or by inoculating impressionable minds continue to this day. Efforts to arm unwary viewers have become quite sophisticated.

In *Cinema and Spectatorship*, Judith Mayne gives a rigorously academic account of the treatment of audience awareness in film theory since the 1970s. She begins with Louis Althusser's seminal work on ideology, which argues that the capitalist mode of production casts individual viewers as ideological "subjects" in movies. The American film industry, with its enormous cinematic apparatus and pervasive Hollywood style, positions spectators within a particular value system. Whether we know it or not, as spectators we identify with the entire system, not just with the story or the characters. Mayne goes on to show how psychoanalytic theorists like Metz and Mulvey place a similar stress on ideological positioning. When the camera identifies with the male gaze, for example, as Mulvey says, it helps situate the viewer's attitudes about men and women.

A problem with this emphasis on implied or imposed ideologies is that it concedes little freedom to the audience. Mayne points to the work of Stuart Hall as an antidote. Hall suggests that real viewers do not automatically accept a given position within a film. They may question, test, resist, and oppose the dominant ideological reading, using a variety of strategies to negotiate the meaning of the cinematic text and the value systems behind it. A recent trend in **reception studies** is to consider historical perspectives. Drawing on documents such as fan magazines, trade journals, and oral accounts, film historians are asking what movies have meant to audiences at different times and in different contexts. How do different generations regard the movie stars of classic Hollywood? How do film genres address niche audiences? What is emerging from these studies is a broader notion of viewing communities—not a "correct" reading of a film or a manipulative machinery to be unveiled but a range of possible responses available within a "horizon of expectations" (Mayne 67).

Cultural Studies

Stuart Hall's concept of negotiated readings is part of a movement generally known as **cultural studies.** The movement began in Britain and Australia during the 1950s and 1960s, reflecting the strong interest abroad in popular culture and particular concerns about the pervasive influence of American popular culture. From the beginning, cultural studies took the form of ideological critique. In contrast to literary studies, which can be seen as narrow-minded and elitist—holding up individual texts for scrutiny against standards of high art—cultural studies focuses on cultural contexts and considers many forms of cultural artifacts as texts. A cultural study of a movie, ad campaign, shopping mall, or Barbie doll looks at the system that produced it as well as the consumers who make use of it. The concerns of cultural studies are pragmatic and political rather than aesthetic. The question is not what does a text mean, but how do people respond to it and what ideological agendas are at work in its production and reception.

Although the scope of cultural studies is broader than the usual province of film theory, it has nudged film theorists in new directions, generating interest in the commercial aspects of movies and in the global networks that are replacing national cinemas. It has also fostered a robust media literacy movement in the United States, one based on the principles that all media are constructed, contain value messages, and have political, social and commercial implications. For film teachers and their students, these key concepts offer a useful set of investigative tools that can be applied to any movie (Bazalgette):

1. Media Agencies. WHO is communicating, and why?
2. Media Categories: WHAT TYPE of text is it?
3. Media Technologies: HOW is it produced?
4. Media Languages: HOW do we know what it means?
5. Media Audiences: WHO receives it and what sense do they make of it?
6. Media Representations: How does it PRESENT its subject?

Derrida and Deconstruction

Metz and Lacan are two of the most important recent European influences on American film theory. The impact of French philosopher Jacques Derrida has been less direct. Derrida's influence on literary studies, generally associated with the term **deconstruction,** is described by Christopher Norris in *Deconstruction: Theory and Practice.* Norris presents deconstruction as a reaction to structuralism. Where structuralists read texts for the universal structures of meaning corresponding to deep-seated patterns of mind, Derrida and his followers contend that no structure can account for all the elements of a text, and that all structures ultimately undo themselves through self-contradiction. Derrida defies the very idea of classification, challenging the foundations of Western thought.

Derrida argues that concepts traditionally considered whole and complete within themselves—like truth and nature—actually rely on opposite concepts (falsehood, culture) for their meaning. The idea of good, for example, is meaningless without the idea of evil. Derrida shows that each concept contains a "trace" of its opposite, contaminating its presumed purity, contradicting the logical principle of unity. Derrida's analysis of texts typically identifies a contradiction in some key term (like the word *pharmakon* in Plato, which means both poison and remedy) or unconscious rhetorical strategy (like Rousseau's metaphor of writing as supplement). These are the "blind spots" that reveal a text's instability, its resistance to being defined or reduced to any final concept. The work of deconstruction, says Norris, is to read texts radically, "not so much for their interpretive 'insights' as for the symptoms of 'blindness' which mark their conceptual limits" (23).

Derrida's approach has been most persuasively applied to film by Peter Brunette and David Wills in *Screen/Play: Derrida and Film Theory.* Brunette and Wills use Derrida to critique contemporary film theory, demonstrating how the "essentializing gestures" of film history and genre theory always require some form of exclusion. Any effort to speak broadly about German expressionism or the Hollywood film, about Westerns or film noir, represses differences within each category as well as similarities between categories. The paradox of studying film by means of genre, history, or any other generalizing principle is that the number of common traits constituting any group is exceeded by the number of uncommon traits or by the number of traits shared across group boundaries. Thus deconstruction offers a critique of structuralist readings that view film texts as exemplars of some class or formula. Brunette and Wills move beyond the deconstructionist critique in Chapter 5, where they offer experimental readings, based on Derridean ideas, of two fascinating films, François Truffaut's *The Bride Wore Black* (1968) and David Lynch's *Blue Velvet* (1986).

Cognitive Studies

Something quite new in film studies emerged in the 1990s. Dissatisfied with theories that seem to be increasingly abstract, a number of film scholars turned to cognitive science. **Cognitive science** is the study of how the human mind processes information. Not a science in the same sense as physics or chemistry, cognition is an interdisciplinary movement concerned with the nature of perception and thought. It uses empirical tests and computer simulations to understand the workings of the mind in terms of mental representations and processes. Taking the computer as an analogy, a cognitive theorist might liken the viewer's brain to a processor, the movie to a program, and the filmmaker to a programmer. Filmmakers may not know much about the operating system (the procedures that govern human perception), but by trial and error they have learned how to program motion pictures that seem real and compelling to their audiences.

Although radically different from the mainstream of film theory, the cognitive approach can be traced as far back as 1916 to Hugo Münsterberg's little book on perception and the photoplay. In the late 1980s, cognitive film studies received a big boost from David Bordwell (*Narration in the Fiction Film*) and Noël Carroll (*Mystifying Movies*). Writing against the grain of psychoanalytic and Marxist methodologies, Bordwell argued that films do not position anybody ideologically; they activate mental operations in the viewer through definable cues (29). Both Bordwell and Carroll proposed a path of empirical research.

The methods and rewards of such research are spelled out by Joseph Anderson in *The Reality of Illusion: An Ecological Approach to Cognitive Film*

Theory. Anderson stresses the principle of veridicality, by which our perceptions of the world need to approximate the world closely in order to ensure our survival. Basing his insights on the work of J. J. Gibson and other cognitive psychologists, Anderson reasons that "we interact with a motion picture in many of the same ways that we interact with the world" (22). This enables him to explain the perception of motion, depth, and color that makes movies so realistic. It clarifies the importance of synchronous sound and editing conventions such as match cuts, point-of-view shots, and the 180 degree rule that constitute the Hollywood style. And it helps him build a case against film theorists who insist that filmgoing is a learned experience. Anderson cites research that shows how much of our response to movies occurs at the lowest levels of the perceptual system, before information reaches the cerebral cortex. Our perceptions of color, perspective, and even pictorial continuity might not be matters of cultural convention but of genetic evolution, built into the way we see and hear. Anderson concludes that motion pictures are illusions, surrogates for the physical world, which we enter with an innate capacity for play. They are the adult's cognitive equivalent to the child's game of "let's pretend," a safe way to practice survival skills.

And so the work of film theory keeps moving on, borrowing from different fields, breaking new conceptual ground, returning to earlier positions with fresh energy, always seeking systematic answers to the questions raised by inquiring minds at the movies.

Further Readings

I began by saying that this chapter would be more of a sampling than a summary of film theories. For a more thorough, detailed survey of the field, you can consult several respected studies and anthologies.

One of the earliest (and still one of the clearest) introductions to film theory is by Dudley Andrew. In *The Major Film Theories*, Andrew offers a critical survey of the first five decades, outlining the broad movements of formalism, realism, and contemporary French semiology and phenomenology. He analyzes eight major theorists along Aristotelian lines, comparing their views on the raw material of film, its methods and techniques, its forms and shapes, its purposes and values. His book provides an orderly map of the field as it appeared in the midseventies.

Andrew surveyed later developments in *Concepts in Film Theory*, noting that modern film theory in the mideighties was no longer organized around individual theorists, but instead pirouetted around key concepts. Andrew organizes his book around several conceptual hubs, including perception, representation, signification, valuation, identification, and figuration. He outlines the arguments between realists and perceptual psychologists, between genre and auteur critics, between psychoanalytic and cultural camps, noting how contemporary thinking on film is tied to other intellectual movements. "In sum," he says, "film theory today consists primarily in thinking through, elaborating, and critiquing the key metaphors by which we seek to understand (and control) the cinema complex" (12).

Another popular anthology is *Film Theory and Criticism,* originally edited by Gerald Mast and Marshall Cohen and regularly updated, most recently by Leo Braudy and Cohen. The fifth edition (1999) spans the field from Pudovkin to Kawin and beyond. The editors frame the issues in seven categories: Film Language; Film and Reality; The Film Medium; Film Narrative and the Other Arts; The Film Artist; Film Genres; and Film Psychology, Sociology, and Ideology. The prefaces to each section are clear and concise, useful guideposts by which to steer a beginning course through the shifting currents of film theory.

David Bordwell and Noël Carroll offer alternatives to what they call "Grand Theory" in an anthology provocatively titled *Post-Theory: Reconstructing Film Studies.* Bordwell divides film studies of the 1970s and 1980s into two broad categories: subject-position theories and cultural theories. Theorists of the former camp (Althusser, Heath, Metz, Lacan) emphasize a notion of self in the movies that is constructed through social and psychological forces. Theorists of the latter camp (proponents of cultural studies, postmodernists, the Frankfurt School) are interested in historical views of cinema, stress the active role of audiences (they are more than subjects manipulated by a dominant ideology), and focus less on texts than on the uses made of texts. The essays in this volume are presented as "middle-range" inquiries, combining reflection and research to address specific issues of film study rather than broad theoretical constructs.

A more recent collection of film theory, edited by Robert Stam and Toby Miller, takes yet another approach. Instead of arranging essays by theoretical schools and allegiances, *Film and Theory* is organized around key conceptual issues: What is cinema? What makes it different from other arts? How does technology contribute to the film experience? What do spectators want? How do movies represent race, gender, and sexuality? By arranging the essays in this way, this comprehensive anthology avoids academic partisanship and presents the work of diverse theorists in terms that nonspecialists can easily appreciate: as answers to important questions about the movies.

7 Film Genres

L
et's start with a few scenes. Imagine walking into a darkened theater or flipping through the television channels and finding yourself in the middle of a movie. How do you get your bearings?

Film 1. A solitary rock formation rises from the prairie against a blue, expansive sky. Two men on horseback ride into the frame in silhouette. One of them is wearing a wide-brimmed hat and leather shirt, a kerchief around his neck. A cutaway shows what he is looking at: a cabin burning in the distance. He waves his rifle in a sweeping gesture and gallops toward the smoldering ruins. Another, younger man with a six-shooter in his holster arrives on foot, surveys the scene, his eyes bulging in disbelief. The man in the hat dismounts, lifts a torn dress from the wreckage, and walks slowly toward the charred door. As he enters, he hangs his head in pain.

Film 2. We see a large suburban house in a picture-perfect setting. As the door opens, the pastoral music takes on a comic gait and a man in a business suit steps out onto the portico, luggage in each hand. Again the music shifts, this time to a romantic sweep, as a woman in a white flowing nightgown glides after him. She is carrying a set of golf clubs and a pipe rack. With a smirk, she drops the pipe rack at his feet, then takes out a golf club and snaps it across her knee before turning back toward the door. After a stunned moment, he marches after her (to a drum roll), taps her shoulder, starts to make a fist, and then opens his fingers on her face and resolutely pushes. She falls backwards through the threshold like a mannequin onto the floor.

Film 3. A man and a woman are speaking to each other in a darkened room. Slabs of light cut through the venetian blinds and big band music filters in from next door. Their speech is clipped, jagged, hard-boiled. The woman, a cheap blonde with a glinting diamond on her ring, has just fired a gun at the man. He grabs his chest but does not fall. "Try it again," he says, moving closer. The camera keeps cutting to new angles. She rises, lowering the gun. "I never loved you," she says, "I used you . . . until a minute ago when I couldn't fire that second shot. Just hold me." A new strain of romantic music swells behind them. "Sorry, baby," he says. "I'm not buying." She embraces him, and then looks at him, startled, as he pulls the trigger, twice. "Goodbye, baby," he says.

Even if you didn't recognize the figure of John Wayne in the first example, you probably would know that you were watching a Western. The frontier setting, the cowboy outfits, and the familiar image of a ravished homestead are all clues. The second scene could be a romance or perhaps a melodrama until the music and the action cue you in to its comic agenda. If you identify the man and woman as Cary Grant and Katharine Hepburn, or if you know something about the history of romantic comedy, you might guess that this is a particular variation of the genre called screwball comedy, which sublimates sexual tensions into a zany battle of the sexes. In this case, you would expect the hostile couple to end up happily married by the end of the film. Not so in the third example. The hostility between the man and woman in the dark is no laughing matter. Their hackneyed speech and cruel behavior, like their tawdry, poorly lit surroundings, suggest a gangster or detective film. A closer look at the characters (a tough guy and a treacherous woman) as well as the film's visual style (the shadowy room, those venetian blinds, the shifting camera angles) mark this as a classic film noir. Fred MacMurray has just paid back Barbara Stanwyck for double-crossing him in Billy Wilder's *Double Indemnity* (1944). The other scenes described above (films 1 and 2) are from, respectively, John Ford's *The Searchers* (1956) and George Cukor's *The Philadelphia Story* (1940).

Although these movies were made well before most students were born, young people today are probably more aware of film **genres** than any previous generation. In video stores, in television listings, and on the Internet, they find movies classified as action/adventure, comedy, drama, romance, and dozens of other categories. Movies are now so easy to see, and see again, that it is natural to look beyond their content to their formal features. Furthermore, in this style-conscious, imitation-loving, postmodern age, the films themselves are often tributes, replicas, or parodies of generic movie forms. Some young people can talk about neo-noirs and pseudo-Westerns as fluently as brand-name clothing. But what really makes a Western a Western? What enables us to tell a slapstick comedy from an *Animal House* comedy or a screwball comedy? And why does it matter?

What Do Genres Look Like?

Most movie genres have distinctive settings. Westerns, for example, take place at the American frontier, the edge of "civilized society" during the second half of the nineteenth century. There are long shots of the wide-open spaces, often filmed among the mesas of Monument Valley, with one-street towns that usually contain a saloon, a jailhouse, and a brothel. Gangster films have a more claustrophobic setting. They take place in an urban underworld of dark streets, speakeasies, and cheap hotels. Each genre has its icons, too: the Western its cowboy hat and six-guns, the musical its top hat and cane, the gangster film its cigars and heavy-duty weaponry. A genre's standard characters and plots go hand in hand. You can usually expect the conflicts of a Western to be between cowboys and Indians, ranchers and settlers, or the town marshal and an outlaw gang. In gangster films, the shoot-outs typically involve the principle gangster and an expendable array of cops or rival mobsters. Science fiction movies have their monsters and mad scientists. In romantic comedies, the man and woman who can't stand each other from the beginning are most likely to end up married. These are the formulas that audiences have come to know and love.

Beyond these elements of setting, iconography, character, and story are the visual and acoustic styles associated with particular kinds of film. Screwball comedy came of age during the 1930s, when Art Deco was still in fashion. The sleek interiors in many of these Depression comedies contribute to the humor and add a touch of class that underscores the social conflicts of the genre. Film noir, a product of the 1940s, bears a distinctively disorienting look. Shadowy lighting, claustrophobic framing, and distorting lenses create a sense of paranoia that complements the genre's themes. The sound tracks are recognizable as well. It's hard to imagine a Western without harmonicas, gunshots, and horses' hooves, or a melodrama without sobs and soaring violins, or a horror film without the piercing screams.

Like a language, a genre can be studied as a formal sign system, with codes and conventions that distinguish it from other genres. Scholars use principles of text analysis or semiotics to understand how genres work and what they mean. Learning how to "read" a Western or a horror film this way requires a familiarity with its distinctive grammar and vocabulary, the elements that have come to constitute the genre and the unwritten rules that govern how those elements work together. Here are some questions to use with students:

- Where do movies of this kind take place? (eras, locations)
- Who are the main characters? (protagonists and antagonists, heroic qualities, male and female roles, secondary types and stereotypes)
- What stories do they tell? (narrative formulas, central conflicts, threats and resolution strategies, standard plot devices)
- What are the familiar scenes? (important moments, typical events)
- What props do they use? (clothing, weapons, vehicles, and other icons of the genre)
- What makes their visual style unique? (décor, framing, camera work, lighting, color)

- What do we expect on the sound track? (music, sound effects, typical dialogue)

Students can generate simple lists like that in Table 7.1, which outlines the conventions of Westerns and film noir.

Table 7.1

	Westerns	**Film Noir**
Settings	The Wild West after the Civil War: mesas, cacti, saloons, Indian territory, jailhouse	Postwar period, seedy side of town, usually at night, rain-drenched streets, tawdry sets
Characters	Lone cowboy hero, the stoic sheriff, outlaws, ranchers, settlers, drunken doctor, schoolmarm, gambler, prostitute with a heart of gold	Detective hero: proletarian tough guy of few words; femme fatale: sexy woman who can't be trusted; amnesiac
Actors	John Wayne, Gary Cooper, Clint Eastwood	Humphrey Bogart, Mary Astor, Fred MacMurray, Barbara Stanwyck
Stories	Clean up the town, avenge a wrong, tame the wilderness, teach the tenderfoot, rustlers vs. ranchers, cattlemen vs. home-steaders	Story unfolds in complex flashbacks; solve the case, find the murderer, unveil a mysterious identity
Scenes	Shoot-out, barroom brawl, Indian attack, cattle drive, riding off into the sunset	Setup, double-cross, revenge, surreal dream sequence
Iconography	White hat, six-guns, spurs, stagecoach, strong box, horses, cattle, lasso, hanging tree	Wet pavement, venetian blinds, cigarettes, trench coat, high heels, revolver
Visual Style	Panoramic long shots, dusty trails	Impressionistic lighting, oblique camera angles, deep-focus photography, tight framing
Sound Track	Galloping horses, gunshots, train whistle, square dance, harmonica and guitar	Voice-over narration, gaudy music, screeching tires, muffled gunshot, clichéd underworld dialogue

Where Do Genres Come From?

Hollywood may not be the mother of all genres, but it has spawned more types of movies than any other filmmaking agency, and its motivating force is profit. In this respect, genres are the children of commercial success. Producers try to duplicate a box office hit by generating spin-offs, copying elements of the original that they believe have audience appeal. LeRoy's *Little Caesar* (1930) was followed first by Wellman's *The Public Enemy* (1931) and then by Hawks's *Scarface* (1932)—and the gangster film was born. While critics sometimes lament the endless, often inferior sequels that follow a popular film, the practice of telling the same story again and again is important for several reasons. First, as John Belton points out, "genres serve to stabilize an otherwise unstable industry" (115). People pay for movies before they know exactly what they're seeing, so the promise of a similar experience helps them make decisions at the box office. From the producer's point of view, a genre's track record minimizes the risk of investment. Genre films also are cheaper to make if studios already have the sets, properties, and actors readily at hand. So the genre system, like the star system, is partly a function of the marketplace. But sequels and genres are also cultural phenomena. They tell us something about the times. Thomas Schatz underlines the genre's status as "a coherent, value-laden narrative system" (*Hollywood* 16). By studying the genesis and evolution of a genre, we gain insights into the concerns and beliefs of those for whom the genre has such a strong appeal. If Hollywood is the nation's dream factory, genres are those recurring dreams that mirror our deepest fears and guilty pleasures.

Even before a movie starts a trend, it usually draws inspiration from outside sources. Before Americans saw their first movie Western, they were reading dime novels that celebrated the Old West while it was still in progress, some published as early as the 1860s. These inexpensive works of fictions were often based, in turn, on newspaper accounts, turning real people like Wild Bill Hickok, Calamity Jane, and Jesse James into legends. Some scholars trace the genre back even further to literary figures, such as Natty Bumppo in James Fenimore Cooper's *Leatherstocking Tales*, written in the 1820s and loosely based on the backwoods adventures of Daniel Boone. Film noir also has its literary precursors, in the pulp novels and popular magazine stories of the 1920s and 1930s. Dashiell Hammett and Raymond Chandler, two of the most widely read practitioners, developed a hard-boiled style of detective story that contrasted with the drawing room tradition pioneered by Arthur Conan Doyle and Agatha Christie. In contrast to the genteel ways of Sherlock Holmes and Hercule Poirot, who were mainly interested in solving puzzles, American detectives like Philip Marlowe and Sam Spade were street-smart proletarians who depended on instinct rather than intellect in order to survive. This highlights an important feature of American movies. Genre films, as entertainment for the masses, tend to find their muses in the attics of pop culture rather than the salons of high art. Most adventure films get their characters and plots from comic books, not the literary canon. The Hollywood musical looks to folk dance, vaudeville, and jazz, not classical ballet.

How Do Genres Evolve?

Studying the distinctive traits of a genre is useful for forming a sense of what it is—what makes a melodrama melodramatic—and what it isn't— what distinguishes melodrama from drama, for example, or from romantic comedy. But this can be misleading. Film genres change over time. They grow, merge with other genres, branch out into divergent forms, and reinvent themselves. Moreover, our notions of a genre may alter. What once looked like a disaster film may look quite different when seen from the broader view of history. A number of film historians have adopted Henri Focillon's analysis of evolving art forms (*The Life of Forms in Art*) to help explain the changing patterns of a genre. According to Focillon, art forms develop through four stages. In the first, or experimental, stage, the formal conventions are established. This is when filmmakers like Thomas Edison (*Cripple Creek Bar-Room Scene*, 1899) and Porter (*The Great Train Robbery*, 1903) made action movies without knowing they were making Westerns. Working with historical materials, imagination, and a sense of what audiences would like, they improvised many of the basics of the genre. Gradually a genre evolves into the second, or classical, stage. At this point, the conventions have reached a kind of equilibrium, a firm platform for telling stories. Aficionados of a genre often look back to this stage with nostalgia, regarding classics like Ford's *Stagecoach* (1939) as part of the golden age of Westerns.

Focillon describes two further evolutionary steps, a stage of refinement and what he calls the baroque phase. In the refinement stage, filmmakers embellish the form with stylistic details. Plots become more sophisticated. The basic elements are elaborated with irony, ambiguity, and thematic complexity. *The Searchers*, with its morally ambivalent hero and mature cinematic style, represents this level of refinement for Ford. In the baroque stage, the formal elaborations take over. Style becomes the content. Movies in this stage tend to be highly self-reflexive; they consciously refer to the fact that they are genre films. In *The Shootist* (1976), a legendary gunfighter hunts down three outlaws who threaten the community of Carson City. John Wayne plays the hero, a familiar role, but what makes the film generically self-aware are the flashbacks of his former showdowns, all taken from earlier John Wayne Westerns. Furthermore, two of the outlaws are well-known actors from television Westerns. At the film's end, instead of galloping into the sunset to fight another day, Wayne's character, who is dying of cancer, is shot in the back—a biographical allusion to the actor, who was dying of cancer when he made the film. Many viewers saw *The Shootist* as Wayne's screen farewell and an elegy to the Western with which he was so closely identified.

While such a neat stage-by-stage account does not work for every genre, Focillon's categories offer useful tools for analyzing change (see Table 7.2). What it leaves out are the historical and cultural factors that influence the direction of a genre. Schatz notes that the Western reached its heyday from the 1930s through the 1950s, when the American West and its values were being threatened by the forces of modernity (*Hollywood* 46). As national attitudes toward technology and manifest destiny changed, the classic Western faded out. Belton correlates specific films with current events (223). During the Korean War, when American troops were not allowed to cross the 48th parallel, the U.S. cavalry in *Rio Grande* (1950) pursued the enemy beyond the Mexican border. During the aftermath of Vietnam, when American soldiers were accused of killing innocent civilians, Westerns like *Little Big Man* (1970) showed the brutal massacre of American Indian families by the cavalry. Revisionist Westerns of the 1990s replaced the white male hero with African American cowboys (*Posse*, 1993) and strong women (*The Quick and the Dead*, 1995). Insofar as filmmakers keep trying to keep pace with their audience, the evolution of a genre can be studied as an index of social change.

Table 7.2

	Western	**Musical**
Sources	Dime novels, pulp magazines, Cooper novels, Buffalo Bill's Wild West show	Vaudeville, folk dancing, stage musicals, jazz
Experimental Stage	*The Great Train Robbery* (1903)	*The Jazz Singer* (1927)
Classical Stage	*Stagecoach* (1939)	*42nd Street* (1933)
Refinement Stage	*The Searchers* (1956)	*An American in Paris* (1951)
Reflexive Stage	*The Shootist* (1976)	*Singin' in the Rain* (1952)
Historical Influences	Changing attitudes about manifest destiny, technology, Native Americans, women	Sound film technology, television

What Do Genres Tell Us?

Knowing what a genre is, where it comes from, and how it has changed over time does not give us the whole story or even the most important. For most of us, the big payoff is in enjoying what a genre film has to offer and in understanding its messages. While some messages may be explicit, others may be stitched seamlessly into the cinematic fabric. A melodrama that seems to be saying one thing about women's roles at the level of plot may be subtly undermining that statement at another level. After studying dozens of family melodramas from the 1950s, Thomas Elsaesser concludes that despite their happy endings, these films are "critical social documents" (378). What messages do 1930s screwball comedies communicate about sex and social class? What philosophies of life are implied by the visual aesthetics of 1940s film noir? What images of men and women are fostered by the action movies of the 1980s or the romantic comedies of the 1990s? Does Carrie-Anne Moss's kick-ass role as Trinity in *The Matrix* (1999) signal a new kind of female hero, or is she a Hollywood stereotype repackaged in a designer catsuit?

It may be helpful here to think in terms of themes, myths, and ideologies. A theme is an idea that underlies a story, some generalization or insight about life. In *Stagecoach,* the small community of passengers learns about the need for compromise and cooperation. It also learns that social status is a poor index of moral worth. The respected banker proves to be a thief, while the town prostitute turns out to be heroic. A myth operates on a broader scale. Behind the individual stories and themes of *Stagecoach* or *The Searchers* is the Western myth, an idealized realm distinct from the historical West, in which an individual hero mediates between the wilderness and civilization. Ford's movies evoke this myth, not so much in the plot as in image after image of the lone cowboy on horseback silhouetted against the sky, of a stagecoach jostling through the desert, of mesas rising like cathedrals from the floor of Monument Valley. An ideology is a way of thinking, a set of beliefs on which a social system is based. The underlying ideology in Ford Westerns is visible in the way characters behave. It is essentially conservative, embodied in the Western hero's code of rugged individualism. Marx Brothers comedies are often said to be anarchic because they subvert the social order by poking fun at the upper class. In 1950s melodramas, the dominant ideology is arguably patriarchal. Everything in these movies—the plots, the sets, the camera work—seems to say that women's lives are ultimately dependent on men. Yet, as Elsaesser and others point out, it is possible to read these films against the grain, as critiques of the ideology that supports them.

This brings us to a final major point about genres and what we do with them. Whatever messages may be intended or implicit in a film—its themes, its myths, or its ideologies—the audience has a lot to say. As viewers, we have the power to accept, resist, embrace, or pointedly ignore such meanings. For many of our students—and us—going to the movies is a pleasure, a matter of entertainment, of escape. In the classroom, we should acknowledge the pleasures of the cinematic text and respect each viewer's right to enjoy each film. This does not necessarily mean, however, that we cannot enlarge those pleasures to include an understanding of a movie's cultural context and, by doing so, to appreciate how each of us fits into the changing patterns of American life.

Useful Genres

A typical video store classifies hundreds of movies in convenient groupings such as action, comedy, and drama. These are broad categories. They help the average person find the film experience that he or she is looking for in the broadest terms: excitement, laughter, tears. This chapter focuses on more specific genres such as Westerns, screwball comedies, and film noir. My purpose is to explore a few representative types of movies within the framework of genre studies. A knowledge of such genres can deepen students' appreciation of contemporary movies, introduce them to new movies, and open a window onto the rich traditions from which these movies draw.

The Western

A good deal has already been said in this chapter about Westerns. We have itemized their basic elements, traced their origins to Natty Bumppo and the dime novels of the nineteenth century, and followed their development from classical films like *Stagecoach* to postmodern reincarnations like *The Shootist*. We have also explored some of the genre's themes, myths, and ideologies. My reason for using the Western as an exemplary genre is its extraordinary popularity and resiliency. Belton has called the Western "the American film genre par excellence" (206). Schatz calls it "without question the richest and most enduring genre of Hollywood" (*Hollywood* 45). From 1926 to 1967, Hollywood produced more Westerns than any other kind of film, about one-quarter of its total output in forty years. Yet relatively few Westerns are made today. Older audiences remember the genre with nostalgia. Younger audiences seem familiar with certain films, especially the more violent products of Sam Peckinpah (*The Wild Bunch,* 1969) and Sergio Leone (*The Good, the Bad, and the Ugly,* 1966). But in the 1970s and 1980s, Westerns suffered a serious decline from which they have never quite recovered. In the1990s, nearly all efforts to revive the genre had revisionist themes, redressing earlier stereotypes of Native Americans (*Dances with Wolves,* 1990), women (*Unforgiven,* 1992; *The Ballad of Little Jo,* 1993), and African Americans (*Posse,* 1993). The classical Western seems to have disappeared like the Old West itself. Or has it only morphed into another genre, one that offers a new frontier to overcome?

Science Fiction

Introducing a volume of essays on science fiction in 1972, William Johnson observed that "science fiction writing . . . is still not fully respectable" (1). The situation has changed in thirty years. Today, the genre has a large, devoted following. Big budget films like *Independence Day* (1996), *Star Wars Episode I: The Phantom Menace* (1999), *The Matrix* trilogy (1999, 2003, 2003), and *A.I.: Artificial Intelligence* (2001) bring in big box office receipts, boosted by aggressive marketing campaigns and award-winning digital effects. Their popularity suggests that the American fascination with wide-open spaces and the need for heroes to explore them are still very much alive. The *Star Wars* cycle deliberately incorporates Western iconography. Han Solo rides his spaceship like a bronco and instigates barroom brawls in space saloons. When Luke Skywalker finds his home in ruins, the scene is taken right from *The Searchers* (film 1 scene at the beginning of the chapter). The Western homestead has become a settlement on another planet, and the Indians now are extraterrestrials.

Imaginary landscapes, futuristic technology, and alien (usually hostile) life-forms are among the hallmarks of science fiction films. They are usually fueled by fears about technology getting out of hand. Some of the earliest examples of the genre, like *Metropolis* (1927) and *Things to Come* (1936), offered visionary images of the city, a reflection of contemporary concerns about urbanization. In the 1950s, cold war anxieties about nuclear warfare generated cautionary tales such as *The Day the Earth Stood Still* (1951), in which a benevolent alien forces earthlings to solve their differences, and a series of low-budget monster films (*Them!*, 1954; *Creature from the Black Lagoon*, 1954; *Godzilla, King of the Monsters!*, 1954/1956), which often featured creatures mutated by nuclear tests. Hollywood ransacked the shelf of classic science fiction novels from Jules Verne and H. G. Wells (*The Time Machine*, 1960) to Ray Bradbury and Arthur C. Clarke (*2001: A Space Odyssey*, 1968), but it also invented new life-forms, like Ridley Scott's *Alien* (1979), Steven Spielberg's *E.T. the Extra-Terrestrial* (1982), and James Cameron's *The Terminator* (1984), which continue to reproduce. Their cinematic offspring remind us that a genre, like a new species, must evolve through a delicate balance of repetition and variation if it is to survive.

Varieties of Comedy

One genre that will never disappear is comedy. Comic movies are our safety valve, a device for releasing tensions through laughter. By making light of our deepest fears, comedy can be good therapy. Comedy also serves a social function, exposing hidden prejudices, poking fun at onerous authorities and institutions, and allowing us to criticize what's wrong with our culture without putting us at risk.

Comic films take many forms, swelling and waning in response to cultural needs. The silent period was a golden age of **slapstick** comedy, pioneered by the Keystone Kops and followed by Charlie Chaplin, Buster Keaton, and Harold Lloyd. These three great silent comedians perfected the physical humor of slapstick—once limited to banana peel falls and pies in the face—into an eloquent vocabulary of pantomime to comment on modern life. Keaton's *Steamboat Bill, Jr.* (1928) and Chaplin's *Modern Times* (1936) both deal with new technology, though the former film embraces it while the latter rejects it. Although slapstick declined with the coming of sound, some comics such as Laurel and Hardy, the Marx Brothers, Jerry Lewis, and Jim Carrey managed to combine the pratfalls and sight gags successfully with verbal humor. For good historical accounts of slapstick comedy, see Raymond Durgnat's *The Crazy Mirror,* Gerald Mast's *The Comic Mind,* and Alan Dale's *Comedy Is a Man in Trouble.*

Each decade seems to have a comic trend that reflects the dominant concerns and interests of its generation. There was screwball comedy in the 1930s, war comedy in the 1940s, comedies of courtship and consumerism in the 1950s, black comedy in the 1960s, Woody Allen and Mel Brooks in the 1970s, teen comedy in the 1980s, and romantic comedy in the 1990s.

Screwball comedy, a variation of romantic comedy, is worth a close look because it shows how a genre gets inflected by the times. *Screwball* is a baseball term, used to describe an erratic pitch designed to confuse the batter. It was applied to movies that gave a zany spin to the standard plot of boy meets girl. What makes these movies "screwy" is the way the male and female leads express their love, usually through a rapid-fire series of hostile acts. The opening golf-club-snapping-knock-her-down tit-for-tat from *Philadelphia Story* (film 2 scene at the beginning of the chapter) is a good example. The genre's peculiar narrative form is credited to a specific, historical event, the application of the **Motion Picture Production Code** of 1934, which sharply limited the ways that sexuality could be expressed on screen. When sexuality is repressed, it usually goes underground to emerge in another form, in this case as a battle between the sexes. In the case of screwball comedy, where the code is to Hollywood as the superego is to the id, there is a perfect match between the desires of an audience and the creation of a genre.

The first screwball comedy was *It Happened One Night* (1934), in which a gruff, working-class reporter (Clark Gable) and a spoiled heiress

(Claudette Colbert) duke out their differences right up to the altar. As Ed Sikov puts it in his witty and informative study of the genre, "Hatred is no reason to give up on a relationship" (15). The film's extraordinary success (it won five top Oscars) was followed by a cycle that includes *My Man Godfrey* (1936), *Bringing Up Baby* (1938), *His Girl Friday* (1940), and *Sullivan's Travels* (1941). All of these films feature the sarcasm, slapstick sparring, rapid-fire verbal duels, and impudent behavior that made Gable's "courtship" with Colbert so much fun. As a child of the Great Depression, screwball comedy reflected the economic preoccupations of the era. Typically, the woman is from a higher social class than the man and she is the one pursuing him. Christopher Beach is one of many scholars who point out that the wedding at the conclusion of a screwball movie reconciles class differences as well as sexual disparities. Depression-era audiences were reassured that honest work is better than being idly rich and that love is more important than money. Like many forms of comedy, screwball ends by neatly wrapping up the frustrations and anxieties it releases in the course of the film.

While classical screwball comedy ended in the 1940s, many of its most endearing features have endured in films like *Some Like It Hot* (1959), *What's Up, Doc?* (1972), *The Hudsucker Proxy* (1994), and *State and Main* (2000). James Harvey gives an affectionate analysis of these traits in *Romantic Comedy in Hollywood from Lubitsch to Sturges.* For a more provocative view from a feminist perspective, read Kathleen Rowe's *The Unruly Woman: Gender and the Genres of Laughter.* Rowe shows how women in screwball comedy use language and laughter to disrupt the order of men's world, wielding exaggeration and hyperbole as weapons against the rational. Drawing on Bakhtin's concept of carnival, she traces a lineage of strong-willed female comedians from Katharine Hepburn and Cher to Roseanne and Miss Piggy.

The Crime Film

Women's roles are less pronounced in movies about criminal behavior. In the classic gangster film, they tend to hover in the background as the saintly mother or the ornamental moll while the real hero, an ambitious tough guy from the streets, steals and murders his way to the top. The stories for these films came from tabloid headlines and romanticized the lurid lives of criminals like Al Capone. The gangster film milieu is the urban underworld at night, a place of fast cars, neon signs, sleazy nightclubs, and backroom poker games. Their speech is mean and brusque, riddled with the clichés of gangland jargon. The gangster hero is headstrong and hard-hitting, driven by a thirst for power and material success. Along the way, he battles rival gangs, squads of police, and sometimes his own megalomania.

While crime films appeared as early as 1912 (Griffith's *The Muske-teers of Pig Alley* is considered the first), the genre really came to life during the early 1930s with the arrival of sound films and Prohibition. Audiences flocked to the theaters to hear a city symphony of tommy guns and screech-ing tires. They enjoyed the familiar scenes of speakeasies, bootlegging, and Valentine's Day massacres. And perhaps they identified with the spectacle of someone pursuing the American dream in the only way he could.

The quick, successive triumphs of *Little Caesar* (1930), *Public Enemy* (1931), and *Scarface* (1932) ushered in a cavalcade of stars like Edward G. Robinson, James Cagney, and Paul Muni. These actors portrayed cunning, self-reliant men of action, often devoted to their families and pals but ulti-mately doomed. One reason the characters were not allowed to outlive their movies was the Production Code, which specified that the law should be upheld, criminals should be punished, and "the sympathy of the audience shall never be thrown to the side of crime, wrongdoing, evil, or sin" (qtd. in Schatz, *Hollywood* 95). The code notwithstanding, many viewers saw the mobster as a tragic figure, a victim of his milieu and his hubris. Others saw the crime film as a comment on capitalism, private enterprise exposed through the wrong side of the societal telescope.

By 1933, when the Production Code began to have real force, the genre was declining. Gangster films gave way to detective films, which shaded into film noir. Humphrey Bogart dominated the field, graduating from small-time gangster parts in the 1930s to play Sam Spade, the hard-boiled private eye of *The Maltese Falcon* (1941). Spade was a creation of Dashiell Hammett's pulp fiction, an unsentimental professional who took on unseemly jobs for cash. He inhabited the same cheap side of town as the gangsters, but he professed a kind of code. He was a good guy, com-mitted to protecting society, although ultimately looking out for himself. Bogart went on to play another detective, Philip Marlowe in *The Big Sleep* (1946), where he paired up with Lauren Bacall, and he co-starred in *Key Largo* (1948) opposite Edward G. Robinson's gangster Johnny Rocco. Be-ing the good guy, Bogart survived while Robinson was killed.

Meanwhile, in Paris, which had survived World War II without American films, French critics were noticing a trend. Watching scores of new Hollywood imports in the summer of 1946, they saw a pattern of sty-listic traits they called *noir,* after the popular *série noire* (black series) of down-beat American novels. Here was an unsettling departure from the buoyant tone of prewar movies. **Film noir** was not a genre in the usual sense; it was more of a cinematic style. It featured chiaroscuro lighting with lots of shad-ows, deep-focus photography, distorting lenses, tilted camera angles, sur-real set designs, and confusing narratives rendered hard to follow by complex flashbacks. All this contributed to a sense of threat, of imminent danger, of paranoia. The detective hero's life was rendered even more uneasy by the women in his world. These *femmes noires* showed up as sirens (Lauren Bacall), temptresses (Rita Hayworth), and black widows (Joan Crawford). They lured him with promises of love and money, and they double-crossed him in the end.

No wonder film historians link the alienated film noir hero to existentialist philosophy and Freudian psychology (Schatz, *Hollywood* 111–49; Belton 184–205). They also emphasize the mentality of men returning from the war, uncertain about their loved one's fidelity and troubled by the new place of women in the workforce. Rosie the Riveter was now a femme fatale. Her man had become cynical, suspicious, and isolated. Here was a perfect formula for a dark new genre. In addition to *The Maltese Falcon* and *Double Indemnity*, the classics from that era include *Murder, My Sweet* (1944), *Scarlet Street* (1945), *The Lady from Shanghai* (1946), and *The Third Man* (1949). Not all noir films had detectives. Some, like *Mildred Pierce* (1945) and *The Postman Always Rings Twice* (1946), were written in a romantic vein. A few, like *Laura* (1944) and *Rebecca* (1940), turned the tables and showed women threatened by men. Scholars still dispute whether film noir is a genre (with a distinct set of conventions), an aesthetic movement (like German expressionism), a cycle (belonging to the same period), or a mode (such as comic, tragic, or melodramatic). They often use the term *neo-noir* to describe more modern movies that contain noirish elements, such as *Chinatown* (1974), *Body Heat* (1981), *Blue Velvet* (1986), *Basic Instinct* (1992), *Fargo* (1996), and *Mulholland Dr.* (2001). Whatever terms we use, the fact is that film noir, detective movies, and crime films in general have left a lasting legacy. Perhaps they will continue to dominate our screens as long as there is crime in our streets and darkness in our hearts.

The Musical

Far from all these sordid images is the Hollywood musical. Emerging during the 1920s and the early 1930s from vaudeville and music hall traditions, the genre rose and fell in popularity at various times and morphed into a multitude of vibrant forms. Musicals celebrate vitality through song and dance. When audiences leave the theater, the world seems a little brighter and the whole planet seems to move to the rhythms in their hearts.

The first full-length talkie, *The Jazz Singer* (1927) is also credited as the first film musical. Sound technology made it possible to bring music to the screen. It made the voice of Al Jolson, a well-known stage performer, available to millions of filmgoers. It also set a precedent for musical plots. In the film, Jolson is the son of a Jewish cantor caught between his father's religious music and his dream of becoming a popular singer. He manages to please his father with a traditional Hebrew service and perform on Broadway in the end. This formula of competing traditions became a staple of the genre. *Swing Time* (1936) celebrates the triumph of swing over Latin dance, *The Band Wagon* (1953) of popular dance over classical ballet, and *Singin' in the Rain* (1952) of sound film over silent movies. The guy who gets the girl (or vice versa) has to play the right kind of music. The goal of putting on a show became another central plot device, repeated again and again in films like *42nd Street* (1932), *Swing Time,* and *Singin' in the Rain.* In these films, a backstage romance develops as the play goes through rehearsals. Dick Powell courts Ruby Keeler, Fred Astaire courts Ginger Rogers, Gene Kelly courts Debbie Reynolds, and their happy unions coincide with the big show—a marriage of true love and entertainment, of story and spectacle.

This opposition of drama and performance is unique to musicals. More often than not during the early years, the plots are silly and the acting static compared to the dynamic interludes of entertainment. In some cases, as in most Busby Berkeley musicals, the story and the choreography are directed by different people. Even today, people who rent videos fast-forward past the talking parts to watch Ginger and Astaire or Rooney and Garland do their stuff. Gradually, though, as the genre evolved, musicals became more integrated. Gene Kelly helped to further this trend, not only by entering the narrative and the choreography with equal zest but also by incorporating pieces of the narrative world into the dance. Grabbing a mop as a partner, using a table for a stage, or dancing in puddles, he seemed to improvise his numbers from materials at hand like a true American inventor.

The Hollywood musical reached its peak in the 1940s under MGM's Arthur Freed Unit, which produced an astonishing number of outstanding films using talents like Vincente Minnelli, Stanley Donen, and Gene Kelly. During the age of television, the studios hedged their bets by borrowing from successful Broadway hits such as *Show Boat* (1951), *Oklahoma!* (1955), and *The King and I* (1956). By the 1960s, musicals like *West Side Story* (1961), *My Fair Lady* (1964), and *The Sound of Music* (1965) were winning top Academy Awards and breaking box office records. Then something happened. One flop followed another. From the late 1960s through the 1990s, the genre seemed extinct, no longer suited to the cultural environment. Only Disney produced a regular output, with animated musicals like *The Little Mermaid* (1989), *Beauty and the Beast* (1991), *Aladdin* (1992), and *The Lion King* (1994). At the beginning of the 2000s, *Moulin Rouge* (2001) and *Chicago* (2002) gave the genre new signs of life, but it is still too early to tell.

Jane Feuer's study *The Hollywood Musical* makes some intriguing observations about Hollywood's most self-reflexive genre, a form of entertainment that celebrates entertainment. She notes that even the earliest musicals employ techniques associated with modernism. They fragment space like cubist paintings, use direct address like Godard, and offer multiple levels of reality like Fellini films. Yet, while formally bold, the Hollywood musical is "culturally the most conservative of genres" (viii). To distinguish between Hollywood's conservative agenda and the cultural avant-garde, Feuer argues that the genre seeks to hide its own status as a mechanically reproduced mass art. The musical film tries to compensate for the fact that it is not a live performance by creating a folksy feel, pretending that the actors are only amateur performers, smuggling in polished song and dance routines under the guise of rehearsals, letting the singers address the camera directly "in the first person," and inviting us to identify with the screen audience through frequent reaction shots. "Unless we put the Hollywood musical in its proper place in the history of entertainment," she concludes, "we may mistake it for a modernist film or, worse, we may never see what its revelations are trying to conceal" (47).

Melodrama

Jane Feuer's work shows how complex and devious a seemingly simple genre can be. Feminist critics have made similar studies of another genre that once appeared so simple as to pass beneath notice. In *A Woman's View: How Hollywood Spoke to Women, 1930–1960*, Jeanine Basinger devotes more than 500 pages to what she calls "women's films." She begins by reminiscing about her own childhood when she was learning what it means to be a woman from the films she saw. Part of her film experience involved choosing what she wanted to pretend was true. The matter of choice is crucial in films of that period that center on the lives of women. Women's films were clearly fictions, but the emotions they evoked were real. And each one contained a paradox. "It both held women in social bondage and released them into a dream of potency and freedom. It drew women in with images of what was lacking in their own lives and sent them home reassured that their own lives were the right thing after all" (6). Basinger shows how it was possible for women to resist the overt messages of these texts. She also shows how the women's film often deliberately subverted itself: "Everything it endorses, it undermines. Everything it destroys, it reaffirms" (7).

Basinger examines movies such as *Possessed* (1931; "A woman can do anything, anything, as long as she doesn't fall in love."), *I'm No Angel* (1933; "Take all you can get and give as little as possible."), *One Girl's Confession* (1953; "They're all alike. They just have different faces so we can tell them apart."), and *Blondie for Victory* (1942; Dagwood: "Blondie's not always right. . . . I let her think she is." Blondie: "All of my thoughts are bright, long as he thinks they're his."). By focusing on hundreds of films that are not part of the academic canon, Basinger develops a strong feel for the genre. She sees that the physical space in these films is "a series of never-ending traps and prisons" (215). She observes that women define their lives in terms of love, men, marriage, and motherhood. She also shows that with two exceptions (Mae West and Marlene Dietrich) the roles available to women are to suffer or be destroyed.

Only half of the women's films explored by Basinger are **melodramas,** a subgenre that has received close attention in recent years. Literally, a melodrama is a play accompanied by music. In the eighteenth century, the term referred to a form of French acting without words, much like mime, which developed its own mute language of gestures. From the start, then, melodrama appealed to the emotions of the middle and lower classes, which made it readily adaptable to silent movies. Today the word is commonly used pejoratively, like "weepie" or "hankie pix," referring to the cheap manipulation of an audience's feelings. As a genre, though, melodrama has come to embrace a form of domestic romance in which someone (usually a good woman) is victimized by social circumstances involving marriage, livelihood, or family (Schatz, *Hollywood* 222). Melodrama is the flip side of romantic comedy. Whereas comedy frees the protagonists from repressive forces, melodrama demonstrates their social bondage. One genre produces laughter, the other tears.

The acknowledged master of silent melodrama was D.W. Griffith, who cast Lillian Gish as the innocent heroine in *Broken Blossoms* (1919) and *Way Down East* (1920). Before the Production Code took effect, Hollywood produced a few "loose women" who made liberated choices, such as those in *Sadie Thompson* (1928) and *The Divorcee* (1930), but during the Great Depression and World War II, a large number of heroines suffered from unrequited love and family crises so that audiences could forget their own domestic problems. Women everywhere identified with the emotional performances of Barbara Stanwyck, Joan Crawford, Greta Garbo, or Bette Davis. In the 1950s, melodrama reached a high point with the work of Vincente Minnelli (*The Cobweb*, 1955; *Tea and Sympathy*, 1956) and Douglas Sirk (*Magnificent Obsession*, 1954; *All That Heaven Allows*, 1956). Their films may seem naive on the surface, but as Thomas Elsaesser argues, they are deeply and self-consciously ironic, "critical social documents" that expose the impossible contradictions of the underlying ideology (378). Their irony lies not so much in the dialogue or narrative as in the camera work and décor, those images of women waiting at home, standing by a window,

caught in a world of objects that "become more real than the human relations or emotions they were intended to symbolize" (372).

Elsaesser returns to the original definition of melodrama, showing
that what counts in the genre is "the *rhythm* of experience," its tone and
emotional tempo, rather than a logically coherent story or intellectual content. In an essentially emotional form such as melodrama, with its broad
appeal, language is used like music, less for its conceptual content than for
its expressive values of pitch and timbre. Mise-en-scène is more important
than ideas or story value, so that the meaning of a moment resides more in
the contrasting colors and textures of décor than in dialogue or narrative
consistency. Actors function mythically—as links to action, locale, and
theme—rather than realistically, as psychological beings; they are chosen
(like Rock Hudson and Jane Wyman) for the inarticulate energy they sup-
press rather than for what they say. From this perspective, it is possible to
see that much of the critical disapproval of melodrama comes from applying the wrong standards. What makes for bad drama may make for per-
fectly good melodrama.

More Genres to Explore

This chapter on film genres is far from complete. I have left out war films,
for example, as well as horror, fantasy, historical epics, action/adventure,
and subgenres like disaster films. There is no way to cover them all. My
intention has been to make a start: to raise some of the more interesting
issues of genre studies, to offer a methodic approach for analyzing what
genres are, how they function, and why it is important to know about them.
My examples illustrate the value of placing movies in a broad historical
context, of seeing them side by side as part of a cultural pattern, and of judging them in terms of their own time and formal principles. Since genres
are generated by commercial success, they tell us something about our
nation's changing tastes, needs, and desires. Audiences vote with their ticket
stubs. The genres we see on the screen are ultimately about us.

8 Representation in Film

When we look into the mirror of the movies, what images look back at us? Do we see an accurate reflection of our faces, or faces like our own? Are the characters with whom we most identify true to our realities? Do the groups that we belong to—ethnic, racial, gender, religious, generational—appear on screen as realistic, multidimensional communities or as simplistic stereotypes?

We don't all watch the same films through the same eyes. Frank Wu, a Chinese American professor at Howard University and author of *Yellow: Race in America beyond Black and White,* remembers growing up during World War II when the only actors who resembled him were piloting Japanese warplanes or being trampled in the Tokyo streets by Godzilla. Another teacher, a Navaho anthropologist, recalls watching cowboys and Indians on his reservation's only television set. As a child, he rooted for the cavalry because they always won. In one of my own film classes, an African American student once surprised the other students with his response to *Casablanca* (1942). They had been enjoying the adventure, the Bogart-Bergman romance, and the corny lines; all he could think of was the black piano player in the background. Like the film's only black actor, Dooley Wilson, this student was confined to the margin of the picture, unable to enter the main story.

This chapter offers a very brief history of representation in American films. It traces the images of African Americans, Asians, Latinos, and other minorities during a hundred years of motion picture history. It also explores how movies have characterized differences in gender and sexual orientation. Behind the history are questions: questions of identification and identity, representation and appropriation, politics and power. How do we fit ourselves into the movies? Who gets to write the scripts, and whose stories are told? How do movies define us? What roles are available? When are stereotypes damaging and when are they benign? Who benefits from these images, who loses, and what can or should be done about the inequities? A chapter like this cannot pretend to be comprehensive or neutral. I have had to be selective, and I am aware that my selections have left out many important questions, areas of focus, and examples. But what follows should provide some useful starting points for further explorations.

Stereotypes work in complex, often perplexing ways. Webster's *New World Dictionary* defines *stereotype* as "a fixed or conventional notion or conception, as of a person, group, or idea, held by a number of people and allowing for no individuality, critical judgment, etc." The key words are *fixed* and *allowing for no individuality.* A *stereotype* was originally a printing term, referring to a metal plate cast from a mold so that each printing produced an identical impression. In popular usage, we speak of stereotypes as one-dimensional generalities, treating all members of a group as if they were cut from the same mold.

Charles Ramirez Berg points out that stereotypes serve a useful cognitive purpose. As human beings, we naturally classify things in order to simplify our lives. By recognizing a few distinctive characteristics of a plant, bird, or person and assigning those traits to categories, we find it easier to manage the world's endless complexities. In psychological terms, Berg relates stereotyping to early child development, when humans first begin to distinguish the self from the outside world, the Other. Berg points out that the qualities we ascribe to others may be projections of our own fears and desires. Our images of outsiders are reduced to a few characteristics that we don't want to see within ourselves. Berg also describes a sociological dimension of stereotypes as cultural categories. When we accept the pre-existing labels inherited from our culture, we run the risk of perpetuating stereotypes. When we act on the strength of these labels, our relationships with other groups and individuals become restricted, confrontational, or oppressive.

While movies often draw on existing categories, they also play a major role in shaping cultural stereotypes. Ask people to picture a *bandido* and they're likely to describe a squat, dark-skinned figure wearing a red bandanna. Their *bandido* is probably unshaven, brandishes a pistol or a dagger, wears a wide sombrero, and slings bullet belts across his chest. Ask where this image comes from and you'll probably trace it back to the popular media: to movies, television shows, and cartoons. Some might say that comic strip *bandidos* are harmless. Stereotypes can be a narrative convenience, a kind of shorthand for adding local color, making a quick joke, or clinching a point. Others might reply that labeling any group, reducing individuals to a set of identifying traits, is always dangerous. They could point to Hitler's treatment of Jews in Europe, the internment of Japanese Americans in the United States during World War II, or racial profiling in recent times. In each case, destructive stereotypes have been reinforced by movie images, repeated on screen after screen like the impressions of a printing press, and ultimately stamped on the collective consciousness of countless viewers.

The persistence of movie stereotypes has confined many actors to typecast roles. In the early days of Hollywood, black actors were generally limited to a few demeaning secondary parts. The title of Donald Bogle's groundbreaking study of these roles, *Toms, Coons, Mulattoes, Mammies, and Bucks,* tells this story in a nutshell. During the twenties and thirties, Latino men were cast as Western villains or romantic lovers, depending on the shading of their skin; Latino women were routinely cast as spitfires or clowns with tutti-frutti hats. During World War II, Chinese American actors were assigned to play the part of the Japanese enemy (would-be actors of Japanese ancestry were being held in U.S. internment camps). Even in our own day, the typecasting continues, though sometimes in odd directions and with unexpected results. In 2001 a Hollywood agent reportedly told Nia Vardalos, the Greek performer, to change her name to Vardalez and market herself as a Puerto Rican. Instead, she wrote the screenplay for *My Big Fat Greek Wedding* (2002) and made one of the highest-grossing independent films in movie history.

Movies have been mirroring Americans for more than a century. During that time, attitudes have altered with the country's demographic complexion. The movies have both reflected these changes and helped mold them. One major change has been in the ethnic origins of moviegoers. Before the 1890s, when the first silent films were being shown to large immigrant populations, the majority of newcomers were from Ireland, Germany, and other western European countries. The pattern soon shifted to southern and eastern Europe as multitudes of Jews, Italians, Greeks, Poles, and Hungarians streamed in through Ellis Island. More recently, the tide has shifted again. Today the largest immigrant groups come from Asia, Latin America, and the Caribbean. It has been estimated that by 2050 more than half of the U.S. population will be Asian, Hispanic, and black. Another significant change has been in the prevailing attitude of minorities themselves. In the first half of the twentieth century, most immigrants wanted to shed their old-world vestments and become Americans. The desire for assimilation took metaphorical shape in the image of the melting pot. Each incoming group added flavor to the mix but ultimately surrendered its differences in the interest of national unity. This popular figure of speech was given a strikingly literal form in the early 1920s when Henry Ford staged a pageant in front of his assembly plant. Ford had groups of colorfully dressed immigrants enter an immense black pot singing native songs; they exited in identical clothing singing the national anthem (Sobchak 329).

Today, in contrast, the trend is to celebrate diversity, to take pride in cultural differences through ethnic holidays, traditional dress, and special-interest group events. The melting pot seems to have given way to the rainbow. At the same time, Americans have grown more vocal about their differences. We speak more openly about our ethnic identities, our sexual preferences, and what used to be called our disabilities. Some would add

---

that we have become more tolerant as a nation, perhaps more sensitive to the rights and feelings of people different from ourselves. Others disagree, claiming that the vogue to be "politically correct" only glosses over deeply ingrained prejudices.

Whatever changes have occurred on screen can often be understood in the light of historical events and trends within the motion picture industry. The United States' entry into World War II, for example, further discredited the images of Asians, especially our Japanese enemy, but improved the image of Latinos, our "good neighbors." Postwar prosperity, the civil rights movement of the fifties, and the period of ethnic pride of the sixties coincided with the appearance of "social problem" films and a generally more sensitive treatment of minorities. Furthermore, as the old studio system broke up, technology reduced the cost of film production, and cameras found their way into the hands of independent filmmakers, more members of minorities were able to tell their own stories in their own ways.

Black Images on Film

What can we learn from the history of African Americans on film? According to Bogle, the first black movie character was Uncle Tom (in *Uncle Tom's Cabin,* directed by Edwin S. Porter in 1903), performed by a white actor in blackface. It was not until 1914 that Sam Lucas appeared as the first black actor in a leading role—in another film version of Stowe's novel. The most notorious depiction of African Americans during the silent period was *The Birth of a Nation,* directed by D. W. Griffith in 1915. Griffith's three-hour epic was based on *The Clansman,* written by a supporter of the Ku Klux Klan. It showed an idyllic Old South giving way to chaos after the Civil War, when "uppity" Negroes from the north pillage plantations, corrupt former slaves, and take over local governments until the Klan restores order once again. The film purports to show "an historical facsimile" of Negro legislators drinking from whiskey flasks with their bare feet on the desks and features a scene in which a white woman leaps from a cliff to her death rather than face rape by a black man. Hailed as a cinematic masterpiece by many, *The Birth of a Nation* was picketed by the NAACP and incited race riots in some cities. Its legacy of racist images left indelible impressions on American movies and audiences for years.

Less generally known was a small body of silent films made by independent black directors with black performers for black audiences. These so-called **race movies,** shown in black ghetto theaters, often mimicked Hollywood genres, but with black actors in the principle roles. These actors appeared as "the black Valentino," "the sepia Mae West," or "the colored Cagney," but they also performed serious dramatic roles. The most celebrated producer of such films was Oscar Micheaux, a resourceful entrepreneur who wrote, produced, and directed some thirty-four movies in thirty years. *Within Our Gates* (1919/1920), his earliest surviving feature, uses flashbacks to tell the story of a hard-working, poor black couple with dreams of education and a better life. The film includes a number of role reversals, including the attempted rape of a black woman by a white landowner—a pointed reply to *Birth of a Nation.*

Back in Hollywood, the coming of "talkies" opened up new roles for black actors, singers, and dancers. The sound of music ushered in a rousing parade of all-black spectacles, from *Hearts in Dixie* (1929) to *Porgy and Bess* (1959). Yet, while these musicals provided lots of jobs for black performers, Bogle points out that they were scripted and directed by whites. So although *Hallelujah* (1929) and *The Green Pastures* (1936) claim to celebrate "real Negro folk culture," they offer quaint caricature instead (Bogle 27). Meanwhile, mainstream films continued to typecast black actors like Stepin Fetchit (as the self-deprecating dimwit suggested by his screen name), Bill "Bojangles" Robinson (as Shirley Temple's kindly "uncle"), and Hattie McDaniel (as the faithful servant in *Gone with the Wind*, 1939). When McDaniel was criticized for accepting such demeaning parts, she replied, "Why should I complain about making seven thousand dollars a week playing a maid? If I didn't, I'd be making seven dollars a week actually being one" (Bogle 82).

As the decades wore on, these molds were broken by a succession of talented black actors like Paul Robeson, Dorothy Dandridge, and Sidney Poitier. Robeson was also a brilliant student, skillful athlete, and gifted singer, but despite his prodigious talents he was blackballed for his political beliefs and forced to make many of his films abroad. Dandridge became a vibrant national star with *Carmen Jones* (1954) and was the first black woman to receive an Oscar nomination for Best Actress, but ended her career tragically, bankrupt and depressed. Sidney Poitier fared much better. In film after landmark film—*The Defiant Ones* (1958), *A Raisin in the Sun* (1961), *To Sir, with Love* (1967)—he played a progression of serious roles with dignity and an unwavering inner strength.

Poitier's performances can be seen as the culmination of a trend that began with postwar "social problem" films and continued during the civil rights period with films such as *Guess Who's Coming to Dinner* (1967). The trend is carefully traced by film historian Thomas Cripps (*Making Movies Black*), who examines how these movies handled issues of racial prejudice in the context of their times. In *Home of the Brave* (1949), a black soldier returns from World War II shattered not only by the shock of battle and survivor's guilt but also by the racism he encountered in his own platoon. In *Pinky* (1949), a fair-skinned black woman returns to the South and tries passing as white before reclaiming her black identity. Elia Kazan, who directed *Pinky*, cast Jeanne Crain, a white actress, in the role of the mulatto woman, but it was Ethel Waters's resilience in the supporting role of Granny that won an Oscar nomination.

A very different kind of film emerged during the black power movement of the 1970s. Melvin Van Peebles, a black filmmaker, was unable to get Hollywood to produce his script, so he directed *Sweet Sweetback's Baad Asssss Song* (1971) himself on a shoestring budget. The film had a fresh, aggressive style and introduced a brash, new urban character with a boundless capacity for violence and sex. It was a sweeping commercial success with black audiences, spawning an outburst of imitations like *Shaft* (1971), *Superfly* (1972), and *Foxy Brown* (1974). The heroes of these films were pimps, addicts, gangsters, and prostitutes, and the villain was often the white establishment. Denounced by the NAACP for reinforcing negative stereotypes, these features were dubbed **blaxploitation films,** but they were immensely popular. Hollywood studios were happy to back the movement financially until it ran out of steam near the end of the decade.

It was Spike Lee who wrote the next chapter in the history of black film images by telling his own stories in his own way. A student of the film school generation, Lee proved that talented black directors could produce independent films with strong personal messages and still make enough money to continue making films. Lee began making feature films with *She's Gotta Have It* (1986), achieved national acclaim with *Do the Right Thing* (1989), and went on to make such highly individual, often politically controversial films as *Malcolm X* (1992), *Clockers* (1995), and *Bamboozled* (2000). His success paved the way for other young directors like John Singleton (*Boyz N the Hood*, 1991) and Julie Dash (*Daughters of the Dust*, 1991).

Meanwhile, a new crop of black actors gained widespread popularity with audiences. Bill Cosby, Richard Pryor, Eddie Murphy, Whoopie Goldberg, Angela Bassett, and Thandie Newton took on both comic and dramatic roles, widening the options available to black performers. In 2002, when Denzel Washington accepted his Academy Award for *Training Day* (2001), he saluted Sidney Poitier, the only other black actor to receive an Oscar, who had just been given Hollywood's Lifetime Achievement Award. Also on stage was Halle Berry, who received an Oscar for *Monster's Ball* (2001). As she became the first black woman to receive the award for Best Actress, she accepted it "for every nameless, faceless woman of color who now has a chance."

Asian Images

While film scholars regularly speak of "Asian" images, they often recognize that this is a misleading, lump-together word, one that perpetuates the view that all so-called yellow-skinned people are alike. Chinese, Japanese, Koreans, and other groups on or near the Asian continent have distinct histories and cultures, and they make further ethnic distinctions within their own national borders. Yet it is precisely because Americans of Chinese, Korean, or Vietnamese ancestry have been regarded by mainstream moviegoers as "Asian Americans" (some would include East Indian and Pakistani immigrants as well) that the term is useful here. In *Orientalism*, Edward Said's breakthrough study of colonial thinking, the Palestinian-born American scholar discussed Western notions of the Middle East. Said emphasized that the exotic images of Eastern peoples constructed in the West are superficial, condescending, and highly artificial. He proposed that these images be systematically deconstructed, not merely denounced, suggesting that by exposing its artificiality, the "Orient" might be dismantled altogether (28).

Asian immigration to the United States began in the mid-1800s to fill a labor shortage created by the gold rush. Chinese workers supplied most of the cheap labor on the transcontinental railroad, but when the job was done they were no longer wanted. The U.S. press warned of a "Yellow Peril," inflaming fears by generating images of hordes of Asians overrunning white civilization. The "Chinese Question" was resolved by expulsion and restriction. Immigration was severely curtailed. Many Chinese immigrants were forced to return to China, while others were confined to noncompetitive jobs as houseboys, in laundries, and in restaurants. Asian women were no longer allowed into the country, and by 1900 the ratio of males to females in the Chinese population was 26 to 1 (Shim).

On America's early movie screens, Asian women often were alluring sexual objects for white males. The pattern of *Madame Butterfly* (1915), in which the Japanese woman dies after a romance with the American, was repeated with minor variations in films like *Sayonara* (1957) and *The World of Suzie Wong* (1960). Asian men typically served as comic figures, like the aphoristic Charlie Chan (who appeared in forty-eight films during the 1930s and 1940s), or as menacing gangsters, like the insidious Dr. Fu Manchu (whose evil doings entertained audiences from the 1920s well into the 1940s). Fu Manchu reflected fears of Asian imperial aggression at a time when Japan had just taken over Manchuria and seemed likely to continue its imperial expansion. When Japan invaded China in 1937, the Chinese suddenly became the good guys. *The Good Earth* (1937), *Dragon Seed* (1944), and *Thirty Seconds over Tokyo* (1944) offered positive portraits of patiently suffering Chinese. Meanwhile, the Japanese became kamikaze villains in films such as *Wake Island* (1942), *Bataan* (1943), and *Bugs Bunny Nips the Nips* (1944). In contrast to films about the United States' European enemies, the Japanese were shown as a subhuman race, the deserving object of ethnic slurs and racist language.

Another role reversal occurred in 1949, when the communists took over China and U.S. forces entered Korea (1950–1953). Now the Japanese became the good Asians (*The Teahouse of the August Moon*, 1956; *Sayonara*, 1957), while the Chinese appeared as insidiously clever torturers in movies like *The Manchurian Candidate* (1962). In the Reagan-Bush era of the 1980s, the pendulum swung again. Competition from a strong Japanese economy created a taste for revenge, a climate in which Americans were happy to watch midwestern autoworkers stand up to management (*Gung Ho*, 1986) and cheer on New York cops while they chased Yakuza gangsters in their own backyard (*Black Rain*, 1989; *Showdown in Little Tokyo*, 1991). Once again, Asians became convenient outlets for national frustrations and fantasies.

As with African American characters, major Asian roles were often taken by white actors, especially in the early years. The Chinese Buddhist in *Broken Blossoms* (1919) was played by Richard Barthelmess. The Chinese peasants in *The Good Earth* (1937) were played by Paul Muni and Luise Rainer in yellow face. A notable exception was Sessue Hayakawa, a handsome Japanese American actor who became a matinee idol during the silent period. His powerful performance in Cecil B. DeMille's *The Cheat* (1915) made him famous, but the role of sadistic villain kept dogging his career (Higashi). To avoid being stereotyped, Hayakawa left Hollywood for New York, France, and England, giving his last great performance as the Japanese commander of a prison camp in *The Bridge on the River Kwai* (1957).

More recently, as Asian Americans began to direct their own films, Asian stereotypes have given way to more complex characterizations. In *The Wedding Banquet* (1993), director Ang Lee places Asians at the story's center. Sometimes they speak Chinese, sometimes English. The banquet scene is an energetic mélange of traditional Chinese customs and New World practices. And Lee adds a surprising twist by making the groom gay. Ultimately, the film treats Asians, Americans, heterosexuals, and gays with equal measures of respect while handling each scene with a light touch. Born and raised in Taiwan, Lee came to the United States to study at the University of Illinois at Urbana-Champaign, and then went on to get an MFA in filmmaking at New York University. Preferring individuals to stereotypes, he continues to evade being typecast himself by making such diverse films as *Sense and Sensibility* (1995), *The Ice Storm* (1997), *Crouching Tiger, Hidden Dragon* (2000), and *Hulk* (2003).

Another Asian filmmaker who honors the complexity of Asian cultures is Mira Nair. Born in India, Nair achieved international acclaim with *Salaam Bombay!* (1988), a wrenching study of street kids in Bombay. After coming to the United States, she broke all molds with *Mississippi Masala* (1992), a story about Indian immigrants and African Americans in the American South. Ironically, the Indians in this film have emigrated from Africa to escape Uganda's racist policies only to reveal their own racial bias against African Americans, who themselves have never been to Africa. Nair explores their attitudes of mutual distrust in one of the few American movies about race relations that does not center on a conflict between white people and people of color.

Latino (Hispanic) Images

As with other ethnic groups, early Hollywood employed Latino actors as narrative conveniences: for comic relief or local color and as identifiable villains, but rarely as protagonists. When they were given leading roles, the men were usually cast as dark-eyed Latin lovers and the women as tempestuous spitfires. Antonio Moreno exemplifies the former in films like *The Temptress* (1926). Dolores Del Rio, the dark lady of *Flying Down to Rio* (1933), and Lupe Vélez, the hot-blooded temptress of *Hot Pepper* (1933), typify the latter. But Hollywood's trend of releasing the occasional Latino film shifted abruptly during the 1940s. Between 1939 and 1945, some eighty-four films were produced with Latin American themes (López 407), and Latinos suddenly appeared in a more favorable light. There were historical reasons for this. The Roosevelt administration wanted friendly relations with South America during World War II and called on the movie industry to help revive its good-neighbor policy. Hollywood was quite willing to comply. The war had closed most European markets, leaving Latin Americans as the only large potential audience for North American films. Will Hayes, president of the Motion Picture Producers and Distributors of America, even hired an expert on South America, Addison Durland, to screen out material that might offend our southern neighbors. With these movies came a stream of Latin stars, but none as bright as Carmen Miranda. Born in Portugal and raised in Brazil, Miranda arrived on American screens with a thick accent and a fruit basket on her head. In Busby Berkeley's hit musical *The Gang's All Here* (1943), she appears as the "girl with the tutti-frutti hat." A Brazilian boat docks in New York, unloading boxes of coffee, sugar, bananas, and Brazil's leading export, Miranda herself, who ends up dancing the "Uncle Sam-ba." According to Ana López, Del Rio and Vélez did not survive the good-neighbor policy because the former was "not ethnic enough" and the latter was "too Latin" (414), but Carmen Miranda was the embodiment of Pan-Americanism: an ethnic fetish of colonial appropriation. She became the highest-paid actress of her time.

It is interesting to compare Carmen Miranda to a later Latina icon, Rita Moreno. Anyone who has seen *West Side Story* (1961) will remember her as the fiery Anita who sings "Puerto Rico, my heart's devotion, let it sink back in the ocean" in the lively musical number "America." The plot of *West Side Story* centers on two rival gangs, the Sharks and the Jets. The Jets see themselves as "Americans," the rightful owners of the streets, and the Puerto Rican Sharks as intruders. By the 1960s, Spanish-speaking people were no longer just friendly neighbors to visit *Down Argentine Way* (1940) or for a *Week-End in Havana* (1941). They were immigrants who appeared to threaten the urban landscape and the status quo (Sánchez). Like Miranda, Moreno accentuates the exotic: she wears colorful dresses, dances flamboyantly, and speaks with an accent. But Moreno did not want to be typecast for life. As a result, it was eight years before she appeared in another movie. It took that long before she was offered a non-Latina role.

Although *West Side Story* deals in stereotypes, it presents an ironic view of the American dream. Musical numbers like "America" contrast the promise of opportunity with the realities of exclusion. They tell us "everything's right in America—as long as you're white in America." Yet in another sense, the film's treatment of Puerto Ricans is almost incidental. The original 1949 play was set in the Lower East Side and centered on the romance between a Jewish girl and an Italian Catholic boy. Robert Wise and Jerome Robbins updated the story by moving it across town and transforming the Jews into Puerto Ricans. A few decades later, Puerto Ricans in the movies were still filling in for lawless Italian immigrants (*Scarface*, 1983) and unruly Native Americans (*Fort Apache the Bronx*, 1981).

Yet some Latinos managed to get behind the camera to tell their own stories in the 1980s. Gregory Nava directed *El Norte* (1983), which follows the efforts of two siblings to flee the political violence of Guatemala for a better life in the north. After desperate life-and-death struggles, they finally arrive in the "promised land," only to be mistreated as illegal aliens. Ramón Menéndez directed *Stand and Deliver* (1987), in which Jaime Escalante, a high school teacher in East Los Angeles, motivates his Latino students to excel in math. Such films present a more complex view of immigrant experience through the eyes of the immigrants themselves.

Hollywood's Jews

At the center of Hollywood's vast studio system lay a paradox. The film industry was founded largely by a minority, one that was barely represented on the screen during Hollywood's golden age. Most of the studio heads were Jews from central Europe who rose from humble beginnings. MGM's Louis Mayer was a junk dealer from Russia. Paramount's Adolph Zukor and Universal's Carl Laemmle were both furriers, emigrating from Austria and Germany respectively. William Fox, of Twentieth Century Fox, was a dressmaker, the son of Hungarian immigrants. Jack Warner of Warner Bros., the son of Polish immigrants, started as a glover. Columbia's Harry Cohn, son of German immigrants, once hustled pool games in the ghettos of New York. As immigrants, they understood what audiences wanted. Their studios became great dream factories, manufacturing pictures of the American dream for millions of other immigrants every week. Yet they knew their power was precariously perched on a throne that could be toppled by resentment and anti-Semitism. So they downplayed their Jewish heritage in their films. So did many Jewish actors, who adopted screen names that sounded more American. Emanuel Goldberg became Edward G. Robinson, Melvyn Hesselberg changed to Melvyn Douglas, Leo Jacoby to Lee J. Cobb, Meshilem Meier Weisenfreund to Paul Muni, and Pauline Marion Levy to Paulette Goddard. Ethnically speaking, as Neal Gabler explains in *An Empire of Their Own,* these producers and performers became "phantoms of the film industry they had created, haunting it but never really able to inhabit it" (2).

While few Jews appeared as Jews in Hollywood films of the 1930s and 1940s, the silent films were full of Jewish stereotypes, often lifted from popular cartoons. Lester Friedman counts 230 films between 1900 and 1929 that include Jewish characters (*Hollywood's Image of the Jew* 9). A typical example is *The Yiddisher Cowboy* (1911), in which a street peddler named Ikey Rosenthal finds himself on a Wyoming ranch, taunted by the cowboys to perform a "Yiddisher dance." Ikey gets revenge by opening a pawnshop and ultimately buying all their guns, which he uses to shoot at them. The silent period came to a close with *The Jazz Singer* (1927), the story of a Jewish cantor's son who wants to discard family tradition and become a popular singer. Al Jolson, in the title role, appeases his father before the old man dies by chanting in the synagogue, but the film ends with Jolson on stage singing "My Mammy" to his mother and a cheering audience. What makes the scene so troubling today is that Jolson's number is performed in blackface. Minstrelsy, the practice of white entertainers painting their faces black and posing as Negroes, was a popular form of mass culture in the nineteenth century, one that had been adopted by Jewish entertainers in Jolson's day. Some cultural critics, like Irving Howe, see blackface as "a mask for Jewish expressiveness, with one woe speaking through the voice of another" (563). Others, like Lester Friedman, find it "blatantly offensive . . . like one group's desperate need to assert its own superiority by mimicking another" (*Hollywood* 50). In his provocative and insightful book-length study on blackface and Jewish filmmakers, Michael Rogin argues that racial masquerading, while seeming to unite Jews and African Americans in a common cause, really deepens the divide between ethnicity and race, "making the former groups . . . distinctive but assimilable, walling off the latter, legally, socially, and ideologically" (12).

Jewish actors in the thirties, rarely given Jewish roles, took on other cultural identities in film after film. Paul Muni, for example, appears as an Italian gangster in *Scarface* (1932), a Mexican revolutionary in *Juarez* (1939), and a Chinese peasant in *The Good Earth* (1937). Occasionally, however, they parodied their role as role-players. In *Animal Crackers* (1930), the Marx brothers play Italians and Jews trying to pass themselves off as WASPs. In *To Be or Not to Be* (1942), Jack Benny is part of a Polish drama troupe pretending to be Nazis in order to fool the invading Gestapo. At one point in this intricately ironic comedy, a character named Greenberg is a Jew who pretends to be a gentile pretending to be Jewish. Director Ernst Lubitsch, himself an émigré from Germany, mocks a world that forces an oppressed people to keep assuming false identities in order to survive.

One of the first Hollywood movies to speak openly about anti-Semitism was *Gentleman's Agreement* (1947). Gregory Peck is a journalist who pretends to be Jewish in order to prepare for a story he is writing. Suddenly, he sees—and experiences—the anti-Semitism all around him, even from his own fiancée. The message was clear to many, but not all. Moss Hart tells of a stagehand who, after seeing the film, told him, "I'll never be rude to a Jew again because he might turn out to be a Gentile" (qtd. in Friedman, *Hollywood's*). During the ethnic pride movement of the 1960s and the nostalgic sentiment of the 1970s, Jewish characters became more outspokenly Jewish, such as Fanny Brice (played by Barbra Streisand) in *Funny Girl* (1968) and Tevye (Topol) in *Fiddler on the Roof* (1971). At the same time, more attention was given to serious Jewish themes, such as the founding of Israel (*Exodus,* 1960) and the Holocaust (*Judgment at Nuremberg,* 1961; *The Pawnbroker,* 1965). Filmmakers like Woody Allen, Mel Brooks, Sidney Lumet, and Paul Mazursky began making movies that accentuated their heritage. Whether their vision was essentially comic or tragic, they found ways to include a wider audience in the experience of being Jewish in America.

The Other Immigrants

We might trace similar patterns with other immigrant groups. Despite continued stereotyping, Italians, Irish, Greeks, and Poles have received more multidimensional treatment in more recent movies, particularly when directed by insiders. A quick survey of Irish American roles, for example, shows a gradual departure from the brawling Irishman and the suffering Irish woman despite a stubborn persistence of these familiar types. In *Angels with Dirty Faces* (1938), the Irish characters are cops, priests, and gangsters fighting for turf in the Bowery during the Great Depression. In *A Tree Grows in Brooklyn* (1945), set in the early 1900s, the Irish family is headed by a sturdy matriarch and her heavy drinking dreamer of a husband. In *Studs Lonigan* (1960), Irish youths reach for the American dream in Chicago's ghetto of the 1920s. But as recently as *The Brothers McMullen* (1995), the title characters are still trying to break out of the mold set by their alcoholic father and suffering mother.

When Italians appear in films, the phantom of the Mafia is usually lurking in the shadows. Gangster movies like *Little Caesar* (1930) and *Scarface* (1932) helped to popularize this mobster image in the 1930s, drawing on the legend of Al Capone. *The Godfather* trilogy revived it in 1972, 1974, and 1990, although protests by Italian American groups forced the producers to delete the words *Mafia* and *La Cosa Nostra* from the script. In contrast to earlier gangster films, director Francis Ford Coppola presented the Corleones as a family, softening their crimes through wedding, funeral, and dinner scenes that made them seem like human beings instead of murderers. Still, a recent survey of 1,220 Italian-related films since 1928 has found that 40 percent of the characters are mobsters—in contrast to an estimated .0034 percent in the actual Italian American population (Italic Studies Institute).

The depiction of Arab Americans calls for particular attention. Hollywood's casting of Arabs as exotic sword-wielding types may be traced back to silent movies from *The Sheik* (1921) up through *Lawrence of Arabia* (1962) and *Aladdin* (1992). Some of the lyrics from *Aladdin* were modified only after Arab groups found them to be racist. More recently, Arabs have been identified with Muslim terrorists in films such as *True Lies* (1994), *The Siege* (1998), and *Rules of Engagement* (2000). At one point in *The Siege,* the U.S. Army marches into Brooklyn and incarcerates all Arabic-speaking people in barbed-wire compounds reminiscent of the Japanese American internment camps of World War II. Images linking Arabs with terrorism are not uncommon. Jack Shaheen has counted more than 300 negative Arab portrayals in major films since 1970. After the real-life terrorist attacks of

September 11, 2001, producers were more careful. Paramount changed the villains in Tom Clancy's *The Sum of All Fears* (2002) from Muslims to neo-Nazis. It remains to be seen how the war on terrorism will influence the screen profiles of Muslim Americans.

Native Americans

In many respects, the plight of Native Americans on screen has followed paths similar to those of immigrants and African Americans. Some Native Americans who have written on the subject find little resemblance between real Indians and their depiction in the movies. In the words of Ted Jojola, a Pueblo-born scholar, "The Hollywood Indian is a mythological being who exists nowhere but within the fertile imaginations of its movie actors, producers, and directors" (12). Stereotypes of the war-whooping redskin abound in the Western, a genre that dominated American movies during its first seventy years. In the earlier Westerns, Native Americans are rarely distinguished from one another. Seldom is one tribe differentiated from another; seldom are Native Americans presented as individuals. Only gradually did Hollywood give them separate identities or voices. This trend can be seen in the films of John Ford, the Western's preeminent director from 1939 to 1964. In *Stagecoach* (1939), the Native Americans are little more than faceless threats and targets, the occasion for an exciting chase. They appear as part of the wild landscape through which the white community must travel from one settlement to another. In *The Searchers* (1956), some of the Native Americans are three-dimensional human beings. The Comanche chief Scar (played by Henry Brandon) is an important character whose single-minded racial hatred and thirst for revenge parallel those of the white hero, Ethan Edwards (John Wayne). In *Cheyenne Autumn* (1964), there is an expressed desire to tell the story from the Cheyenne nation's point of view (Nolley 82). Although Ford uses a white actor to narrate that story and employs white actors in the lead parts, he lets viewers enter the Native campgrounds to witness their private lives and overhear their untranslated conversations. We watch them and their families make the grueling 1,800-mile trek to Oklahoma, hounded by cavalry, hunger, and disease.

The American Indian Movement (AIM) of the 1960s and1970s brought national attention to the plight of Native Americans. Following incidents like the occupation of Alcatraz prison (1969) and the siege at Wounded Knee (1973), the Hollywood image of Native Americans began to reflect a growing sensitivity. *Little Big Man* (1970) presented a sympathetic portrait of the Sioux people. *Dances with Wolves* (1990) revisited the same historical period with the story of a former cavalry officer (Kevin

Costner) who is gradually accepted into the Sioux community. *A Man Called Horse* (1970) and *Black Robe* (1991) sought more multifaceted cultural depictions that are not as easy to digest. Some of these films featured Native actors in more prominent roles, notably Chief Dan George as Old Lodge Skins in *Little Big Man* and Tantoo Cardinal as Black Shawl and Floyd "Red Crow" Westerman as Chief Ten Bears in *Dances with Wolves.*

To date, few films have been directed by contemporary Native Americans. The first to get mainstream billing is Chris Eyre, whose *Smoke Signals* (1998) and *Skins* (2002) also break new ground by focusing on contemporary issues. *Smoke Signals* follows two Coeur d'Alene Indians from Idaho to Phoenix in search of family remains and their own identity. *Skins* is about two brothers on a Lakota reservation: a policeman and an alcoholic Vietnam vet. Both films feature indigenous actors in the starring roles.

Hollywood and Gender

Since the beginning of the women's movement, much attention has been focused on gender issues in the movies. Film studies and feminist studies have developed side by side as academic subjects, and cross-pollination between these fields of study has produced some of the most vigorous scholarship of our times. As we come to understand the power of motion pictures to shape our sense of sexual identity, these explorations include issues of gender orientation as well. What do the movies tell us about who we are as women and men?

Women and Film

One way to follow the changing roles of women in film is to survey the stars and genres of each era. The typical heroines of cinema's two first decades were paragons of Victorian virtue: pure, pious, and submissive. They often appeared as ethereal, childlike creatures in peril, like Lillian Gish stranded on an ice floe or Mary Pickford, "America's sweetheart," cowering before some brutish lout. Such delicate images of femininity appealed to the protective side of male audiences, confirming women's place in a patriarchal society. The Roaring Twenties introduced a bold new kind of woman. Liberated from her whalebone stays and domestic setting, the flapper girl spoke frankly, acted audaciously, and enjoyed a ripe good time. Actors like Clara Bow (the "It" girl), Jean Harlow ("I like to wake up each morning feeling a new man"), and Mae West ("Is that a gun in your pocket, or are you just happy to see me?") flaunted their sexuality and their independence, playing in tune with the Jazz Age.

Some of these women pursued their wicked ways into the 1930s, although the Great Depression transformed many into working girls. Screwball comedy, a popular genre of the time, sidestepped the Production Code by transposing sexual energy into a battle of the sexes. Katharine Hepburn (*The Philadelphia Story,* 1940) and Rosalind Russell (*His Girl Friday,* 1940) portrayed strong women who stood up to their male counterparts with equal vigor and considerably more wit. By the end of World War II, however, the gender war was no longer a laughing matter. A new genre, dubbed film noir, represented women as treacherous femmes fatales. In movies like *The Maltese Falcon* (1941) and *Double Indemnity* (1944), Mary Astor and Barbara Stanwyck used men to do their dirty work, offering their feminine charms as bait. Viewed historically, these noir films can be seen as dark mirrors reflecting the fears of returning soldiers who worried about the fidelity of their wives and resented the women who had taken their jobs on the home front. But the 1940s also offered more reassuring images of the girl back home, such as Ginger Rogers and Jennifer Jones, just as the 1930s had offered the spunky wholesomeness of Shirley Temple and Judy Garland. Whatever the nation's historical mood may be, Hollywood always seems to find comfort in traditional roles.

By the 1950s, the movies were losing viewers to television and other postwar forms of entertainment. Hollywood lamented the fading female star in films like *Sunset Boulevard* (1950) and *All about Eve* (1950) but soon introduced a cluster of sexy new stars such as Ava Gardner, Kim Novak, and Marilyn Monroe. Meanwhile, in the conservative spirit of the times, the movies provided domestic images with actors like Doris Day and Debbie Reynolds. In the 1960s, these two trends found expression in Jane Fonda and Julie Andrews, one reflecting a new spirit of liberation, the other embodying old-fashioned family values. During the following decades, changing trends in women's roles—often a response to the feminist movement and its backlash—can be traced in the actors who perform them, from the 1970s (Faye Dunaway, Sally Field, Cicely Tyson) and 1980s (Demi Moore, Meryl Streep, Pam Greer, Whoopi Goldberg) to the 1990s (Barbra Streisand, Jodie Foster, Angela Bassett, Geena Davis, Susan Sarandon) and beyond (Julia Roberts, Halle Berry). These actors appeared on screen as a procession of single women learning how to make it on their own, from Jill Clayburgh's *An Unmarried Woman* (1978) and Sally Field's *Norma Rae* (1979) to Melanie Griffith's *Working Girl* (1988) and Julia Roberts's *Erin Brockovich* (2000). They also supported one another in close-knit circles, like the southern white conservatives in *Steel Magnolias* (1989) or the rookie baseball players in *A League of Their Own* (1992). They engaged in intimate, sometimes erotic relationships (*Personal Best,* 1982; *Lianna,* 1983; *Entre Nous,* 1983). And they showed that women could be dangerous and even deadly when their passions were aroused (*Thelma & Louise*, 1991; *Single White Female*, 1992; *Basic Instinct*, 1992).

The Women's Film

It might be said that most of the early female stars were marketed primarily for a male audience. When Lillian Gish, Clara Bow, or Marilyn Monroe appear on screen, they are viewed from a male perspective, figures dressed and positioned to appeal to men. Some film historians argue that the great majority of movies have been directed by men for men, using essentially masculine storytelling methods and visual techniques. A noteworthy exception is the so-called women's film, condescendingly referred to as the "weepie." Jeanine Basinger's comprehensive study of this genre from the thirties through the fifties examines hundreds of women's films such as *Stella Dallas* (1937), *Now, Voyager* (1942), *Mildred Pierce* (1945), *Gilda* (1946), and *Imitation of Life* (1959). Basinger observes that such melodramas provided female audiences with sentimental entertainment centered on relationships, but she also notes a fundamental ambivalence at the heart of all these films. They offered impossible plots—women escaping from assigned roles in marriage and motherhood to positions of incredible glamour, excitement, and power—but they contained real passion and anger. In this way, women's films were liberating. Perhaps the most important feature of these movies was the way they claimed a space for women, a screen of their own, placing their joys and miseries at the heart of the story, "putting them front and center as terribly important and terribly real" (Basinger 14). In this respect, films for and about women have persisted well beyond the 1950s, often interweaving themes of regional and cultural identity into episodic narratives, as in *Fried Green Tomatoes* (1991), *The Joy Luck Club* (1993), *How to Make an American Quilt* (1995), or *Waiting to Exhale* (1995).

Women Filmmakers

Historically, relatively few women have directed movies. According to one estimate, fewer than one-fifth of one percent of Hollywood's directors between 1949 and 1979 were women (Quart 1). Yet researchers have discovered some surprises. Alice Guy-Blaché, born in France and credited with making the first story film, dominated the Gaumont studio from 1896 to 1906. She gave up directing when her husband was transferred to the United States. In California, Lois Weber directed for Universal Studios during the early silent years, making more than a hundred films in her career. Once the highest-paid director in Hollywood, she was as famous as Griffith or DeMille in her time. Dorothy Arzner, the only woman to span the shift from silent films to sound, wrote and directed a succession of successful films until 1944. Her movies featured strong-willed, independent women like Katharine Hepburn in *Christopher Strong* (1933) and Maureen O'Hara in *Dance, Girl, Dance* (1940). Ida Lupino made seven features between 1949 and 1954 before moving on to television. On the whole, however, moviemaking was a male-dominated industry. Not until recently have women directors become numerous enough not to be singled out as "women" directors.

Elaine May was the first major woman writer-director after Arzner and Lupino. She directed films like *The Heartbreak Kid* (1972) and *Mikey and Nicky* (1976) with "a woman's vision." Others soon followed with a more distinctly feminist agenda: Joan Micklin Silver (*Hester Street*, 1975), Claudia Weill (*It's My Turn*, 1980), Susan Seidelman (*Desperately Seeking Susan*, 1985). Some of these directors were industry insiders, actors or writers who worked their way into the director's chair, like Barbra Streisand (*Yentl*, 1983), Penny Marshall (*A League of Their Own*, 1992), and Nora Ephron (*Sleepless in Seattle*, 1993). Some were outsiders, independent filmmakers with a tenacious commitment and a story to tell, like Donna Deitch (*Desert Hearts*, 1985) and Julie Dash (*Daughters of the Dust*, 1991). They all contributed to a national cinema in which women's voices and images are becoming arguably more central, powerful, and diverse.

Men and Film

What about the images of men on film? How have they changed over time? The question has been explored in several books, though with considerably less notice by the academy. John Mellen's *Big Bad Wolves* traces male actors decade by decade, from the glamorous masculine stars of silent films (Errol Flynn, Rudolph Valentino) to the smooth-talking stars of the thirties and forties (Clark Gable, Humphrey Bogart), the Western heroes (Gary Cooper, John Wayne) and young rebels (James Dean, Marlon Brando) of the fifties, and those more sensitive men of the seventies and eighties (Robert Redford, Paul Newman). Susan Jeffords's *Hard Bodies* carries the inventory into the Reagan era, documenting the resurgence of male muscularity in the popular cycles of *Rambo, Lethal Weapon, Star Wars, Indiana Jones,* and *Batman* films. Steven Cohan and Ina Rae Hark's *Screening the Male* seeks to complement the work of feminist studies by examining individual male stars, films, and genres, concluding that Hollywood "puts [the male] on screen, hides him behind a screen, uses him as a screen for its ideological agenda, and screens out socially unacceptable and heterogeneous cultural constructions of masculinity" (3). According to this view, the movie industry constructs and manipulates male stereotypes just as it does stereotypes of women.

Sexual Orientation

"In a hundred years of movies, homosexuality rarely was depicted on the screen, and when it did appear it was depicted as something to laugh at, or to be pitied or feared." This pronouncement from *The Celluloid Closet,* an award-winning documentary on gay images in American movies, introduces a fascinating study on stereotyping, well-kept secrets, and denial. Based on Vito Russo's book of the same title, the film uses interviews and clips of little-known and familiar movies to show how Hollywood has treated gay and lesbian characters. In it, Gore Vidal talks about writing the script for *Ben-Hur* (1959), in which the Roman tribune Messala wants to restart a childhood romance with Ben-Hur, a back story known to actor Stephen Boyd (Messala) but not to Charlton Heston (Ben-Hur) during the shooting. Stewart Stern, the screenwriter of *Rebel without a Cause* (1955), explains his efforts to write a story "about tenderness and intimacy . . . , an attempt to widen the permission to love when men were supposed to be one way with each other." In *Rebel,* Sal Mineo's effeminate behavior marks him as a misfit who has to be killed off in the end. We see a film clip of Marlene Dietrich, dressed like a man, kissing a woman on the lips in *Morocco* (1930) to arouse Gary Cooper's ire and appetite. We watch the ironic performance of Rock Hudson in *Pillow Talk* (1959), a gay actor playing a straight man impersonating a gay man in order to get a female character (played by Doris Day) into bed. And we observe Laurel and Hardy's playful physicality in a new light.

Russo offers a more commodious compendium of stories and scenes. Gays in the movies, he points out, were always good for a joke; a quick laugh at the effeminate male or the mannish woman was reassuring to the mainstream audience. "In a society so obsessed with the maintenance of sex roles and the glorification of all things male," Russo explains, "sissies and tomboys served as yardsticks for what was considered normal behavior" (63). Under the Motion Picture Production Code and its successors, "sexual perversion" was explicitly prohibited on the screen. The censor's hand twisted story after story, relegating gay men and women to a celluloid closet and preventing any serious film treatment of homosexuality for years. Even during the liberating sixties, "lesbians and gay men were pathological, predatory and dangerous; villains and fools, but never heroes" (Russo 122). As a result, the lesbian relationship in Lillian Hellman's play *The Children's Hour* was rewritten for the screen as a heterosexual triangle in *These Three* (1936), and Richard Brooks's *The Brick Foxhole*, a novel about homophobia, was transformed into a film about anti-Semitism in Edward Dmytryk's *Crossfire* (1947). The 1961 remake of *The Children's Hour*, with Shirley MacLaine and Audrey Hepburn, reestablished the main characters as lesbians. Dmytryk's *Walk on the Wild Side* (1962) explored the gay underworld. But for the most part, these were explorations of neuroticism and self-destruction.

This is not surprising given the climate of those times. The gay and lesbian rights movement did not begin in earnest until 1969 with the Stonewall riots in Greenwich Village. The American Psychiatric Association did not remove homosexuality from its list of mental disorders until 1973. Even then, emerging from the closet was not an easy matter. William Friedkin's *The Boys in the Band* (1970) offered an upbeat, sympathetic look at gay culture, but his *Cruising* (1980) presented gay culture as threatening, degenerate, and sick. *Making Love* (1982) featured positive gay roles, but it did not get widespread distribution. The lesbian relationships in *The Color Purple* (1985) and *Thelma & Louise* (1991) were muted rather than developed, a compromise with producers' notions of what audiences were willing to accept. Perhaps the breakthrough mainstream film was *Philadelphia* (1993). Tom Hanks won an Oscar playing a gay lawyer with AIDS, and the movie was a box office hit. In the 1990s, characters of different sexual orientations appeared in a widening variety of roles and genres, from *The Adventures of Priscilla, Queen of the Desert* (1996) and *The Birdcage* (1995) to *My Own Private Idaho* (1991), *The Wedding Banquet* (1993), and *Boys on the Side* (1995). Such movies may be harbingers of a time when gay and lesbian people can be accepted as part of everyday life on screen and off.

Conclusions

One of the challenges of studying issues of representation is to know which groups to study. I have chosen to concentrate on race, ethnicity, and gender in this chapter because these groups seem to have received the most attention in the literature on film. Many other categories invite analysis. The movies reflect our attitudes toward people of different classes, generations, and religions. They model our behavior toward people whose bodies resemble or differ from our own. They show us how to act with people who have hearing impairments or physical or mental disabilities. For each group, we could make extensive surveys of Hollywood's stock characters to explore how films have depicted teenagers and old people, the wealthy and the working class, or slim and portly people over time.

Another challenge is to find appropriate language for naming these groups. In the course of history, words such as *Negro, colored, black,* and *Afro-American* have been introduced, adopted, and abandoned as the accepted terms for those we speak of as African American today. There is a similar history with terms such as *Hispanic* and *Latino; old folks, senior citizens,* and the *aged; crippled, handicapped,* and *disabled.* The struggle seems to continue as each new term gathers negative connotations and hardens into stereotyped thought. Examining the value-laden history of language and searching for fresh terms can be an eye-opening exercise for students of the movies. A third challenge is to locate good sources of information and ideas, books and films that give us access to a wider reach of history, movie images, and points of view. I have made a special effort to point out promising primary and secondary sources in the film lists and parenthetical citations of this chapter.

Beyond analysis and theory, we might ask questions of action. What can or should be done about misrepresentation in the movies? Some people take the course of social action. They create special-interest groups, raise awareness by writing film reviews in campus or community publications, or establish a presence on the Internet through discussion groups or a personal Web site. Some people vote at the box office. Since producers and distributors want to make movies that will sell, they respond to trends in ticket sales. When filmgoers avoid movies that perpetrate demeaning images, when they turn out in large numbers for independent films that have something new to say, moviemakers take notice. Finally, some people become moviemakers themselves. Spike Lee, Julie Dash, Gregory Nava, Joan Micklin Silver, Mira Nair, Chris Eyre, Jim Jarmusch, and many more took cameras into their own hands because they were dissatisfied with the images they saw in mainstream films. Their visions have created new mirrors for searching eyes.

9 Film in the English Class

As early as 1911, when the National Council of Teachers of English (NCTE) was founded, English teachers recognized the educational significance of motion pictures. Dale Adams has traced the shifting tides of film study within the profession from the first days of condescending skepticism to more recent signs of its acceptance in the schools (Costanzo, *Report* 3–7). In the 1920s and 1930s, NCTE was primarily concerned with raising standards of film appreciation and arming students with critical perspectives. After World War II, when movies were considered merely one of several "visual aids," and during the Sputnik era, when movies were regarded as diversions from the national agenda, film study declined in popularity. It was not until the 1970s that a fresh wave of media awareness found its way into the schools, inspired by creative trends in European cinema, fostered by visionary critics like Marshall McLuhan and Andrew Sarris, and sustained by a young generation of enthusiastic teachers who discovered how to apply their literary training to the new discipline of film. By 1978, *The American Film Institute Guide to College Courses in Film and Television* listed over a thousand institutions of higher learning in the United States that together offered more than nine thousand courses in film and television (Bohnenkamp and Grogg). Today, after several steps "back to basics" in the early 1980s and a great leap forward in the 1990s, the study of film is growing once again, supported by advances in technology and strengthened by developments in theory, pedagogy, and experience. A significant trend is the growth of graduate film programs. The *American Film Institute Desk Reference* highlights more than forty institutions offering an MA, MFA, or PhD as well as several highly respected nondegree programs (571–75). From high school to higher education, it seems that more students than ever before are serious about studying the movies.

Sample course syllabi for undergraduate film courses can be found in several sources. *The Journal of Film and Video* regularly lists course files on a wide variety of film topics. A number of anthologies on film study include sections that highlight successful courses. In *Multiple Voices in Feminist Film Criticism*, Diane Carson describes a course at St. Louis Community College on "Women Filmmakers," organized chronologically from the silent years to the present (Carson, Dittmar, and Welsch). Frances Subbs uses a thematic arrangement in her "Black Women in American Films" course at Howard University (Carson, Dittmar, and Welsch). At Northeastern University, Elizabeth Freyberg's syllabus for "Women of Color" features units on African Women, Aboriginal Women, Asian Women, Latina Women, Lesbians, Native American Women, Caribbean Women, and Interracial Alliances and Concerns (Carson, Dittmar, and Welsch). The Spring/Summer 2002 issue of *Women's Studies Quarterly* also includes syllabi for feminist-oriented courses (Kolmar). A larger sampling of course files is available on the Internet at Web sites like the University of Alabama's ScreenSite. Appendix 1 of this book suggests some popular ways to organize a course on film.

Activities for Class and Home

One difference between film courses and other subjects is that the films are often screened in class, whereas novels, plays, and other texts are usually read outside of class. Fitting a two-hour feature film into standard fifty-minute periods can be a challenge. Screening a film in two consecutive classes disrupts its continuity and takes away from valuable discussion time. For this reason, some film classes are scheduled in longer time blocks, or special screenings are arranged outside of class. Now that most films are available on videocassette and DVD, it is easier to assign movies like books, to be viewed individually at home or in a section of the library equipped with playback units. Still, many teachers feel that the experience of watching films as they were intended to be shown—on a large screen with a large audience—is worth the extra effort to preserve class screenings.

Discussion is often the heart of class. It pumps up the mental energy, gets the juices flowing, circulates ideas, and nourishes the group's collective insight. Discussing a film enables students to articulate their personal experiences, to compare their first impressions to other points of view, to connect what they have seen to larger social, political, and cultural events. A good discussion also clarifies the facts, establishing boundaries between what was seen and what was imagined, between private reactions and cultural norms. The tenor of discussion can be factual: What happened in the movie? What did you see and hear? It can be personal: How did you feel during each scene? What was going through your mind? It can be contextual: How did this remind you of other movies, other scenes, other moments in art or life? The discussion can be analytic, focusing on specific elements within the film that contributed to a given effect. It can be evaluative, with students judging how well the effect was achieved. Or it can be dialectic, with students taking sides on a given issue.

Before screening the film, it often helps to give a brief introduction. Students may want to know about the historical context of *The Grapes of Wrath* (1940), or the musical tradition that preceded *Singin' in the Rain* (1952), or Orson Welles's career before he directed *Citizen Kane* (1941). Some teachers like to point out things to look for, like the use of colors in *The Matrix* (1999) or parallel editing in *The Godfather* (1972). Handouts describing the film's production team and cast are also useful, as are excerpts from film reviews, lists of related films, and bibliographies. These can serve as prompts for the discussion and guides to student projects.

Teachers have varied the pattern of introduction, screening, and discussion depending on the film. Sometimes it makes sense to show the entire film before discussion. Sometimes it seems best to stop the film at several points, discussing students' expectations and assumptions before moving on. When time permits, a key scene might be screened again during discussion. This enables students to do a close textual reading, applying their analysis inductively to the film as a whole. Many teachers have experimented with the technical features of a film. They show a scene without the sound track, asking students what sounds they imagine; they play the sound track without the picture, asking students to visualize the scene. Some teachers have their students read the script or story first and then compare it to the film experience. Others show an adaptation before reading the original to make it clearer how a filmed interpretation affects the reader's imagination.

Responses to the film do not always take the form of a discussion. Sometimes students write down their immediate reactions. Sometimes they complete questionnaires and then pool the results to form a class profile. The class response may be in the form of role-playing (with students imagining new situations for the characters), panels (with different students concentrating on camera work, directing, sound, or other elements of the film), or even an original film (with students filming their own local adaptation or sequel to the film).

My own inclination is to let students take more responsibility for the introduction and discussion through group presentations. After I lead several classes, students sign up in groups of two to four for one of the remaining films on the syllabus. Each group prepares introductory material and discussion questions. During the class session, they present the film and lead the discussion. In this way, they have a chance to study one film in depth, screening it together, investigating the background, sampling reviews, and learning about the principal artists, technicians, and performers. They also have a chance to practice public speaking skills. What I find is that the prospect of a performance before peers draws out even the most withdrawn of students. With some tactful guidance and enough time to prepare, they become the class experts on at least one film. Their research and their study questions become part of the course content, a fact that contributes to the quality of research and discussion. And since all students get a turn, their responsiveness to one another tends to be high.

Individual and group projects can take many forms. Ralph Amelio describes students in his classes who responded most creatively to film. One talented young woman wrote, scored, and played an original mood piece in response to her favorite film. Another student took photographs and mounted them in a collage, which he unified with an original poem. A third student used a movie camera to film hundreds of photographs in quick succession, adding an original sound track to express his response to a unit on violence in society (63–64). Group work is particularly well suited for film study since both film production and spectatorship are collaborative activities. A good way to begin a course is to ask students to prepare group viewing profiles based on their preferences and habits. Each group polls its members about their favorite movies, genres, actors, and viewing venues (TV, VCR, DVD, or multiplex) and then reports what it has learned to the class. Groups are also useful for scene analysis. When you show a scene in class, divide each group into technical experts. One student counts the length of each shot, another listens to the music, a third pays close attention to the lighting, and so on. After several screenings of the scene, each group creates a shot-by-shot description, with all members contributing their expertise. If the class is studying how films are made, try dividing the class into rival production groups. Challenge each group to list as many steps of the filmmaking process as it can in the right order. When I made this a competition, my students surrpised me with their combined energy and knowledge. One group divided the task into its component parts, one student listing the steps of preproduction, another listing postproduction activities, and so on. The group won the contest by reinventing Hollywood's historic strategy for efficient film production, thus serving as a neat segue to our unit on the studio system. See Appendix 2 for more ideas on teaching film with groups.

More traditional assignments include film comparisons and film reviews. In a film comparison, students compare one film from the syllabus to another film not necessarily on the syllabus. The second film may be a current release or an earlier film that bears some relationship worth exploring. The original *King Kong* (1933), for example, might be paired with one of its many sequels. *Blackboard Jungle* (1955) might be matched with *Stand and Deliver* (1987) or another film about city schools. Two films by the same director or featuring the same performer might be studied side by side for what they reveal about his or her artistic style and growth.

A film review is an opportunity for students to apply what they have learned in class to a fresh film experience. Students might begin by reading and reporting on several reviews of a new film culled from different sources. This acquaints them with the form and scope of film reviews. Or they could write an original review of a contemporary film. It is sometimes entertaining and enlightening to hear from student reviewers who take different views of the same film.

Appendix 2 contains descriptions of several other projects. The Shot-by-Shot Analysis involves students in a close reading of one scene. They examine the technical elements in each shot and then see how those elements contribute to the broader meanings of the scene. Behind the Scenes gives students a chance to investigate one aspect of filmmaking in depth, such as directing, acting, scriptwriting, photography, music, or set design. By looking behind the scenes of a particular film to the work of a particular technician or performer, they learn about the craft as well as the art of filmmaking. Fiction into Film is a more ambitious venture. Here students get involved in all stages of film production from scripting to editing. They begin by selecting a short story or poem for adaptation to the screen. Then they scout locations, cast the characters, and prepare a storyboard or shooting script outlining each scene. If there is time to film the script, a production crew does the shooting, editing, and sound track. Not only does the group learn about moviemaking through hands-on experience, but it also learns about the intricacies of adaptation. In the process, students learn to pay close attention to the details of a narrative. In transforming settings into actual locations, characters into a cast, description into action, or tone and point of view into photography and sound, they become involved in literature—and cinema—as never before (see Costanzo, "Fiction," for a more complete discussion of this approach).

Curriculum Design and Assessment

Using a lot of lessons and activities, even great ones, does not necessarily add up to a great course. It takes some reflection and careful planning to fashion a curriculum that will support your educational philosophy and meet the goals of your students, department, and institution. Are you thinking of a film to fit into a regular English class? Do you want to redesign your fiction course to include the literature of film, perhaps with an emphasis on adaptations? Will you be exploring movies as historical documents or cultural barometers? Can you sustain an entire course on science fiction films or global cinema?

Renee Hobbs, a national leader in the field of media education, identifies seven vital steps in the process of curriculum design. First, consider your teaching philosophy, motives, and goals. Why are you interested in movies, and why is the answer to this question important? Are movies a way to get your students talking about significant issues and choices in their lives? Is your aim to focus on the artistic and technical sides of filmmaking, helping students develop thoughtful standards for what they watch? Do you want to build critical thinking and communication skills? Are you more interested in motivating their curiosity and challenging their imagination with new kinds of films?

Being clear about your educational objectives builds a foundation for the second step, determining desired outcomes. What should your students know and be able to do by the end of your course? Do you want them to be familiar with common film terms such as *film noir* and *Foley editing*? Should they be able to analyze the framing, lighting, and camera work of any scene? Do you want them to recognize the cultural assumptions that underlie the movies they watch, examining their beliefs and attitudes about money, sexuality, age differences, or minorities? It helps to establish your priorities at this point. Which outcomes are most important? It also helps to state these outcomes as skills and actions, what students will be able to do rather than what they should know. This makes it easier to judge the success of your curriculum design.

Step 3 looks ahead to assessment. What will you accept as evidence that students have acquired the skills and understanding you want them to develop in your course? Will their performance during class discussions and exams be enough? What projects might exercise their skills and enable them to demonstrate an appropriate level of understanding? Many teachers have found a useful guide in Bloom's taxonomy for classifying different levels of abstraction. Bloom distinguishes between knowledge (recalling information, listing, defining, identifying, or labeling), comprehension (interpreting facts, translating into new contexts, comparing and contrasting, inferring causes, predicting consequences), application (using knowledge to solve problems, applying theory to new texts, making a movie), analysis (identifying a movie's component parts, finding hidden meanings, discovering ideological assumptions), synthesis (creating new ideas out of old ones, generalizing from given facts), and evaluation (making judgments, assessing value). The literature on assessment can be heavy going, a trek through jargon-laden passageways and endless tunnels of refinement. Some teachers cut through the thickets with simple "I can" statements, which students can apply to individual portfolios. "I can create a storyboard that demonstrates the artistic use of camera angles, color, action, sound, and special effects in a scene from *The Matrix*." "I can connect *It Happened One Night* to research on social and economic conditions of the 1930s." "I can explain why *The Godfather* is a better film than any of its imitators."

With tentative objectives, outcomes, and assessment tools in place, Hobbs identifies five final steps: (4) plan learning experiences and instruction; (5) create and find materials and resources; (6) implement instruction; (7) reflect on the process and revise. Of course, the real planning process is as messy and recursive as any creative endeavor. Good curriculum development takes time, plenty of patience, and an open mind, but students have a better chance of learning by design than by accident or luck.

Equipment and Resources

Projection equipment is no longer the impediment it used to be. As recently as 1983, the MLA publication on film study echoed a familiar lament that "because of the nature of the medium, it is impossible without access to special equipment (analytic projectors, moviolas) to engage in a close textual analysis of film" (Grant, *Film Study* ix). Today, anyone with access to a VCR or DVD player can quickly scan backwards or forwards through a film, play a scene in slow motion, or freeze a single frame. No longer must viewers rely on photographic memories and notes scribbled in the dark. Film texts can be studied with the same deliberate concentration that scholars and students have given to literary texts. No longer must they rely on theatrical screenings or TV's *Million Dollar Movie* to see a certain film. With thousands of titles available at libraries and rental stores, through mail catalogs and Web sites, on cable television and pay-per-view channels, films can be chosen like books. What's more, specific moments of a film can be selected like any literary passage and viewed repeatedly. With the right equipment, film excerpts can even be incorporated into essays as still images or in multimedia projects as full-motion video.

Digital video discs (DVDs) are rapidly replacing videocassettes as the preferred medium for home viewing and increasingly by schools. The digital images and sounds are sharper, the discs are more compact than tapes, and it's much easier to locate a section of the movie on a DVD than winding through a tape. As more computers are equipped with DVD drives, more people are watching movies on their laptops and using their keyboards to navigate the movie and access other information that accompanies the film. These "bonus features" have become a real boon to teachers and students of film. Today's DVDs regularly feature audio commentaries by directors, actors, and others involved in the film's production. They may include the original trailer, interviews, behind-the-scenes documentaries, deleted footage, filmographies, storyboards, archive materials, and Web links—a wealth of resources for serious film study.

Currently, however, DVD technology does not yet offer some of the advantages that made videodisks (laser discs) so promising in the early 1990s. With videodisk technology, any frame can be projected instantly by keying in its reference number by remote control. This allows a film class to jump precisely from frame to frame, comparing the acting or lighting in one scene to similar elements in another scene, or to advance the film one frame at a time, disclosing the mysteries of animation or fine points of editing. This makes it possible to see how Orson Welles achieved that extraordinary crane shot through the skylight of the El Rancho nightclub in *Citizen Kane* or how King Kong interacts with Fay Wray. Because of their relatively high cost and cumbersome size and the annoying need to change disks in the middle of a movie, videodisks never really took root in the home market, but many schools and libraries still have them, and they can be invaluable tools until DVDs or some new technology acquires their interactive features.

The Internet is emerging as a leading resource for film studies, perhaps the one used most by students. Huge archives like the Internet Movie Database (www.imdb.com) and TV Guide (www.tvguide.com) give instant plot summaries, credits, production notes, and other information related to thousands of films, all interlinked and updated every day. Film reviews are available from Web sites like the *New York Times* (www.nytimes.com) and Rotten Tomatoes (www.rottentomatoes.com), which compiles reviews from scores of newspapers, journals, and electronic magazines, rating each film on a scale from fresh to rotten. New Web sites appear almost daily for filmmakers, movie fans, and researchers. A particularly ingenious tool for studying the motion picture industry interactively is the Hollywood Stock Exchange (www.hsx.com). Users who sign up get two million Hollywood Dollars to invest in their favorite movies, stars, and musical artists. It's only electronic money, but the game is free, and students can learn a lot by watching their investments rise and fall as other users trade stocks. Like Wall Street Web sites, the Hollywood Stock Exchange features graphs, portfolios, and related articles to help users make informed choices. On other Web sites, students can find film clips, photographs, and entire screenplays. They should be advised, however, to consider the reliability (and legality) of source material. For serious study, they are best served by dependable groups such as research colleges, recognized film journals, and organizations like the American Film Institute (www.afi.com), the Society for Cinema & Media Studies (www.cmstudies.org), the University Film & Video Association (www.ufva.org), and the National Council of Teachers of English (www.ncte.org). A listing of reliable film-related Web sites is given in Appendix 3.

Respecting Copyright Laws

When teachers were limited to 16mm films, there was little risk of violating copyright laws. The great majority of 16mm prints were legally purchased or rented by the schools; for the most part, it was technically infeasible to copy them. With the advent of VCRs and DVDs, however, the technical options have increased, as have the legal issues. It is relatively easy to copy movies off the air (i.e., off broadcast television), but is it lawful to show the copies to a class? Inexpensive films on a variety of media can now be bought or rented for home viewing, but can they be shown legally in school? What about downloading movies from the Internet or adding digital film footage to a multimedia presentation? Technology is changing so rapidly that the courts can barely keep pace. While interpretations differ and the legal terms are not always clear, any teacher who shows movies in the classroom should be aware of copyright restrictions. This section is an introduction to the basics.

Under the Copyright Act of 1976, authors are protected against unauthorized copying of their original works. The intent, in keeping with the Constitution, is to benefit the public as well as the author. Copyright protection is presumed to promote the production of books, music, films, and other works that contribute to public knowledge and intellectual pursuits (Congress of the United States 5). By guaranteeing the right of authors to profit from their work, the law seeks to encourage work that serves the general good. The 1976 act gave automatic protection to works created after January 1, 1978, for fifty years after the author's death (Sinofsky 39). A later ruling, the Sonny Bono Copyright Extension Act of 1998, lengthened the period to seventy years and gave an even longer extension (ninety-five years) to certain earlier works. After this protection period, works fall into the "public domain"; then the restriction no longer applies.

The Copyright Act of 1976 does not set precise limits for using new technologies like videocassettes or DVDs. Nor does it offer detailed guidelines for fields like education. It does, however, allow copying for certain purposes under the category of "fair use." Fair use, described in Section 107 of the 1976 Copyright Act, permits special exemptions for education, criticism, scholarship, and similar reasons (Bielefield and Cheeseman 63). It is a kind of "escape clause" that, like any legal concept, is subject to testing in the courts.

Several important cases have helped define the limits of fair use. One case began in 1978 when several film distributors sued the New York State Board of Cooperative Educational Services (BOCES) for taping hundreds of movies off the air and distributing copies to public schools. The court ruled that such large-scale, systematic videotaping was illegal, even for educational purposes. A key point of the decision was that most of the movies were available for purchase or rental. The financial harm to copyright owners was judged to be more important than the convenience to schools of copying these movies off the air (Sinofsky 68–78). Another case began in 1979, when Sony was sued for manufacturing its Betamax machine on the grounds that this technology permitted users to tape copyrighted material off the air. Sony took the case all the way to the Supreme Court. Although the Court ruled in Sony's favor, its 1984 decision applied primarily to home use for the purpose of "time shifting"—taping material to be viewed at a more convenient time (Sinofsky 78–88). The implications for teachers remained largely unsettled.

In the absence of precise criteria, Congress has sought standards of fair use. A committee appointed by Congressman Robert Kastenmeier in May 1979 suggested a set of guidelines for education. While these guidelines do not have the force of law, they represent a serious governmental effort to set standards for taping off the air (Sinofsky 119–20). Who decides to do the copying is a factor in these guidelines. An individual teacher in a nonprofit school who decides to copy something from television to use in class has a better case than someone who is asked to do the copying by the school administration (J. Miller 13). The key concept here is "spontaneity": if it is not feasible to rent or purchase certain material in time for a teachable moment, it may be fair to copy the material. By contrast, stockpiling copied tapes just because they may prove useful in the classroom someday is not considered fair use.

Another factor is how and where copies are "performed" (shown in sequence as a movie or as clips) or "displayed" (shown nonsequentially as separate images). Section 110 of the Copyright Act specifies that a copy be displayed during a face-to-face teaching activity in a regular classroom (J. Miller 59). Sending students to the library to see copied tapes on their own may not meet these critiera.

In addition, any copy should be temporary. After its use in the classroom, it should be erased or destroyed. The Kastenmeier committee recommended that off-the-air recordings may be kept for up to forty-five days. It specified that such copies could be used once in class and repeated only for instructional reinforcement within a ten-day period. Copies should include the program's copyright notice and not be altered in any way.

Teachers who show films to a class on a VCR or DVD player should be aware of the distinction between "public performance" and "home use." Just because you or your school owns a film does not mean that you can show it anywhere to any group. Videos and DVDs are sold and rented with licensing agreements, usually shown on screen before the film, which specify the circumstances under which the film may be shown or "performed." Any movie purchased with public performance rights may be shown legally to public audiences, in or out of class. A movie purchased "for home use only" is more restricted. Under Section 110(1) of the copyright law, showing such a movie can be considered fair use if the copy was purchased legally and is shown only to teachers and students during face-to-face instruction in a classroom setting of a nonprofit educational institution (Bielefield and Cheeseman 84). The same movie, however, may not be shown outside of class without permission from the publisher.

As media technologies expand and become more integrated, the educational uses of multimedia pose further complications for copyright law. What if a student wants to include film clips in a PowerPoint project for school? What if a teacher wants to combine film stills, graphics, and motion video in a multimedia lecture demonstration? In 1997 the Conference on Fair Use (CONFU) released "Fair Use Guidelines for Educational Multimedia" with the endorsement of the U.S. Copyright Office (see www.utsystem.edu/ogc/intellectualproperty/ccmcguid.htm). While these new guidelines are still undergoing trial use, they set forth some helpful principles to follow. Essentially, students are permitted to create educational multimedia projects for a course and show them to the class or save them in a portfolio of their academic work. Educators may create multimedia presentations for use in face-to-face instruction, student self-study assignments, or their own professional portfolios. The CONFU guidelines spell out certain limits. Students and educators may use no more than 10 percent of a copyrighted work or a specified amount of material from it, whichever is less: 3 minutes from motion media, 1,000 words from text material, 30 seconds of music, or 15 images from a published work of illustrations and photographs. Only two copies of the project can be made, and these may be kept for up to two years, after which permission is required from the copyright owners (Bielefield and Cheeseman 92).

To summarize, the law on copyright is still in the process of being applied specifically to technologies such as television broadcasting, cable, the Internet, and DVDs. Although the concept of fair use allows some flexibility for educational uses of films and off-the-air programs, the limits of fair use are subject to interpretation and testing in the courts. It is a good idea to keep in mind the spirit as well as the letter of the law:

1. The intent of copyright legislation is to prevent loss of income to copyright owners. Taping should not be a way to avoid renting or buying a film; if it is feasible to buy or rent it for classroom use, it probably should not be copied.

2. Just because it's technically feasible to copy something doesn't mean it's lawful, even for educational purposes.

3. Many schools have a policy on copyright. Consult your media specialist, district office, or library for local guidelines.

Dealing with Censorship

Censorship has always been a serious concern of teachers, especially English teachers. In a society where education is traditionally viewed as serving public needs, the schools have been subjected throughout history to public pressures. During the early 1970s, when nonprint media began to be used more widely in classrooms, Ken Donelson ("Ruminating") warned that audiovisual materials were coming under the same kind of attack that novels, textbooks, and other printed forms had undergone for years (12–26). An NCTE survey of censorship in 1977 confirmed this, revealing that people were complaining about certain films and AV materials being shown in the schools. Among the films were John Boorman's *Deliverance* (1972), Arthur Penn's *Bonnie and Clyde* (1967), Larry Yust's *The Lottery* (1969, a short film; see www.afana.org/yust/htm), and Franco Zeffirelli's *Romeo and Juliet* (1968). In most cases, the complaints came from parents, and to a lesser extent from school staff, who cited violence, sexual references, offensive language, and unacceptable ideas as their chief objections (Burress 31–34).

From time to time, the film industry has responded to public complaints and sought to preempt outside censorship by policing itself. The Motion Picture Production Code of 1930, described in Chapter 7, restricted the depiction of topics such as nudity, sex, childbirth, adultery, and homosexuality (see Hull 1999 129 for the entire document). In 1968 the code was replaced by a ratings board charged with classifying films for different audiences. The earliest ratings were G (general audiences), M (mature audiences), R (restricted), and X (pornographic; shown only in special theaters). In 1984, when parent groups protested a particularly bloody scene in an *Indiana Jones* film, the Motion Picture Association of America added the PG-13 rating (parental guidance for children under the age of thirteen). The NC-17 rating, barring children under the age of seventeen from adult movies, was introduced in 1990. While these ratings seem to work for theatrical performances, community groups continue to have a say in what is shown in schools.

Dealing with censorship requires some understanding of the motives behind it. Robert Small articulates the view of parents who believe that since they pay for the schools and send their children to them, they ought to have a say in what is taught. Small points out that efforts to censor the curricu-

lum often grow out of a sense of frustration by communities that feel powerless to defend their deeply held beliefs. He cites a sign carried by protest-
ors during the famous 1974 censorship campaign in Kanawha County, West
Virginia: "Even hillbillies have rights." These protesting citizens, Small
observes, "are to a very considerable extent fulfilling the role assigned to
them by the historical development of the American school" (61). Robert
Hogan enlarges this perspective. Hogan agrees that much of the drive to
limit schools comes from a basic distrust of those who set the educational
agenda. He asks teachers to consider whether they can trust their own agendas. "The uncomfortable truth," he says, is that "we are all censors. The
difference is that when English teachers practice censorship, we call it 'book
selection'" (88).

Many of the arguments against school censorship are also rooted in
American history. Chief among these is the argument for intellectual freedom, traditionally linked to the First Amendment. Edward Jenkinson expresses this view when he says, "I hope that my children will not have to
grow up in a society in which they are denied the right to study any subject, to read any book they deem worthy of attention, and to speak out on
any topic they think worthy of discussion" (12). Another argument questions the claim of censors that objectionable works may be harmful to young
minds. Reviewing the research on reading, Richard Beach concludes that
books rarely change people's attitudes because "the relatively stable and
defined characteristics of readers shape the experience with a work to a
greater extent than the work affects characteristics of the reader" (144). Beach
extends his observations to visual material, finding no significant evidence
that exposure to obscenity changes the viewer's attitudes toward sex or
violence. On the contrary, he cites studies suggesting that "erotica is generally beneficial to adolescents' normal sexual development" (151).

Given such arguments and pressures, what can teachers do about
selecting films for study and justifying their selection? Many of the steps
suggested by Ken Donelson ("Censorship") to handle censorship of print
media in the 1970s can help you deal with censorship of visual media today. First, develop a departmental rationale statement for teaching film. By
supporting your educational objectives with clear, convincing reasons, you
strengthen your case for including any film that helps your students realize those objectives. Rationales for specific films can further reinforce your
case. Second, set up a committee to recommend film titles. By discussing
films that might best suit your students and objectives, you create opportunities to predict potential problems and to anticipate solutions. Third,
cultivate community understanding and support before censorship becomes an issue. Parents and public groups are less likely to act on partial

information if they have an accurate, full picture in advance. Fourth, encourage your school to form a policy on censorship if it does not already
have one. Threats become less urgent when procedures are worked out
ahead of time (162–67). Donelson's suggestions underline the value of
thoughtful preparation. Prevention is the most expedient way to settle conflict. The National Council of Teachers of English has also prepared an excellent teacher's guide on film censorship. Prepared by the NCTE Task Force
on Guidelines for Dealing with Censorship of Nonprint Materials, the guide
is available online from the NCTE Web site (NCTE Task Force).

II Study Guides for 14 Great Films on Video and DVD

10 Casablanca

Directed by Michael Curtiz; screenplay by Julius Epstein, Philip Epstein, and Howard Koch; based on the 1940 play Everybody Comes to Rick's *by Murray Burnett and Joan Alison; produced by Hal B. Wallis; cinematography by Arthur Edeson; edited by Owen Marks; art direction by Carl Jules Weyl; set decoration by George James Hopkins; music by Max Steiner (except for Herman Hupfeld's 1931 song "As Time Goes By"); costume design by Orry-Kelly; first release by Warner Bros. in 1942; general release in 1943. [102 minutes]*

Rick Blaine	Humphrey Bogart
Ilsa Lund	Ingrid Bergman
Victor Laszlo	Paul Henreid
Captain Louis Renault	Claude Rains
Major Heinrich Strasser	Conrad Veidt
Signor Ferrari	Sydney Greenstreet
Guillermo Ugarte	Peter Lorre
Sam	Dooley Wilson
Carl	S. Z. Sakall
Yvonne	Madeleine LeBeau
Annina Brandel	Joy Page
Jan Brandel	Helmut Dantine
Berger	John Qualen
Emil the croupier	Marcel Dalio

Casablanca is a film of memorable lines and images even for those who have never seen the whole movie. When someone mentions *Casablanca*, we're likely to picture Humphrey Bogart in his trench coat and fedora. We see him as the tough-but-sentimental nightclub owner, Rick Blaine, peering into Ingrid Bergman's liquid eyes while an airplane revs its engines in the distance. Or we start to imitate his shaggy voice: "Here's looking at you, kid" or "We'll always have Paris" or "Play it again, Sam." (What he really said was "Play it, Sam," a telling instance of the gap between our collective memory and what actually occurred.) Few who have watched the film forget the stirring nightclub scene when a roomful of wartime refugees unites to drown out a German military song with a chorus of "La Marseillaise." Few forget the figure of Claude Rains as the jaunty French police chief ordering his men to "round up the usual suspects." And who can fail to mouth the movie's final line of dialogue when Bogart and Rains stroll off into the fog saying, "I think this is the beginning of a beautiful friendship"?

A timeless icon of American popular culture, *Casablanca* represents Hollywood at its best. It has all the ingredients we associate with the classic Hollywood style: a forward-driving narrative; a love story at the center of its tightly scripted plot; strong, sympathetic characters; an exotic atmosphere; an urgent historical backdrop; and a host of stars. The studio system that produced it was at its height in the early forties, turning out a record number of movies for some ninety million filmgoers a week, attendance figures that have never been surpassed. The powerful studio heads that ran film factories such as Warner Bros. had at their disposal all the talent they needed to mass-produce these films. They could draw on a stable of writers to work on the scripts; a pool of actors bound to the studio by seven-year contracts; thousands of skilled craftspeople and technicians; and spacious back lots filled with sets, costumes, and props. Even the directors were owned by the system, routinely assigned to make whatever films the studio deemed profitable. Many of the films that came off this assembly line were run-of-the-mill products. But often enough the "genius of the system," as André Bazin called it, produced a miracle.

Given the unpromising start of *Casablanca*, its current place in the pantheon of cinema certainly seems miraculous. Hastily assembled to exploit current events (the idea was approved soon after the attack on Pearl Harbor), the film was originally conceived as a B movie but grew into something greater. The script was written and rewritten by many hands, and nobody knew exactly how it would end even after shooting had begun. The project ran past its shooting schedule and over budget, only to be rushed into release before the original show date to coincide with the Allied landings in Morocco. In the shuffle, even the roles were radically recast. Although it is difficult to imagine anyone but Humphrey Bogart and Ingrid Bergman in the leading roles, the part of Rick was reportedly offered first to Ronald Reagan and George Raft, and both Ann Sheridan and Hedy Lamarr were considered for the role of Ilsa. The task of directing was assigned to Michael Curtiz, who had directed several swashbucklers for Warner, including *Captain Blood* (1935), *The Adventures of Robin Hood* (1938), and *The Sea Hawk* (1940). A veteran of more than a hundred films, Curtiz could be trusted to turn out a solid romantic melodrama for the studio.

The production process began officially on December 27, 1941, when Warner Bros.' chief producer, Hal Wallis, purchased the film rights to a play entitled *Everybody Comes to Rick's* for $20,000. Never staged (James Agee dubbed it "one of the world's worst plays"), the play was the work of Murray Burnett and Joan Alison. The idea had come to Burnett while he was traveling through Nazi-occupied Austria with his wife in 1938. The Burnetts were stunned by what they witnessed on the continent: the

Nazis' brutal anti-Semitism, the escalating violence, the flood of refugees desperate to escape. One evening they listened to a black piano player entertain a crowd of exiles in a French café called La Belle Aurore. The piano player eventually became Sam, who sings "As Time Goes By" in the play, rekindling the passion between Rick, a self-pitying, adulterous American lawyer, and his former girlfriend, an American tramp named Lois. The play's other characters included Victor Laszlo, a wealthy Czechoslovakian and Lois's latest lover; Captain Rinaldo, a disagreeable French police prefect who pursues women tirelessly; and Major Strasser, a conventionally rigid German officer who is hunting Laszlo. These characters may not have seemed like the makings of a landmark film, but Wallis assigned the task of adapting the stage play to two of the studio's best writers, Julius and Phil Epstein. The Epstein twins transformed Rick into a complex blend of cynicism and romanticism, and they enlarged Rinaldo's character with urbanely witty dialogue, renaming him Renault. Another writer, Howard Koch, also had a strong hand in the development of the screenplay, adding weight and political significance to the story and completing much of it when the Epsteins were called away on another assignment.

In the final shooting script, Rick's American past is obscure, but a flashback reveals his more recent past in Paris, where he and Ilsa fell in love just before the Germans invaded France, forcing them to leave. When Ilsa failed to meet him at the train station, he left alone, feeling bitter and betrayed, eventually becoming the successful though reclusive owner of Rick's Café Américain in Casablanca. It is here the film begins. The nightclub is the hottest spot in town. Everybody comes to Rick's to gamble, exchange goods and stories, and wait for an exit visa. Rick himself, impeccably dressed and clearly in command, prefers to sit alone. Then Ilsa arrives with Laszlo. The couple has come to Casablanca looking for letters of transit that will allow them to leave French Morocco and resume the fight against the Nazis. Unaware that her former lover is there, Ilsa encounters Sam in the café and asks him to play the old song he used to sing for her and Rick in Paris. When Rick hears the first strains of "As Time Goes By," his cynical composure falls apart. He confronts Ilsa, neglects his business, and starts to drink again. Yet, for all his protests of political neutrality ("I stick my neck out for nobody"), he finally decides to take action, though his plan is not revealed until the final scene.

By acting, Rick steps into history. Some viewers draw parallels between Rick and the United States before entering World War II. They note that *casa blanca* is Spanish for "white house," equating Rick's emergence from self-imposed exile to America's shift from neutrality to active participation in the war. At one point, Rick asks, "If it's December 1941 in

Casablanca, what time is it in New York?" adding, "I bet they're asleep all over America." The reference to Pearl Harbor as a wake-up call is unmistakable. When Ilsa and Laszlo arrive, Rick himself awakens to his earlier commitments (he once fought in Spain and Ethiopia) just as the United States roused itself from twenty years of isolationism. And Rick forges a new bond with Renault just as the United States allied itself with unoccupied France.

Even without these historical readings, Rick's brand of solitude holds a particular appeal for Americans. Some, like Michael Wood in *America in the Movies*, associate his cool detachment with Yankee individualism. In contrast to Laszlo's heroically infectious zeal, Rick may appear cynical and detached, but he is also self-reliant and admirably free from entangling alliances. He refuses to compromise his code by admitting German bankers to the gambling tables or by doing business with shady characters like Ugarte and Ferrari. Yet he rigs a roulette wheel—against himself—to help out a young couple in need of cash. Despite the world's intrusions into his personal life, he manages to meet it on his own terms. In the end, what makes him so attractive is his principled independence.

In the cast of major characters, Bogart is the only American. Before *Casablanca,* he was best known for his minor gangster roles, from which he builds the character of Rick Blaine. Most of the other actors are European. Ingrid Bergman was from Sweden, Claude Rains from England, Peter Lorre from Hungary, Paul Henreid from Austria-Hungary, and Conrad Veidt from Germany. Michael Curtiz himself was a Hungarian whose heavy accent imbued the set with a cosmopolitan tone. All these émigrés gave the film an appropriately multiethnic flavor. They also made the theme of escape more authentic. Lorre, Henreid, and Veidt were all refugees from Hitler's regime. Madeline LeBeau had escaped from occupied France only months before filming.

Shooting began on May 25, 1942, and wrapped on August 22 of the same year. The film opened in New York on November 23, 1942, fifteen days after the Allied landing at Casablanca, but its general release was delayed until January 1943, during the Roosevelt-Churchill conferences in Casablanca. Although some critics were unimpressed, the film did well at the box office and was nominated for eight Academy Awards. It won three Oscars: Best Picture, Best Director, and Best Screenplay. Today, *Casablanca* regularly appears on critics' ten-best lists. It has been colorized, serialized, and novelized; it is regularly quoted, misquoted, and parodied. In the American Film Institute's 1998 poll of the top 100 movies of the century, *Casablanca* was ranked second only to *Citizen Kane*.

Suggested Films and Readings

More Films with Humphrey Bogart (more than 90 film credits in his career)

Dead End (1937), as Baby Face Martin

Angels with Dirty Faces (1938), as James Frazier

The Roaring Twenties (1939), as George Hally

High Sierra (1941), as Roy Earle

The Maltese Falcon (1941), as Sam Spade

Sahara (1943), as Sergeant Joe Gunn

To Have and Have Not (1944), as Harry Morgan (Steve)

The Big Sleep (1946), as Philip Marlowe

The Treasure of the Sierra Madre (1948), as Fred C. Dobbs

Key Largo (1948), as Frank McCloud

The African Queen (1951), as Charlie Allnut

Beat the Devil (1954), as Billy Dannreuther

The Caine Mutiny (1954), as Captain Queeg

Books about *Casablanca*

Anobile, Richard J., ed. *Casablanca*. New York: Universe Books, 1974.

Harmetz, Aljean. *The Making of Casablanca: Bogart, Bergman, and World War II*. New York: Hyperion, 2002.

Koch, Howard. *Casablanca: Script and Legend*. Woodstock, NY: Overlook Press, 1973.

Robertson, James C. *The Casablanca Man: The Cinema of Michael Curtiz*. London: Routledge, 1993.

Rosenzweig, Sidney. *Casablanca and Other Major Films of Michael Curtiz*. Ann Arbor, MI: UMI Research Press, 1982.

Siegel, Jeff. *The Casablanca Companion: The Movie and More*. Dallas: Taylor, 1992.

Wood, Michael. *America in the Movies: or, "Santa Maria, It Had Skipped My Mind."* New York: Basic Books, 1975.

Questions for Reflection and Discussion:

1. How does the film measure up to your criteria for a good story? What features of successful storytelling does it have or need? How can you account for its enduring popularity?

2. What do you already know about World War II and the political climate of the 1940s? What historical references can you find in the film? What political messages come through?

3. How are different nationalities and ethnic groups represented in the film? Are any groups notably absent? If so, how might their absence be explained?

4. When Rick says, "I stick my neck out for nobody," Captain Renault calls this "a wise foreign policy." Later Renault tells Rick, "I suspect that, under that cynical shell, you're at heart a sentimentalist." Ilsa accuses Rick of being self-absorbed. "With so much at stake," "she tells him, "all you can think of is your own feeling." Strasser expresses yet another view: "My impression was that he was just another blundering American." How do you see Rick Blaine? If your judgment changed during the film, explain when it changed and why.

5. When Ilsa arrives at Rick's Café Américain, she brings the past with her. How much of the past can you reconstruct from references in the film? What do you learn about Rick and Ilsa in Paris and about Rick's earlier life? How does this knowledge help to explain what happens in the film?

6. Explore some of the other relationships in *Casablanca*. What kind of marriage do Ilsa and Laszlo have? How well do Renault and Strasser share the power? What is the basis for Rick's association with Renault? Describe the bond between Rick and Sam.

7. Contemporary viewers often notice the quantities of alcohol and tobacco consumed in the movie. Compare the use of these products on film in the forties to today's films. What accounts for the differences you find?

8. At the end of the movie, Rick turns to Renault, saying, "I think this is the beginning of a beautiful friendship." What do you think he means? What would you expect to see in a sequel to the movie?

Topics for Further Study

1. Investigate the period by reading about the forties, watching wartime documentaries, or checking the Internet. What can you learn about the Cross of Lorraine, Morocco, Vichy, the Resistance movement, Nazis, American neutrality?

2. Try recasting the roles in *Casablanca* with actors today. Who would you choose for the lead parts? Where did your image of these actors come from? Justify your choices. Remember: film is a business as well as an art. Consider the actors' box office appeal as well as previous performances, dramatic range, and requirements of the role.

3. "The Lisbon plane soared away from the dense, swirling fog of Casablanca, up and into the night. Below, the airport was plunged deep into the North African darkness, its only illumination the revolving beacon that perched atop the conning tower. The sirens of the French colonial police cars had faded into the night. Everything was quiet but the wind." So begins the first chapter of *As Time Goes By*, a novel written by Michael Walsh and published by Warner Books in 1998. Read Walsh's story (the first chapter is available free online at www.twbookmark.com) or write your own imagined sequel to the movie.

4. Bogart and Bergman gained immense popularity with *Casablanca*, but they were not unknown in 1941. Learn more about these two famous actors: their public performances and private lives. Trace the roles they played in earlier and later films. Consider why they appealed to audiences in their day and whether these same traits apply to actors today.

5. Watch the documentary that accompanies the DVD. Lauren Bacall narrates this exploration of the film's history, production, reception, and themes. Interviews with playwright Murray Burnett, screenwriter Julius Epstein, story editor Irene Lee Diamond, critic Pia Lindstrom, and film historians Rudy Behlmer and Ronald Haver offer insights into what made *Casablanca* stand out from its many competitors in the golden age of cinema.

Scenes to Analyze

1. **Opening Scene.** [2:00] Key features of the location, atmosphere, and plot are established in this scene of the Casablanca streets. Notice how the scene combines narration and action to introduce what is to come.

2. **Rick's First Appearance.** [8:52] How do we read a character? How do we read a movie? For those who have never seen *Casablanca*, this can be a good demonstration of viewing skills. Begin the scene just as the waiter brings the check to Rick. Step forward through the scene frame by frame, stopping to ask what assumptions about the character we make at each step. What can we tell from the chessboard, the champagne glass, the ashtray, or the white suit? What does the close-up of the check reveal: the language, the face amount, the address, the date, and the handwriting style? How much of our speculation is confirmed as the camera tilts upward to show Rick's face?

3. **Ugarte's Arrest.** [20:40] We learn about the arrest before Ugarte or Sam does. What kind of relationship does Captain Renault seem to have with Major Strasser? How does this reflect the historical relationship

between France and Germany at this time? Why doesn't Sam "do something" to help Ugarte?

4. **"Play it, Sam."** [31:15] Replay the scene in which Ilsa tells Sam to play the song he used to play for her and Rick in Paris. What emotions does Ingrid Bergman convey? How are they conveyed through her performance—and Rick's?

5. **Memories of Paris.** [38:55] The long flashback in Paris reveals a very different side of Rick and Ilsa. Compare this montage to romantic sequences you have seen in other films. How is the mood (or moods) created? What is the effect on you?

6. **"Les jeux sont fait."** [1:07:01] Rick helps a young couple at his own expense. Notice the use of reaction shots to comment on his action. Why does he perform this unusual act of generosity at this point in the story? What does the subplot contribute to the film?

7. **"La Marseillaise."** [1:12:05] Laszlo leads a chorus of the French national anthem over the voices of the German officers. How is the feeling built up? What does the scene tell us about Laszlo, the refugees, and Rick at this point?

8. **At the Airport.** [1:35:25] The final scene is famous for many things, among them its use of lighting, music, camera work, dialogue, and acting styles. Notice how all these elements contribute to the atmosphere and tension of the film's climactic moment.

11 North by Northwest

*Directed by Alfred Hitchcock; screenplay by Ernest Lehman; produced by
Alfred Hitchcock and Herbert Coleman; cinematography by Robert Burks;
edited by George Tomasini; art direction by William Horning and Merrill
Pye; production design by Robert Boyle; set decoration by Henry Grace
and Frank McKelvey; music by Bernard Herrmann; title design by Saul
Bass; released by MGM in 1959. [136 minutes]*

Roger O. Thornhill	*Cary Grant*
Eve Kendall	*Eva Marie Saint*
Phillip Vandamm	*James Mason*
Leonard Adam	*Martin Landau*
Clara Thornhill (Roger's mother)	*Jessie Royce Landis*
Professor	*Leo G. Carroll*
Lester Townsend	*Philip Ober*
"Mrs. Townsend" (Vandamm's sister)	*Josephine Hutchinson*
Man Who Misses Bus	*Alfred Hitchcock*

Alfred Hitchcock (1899–1980) liked to tell a story about his first encounter
with the law:

> I must have been about four or five years old. My father sent me to
> the police station with a note. The chief of police read it and locked
> me in a cell for five or ten minutes, saying, "This is what we do to
> naughty boys." (Truffaut 17).

Hitchcock's story, in one form or another, is reenacted in many of his films.
An ordinary person, someone with whom the viewer can identify, is caught
in extraordinary circumstances, often treated as a criminal or spy. When
bad things happen to decent people, we begin to wonder what lies beneath
the veil of decency. This is one of Hitchcock's most persistent themes.

Roger Thornhill, the protagonist of *North by Northwest,* is enjoying a
typical day. A successful advertising executive in a gray flannel suit, he
hurries confidently through the Manhattan crowd and grabs a taxi for his
lunch appointment at the Plaza Hotel. More accurately, he swipes the cab
from another would-be passenger, explaining to his secretary, "I made him
a happy man. I made him feel like a Good Samaritan." At the Plaza, however, a series of coincidences changes the direction of his life. He is mistaken for someone else, a man named George Kaplan, who is being hunted
by a group of stolidly determined men. Soon, Thornhill is running for his
life. The chase takes him on a four-day journey to the United Nations, to
an estate on Long Island, and to Chicago and North Dakota. As he learns

more about the mysterious Mr. Kaplan, he finds himself pursued by the police, a gang of spies, and a shadowy government agency. He also meets a temptingly beautiful blonde named Eve. By the time he reaches the Mount Rushmore monument, his identity has been thoroughly questioned. He has been accused of theft, murder, espionage, and driving while intoxicated, among other things.

North by Northwest is a big picture that embraces many genres. It has been called an epic, a spy chase thriller, a comic romance, an ironic comment on cold war politics, and a precursor to James Bond. Made in 1959 at the peak of Hitchcock's career, between *Vertigo* (1958) and *Psycho* (1960), it sums up the state of Hitchcock's art, themes, motifs, and technical achievements. As François Truffaut observed, "the picture epitomizes the whole of [his] work in America" (190).

Film historians like to compare *North by Northwest* to its earlier British counterpart, *The Thirty-Nine Steps* (1935), in which an innocent man named Hannay (played by Robert Donat) is chased from London to Scotland. Like Thornhill, Hannay gets entangled in an enemy spy ring. Both protagonists are suave, resourceful men who don various disguises to foil their pursuers; both become romantically involved with an attractive blonde. But while *The Thirty-Nine Steps* is markedly British in setting, tone, and character, *North by Northwest* is thoroughly American. Technically, it is a big Hollywood production, filmed in Technicolor and making full use of the wide-screen VistaVision process. The film travels through the American landscape, from the skyscrapers of New York to the vast cornfields of the prairie, yet far from being a travelogue, it offers Hitchcock's barbed critique of what Americans have made of their environment. Manhattan is a grid of crowded streets and boxy buildings locked in a senseless dance of urgent haste. The sculpted outcrops of Mount Rushmore bear stony witness to cold war politics as tiny figures play out their petty intrigues amid the great silent faces of the nation's former heroes. Every landmark is an ironic commentary on the American way of life.

Some critics emphasize the film's mythic qualities, characterizing Thornhill's journey as a quest, a series of tests through which he grows until he achieves ultimate deliverance. As he gets farther from New York, his protective veneer is stripped away, leaving him to discover his own courage and resourcefulness in order to survive. From this perspective, Thornhill emerges from the urban crowd as a kind of Everyman, an ordinary person thrust into extraordinary circumstances. Other critics see him as a particular kind of man, a figure of corporate America: slick, self-serving, and manipulative. Seen in this way, Thornhill lacks a genuine identity. The stereotypical business suit he wears throughout the film is one index of his superficiality. His relationships seem to be as shallow as his conversation. At one point, he explains to Eve that the middle initial on his cigarette lighter, R.O.T., stands for nothing. There is a zero at the center of his name. No wonder he is so easily mistaken for the nonexistent Mr. Kaplan.

Freudians have made much of Thornhill's relationships with women. He lets himself be controlled by his mother and depends on Maggie, his secretary, to handle the "details" of his life. It is no accident that the domineering "Mrs. Townsend" bears a physical resemblance to his mother and that Eve, like Maggie, is a blonde, one more in a succession of Hitchcock temptresses. Like her biblical counterpart, Eve Kendall lures Thornhill into temptation and possibly his own death, but she is not a free agent. It was Vandamm's sinister spell that got her into trouble in the first place and the Professor's appeal to patriotic duty that fixed her plight. The protagonist, however, is Roger Thornhill and, as Thomas Leitch argues, his northwesterly journey can be seen as the passage of an irresponsible mama's boy to independence and maturity (211).

Politically minded viewers have interpreted the story as a parable of cold war politics. They point out that the foreign spies and the FBI pursue like goals with the same disregard for civilian life. When the Professor learns that Thornhill has been caught in his net, he cavalierly bids him farewell, and he is quite willing to sacrifice Eve to the cause. More than one historian has pointed out the Professor's resemblance to Allan Dulles, director of the CIA when the film was made. Robert Corber takes the political critique further, finding 1950s sources for the film's oblique references to communism, homosexuality, and "mamaism" (196). Even without these ideological readings, it is easy to see how the netherworld of political intrigue is a match for Thornhill's career. Advertising is the art of "The Expedient Exaggeration," he boasts, and deception—whether manipulating language for profit or stealing taxis for the fun of it—is his favorite game. Part of our pleasure as viewers is watching how the deceiver gets deceived, by Eve, by Vandamm, and by the Professor. Of course, at the same time, we enjoy being manipulated by Hitchcock, the master of cinematic deception.

Hitchcock's mastery of surprise and suspense owes much to his control of information in the film through what David Bordwell and Kristin Thompson call a "hierarchy of knowledge" (372). For much of the story, we know as little as Thornhill does about the people who are chasing him. Our shared ignorance often leads to stunning surprises, like the knife scene at the United Nations. At other times, we know what Thornhill knows but what other characters do not, as when he sees the gun behind Leonard's back at Vandamm's hideaway. Here, knowledge creates expectations, which sustain suspense. We are keen to see how Leonard will use the gun. But the moment holds yet another surprise for those of us who failed to recognize the weapon from an earlier scene.

Hitchcock limits and releases knowledge largely through point of view. The narrative perspective in *North by Northwest* is mostly limited to the protagonist. Only rarely do we leave Thornhill entirely to eavesdrop on the Professor and his cohorts. More often, the camera shifts within a scene. When Thornhill first encounters Vandamm, in the Townsend library, the camera cuts back and forth as the two men eye each other warily. It even rises above them for a moment to show their confrontation from above. This "bird's-eye view" shot is a Hitchcock trademark. A striking example occurs when Thornhill runs from the United Nations. We observe him as a tiny speck from high above the building, as though we are some superior, watchful being.

Hitchcock controls the flow of action with a well-used palette of plot devices. Count the number of times a vehicle is stopped or exchanged. Thornhill takes someone else's cab in Manhattan, crashes into another motorist on Long Island, and steals a pickup truck when the crop duster collides with a tanker at the bus stop among the cornfields. Detectives stop his train to search for him, and the Professor stops the police when they arrest him in Chicago. Or count the number of messages interrupted in the course of the film. Thornhill inadvertently interrupts a page for Kaplan at the Plaza, setting the whole plot in motion. He intercepts Vandamm's phone message to Eve in the Ambassador East, and Vandamm discovers Thornhill's matchbook message to Eve in the hideaway. In this film, transportation and communication are unreliable necessities. What counts more is strength of resolve. Yet the motivating element behind the whole story, the state secret hidden in a statuette, turns out to be a trick. In his interview with Truffaut, Hitchcock calls this gimmick a MacGuffin: "[I]n the picture the plans, documents, or secrets must seem to be of vital importance to the characters. To me, the narrator, they're of no importance whatever" (98). Ultimately, although the secrets are rescued and the villains neatly neutralized, the romantic plot wins out over the spy thriller. Political intrigue and adventure conclude happily in love and marriage, a conventional Hollywood ending. Yet, with his clever match cut from Mount Rushmore to the sleeping berth and his sly cutaway to the train roaring through a tunnel, Hitchcock is winking at us to the very end.

While a great deal has been written about Hitchcock the director, Hitchcock the man remains elusive, hiding in the darker shadows of his genius. As a child, he was a loner. Quiet and generally well behaved, he played mostly by himself, inventing his own games. In college he studied art and engineering, interests that persist in the technical and visual preoccupations of his films. In interviews he talked about his early fascination with the movies, how he devoured the cinema journals and frequented the local theaters. Entering the film industry in 1920 as a title designer, he worked his way up to directing in 1925. *The Lodger* (1926) contained many of the hallmarks of Hitchcock's visual style and introduced the motif of a man pursued for a crime he did not commit. It was also in *The Lodger* that Hitchcock filled in briefly when an extra was needed on the set, making the first of those screen appearances that became his personal signature. During his apprenticeship in Germany in the 1920s, he drew lessons from expressionist filmmakers like F. W. Murnau. He learned how to use the camera subjectively, identifying the lens with characters under stress. He also created some methods of his own. In *Blackmail* (1929), Hitchcock orchestrated a climactic pursuit over the rooftops of the British Museum, the first of many landmark chase scenes that include the Statue of Liberty (*Saboteur*, 1942) and London's Royal Albert Hall (*The Man Who Knew Too Much*, 1934, 1956). But he could also confine his action, as he did in *Lifeboat* (1944), in which nearly the entire film takes place in a small boat. In time, Hitchcock became less interested in the plausibility of his stories than in creating a mood. By the 1950s, he had reached directorial maturity with moody thrillers such as *Rear Window* (1954) and *Vertigo* (1958). More successes, including *Psycho* (1960) and *The Birds* (1963), were yet to come.

After *Vertigo*, Hitchcock was supposed to make a film based on a novel by Hammon Innes. He hired Ernest Lehman to write the script, but both men dropped the idea in favor of something else. According to Lehman, Hitchcock mentioned his long-standing desire to use the United Nations as a set and to shoot a chase scene on the faces of Mount Rushmore (Fitzgerald; Brady). Lehman wrote the first sixty-five pages of a script that included those locations. The script evolved through many collaborative conversations, with Hitchcock rolling out his thoughts and occasionally sketching out scenes. Lehman went to New York, visited the United Nations and a mansion in Glen Cove, and then took the Twentieth-Century Limited from Grand Central Station to Chicago, checked in at the Ambassador East, and traveled on to Rapid City, South Dakota—familiarizing himself with all the locations that Roger Thornhill would encounter. He spent a day on the monument, where he tried to draft the chase scene. "It was impossible. No way you could do a sequence on top of Mount Rushmore. But I wrote it anyway, and Hitchcock constructed it at the studio" (Brady 198).

According to Spoto, the script was written with Cary Grant in mind (436). Naremore suggests that Grant "coauthored" the film, contributing to its tone and content with the force of his personality (5). It is certainly hard to imagine Roger Thornhill without Grant's sophistication and classical good looks. He manages to bring confidence and cunning to the role yet allows ample room for comedy and vulnerability. Somehow we believe that this urbane ad executive and lady-killer is also a funny drunk and a mama's boy. There was less unanimity about the casting for Eve Kendall. Eva Marie Saint's previous roles, such as the waif in *On the Waterfront* (1954), had hardly been glamorous, but Hitchcock insisted on using her and directed her every gesture. He even picked out her wardrobe himself. Viewers must decide whether she successfully combines the three faces of Eve: the wicked woman who falls in love, the treacherous double-dealer, and the good woman being used (Wood 105). Other actors gradually came on board. Hitchcock chose Leo G. Carroll (a fixture in nearly all his films) as the Professor, James Mason as suave villain Phillip Vandamm, and Martin Landau (in his first screen role) as Leonard Adam, Vandamm's unctuous assistant. In an ironic bit of casting, he selected Jessie Royce Landis as Thornhill's mother, although the actress was only a year older than Grant.

Filming began on August 27, 1958, at the United Nations and proceeded more or less in a northwesterly direction. Hitchcock used the actual locations for Grand Central Station, the Plaza Hotel, Glen Cove, and the Ambassador Hotel. He was denied permits, however, for the United Nations and Mount Rushmore. From a camera hidden in a truck, he secretly filmed Grant entering the UN, later shooting the interior scenes in a studio. Since the National Parks Department feared "patent desecration" of Mount Rushmore, he had to reconstruct the monumental faces of the presidents in an immense MGM soundstage. The concrete set was 30 feet high and 130 feet wide, but Cary Grant and Eva Marie Saint were never far from the ground. Hitchcock's special effects team used the complex Schüfftan process for the high-angle views, coordinating live action and models through an intricate arrangement of painted glass and mirrors. To some eyes, the artificial look adds an appropriately hallucinatory tone to the scene. The famous crop-dusting scene was filmed in Baker's Field, California, over three days. Here, too, trick photography made things safer for the actors. In this case, Grant (or a stand-in) dived into a fake ditch on the soundstage while a movie of the oncoming plane was screened behind him. With take after take, the script supervisor had a hard time keeping track of the dust on Grant's suit. Shooting was completed on December 16 after seventy-eight days. The film was edited to Hitchcock's tightly planned shooting script by George Tomasini and scored by Bernard Herrmann, the celebrated musical composer of *Citizen Kane* (1941).

Alfred Hitchcock died in 1980, leaving a legacy unmatched in motion picture history. Few directors have experienced the same measure of critical appreciation and popular success. His work (some nine silent movies, forty-three sound features, and twenty television films) is both studied for its artistry and enjoyed as entertainment around the world. Although he never won an Oscar, Hitchcock became a household figure, partly through his popular TV series, *Alfred Hitchcock Presents*, in which his exaggerated profile is accompanied by the music from Gounod's "Funeral March of a Marionette." His films could be thrilling and romantic yet ironic and surreal. He made fun of Hollywood, his sponsors, and himself while making money for all three. He once boasted to Lehman that the audience was like a giant organ, and he pictured himself manipulating all the keys and pedals. His lens was both a source of pleasure and an instrument of guilt. Perhaps all his films are variations of that childhood anecdote of being locked in jail. For the brief space of a motion picture, we are locked in the frame of Hitchcock's artful imagination, good people to whom bad things happen, face to face with our guilty pleasures, and running, like Roger O. Thornhill, for our lives.

Suggested Films and Readings

More Films by Alfred Hitchcock

The 39 Steps (1935)

Secret Agent (1936)

Sabotage (1936)

Rebecca (1940)

Suspicion (1941)

Shadow of a Doubt (1943)

Lifeboat (1944)

Spellbound (1945)

Notorious (1946)

Strangers on a Train (1951)

Rear Window (1954)

To Catch a Thief (1955)

The Man Who Knew Too Much (1956, 1934)

The Wrong Man (1956)

Vertigo (1958)

Psycho (1960)

The Birds (1963)

Marnie (1964)

Frenzy (1972)

Family Plot (1976)

Books and Other Resources

Bordwell, David, and Kristin Thompson. "North by Northwest." *Film Art: An Introduction.* 4th ed. New York: McGraw-Hill, 1993. 370–75.

Brady, John. "Interview with Ernest Lehman." *The Craft of the Screenwriter: Interviews with Six Celebrated Screenwriters.* New York: Simon & Schuster, 1982. 198–206.

Corber, Robert J. *In the Name of National Security: Hitchcock, Homophobia, and the Political Construction of Gender in Postwar America.* Durham, NC: Duke UP, 1993.

Fitzgerald, Peter. "Destination Hitchcock: The Making of *North by Northwest.*" Documentary film available on the DVD of *North by Northwest.*

LaValley, Albert J., ed. *Focus on Hitchcock.* Englewood Cliffs, NJ: Prentice Hall, 1972.

Lehman, Ernest. *North by Northwest.* The MGM Library of Film Scripts. New York: Viking, 1959.

Leitch, Thomas M. *Find the Director and Other Hitchcock Games.* Athens: U of Georgia P, 1991.

Naremore, James, ed. *North by Northwest: Alfred Hitchcock, Director.* New Brunswick, NJ: Rutgers UP, 1993.

Spoto, Donald. *The Dark Side of Genius: The Life of Alfred Hitchcock.* Boston: Little, Brown, 1983.

Truffaut, François, with Helen G. Scott. *Hitchcock.* New York: Simon & Schuster, 1967.

Wood, Robin. *Hitchcock's Films.* New York A. S. Barnes, 1969.

Questions for Reflection and Discussion

1. The working titles for this film were *Breathless, In a Northwesterly Direction,* and *The Man on Lincoln's Nose.* Why do you think Hitchcock settled on *North by Northwest*? Some critics see an allusion to Shakespeare, when Hamlet tells his former friend Guildenstern: "I am but mad north-north-west. When the wind is southerly I know a hawk from a handsaw." Do you see any justification for this literary reading of the title?

2. Find a few key words to describe Roger Thornhill at the beginning of the film. Describe his appearance, mannerisms, and personality. Do you notice any changes as the film progresses? If so, when? To what extent does he emerge as a new man by the final scene?

3. Hitchcock used the term *MacGuffin* to describe a plot device that is important to the characters but not to the audience, like the microfilmed secrets hidden in the statue. If the secrets are not important to you, what is? What keeps you interested in the movie?

4. Hitchcock is often called the Master of Suspense. Identify some scenes that you found especially suspenseful. How does Hitchcock create suspense in these scenes? Where in the story were you surprised? What surprised you? What is the difference between suspense and surprise?

5. Some viewers think it's hard to tell the good guys from the bad guys in this film. Compare the Professor and Vandamm. Who are they, what are their objectives, and what do they represent? Describe their use of force, deception, and ordinary citizens in the service of their goals.

6. When the Professor says, "War is hell," to what war is he referring? Why does Thornhill reply, "Perhaps you ought to start learning to lose a few"? To what extent does this exchange—and the film in general—reflect Hitchcock's views on world events?

7. Take a close look at the women in Thornhill's life. How do you characterize his relationships to his secretary, his mother, Mrs. Townsend, and Eve Kendall? What evidence of personal growth do you see, if any, in these relationships?

8. Some viewers notice that there are few minorities in the film. Where do they appear? What do their roles tell you about the United States in the 1950s? How do you think minorities would be represented if the film were remade today?

9. *North by Northwest* has many comic moments. Which lines or scenes did you find funny? Does the humor detract from the film's serious elements or make it a better film? Explain.

10. Thornhill's business suit gets stained with bourbon, rumpled by the police, soiled by a crop duster, and cleaned by Eve. Trace this sartorial odyssey through the story. Aside from the fact that Thornhill has no time for luggage, what case could be made for the suit's symbolic function? What might the suit represent for Thornhill, for Hitchcock, or for you?

Topics for Further Study

1. A great deal has been written about the production of this film. Read one of the published interviews with Alfred Hitchcock, Ernest Lehman, or others involved in the making of *North by Northwest* (Truffaut; Brady).

Or watch the documentary (Fitzgerald) that accompanies the DVD. Compare their accounts to what you know about filmmaking today.

2. As in literature, movies use motifs, or repeated elements, to give the story unity and meaning. Notice the motifs of intercepted messages and vehicles. Notice, too, the use of colors, clothing, and locations in the film. What clues do these motifs offer toward the film's deeper meanings?

3. Although *North by Northwest* can be enjoyed entirely as entertainment, it has been seriously studied as a commentary on human nature and on American culture in particular. Explore some of these interpretations discussed in the books, articles, and Web sites devoted to the film. Or come up with your own reading of the film's main themes.

4. Do a storyboard analysis of one scene, like the analysis of the cornfield chase scene by Albert LaValley in *Focus on Hitchcock* (145–73). Begin with a drawing for each shot, showing the action and composition within the frame. Below the drawings, give the length (in seconds) and a brief written description of what you see and hear. A storyboard enables you to see the director's artistry in action: how he organizes elements within the frame, how he edits a series of buildups and false starts to create suspense and surprise, and how the scene furthers the action while developing the movie's thematic interests. What does your storyboard teach you about Hitchcock's film technique?

Scenes to Analyze

1. **Opening Credits.** [0:14] Saul Bass's striking credit sequence begins with a blank green screen. Parallel lines invade the frame from three sides to the vigorous tempo of Bernard Herrmann's "fandango" theme. The lines form a grid, which becomes a tilted surface for the credits and then turns into the glass facade of an office building, reflecting the city traffic below. Describe the mood created by this opening. What expectations are created by the music, the perspective, and the images?

2. **Missing the Bus.** [2:06] Hitchcock's signatory appearance comes early in this film. Why? How can his predicament of missing the bus be seen as a sign of things to come?

3. **Thornhill in Manhattan.** [2:15] Note how Roger Thornhill is introduced. What makes him part of the city's jostling flow? What makes him stand out from the crowd? What does his method of getting a taxi reveal about his character?

4. **In the Library.** [8:38] The first confrontation between Thornhill and Vandamm takes place at the Townsend estate. What does the setting contribute to the confrontation? How similar are the two men in dress, mannerisms, and speech? Watch how Hitchcock stages the scene. Thornhill examines the room. Vandamm closes the curtains and arranges the lighting as he sizes up his prey. The two men circle each other like animals. Notice the use of point-of-view shots to shift perspective throughout the scene.

5. **Driving Drunk.** [14:25] The scene's mixture of tension and humor is reflected in the sound track, camera work, and Cary Grant's performance. When does it seem like a thriller; when does it seem like a comedy? How do the lighting and special effects influence your experience?

6. **"Do you know this man?"** [36:14] The scene at the United Nations building where Thornhill goes to speak with "Mr. Townsend" ends in some surprises. How does Hitchcock prepare us for the unexpected? Do Thornhill's reactions seem realistic to you? The extreme high-angle shot of Thornhill running from the building has been much discussed by film students. What points of view (and ideological perspectives) might it represent?

7. **"It's a nice face."** [46:22] When Thornhill joins Eve for dinner on the train to Chicago, they begin a sophisticated game of romance. Trace the evolution of their dialogue and body language. The scene in which Cary Grant lights Eva Marie Saint's cigarette entranced audiences in the 1950s. How do their words and actions strike us today? In such close quarters, there is little room to maneuver a camera. What other cinematic resources does Hitchcock use to keep our interest high?

8. **Crop Dusting.** [1:06:14] The film's most celebrated scene takes place in an unlikely locale. A midwestern prairie in broad daylight seems like the last place for suspense or surprise, but Hitchcock delivers both with ingenuity and skill. There is no music and little sound. Nothing much happens during the first five minutes, yet viewers perch on the edges of their seats. Examine the scene's editing decisions to see how it prompts this reaction: how the shots are framed, composed, and timed to the rhythms of a chase scene, creating tension and false starts and involving the audience in Thornhill's extraordinary experience in an ordinary space.

9. **Auction.** [1:25:30] When Thornhill sees Vandamm's hand on Eve's bare neck, he feels betrayed. Who has the power in this scene? Take note of how the characters are dressed and placed in relation to one another.

Follow the metaphor of acting through the dialogue. How does Thornhill use the situation—a public auction—to ensure his "survival" and gain the upper hand?

10. **Vandamm's Hideaway.** [1:58:45] Thornhill is peeping through the window of Vandamm's house, where the spies are about to fly off with Eve and the stolen secrets. From his dangerous vantage point, he cannot hear everything, and Eve is out of reach, but he sees what Vandamm himself does not: Leonard's gun. This is a good scene to study how Hitchcock reveals information to the audience, feeding them details yet always keeping them off balance. It also shows how relationships are subtly managed, with strong feelings working just below the surface of composure.

11. **Cliff Hanger.** [2:10:26] Hitchcock was obliged to shoot the final chase scene on the Mount Rushmore monument on a soundstage using immense models and rear-projection special effects. Some modern viewers find these effects artificial and distracting. Others think they give the scene a surrealistic look in keeping with the movie's themes. What is your impression of the setting in this scene? Aside from the thrill of the chase, what messages are conveyed by the image of these tiny figures scrambling over the stony faces of America's great presidents?

12. **"Come along, Mrs. Thornhill."** [2:15:40] The film ends with one of the most famous match cuts in film history. Thornhill pulls Eve, dangling from the edge of Mount Rushmore, into their berth aboard the Twentieth Century Limited. Hitchcock once said that movies are not a slice of life but a piece of cake. Does he get to have his cake and eat it too? What makes this finale both a typical Hollywood ending and a parody? Consider the lighting, music, costuming, and that parting shot of the train plunging into the tunnel.

12 To Kill a Mockingbird

Directed by Robert Mulligan; screenplay by Horton Foote; based on the 1960 novel by Harper Lee; produced by Alan Pakula; cinematography by Russell Harlan; edited by Aaron Stell; art direction by Alexander Golitzen and Henry Bumstead; set decoration by Oliver Emert; music by Elmer Bernstein; title design by Stephen Frankfurt; released by Universal in 1962. [129 minutes]

Atticus Finch	*Gregory Peck*
Scout Finch	*Mary Badham*
Jem Finch	*Philip Alford*
Dill	*John Megna*
Tom Robinson	*Brock Peters*
Calpurnia	*Estelle Evans*
Bob Ewell	*James Anderson*
Mayella Ewell	*Collin Wilcox*
Boo Radley	*Robert Duvall*
Sheriff Tate	*Frank Overton*
Miss Maudie	*Rosemary Murphy*
Mrs. Dubose	*Ruth White*
Narrator	*Kim Stanley*

To Kill a Mockingbird is one of those rare films that measures up to the popularity and critical acclaim of the original book. Harper Lee's novel remains one of the most frequently read books in English. Since its publication in 1960, it has never been out of print, and readers from all walks of life regularly cite it as the novel that made the most difference in their lives. For some the story evokes nostalgic memories of childhood, of simpler times in the rural South when family life centered on the front porch and kids entertained themselves by swinging on a tire hanging from a tree. For others it is an awakening to the cruelties of prejudice. The book continues to be alternately championed and challenged for its messages about history, politics, and social values.

When the film first appeared in 1962, it was honored by five Oscar nominations, winning Academy Awards for Best Actor (Gregory Peck), Best Adapted Screenplay, and Best Black-and-White Art Direction. It also won special humanitarian awards for its treatment of racial injustice. Harper Lee herself, who rarely comments on her work, praised the adaptation of her story for its integrity and its fidelity to her original intent. "Mr. Foote's screenplay," she said, "should be studied as a classic" (Foote).

Lee's story is told from the perspective of Scout Finch looking back on her early years in Maycomb County, Alabama. It is the 1930s, a time of dire poverty in the United States and perilous rumblings abroad, when people exchange goods and services instead of money, and when suspicion of outsiders runs high. Scout—the family nickname for Jean Louise—is six years old when the story begins. Spunky and strong-minded, an inquisitive youngster who has learned to read before attending school, Scout tags along with her older brother, Jem, and an unconventional boy from out of town called Dill (modeled on Truman Capote, a longtime friend of Harper Lee). Scout's mother died years ago. Her father, a hard-working and respected lawyer whom she calls Atticus, often leaves the children in the capable care of Calpurnia, the black housekeeper. In this community, where doors are left unlocked, Jem and Scout are free to explore on their own. One of their interests is Boo Radley, an unseen neighbor reputed to have stabbed his father in the leg. Another is the trial of Tom Robinson, a black man whom Atticus agrees to defend against the accusation of rape.

Maycomb, a fictionalized version of Monroeville, Lee's hometown, bears much of the character of the Old South. Although the Civil War contributed to its economic problems, its people still celebrate the traditional values of ancestral pride, courtly paternalism, and gracious hospitality. Women continue to wear print dresses on hot days and men bow politely on the street. But in their explorations, the children find other truths behind the face of civility. They learn that their community is rigidly divided by race, social caste, gender roles, and suspicion of outsiders.

Over the course of two and a half years, Scout comes to understand something of the pain of prejudice, the rarity of courage, and the price of maturity. Her story, an initiation into adulthood, covers many themes. There are issues of family. Many of the families in Maycomb are missing a parent. Jem and Scout have no mother, Dill's father is mysteriously missing, and Mayella, the young woman who claims to have been raped, has only an alcoholic father to take care of her and her siblings. There are issues of gender. Scout dresses and acts much like a boy until school age, when she is suddenly expected to dress and act like a young lady. Her discomfort in her first school dress is played for laughs, but the ideal of southern womanhood is seriously questioned more than once. Among the most disturbing issues is the damaging consequence of prejudice. Initially, the children accept the town's judgments of Boo Radley as a dangerous maniac, testing their nerve with rapid raids on his front porch. The town's judgment of Tom Robinson is even more troubling. As a Negro (one of several terms used for African Americans in the book and the movie), Tom has very little chance of a fair trial from a jury of twelve white southern men. What Jem and Scout learn about both Boo and Tom teaches them to see beyond conventional opinions. They learn to face their fears. They learn to "walk around in some-one else's shoes," as Atticus so memorably puts it.

The story's historical dimensions reach back to the thirties, when it is set, and into the fifties, when it was written. The trial of Tom Robinson, for example, recalls the famous Scottsboro Trials that began in 1931, when nine young African Americans were accused of raping two white women on a southern train. One of the "Scottsboro boys," as they were called, was sentenced to death, although the case was based entirely on dubious testimony. The women who made the accusation would have been prosecuted for prostitution if the case had not deflected attention onto the young men. The trial inflamed headlines in North and South until 1950, when the last defendant was finally freed. But the ugliness of racial prejudice persisted as lynch mobs continued to execute black people without trial and segregation remained official policy in southern states. Not only did blacks and whites live in different areas, but also they were not permitted by law to use the same schools, restaurants, or public restrooms. It was the civil rights movement of the 1950s and 1960s that challenged these conditions most directly. In 1955, Rosa Parks refused to take a back seat on a public bus, launching the Montgomery bus boycott. In 1956, Autherine Lucy became the focus of racist violence when she tried to attend classes at the University of Alabama in Tuscaloosa, where Harper Lee had gone to school six years earlier. It was in this cauldron of humiliation, hostility, and courage that the novel was born.

Within a year of its 1960 publication, Lee's book had sold half a million copies and was translated into ten languages. Yet the major Hollywood studios passed it by. It was a young producer named Alan Pakula whose enthusiasm for the book set the reels in motion. Pakula had worked on an earlier film with director Robert Mulligan and composer Elmer Bernstein. They sent the novel to actor Gregory Peck, who later said, "It was the luckiest day of my life." Peck was immediately drawn to the part of Atticus, whom he later modeled on the character of Harper Lee's father. With Peck on board, Universal Studios agreed to the project. Pakula asked Horton Foote to write the screenplay. As a southerner, Foote understood Lee's nostalgic message about childhood and a time gone by. Later he would say that two things helped him re-create the story in cinematic terms. One was Pakula's suggestion to concentrate the novel's time frame into the span of a single year. The other was an article that pointed to the book's roots in *Tom Sawyer* and *Huckleberry Finn* (*To Kill a Mockingbird: Then and Now*).

Pakula's assistant, Boaty Boatwright, interviewed thousands of children throughout the South for the roles of Scout and Jem, finally locating

Mary Badham and Philip Alford. The two children lived in Birmingham within four blocks of each other. Watching them alternately tease and protect each other on the screen, it's easy to believe they are brother and sister. This is the result of good casting and directing as well as acting. Mary grew up with an older brother (John Badham, the film director) and describes herself as a tomboy as a child. She remembers being partly raised by two black women who taught her church values, and she describes her bewilderment when these women were forced to sit in the back of the bus. Philip recalls the natural antagonism that existed between himself, a fourteen-year-old boy, and this nine-year-old girl who kept mouthing her lines. "We argued constantly," he recalls. Mulligan used their personalities, imaginations, and the energy between them to get credible performances (*To Kill a Mockingbird: Then and Now*).

Other actors also identified with their roles. Brock Peters, naturally kind and gentle like Tom Robinson, was able to reach back to the horror of racism in his own life. Kicked and beaten by bigots, he had to "step back from the brink of an anger that would have engulfed me." Collin Wilcox modeled Mayella on people she knew growing up, "girls who took for granted they'd be molested by twelve" and who were locked in their poverty, prejudice, and guilt. After the film was released, neighbors were so incensed by Wilcox's part in the film that they burned crosses on her lawn (*Fearful Symmetry*).

Monroeville had changed too much for location shooting, so Maycomb was re-created on a Universal back lot in California. The most challenging scene was the trial, filmed in three weeks on a set modeled on the Monroeville County Courthouse. Henry Bumstead won an Academy Award for his work on the set. For the title sequence, Pakula asked Stephen Frankfurt to capture the secret world of childhood without words. Frankfurt shot the sequence on a kitchen table, photographing the prized possessions kept by Scout and Jem in a cigar box. As the camera pans across a watch, a necklace, a whistle, and two soap dolls, we hear a girl humming. A light marble rolls toward a dark one, clicks, and Elmer Bernstein's gentle music swells. Bernstein describes the film's lyrical melody as "something children do" with a piano. His score consistently represents the children's point of view, expressing their curiosity, their fears, and their wistful dreams.

If you were to follow Harper Lee's suggestion to study the film as a classic literary adaptation, you might begin by observing how it handles the elements of storytelling common to both written and cinematic fiction. You might notice, for example, how the main characters are introduced. Scout swings into the frame from a tree. Dill is first viewed from a high angle as a small figure almost lost among the leaves of a cabbage patch.

Before we see Jem, we hear his voice coming from the tree house, where he has decided to stay until Atticus agrees to play football for the Methodists. Each entrance tells us something distinctive about each personality. You might also notice how the novel's meandering plot is streamlined, condensing more than three hundred pages of narrative for a single sitting. The film omits characters like Uncle Jack and Mr. Avery, subplots like Mrs. Dubose's morphine addiction, and entire sequences like the children's visit to Calpurnia's church, concentrating instead on the story's two main strands: Boo Radley and Tom Robinson. As for setting, the film establishes the story's time and place with a voice-over narration taken directly from the novel. Kim Stanley's mellifluous voice sets the film's nostalgic tone in an unhurried southern accent spoken over images of rural Maycomb. Soon the narrative voice gives way to dialogue, and the camera takes over the task of setting scenes, reminding us that a picture is worth a thousand words.

Point of view in film is often conveyed literally, by the position of the camera. We glimpse Jem in his tree house in a low-angle shot from Scout's point of view. We see Dill in a high-angle shot from Jem's position in the tree. Since most of the story is narrated from Scout's perspective, the camera usually shows us only what she would see. A good example occurs when the three children enter the courthouse to find Atticus. Scout and Jem lift up Dill so he can peer into the courtroom, and we are limited to what Dill sees and what they hear. That makes the shift in perspective all the more striking after the children leave and Atticus faces Bob Ewell directly, as one adult to another.

As for symbolic objects and actions, these often have a more literally limited life on the screen than on the page. Take the mad dog that threatens Jem and Scout in Chapter 10. Whereas in the book the dog can loom as large as the reader's imagination, its size and shape are limited on the screen. Yet talented filmmakers can take creative liberties with symbols too, as we see in the opening title sequence where a cigar box of trinkets is transformed into a treasury of precious keepsakes through the magical power of memory.

The dialogue and basic actions are the scriptwriter's responsibilities. Sometimes Foote lifts dialogue word for word from the novel, often abbreviating speeches in the interest of economy. Sometimes he takes lines from Harper Lee's narrative and gives them to her characters, transmuting story into drama. The scene in which Scout reads to Atticus is drawn from moments scattered throughout the novel. Here he uses Atticus's watch as an occasion to reveal delicate feelings about Mrs. Finch, the missing center of the family.

But the script is only a blueprint. The actors must construct performances from Foote's words, interpreting them as nuances and gestures.

Mary Badham, playing the innocent six-year-old, speaks primarily in questions, pausing as she reflects on things she is just beginning to understand. Gregory Peck, as Atticus, always formal and controlled, manages to betray just a trace of emotion when Scout reads his watch. When he sits motionless on the porch, listening to the voices of his children reminisce about their mother, his feelings seem all the stronger for not being outwardly expressed.

Robert Mulligan, the film's director, bears the ultimate responsibility for guiding the actors and the technical crew. This includes cinematographer Russell Harlan's camera work, Oliver Emert's set design, Alexander Golitzen and Henry Bumstead's artwork, and Elmer Bernstein's music. Notice how the lighting helps to set the time and mood in the scene in which Scout reads *Robinson Crusoe* to Atticus. Watch how the camera moves in through the curtained windows and then cuts to a position inside the room, always keeping Scout on the left side of the frame and Atticus on the right, even when it shifts back and forth between their points of view. Cutting (splicing separate shots together into a continuous sequence) is the task of the editor, Aaron Stell, who matches particular actions—such as the closing or placement of the book—so seamlessly that few viewers ever notice the cuts. Pay close attention to the sounds, not only to the dialogue, which fades as the children fall toward sleep ("Did you love her?" "Did I love her?"), but also to the music, which resumes its nostalgic motif at certain moments, and the sound effects, like the faint chirping of crickets, which anchor the moment in an audible world.

Suggested Films and Readings

Related Films and Videos

Fearful Symmetry. Documentary film about the making of the film, directed by Charles Kiselyak. Available on the DVD Collector's Edition of *To Kill a Mockingbird.*

To Kill a Mockingbird: Then and Now. Lyceum 2: The Film. Videotape of satellite broadcast, April 25, 1997. Hosts Charlaine Hunter-Gaulte and William Costanzo interview members of the film's cast and crew, who answer questions live from students nationwide. Sponsored by the National Council of Teachers of English. Produced by Prince William Network, P.O. Box 386, Manassas, Virginia, 20108, 1997.

Books

Foote, Horton. *The Screenplay of* To Kill a Mockingbird. New York: Harcourt, Brace, & World, 1964.

Johnson, Claudia Durst. *Understanding* To Kill a Mockingbird: *A Student Case-book to Issues, Sources, and Historic Documents.* Westport, CT: Greenwood Press, 1994.

Lee, Harper. *To Kill a Mockingbird.* New York: HarperCollins, 1995.

Questions for Reflection and Discussion

1. Before the movie: If you were to make a film about your early life, when you were about six to nine years old, what might you include? Who would be the main characters? What would be the major scenes? What tone or themes would be likely to dominate the film?

2. Some people think that an adaptation should be faithful to the book in letter or in spirit. Others think that a film should be faithful only to the art of film, refashioning the story in its own terms. What obligations do you think the filmmaker owes to the original source?

3. Compare Scout's memories of growing up in Alabama during the 1930s to your own experiences of childhood. How does the film compare to the images of childhood represented in other movies or television programs you have seen? How do you account for the differences and similarities?

4. How much of Harper Lee's story could still take place today? Think about the changes that have taken place between the times when the novel is set (1930s) and written (1960s) and our own time. Consider the use of language, the nature of families, the role of women and children, race relations, violence, and justice in these times.

5. What makes a hero? Apply your definition to the characters in *To Kill a Mockingbird.* Are there any heroes in the film? If so, how do these heroes compare to the characters in other films you know?

6. Much of the film's drama centers on Tom Robinson, the black man accused of raping a white woman. What makes such a crime so consequential in his time and place? What is the evidence for and against Robinson? Trace the way he is treated both in and out of court. How do you think his case would be handled today?

7. Some viewers consider Atticus to be a perfect father and attorney. Others think he's too good to be true—or not good enough. Considering the way he raises the children, conducts Tom Robinson's defense, and acts toward Boo Radley, how would you evaluate him as a parent, lawyer, and human being?

Topics for Further Study

1. Read about the Scottsboro Trials and the civil rights movement. Make a time line of historical events from 1930 to 1960 that you can relate to the novel.

2. Some readers find elements of gothic storytelling in both the novel and the film. The gothic tradition, which includes works by Hawthorne, Poe, and Capote, is characterized by horror, violence, and supernatural effects. It often features insanity, degeneracy, imprisonment, and dangerous taboos. Learn more about gothic stories and make a list of gothic elements in *To Kill a Mockingbird*.

3. Lee's novel has been the center of several heated censorship debates. Why do you think anybody would want to ban the book? Do you believe these points have merit? Research the issue of censorship and the historical cases brought against *To Kill a Mockingbird*.

4. If you've read the novel, compare it to the film. How did your viewing experience compare to your experience of reading the book? Notice what the film changed or left out. Why do you think these characters and moments were altered or deleted?

   Consider the following elements of filmmaking:

   Acting: Do the actors look and act as you imagined the characters to be when you read the book? How are their roles interpreted? How believable are their performances?

   Camera Work: How does the camera frame events? Notice when it moves, shifts angles, or otherwise changes the focus of attention. What does this camera work emphasize in each shot?

   Lighting and Set Design: Consider the location chosen for each scene. How was the place made to look as if it belonged to the 1930s? How would you describe the overall tone or atmosphere? How does the lighting contribute to this atmosphere?

   Editing: How are the separate shots within a scene combined into a continuous sequence? Notice how often the camera cuts, fades, or dissolves into a new view of events. What are the reasons for each of these transitions?

   Sound: *To Kill a Mockingbird* uses all four forms of sound available to filmmakers: music, sound effects, voice-over, and dialogue. Notice how Elmer Bernstein's original music helps to create and guide the story's moods. Listen for the creaking stairs, the crickets, and other sound effects that contribute to these moods. What does Kim Stanley's voice-over narration add above and beyond the dialogue?

Script: Horton Foote, the scriptwriter, had to capture the three hundred-plus pages of Harper Lee's story in a 129-minute film. What key decisions did he make? Notice where he trimmed the story or rearranged its parts. Can you justify these changes? How successful is his adaptation on the whole?

Scenes to Analyze

1. **Opening Credit Sequence.** [2:09] The objects that appear behind the opening credits include a pocket watch, harmonica, pearl necklace, whistle, marbles, and a child's drawing of a bird—items that gain meaning as the story unfolds. The sequence is a good introduction to the story's symbolism and themes. It also shows how a film can have (to quote Harper Lee) "a life of its own as a work of art." Notice how the camera moves in, like a child's vision, to close-ups of these valued objects, tracking from left to right along the row of treasures carefully arranged. Notice how the nostalgic music and humming of a child create a mood. And notice what happens to the drawing at the end of the sequence.

2. **Bedtime.** [13:10] The scene in Scout's bedroom presents an intimate bedtime portrait of father and daughter. Reading to Atticus from *Robinson Crusoe,* Scout asks about Boo Radley and is admonished to "leave those poor people alone." When Atticus tells her it is getting late, Scout asks to see his watch and reads the inscription to "my beloved husband." Atticus explains that the watch will go to Jem one day, as is "customary," and assures Scout that she will get her mother's pearl necklace and ring. As Atticus says good night to the children and sits on the porch, we hear Scout asking Jem about the woman who died when she was too young to remember. What do we learn from this scene about these characters and their relationships?

3. **Boo Radley's Porch.** [23:43] The night scene in which the children sneak up to the Radley house dramatizes their fascination with and their fear of the unknown. Compare this moment in the film to its counterpart in the book. How do the filmmakers use lighting, music, sound effects, and camera work to heighten suspense? How suspenseful does the scene seem to you today?

4. **The Mad Dog.** [41:20] The scene in which Atticus shoots the mad dog is a self-contained story within the film, yet it contributes to the ongoing

drama. Notice the position of the camera and the characters throughout the scene. Why is this an important moment for Atticus and Jem? Although few words are spoken, much is communicated in their body language. If father and son could speak their minds, what might they say?

5. **Lynch Mob.** [1:00:00] When a lynch mob confronts Atticus before the trial, Scout's innocent interference dispels the threat of violence. Compare the scene as it occurs in Chapter 15 of the novel to the screenplay (pages 70–75) and the final film.

13 Romeo and Juliet

Directed by Franco Zeffirelli; screenplay by Franco Brusati, Maestro D'Amico, and Zeffirelli; based on the play by William Shakespeare; produced by John Brabourne and Anthony Havelock-Allan; cinematography by Pasqualino De Santis; edited by Reginald Mills; art direction by Emilio Carcano and Luciano Puccini; production design by Lorenzo Mongiardino; set decoration by Christine Edzard; music by Nino Rota; costumes by Danilo Donati; released by Paramount in 1968. [140 minutes]

Romeo	*Leonard Whiting*
Juliet	*Olivia Hussey*
Mercutio	*John McEnery*
Friar Laurence	*Milo O'Shea*
The Nurse	*Pat Heywood*
The Prince	*Robert Stephens*
Tybalt	*Michael York*
Benvolio	*Bruce Robinson*
Lord Capulet	*Paul Hardwick*
Lady Capulet	*Natasha Parry*
Lord Montague	*Antonio Pierfederici*
Lady Montague	*Esmeralda Ruspoli*
Paris	*Roberto Bisacco*
Peter	*Roy Holder*
Balthazar	*Keith Skinner*
Prolog Narrator	*Laurence Olivier*

More movies have been based on Shakespeare's works than on any other writer's. Some critics explain this in terms of the playwright's sense of audience. Shakespeare knew how to play to a diverse crowd. The nobility, merchants, and common groundlings who attended his performances expected a menu of murder and mayhem, sexual misconduct, and supernatural phenomena—not unlike filmgoers of today. Other critics point to a cinematic quality in his writing. Douglas Brode, for example, observes that Shakespeare's unit of construction was the filmic scene, not the theatrical act, noting that the five-act divisions in editions of his plays were added after his death (6). Actors and directors from Orson Welles to Laurence Olivier regularly speculate that if the bard were alive today, he'd be writing and directing movies, not plays.

Of course, plenty of Shakespeareans object to cinematic presentations of his plays. They argue that Elizabethan theater lacked elaborate set designs, costuming, or special effects, which obliged Shakespeare and his

contemporaries to rely principally on words. This need for imaginative language, together with the bard's extraordinary talent, produced the richest literary texts in English. By contrast, film is primarily a visual medium. By duplicating on screen much of the descriptive function of Shakespeare's words, a filmed version of one of his plays often threatens to short-circuit the viewer's imagination and either overwhelm the text or render it irrelevant. Yet it is also true that Shakespeare intended his works to be performed, not read. They were never published in his lifetime, and he might well wonder at the many editions of his works in print today.

In any case, people have been directing filmed performances of Shakespeare plays since the earliest days of motion pictures (Ball). These performances have never been so popular as they are today. It was Kenneth Branagh's *Henry V* (1989) that reopened the movie market for Shakespeare in the 1990s. Within ten years, there were two major *Hamlets* (Zeffirelli's film with Mel Gibson in 1990 and Kenneth Branagh's version in 1996), two films about Richard III (Richard Loncraine's 1995 version of the play starring Ian McKellen and Al Pacino's *Looking for Richard* in 1996), an *Othello* (directed by Oliver Parker in 1995 with Laurence Fishburne in the title role and Kenneth Branagh as Iago), and Baz Lurhmann's *Romeo + Juliet* (1996, with Leonardo DiCaprio and Claire Danes). Modern filmgoers have also had a rich helping of the comedies, including Branagh's *Much Ado about Nothing* (1993), Trevor Nunn's *Twelfth Night* (1996), Michael Hoffman's *A Midsummer Night's Dream* (1999), and Branagh's *Love's Labour's Lost* (2000). In 1998, audiences got to meet the bard himself in John Madden's ingeniously entertaining *Shakespeare in Love* (1998). It is not surprising, then, that high schools and colleges around the country offer courses in Shakespeare on film. With scores of great screen performances to choose from and a plentiful reservoir of resources—the books, articles, videos, Web sites, and DVDs keep coming—teachers everywhere are building on Shakespeare's growing popularity with yet another generation of viewers and readers.

Franco Zeffirelli's 1968 version of *Romeo and Juliet* is a good place to start for many reasons. First, the play itself has proved to be perennially appealing and accessible to young people. They relate easily to the story of young love thwarted by the messed-up world of adults. They understand the conflicts facing Romeo and Juliet, the divided loyalties to family and friends on the one hand and to each other and themselves on the other. Second, although Zeffirelli's film is now more than twenty-five years old, it is still arguably the most engaging rendition of the play. The best earlier screen performances (directed by George Cukor in 1936 and Renato Castellani in 1954) have not dated well, perhaps because their lead actors were already far past the ages of Shakespeare's teenage lovers. Baz Lurhmann's treatment (1996) is a vigorously bold and ingenious updating of the story, but its use of contemporary culture—designer clothes, gang shootouts, television newscasts, and drug deals in Venice Beach—upstages Shakespeare's language and conception in ways that Zeffirelli's film does not.

Those who defend Shakespeare adaptations regularly point out that the playwright himself freely adapted his material from other sources, as did other writers of his time. Elements of *Romeo and Juliet,* first performed about 1597, have been traced back to Greek, Latin, Italian, and French sources. The most direct influences are two English versions of the story, by Arthur Brooke (*The Tragicall Historye of Romeus and Juliet,* 1562) and William Painter ("Rhomeo and Julietta," 1567), which included most of the characters and much of the plot about the tragic deaths of two young lovers caught in a blood feud. Shakespeare condensed the time from nine months to four days and nights, reduced Juliet's age from sixteen to thirteen, enriched the characters, expanded certain roles (especially Mercutio's), and transformed a slight tale into an enduring classic through the brilliance of his language.

Students are sometimes surprised to discover that Shakespearean English is really a supple spectrum of linguistic styles that continually shifts to refract peculiarities of character, mood, and social class. The servants Gregor and Samson speak an earthy street talk of bawdy puns. Mercutio's witticisms are of a higher class, playing off conventions of Elizabethan verse and fluttering into imaginative flights of fancy like the celebrated Queen Mab speech. The Capulets and Montagues use the formal language of adult society. A character's speech patterns can also vary with his mood. Friar Laurence moralizes with the gravity of a spiritual father, but he is also capable of teasing Romeo good-naturedly about the young man's juvenile fantasies of love. Romeo himself enters spouting sonnets, but as his experience of love matures, his poor imitations of love poems ("O heavy lightness, serious vanity / Misshapen chaos of well-seeming forms" [1.1.169–70]) give way to genuinely heartfelt lines addressed to Juliet ("O she doth teach the torches to burn bright" [1.5.43]).

The play's most interesting characters seem multidimensional because they undergo change (like Romeo and Juliet) or embrace contrary natures (like Mercutio, the Nurse, and Friar Laurence). Romeo's love changes from a boyish infatuation with Rosaline (or, since he has never actually met the woman, from being in love with love) to an adult commitment to Juliet. Yet even halfway through the play, when Romeo tries to stab himself in desperation, Friar Laurence can berate him for being unmanly, "unseemly woman in a seeming man" (3.3.112). For her part, Juliet combines the qualities of a little girl and a mature woman. With her Nurse, she acts like an adolescent, but with Romeo, she can spar like an experienced lady of the court. The Nurse is garrulous and secretive by turns, now self-sacrificing, now opportunistic. Friar Laurence, Romeo's father surrogate, treats the boy with a mixture of indulgence and admonishment. The Friar's role as catalyst is especially troubling. While he goes out of his way to help Juliet with his potion, he abandons her at the tomb when she is most in need. Such tensions of character, when played out in performance, make for dynamic acting on stage or on screen.

There are similar tensions in Shakespeare's very language. In a play in which "all things change them to the contrary" (4.5.90), the words themselves seem to be at war with one another. The contrasting imagery of darkness and light, night and day, runs throughout the text. To Romeo, Juliet is like a torch that "hangs upon the cheek on night / As a rich jewel in an Ethiop's ear" (1.5.44–45). Juliet later evokes Romeo, her "day in night," who "will lie upon the wings of night, / Whiter than new snow upon a raven's back" (3.2.17–19). Their secret meetings—at the masked ball, on the balcony, in Juliet's bedchamber, and at the tomb—all take place in darkness, so that the sun itself seems "envious" (3.4.7). In the final scene, after their double suicide, "the sun, for sorrow, will not show his head" (5.3.306). Love and hate also are in conflict in the language of the play. Romeo announces this quarrel early in scene 1—"o brawling love, o loving hate" (1.1.181)—and Juliet takes up the refrain when she learns that Romeo is the son of her father's rival: "My only love, sprung from my only hate" (1.5.140). Friar Laurence, who knows his chemistry, casts the conflict in a laboratory metaphor. For such a love, born in the crucible of hatred, "violent delights have violent ends / And in their triumph die like fire and powder, / Which as they kiss consume" (2.6.9–11). Or, as Capulet concludes,

> All things that are ordained festival,
> Turn from their office to black funeral:
> Our instruments to melancholy bells,
> Our wedding cheer to a sad burial feast;
> Our solemn hymns to sullen dirges change;
> Our bridal flowers serve for a buried corse;
> And all things change them to the contrary. (4.4.84–90)

Capturing *Romeo and Juliet* on film without losing the power of such language presents a daunting challenge, but Zeffirelli had some instructive precedents. The MGM version, produced by Irving Thalberg in 1936, was a major Hollywood spectacle, meticulously researched and generously financed. Thalberg wanted to compete with *A Midsummer Night's Dream*, the big budget art film rolled out by Warner Bros. in 1935. He hired George Cukor as director and a big-name cast, which included Leslie Howard (then age forth-three) as Romeo, Norma Shearer (age thirty-six) as Juliet, John Barrymore as Mercutio, Basil Rathbone as Tybalt, and Andy Devine as Peter. The film received a mixed reception. Critics appreciated this serious effort to film Shakespeare but criticized Cukor for "framing an old picture rather than executing a new one" (Brode 45). In fact, as Brode notes, the emphasis on high art made the film more highbrow than Shakespeare's play. Instead of starting with a crowd-pleasing brawl, as Shakespeare does, Cukor's film begins with a Renaissance painting come to life in pomp and pageantry. Not surprisingly, the film was not a popular success.

Renato Castellani's version, produced for Verona Productions in 1954, approached the challenge differently. Taking his cue from the current interest in James Dean, Castellani chose actors closer in age to Shakespeare's characters: Laurence Harvey (age twenty-five) and Susan Shentall (nineteen). He shot much of the film on location in Italy, hiring Robert Krasker (the cinematographer for Olivier's *Henry V*) to photograph it in sumptuous color. The script takes liberties with Shakespeare's text, deleting Mercutio's Queen Mab speech, most of the low-comedy exchange between Peter and the Nurse, and even lines from the balcony scene. In short, Castellani regarded himself as an interpreter of Shakespeare, transforming the original material to a new medium, not unlike Verdi fashioning the opera of *Otello*. The results were acknowledged as good cinema but bad Shakespeare.

More successful, perhaps because it made no claims of being faithful to Shakespeare, was *West Side Story* (1961). Directed by Robert Wise, stunningly choreographed by Jerome Robbins, and with an unforgettable score by Leonard Bernstein and Stephen Sondheim, the film was adapted from the Broadway musical set in Manhattan's Upper West Side. Based only loosely on *Romeo and Juliet*, it featured Natalie Wood (age twenty-three) as a Puerto Rican who falls in love with Anglo Richard Beymer (twenty-two) amid the racial tensions between two rival gangs, the Jets and the Sharks, who fight with switchblades in 1950s style. *West Side Story* may have been an inspiration for Baz Luhrmann's *Romeo + Juliet*, filmed in 1996 for Twentieth Century Fox. The Australian director updated the story for a Gen-X audience. His Montagues and Capulets are mobsters in Verona Beach, Florida. They fight with outsize guns (which they call "swords"), drive custom cars, and wear heavy gold chains with designer clothes. Luhrmann cast popular young stars as the star-crossed lovers: Claire Danes (age sixteen) and Leonardo DiCaprio (twenty-one). If they had trouble mouthing Shakespeare's dialogue, their efforts were aided by the pulsating energy of hip-hop music and MTV visual effects. Some of Lurhmann's innovations seem strikingly apt (the Prologue is a television newscast), some slyly amusing (a FedEx mishap explains why Romeo never gets the Friar's message), and some gratuitously hip (the apothecary scene is played as a drug deal). Ultimately, this 1990s version of *Romeo and Juliet* is more about drugs and violence than romantic love, reflecting issues of the times. It was a big hit with teenage viewers.

Zeffirelli's film reflects the spirit of its own time, the 1960s, when the youth movement was celebrating freedom, love, and peace. The director had already staged a lively version of the play at London's Old Vic (with a young Judi Dench as Juliet), and he had just filmed a delightfully rowdy *The Taming of the Shrew* (1967) with Richard Burton and Elizabeth Taylor. For the screen version of *Romeo and Juliet,* he drew on the most successful features of Castellani's film (young actors, Italian locations, vibrant photography) and refashioned the play for the generation of *The Graduate* and *West Side Story.* His Romeo and Juliet are pacifists, victims of their parents' wars, who love each other with the innocence of flower children. To stress the theme of youth, Zeffirelli cast Leonard Whiting and Olivia Hussey in the title roles. Both were exceptionally young (sixteen and seventeen respectively), although well trained and experienced. Whiting was a member of Britain's National Theatre; Hussey (half-Argentinean, half-English) had studied and performed in London. Their delicate good looks and guileless performances made them attractive protagonists.

Zeffirelli moves the action forward at a lively pace. The mobility of De Santis's camera keeps up the excitement from the dance scene to the street fights with quick cuts and rapid pans, adding realistic touches in the style of cinéma vérité. Certain scenes use documentary lighting to bring Shakespeare's poetry down to earth. Yet, while the young actors sometimes seem to act like modern teenagers, Zeffirelli chooses lavish Renaissance sets and costumes. Danilo Donati (who won an Oscar for his costume designs) dresses the Capulets in bright red and gold, colors to contrast their nouveau riche status with the more subdued gray and black of the established Montagues. The Nurse is decked in billowy fabrics, like a sailboat, while Juliet wears simple dresses that set off her unspoiled beauty. For their part, the young men strut around in codpieces and tights with all the bravado of their age and class. To these production values, Nino Rota's enduring score adds music that sounds both Elizabethan and contemporary.

Critics of the film chide Zeffirelli for sacrificing the beauty of Shakespeare's poetry to the spectacle and speed of cinema (Manvell 99). The director deliberately cut portions of the play that duplicated the camera work or slowed the action. Lengthy descriptions of Verona have been excised because we can see the city on the screen. The plot is streamlined by trimming clown scenes and details like the pestilence in Mantua. Some of the changes, though, seem more thematic. From act 5, Zeffirelli deletes the apothecary scene, the duel with Paris in the tomb, Lady Montague's death, and Friar Laurence's final explanation—deletions that leave the older characters more culpable and the youth more victimized than they are in the play. The last scene shows the two families, in separate corteges, coming together with their caskets. The overall impression is of innocence sacrificed to a hostile adult world.

Donaldson sees another theme emphasized in Zeffirelli's production, what he calls the "homoerotic aspects" of the play (145). He notes that the camera duplicates the phallic innuendos in the dialogue by showing the men's bodies as "objects of an engrossed, sensual appreciation" (154). John McEnery's Mercutio is the most aggressive practitioner of phallic puns. He continually accuses Romeo of being soft, of abandoning the male group. His clowning has a manic, driven quality, especially in the Queen Mab speech, which leaves him breathless and confused. When he realizes that he is dying, he reveals the fact to Romeo in a gesture suggesting an intimacy of which Romeo himself seems unaware. Donaldson also points out that the conventional gender roles (man watching woman) shift when Romeo becomes the object of Juliet's attentive gaze during the dance scene and later in her bedroom.

The impetus for Zeffirelli's special interest in Shakespeare is clarified in his autobiography (Zeffirelli). The illegitimate child of a successful fashion designer and a fabric merchant, Zeffirelli (his name was taken from a Mozart opera) was tutored in English at an early age. Although educated to become an architect, he was so moved by Olivier's *Henry V* when he saw it in 1945 that he changed career goals. He became a stage actor and then apprenticed himself to Luchino Visconti on several films, developing a close professional and sexual relationship with the great director of *La terra trema* (1948) and *Senso* (1954). During the fifties and sixties, Zeffirelli worked on operas, designing, costuming, directing, and ultimately filming some of the most lavish performances. "I have always been a popularizer," he has said. Nearly all his films are adaptations, thoroughly researched, with extravagant sets and colorful costumes, always motivated by a personal vision. Undaunted by those who berate him for watering down established masterpieces, he describes his mission "to make the audience understand that the classics are living flesh" (qtd. in Hapgood 80). His efforts to bring great art to ordinary people include his three Shakespeare films, a romanticized life of Francis of Assisi (*Brother Sun, Sister Moon*, 1973), a TV miniseries on Jesus of Nazareth (1977), and several Italian operas.

Suggested Films and Readings

More Films by Franco Zeffirelli

The Taming of the Shrew (1967)

The Champ (1979)

Endless Love (1981)

Otello (1986)

Hamlet (1990)

Jane Eyre (1996)

Tea with Mussolini (1999)

More Film Adaptations of Shakespeare

Hamlet (1948; dir. Laurence Olivier) w/ Laurence Olivier, Eileen Herlie

Hamlet (1969; dir. Tony Richardson) w/ Nicol Williamson, Anthony Hopkins

Hamlet (1990; dir. Franco Zeffirelli) w/ Mel Gibson, Glenn Close

Hamlet (1996; dir. Kenneth Branagh), w/ Kenneth Branagh, Derek Jacobi

Macbeth (1948; dir. Orson Welles) w/ Orson Welles, Jeanette Nolan

Macbeth (1960; dir. George Schaefer; made for television) w/ Maurice Evans, Judith Anderson

The Tragedy of Macbeth (1971; dir. Roman Polanski) w/ Jon Finch, Francesca Annis

Romeo and Juliet (1936; dir. George Cukor) w/ Leslie Howard, Norma Shearer, John Barrymore

Romeo and Juliet (1954; Renato Castellani) w/ Laurence Harvey, Susan Shentall

Romeo + Juliet (1996; dir. Baz Luhrmann) w/ Leonardo DiCaprio, Claire Danes

West Side Story (1961; dir. Robert Wise; Leonard Bernstein musical loosely based on *Romeo and Juliet*) w/ Natalie Wood

Julius Caesar (1953; dir. Joseph L. Mankiewicz) w/ Marlon Brando, James Mason

Julius Caesar (1970; dir. Stuart Burge) w/ Charlton Heston, Jason Robards

The Tragedy of Othello: The Moor of Venice (1952; dir. Orson Welles) w/ Orson Welles, Micheál MacLiammóir, Suzanne Cloutier

Othello (1965; dir. Stuart Burge) w/ Laurence Olivier, Frank Finlay, Maggie Smith

Otello (1986; opera by Verdi, dir. Franco Zeffirelli) w/ Plácido Domingo, Katia Ricciarelli

Othello (1995; dir. Oliver Parker) w/ Laurence Fishburne, Kenneth Branagh

King Lear (1971; dir. Peter Brook) w/ Paul Scofield

Henry V (1945; dir. Laurence Olivier) w/ Laurence Olivier

Henry V (1989; dir. Kenneth Branagh) w/ Kenneth Branagh

Richard III (1955; dir. Laurence Olivier) w/ Laurence Olivier, Claire Bloom, John Gielgud

Richard III (1995; dir. Richard Loncraine) w/ Ian McKellen, Kristin Scott Thomas

Looking for Richard (1996; dir. Al Pacino) w/ Al Pacino, Winona Ryder, Kevin Spacey

The Taming of the Shrew (1967; Franco Zeffirelli) w/ Richard Burton, Elizabeth Taylor

Much Ado about Nothing (1993; dir. Kenneth Branagh) w/ Kenneth Branagh, Emma Thompson

Twelfth Night: Or What You Will (1996; dir. Trevor Nunn) w/ Imogen Stubbs, Helena Bonham Carter, Toby Stephens

Love's Labour's Lost (2000; dir. Kenneth Branagh) w/ Kenneth Branagh, Alicia Silverstone, Natascha McElhone, Nathan Lane, Richard Briers

A Midsummer Night's Dream (1935; dir. Max Reinhardt, William Dieterle) w/ James Cagney, Olivia de Havilland

A Midsummer Night's Dream (1968; dir. Peter Hall) w/ Diana Rigg, David Warner

A Midsummer Night's Dream (1999; dir. Michael Hoffman) w/ Kevin Kline, Michelle Pfeiffer, Stanley Tucci, Calista Flockhart

Tempest (1982; dir. Paul Mazursky; modern version) w/ John Cassavetes

Titus (1999; dir. Julie Taymor; based on *Titus Andronicus*) w/ Anthony Hopkins, Jessica Lange, Colm Feore, Harry J. Lennix

Books and Articles

Ball, Robert. *Shakespeare on Silent Film: A Strange Eventful History.* New York: Theater Arts Books, 1968.

Brode, Douglas. *Shakespeare in the Movies: From the Silent Era to* Shakespeare in Love. New York: Oxford UP, 2000.

Cartmell, Deborah. *Interpreting Shakespeare on Screen.* New York: St. Martin's, 2000.

Donaldson, Peter S. *Shakespearean Films/Shakespearean Directors.* Boston: Unwin Hyman, 1990.

Hapgood, Robert. "Popularizing Shakespeare: The Artistry of Franco Zeffirelli." *Shakespeare, the Movie: Popularizing the Plays on Film, TV, and Video.* Ed. Lynda E. Boose and Richard Burt. London: Routledge, 1997. 80–94.

Manvell, Roger. *Shakespeare and the Film.* London: Dent, 1971.

Shakespeare, William. *Romeo and Juliet.* Ed. G. Blakemore Evans. The New Cambridge Shakespeare. Cambridge, UK: Cambridge UP, 1984.

Zeffirelli, Franco. *Zeffirelli: The Autobiography of Franco Zeffirelli.* New York: Weidenfeld & Nicolson, 1986.

Questions for Reflection and Discussion

1. Romeo and Juliet seem isolated in their love for each other. How would you describe their love? What contrasting attitudes toward love surround them? Consider the attitude of Mercutio (who uses his wit as a weapon), Lord Capulet (a man of practical affairs), the Nurse (who is full of bawdy jests), and Friar Laurence (a holy man with worldly sympathies).

2. Shakespeare called his play *The Tragedy of Romeo and Juliet.* What makes the story tragic? Do you blame any of the characters for what happens? If so, explain your judgments.

3. Trace Romeo and Juliet's relationship through the play's key scenes, from the ball to the balcony, from the bed to the tomb. What changes as their love evolves? How do you explain these changes?

4. People who watch Shakespeare plays on film sometimes say, "The story was great once I got past the language." Describe your experience of the language in *Romeo and Juliet.* Where was it a problem, and where did you find yourself appreciating the words? To what extent did the film assist your understanding of the words or interfere with Shakespeare's poetry?

5. Shakespeare's characters have different ways of speaking. Compare the speech patterns of Mercutio, the servants (Gregor and Sampson), the lords and ladies (Capulets and Montagues), and Romeo and Juliet themselves. What differences do you notice in their use of language? What does their speech tell you about their social status, personalities, and moods at various moments in the story?

6. At the dance, Romeo says of Juliet, "O she doth teach the torches to burn bright." Later, on the balcony, he says, "It is the east and Juliet is the sun." In bed, the two young lovers argue playfully about whether they hear a lark (a bird of morning) or a nightingale. What other references can you find to day and night, to light and dark? What might be the purpose of this imagery?

7. At the play's beginning, the Chorus speaks of "a pair of star-crossed lovers." What does this mean? Notice the references throughout the play to heavenly bodies (stars, sun, moon). Note also the number of incidents that seem to hinge on chance. Do you think the source of tragedy lies chiefly in the influence of heaven, in some blind fate, or in the characters themselves? What general view of the nature of tragedy seems to be involved here? How does this compare to your own beliefs about chance, destiny, and individual responsibility?

8. Zeffirelli's film was made in 1968. In what respects does it seem dated now? Considering the nature of acting, filmmaking, and people's interests today, how well has the film held up? What makes it still appealing to viewers like you?

Topics for Further Study

1. In *Interpreting Shakespeare on Screen,* Deborah Cartmell reproduces sections of Shakespeare's text (act 5, scene 3, lines 74–309) using boldface and underlining to show which words were retained by Zeffirelli and Luhrmann in their films (55–66). Consult Cartmell's book, or mark up your own text of the play to see what changes were made in the two movies. What reasons can you give for these changes? What is lost or gained?

2. Read about life in sixteenth-century Italy and England. What kinds of clothing did people wear (men with swords and codpieces, women in wide dresses)? What were their social customs (about dancing, marriage, and sexual conduct)? How did their language differ from our own? Does Zeffirelli's film do a good job of re-creating the world of Shakespeare's time?

3. You've seen the movies, but how was *Romeo and Juliet* staged in Shakespeare's time? Consult a drawing of the Globe Theatre and note what his contemporary actors had to work with. There was an upper stage (for the balcony scene), a curtained inner stage (perhaps for Juliet's bedchamber), a trapdoor (the tomb?), and two pillars holding up the roof (which might serve as trees in Juliet's orchard or as columns to hide behind for the "pilgrims" scene). If you were a director in Shakespeare's day, how would you block each scene of the play?

4. Now imagine you're a filmmaker. What would your movie of *Romeo and Juliet* look like? Who would you cast in the major roles? What sets or locations would you choose? What kind of music, camera work, or special effects would you use? What changes would you make to Shakespeare's text? What kind of audience would your film appeal to?

5. Read one of Shakespeare's earlier sources, such as Arthur Brooke's *The Tragicall Historye of Romeus and Juliet* (1562) or William Painter's "Rhomeo and Julietta" (1567). To what extent was Shakespeare "faithful" to this source? What did he add, leave out, or alter?

6. Compare Zeffirelli's film to one of the other movie versions of *Romeo and Juliet.* Select one or two scenes for close analysis. Compare the set-

ting, props, costumes, acting, cinematography, and sound track. Which version do you prefer? What reasons can you give?

Scenes to Analyze

1. **Chorus.** (act 1, scene 1, lines 1–14) The function of the Prologue, a remnant from Greek tragedy, is to introduce the play to the audience. The words of the Chorus (written as a sonnet) are read by Laurence Olivier (who also reads the final lines in Zeffirelli's film). What expectations about plot and theme are created by these words?

2. **The Dance.** (1.5) The Capulet's ball is a cinematic opportunity for pageantry. Notice how Zeffirelli re-creates the splendor of Renaissance Verona with colorful costumes, lavish set décor, and memorable music. Pay particular attention to the moment when Romeo first sees Juliet ("O she doth teach the torches to burn bright" [1.5.43]) and when he begins their playful exchange about pilgrims ("If I profane with my unworthiest hand / This holy shrine" [1.5.92]). The camera repeatedly focuses on hands in this scene. How much of this attention to hands is justified by Shakespeare's text? Where else are you aware of hands in the movie?

3. **"A sail, a sail!"** (2.4) When Romeo's friends spot Juliet's nurse in the public square, they tease her openly, likening her white smock to a sail (2.4.83). Some viewers find their mockery offensive. Others find it harmless: boys will be boys. Why do you think Shakespeare included this scene? Watch how Zeffirelli captures the moment with fluid motions of the camera and shifts between foreground and background. What does Zeffirelli achieve by moving the conversation between Romeo and the Nurse from the public square into a church?

4. **Queen Mab.** (1.4.54–94) Zeffirelli shifts Mercutio's Queen Mab speech from act 1 to a later scene, just before the fight with Tybalt (3.1). Why do you think he makes this change? Who is Queen Mab and why does Mercutio describe her at such length? Different actors have interpreted the speech differently. How would you characterize John McEnery's performance? How does Romeo fit in with his interpretation?

5. **The Balcony.** (2.2) Watch how Zeffirelli directs this famous scene. What does the camera allow him to do that would not be possible on stage? How are the romantic sentiments of Shakespeare's poetry translated into physical activity? Compare this ritual of courtship to the "pilgrims" scene when Romeo and Juliet first meet.

6. **Sword Fight.** (3.1.1–99) In the film, the duel itself is enacted as playful bravado that turns deadly serious. Mercutio's friends laugh throughout the scene, but we see that more is at stake. How does Zeffirelli let us see what is really going on? At what point do you know that Mercutio will die? When do you recognize the nature of the intimacy between Mercutio and Romeo? What does Mercutio mean when he says, "A plague a' both your houses!" (3.1.97)?

7. **Juliet's Bedchamber.** (3.5.1–36) Shakespeare's text makes no mention of a bed in this scene. Do you think that Zeffirelli is justified in showing the lovers waking up naked? When Juliet says, "It was the nightingale, and not the lark" (3.5.2), what is her intention? How does Romeo respond? Some viewers see this scene as a form of verbal jousting between lovers, like their earlier exchanges at the ball and on the balcony. Others point out the serious threat that daybreak represents, noting the persistent imagery of day and night throughout the play. How does the scene affect you?

8. **In the Vault.** (5.3) The double suicide comes as no surprise since the Chorus anticipated it, but now the final death scene bears the emotional weight of the entire play. What does the film add to this moment beyond the words? Notice how the lovers' bed has been replaced by a tomb, how their love is consummated in death. What is Friar Laurence's role in all of this? Can he be held responsible in any way?

14 The Godfather

Directed by Francis Ford Coppola; screenplay by Coppola and Mario Puzo; based on the book by Mario Puzo; produced by Albert Ruddy; cinematography by Gordon Willis; edited by William Reynolds and Peter Zinner; art direction by Warren Clymer; production design by Dean Tavoularis; set design by Philip Smith; music by Nino Rota; costume design by Anna Hill Johnstone; makeup by Dick Smith and Philip Rhodes; released by Paramount in 1972. [175 minutes]

Don Vito Corleone	*Marlon Brando*
Michael Corleone	*Al Pacino*
Sonny Corleone	*James Caan*
Clemenza	*Richard S. Castellano*
Tom Hagen	*Robert Duvall*
Captain McCluskey	*Sterling Hayden*
Jack Woltz	*John Marley*
Barzini	*Richard Conte*
Sollozzo	*Al Lettieri*
Kay Adams	*Diane Keaton*
Sal Tessio	*Abe Vigoda*
Connie Corleone Rizzi	*Talia Shire*
Fredo Corleone	*John Cazale*
Johnny Fontane	*Al Martino*
Luca Brasi	*Lenny Montana*
Paulie Gatto	*John Martino*
Amerigo Bonasera	*Salvatore Corsitto*
Mama Corleone	*Morgana King*
Carlo Rizzi	*Gianni Russo*
Moe Greene	*Alex Rocco*
Bruno Tattaglia	*Tony Giorgio*
Apollonia	*Simonetta Stefanelli*

For more than thirty years, *The Godfather* has captivated American and international audiences alike. Part of the appeal is Marlon Brando's memorable performance in the title role. Nobody who has seen the film forgets his dominating presence as Mafia patriarch Don Corleone: those deep-set eyes, those sagging jowls, that raspy voice making offers that cannot be refused. Another reason for its popularity is the way this movie plunges us into a fascinating subculture, the underworld of Italian American gangsters of the 1940s, where brutal violence and traditional family values go hand in hand. Francis Ford Coppola's directing gives a kind of epic grandeur to the Corleones and their efforts to maintain first rank among the prominent crime families of New York. Critics have likened the Corleone

family to a dynasty, and they have compared the film's classical plot to the structure of Greek tragedy. But the main reason for *The Godfather's* persistence in the pantheon of cinematic classics is that it is so well made. Repeated viewings reward us with brilliant examples of film editing, scriptwriting, acting, music, and set design. Students of film have a lot to learn from Coppola, his talented cast, and his first-rate crew. So do students of psychology and sociology. Yet for all its instructional significance, *The Godfather* never loses its power to provoke, disturb, and entertain.

The film begins in 1945, just after the end of World War II. Vito Corleone, a Sicilian immigrant, has risen to a position of power and prestige among the five "families" that run a lucrative crime syndicate in the boroughs of New York City. Although his "business" involves bribery and murder, Vito is respected for his scrupulous code of honor. He never wavers from the old Sicilian values of family, friendship, and religion. But he is aging, and his authority is being threatened. A young "Turk" named Sollozzo wants to extend the syndicate's operations—previously limited to businesses such as olive oil, unions, and gambling—to include the profitable new drug trade. Sollozzo wants the assistance of Vito's wealth and political influence, but when the old man refuses to cooperate, Sollozzo arranges to have him killed. Vito is gunned down on the street. While Vito struggles to recover, with five bullets in his body, his oldest son, Sonny, maneuvers the family and its loyal soldiers for a bloody retribution.

The story's structure has been likened to a five-act play (Kawin 275–85). In the first part, Vito is presented at the height of his reign. We see him at the marriage celebration for his daughter Connie, seated at his desk like a king on his throne, granting favors to a succession of supplicants who know that a Sicilian cannot refuse requests on his daughter's wedding day. Michael, his youngest son, has just come home from the war. Unlike his older brothers, Michael has gone to college, served in uniform, and found a non-Italian—an Irish girl named Kay—whom he wants to marry. Kay is curious about the family, but Michael only hints at the dark side that will soon emerge. In act 2, Sollozzo makes his offer to the Don. Sonny, the rash older son, makes the fatal error of showing interest in Sollozzo's proposed drug deal despite his father's clear refusal. Sollozzo sees this as a sign of family disunity and makes his move: with the Barzini family on his side, Sollozzo orders Vito's murder. In this way, he expects to replace the old-world values with modern ones. But this is not as easy as he thinks. In act 3, Michael foils another effort to kill Vito in the hospital. Unlike Sonny, Michael shows cool judgment in the face of danger and patience in preparing his next move. He plans and executes the killing of Sollozzo and Captain McCluskey, a crooked cop, in their favorite restaurant and then flees to Sicily. In this romantic setting, in the land of his roots, Michael falls in love with a beautiful Sicilian girl named Apollonia, marries her, and loses her when she triggers a car bomb intended for him. The pastoral Sicilian interlude is contrasted with events back in New York, where the blood feud heats up. Sonny gives a brutal beating to Carlo, Connie's husband, for abusing her, but is ambushed at a tollbooth in a fusillade of machine-gun fire. In act 4, Michael returns to the United States. Vito gives him some final advice about the Barzini threat and dies of a heart attack in his garden, leaving Michael as his heir. Michael takes charge in act 5. He consolidates his power, extends the family operations to Las Vegas, and methodically eliminates his enemies, but at a price. He has violated the old standards, placing his own dark motives above family, friendship, and church.

The Godfather is based on Mario Puzo's novel, first published in 1969. Puzo had set out to write a bestseller, doing intensive research on the *Mafia* (the book's original title) and including plenty of sex and violence in his story. When he had completed the first hundred pages of the manuscript, Paramount's producer Robert Evans brought him to Hollywood to finish the book, paying him $80,000 for the movie rights. The investment paid off. Puzo's potboiler became an instant success, selling more than thirteen million copies even before the film opened.

Evans hired a promising new talent to produce the picture, Al Ruddy. Ruddy courted several established filmmakers, including Costa-Gavras and Peter Yates, before he recruited Coppola for the job of director. At the age of thirty-one, Coppola was at a low ebb in his career. His dream of creating a new studio (Zoetrope) had failed, his most recent film (*The Rain People*) was a box office dud, and his new film ideas had all been rejected by the studios, so Ruddy reasoned that his services would be cheap. Besides, Ruddy thought that Coppola's Italian name and ethnic background might prove useful. There was already a strong movement in the Italian American community against the *Godfather* project. One group launched a high-profile campaign among politicians and staged a rally in Madison Square Garden featuring Frank Sinatra (widely regarded as the model for singer Johnny Fontane in the book). The protests eventually died down when Ruddy agreed to delete the words *Mafia* and *Cosa Nostra* from the script. When the film finally appeared, filmgoers of Italian descent were among its strongest supporters at the box office. Mobsters reportedly enjoyed watching it on videocassettes and played Nino Rota's music on the jukebox.

At first, Coppola was reluctant to direct the film, referring to Puzo's novel as "this hunk of trash" (Cowie 63). He considered himself an auteur and preferred to do art films. From the beginning, he and Ruddy disagreed on key decisions. Coppola wanted to shoot the New York and Sicilian scenes on location; Ruddy wanted to shoot in less expensive settings to keep costs down. Coppola wanted Marlon Brando and Al Pacino in the roles of Vito and Michael; Ruddy was wary of Pacino's inexperience and Brando's reputation for time-consuming behavior on the set. Coppola wanted to downplay the story's violence; Ruddy thought more violence meant more sales. It was a classic case of movies as an art versus movies as a business.

Eventually, the director won out. He excised some of the more lurid scenes, fleshed out the relationships among the Corleone brothers, and focused more on ethnic details. He devoted more screen time to the rituals of marriage and baptism. He made the mobsters more human. In interviews, Coppola later said that he modeled Vito Corleone on the real lives of Vito Genovese and Joseph Profaci (Cowie 70). He also explained, "every aspect of the story is tied into our own family in some way" (68). Not only did he use his knowledge of Italian customs to authenticate the family scenes, but he also included members of his family in the film. His father Carmine composed some of the music, his brother August served as a consultant on the script, and other Coppolas are scattered throughout the credits. The director's nephew, Nicholas Cage, has a role, as does his sister, Talia Shire, and his parents appear in several scenes (Carmine plays the piano, Italia operates the switchboard, and both can be seen eating dinner at the Luna restaurant where Michael kills Sollozzo).

Coppola's extended family of filmmakers made many contributions to the film. Gordon Willis, the cinematographer, was responsible for the movie's distinctive color scheme. Willis wanted a grainy, slightly faded look, like the texture of old photographs. Although the film's lighting varies with the mood, his amber tones remain constant, unifying the narrative and lending to each scene a somber beauty. Nino Rota's score deepens this effect. From the nostalgic opening trumpet solo to the lively wedding theme, from the ominous minor chords of the baptism scene through the heart-pounding modulations of Bach's "Passacaglia and Fugue in C minor," the sound track amplifies the film's emotional range. A good deal of the rhythm and pacing was achieved in the editing room. The romantic sequence in Sicily and the masterfully orchestrated scenes of violence in New York owe much of their power to the editing skills of Peter Zinner. It was Zinner who hit on the idea of intercutting footage of the baptism with footage of executions for the film's grand finale, creating one of the most celebrated examples of parallel montage in movie history.

Some of the most memorable moments in *The Godfather* are due to members of the production team trying to solve little problems in their own way. It was set designer Dean Tavoularis who rescued the scene in which

Sonny is trapped and killed at a Long Island tollbooth. When traffic at the real tollbooth proved too busy for location shooting, Tavoularis created a replica on a deserted runway on Floyd Bennett Field, erecting a billboard to hide apartments in the background. Vito's death scene in the garden was written by Robert Town, who was hired as an uncredited script doctor (Goodwin and Wise 129). It was Brando, however, who added the business with the orange in that scene. Vito cuts the fruit and holds up the peels like a mask before his frightened grandson, making his last appearance both playful and monstrous. Coppola did some improvising too. Early in the shooting, the nonprofessional actor hired to play Luca Brasi, Lenny Montana, was having trouble with his part. He kept forgetting the lines when he pays tribute to Vito at the wedding. So Coppola rewrote the script to make it seem as though Brasi himself was trying to rehearse his speech. Montana's limitations as an actor thus became part of the character and added an endearing touch of humor to the role.

By October 1971, the crew had produced more than ninety hours of footage, which were edited to a 175-minute release print. When the film opened, it was greeted with rave reviews. Vincent Canby of the *New York Times* called it "one of the most brutal and moving chronicles of American life ever designed within the limits of popular entertainment" (Goodwin and Wise 138). Pauline Kael praised its intelligent direction and novelistic depth, observing that Coppola gave a "classic grandeur to the narrative flow," expressing "a new tragic realism" (138). At the Academy Awards, the film won three Oscars: Best Picture, Best Actor (Marlon Brando refused to accept the award), and Best Screenplay. By 1975, *The Godfather* had made more money at the box office than any film in history.

While *The Godfather* rejuvenated the motion picture industry, it also reinvented a classic American genre, the gangster film. In the 1930s, actors like Edward G. Robinson, James Cagney, and Paul Muni had made gangsters famous in movies like *Little Caesar* (1930), *The Public Enemy* (1931), and *Scarface* (1932). These were usually low-budget films whose grainy film stock and dimly lit sets gave them a tough, realistic quality. Audiences were drawn to the straightforward treatment of sex and violence in these films, but to something else as well. The gangster figure was a tragic hero, a guy from the streets who aspired to the American dream with the closest means available.

Coppola's film has many of these elements and more. It raises the simple crime film to a new level, an epic study of power in America: of family and business, justice and violence, honor and corruption—themes that cut across genres and social milieus. It is possible to see the Corleones as an "honorable" crime family, compelled by social prejudice and conflicting values to work outside the system. The old Sicilian codes of loyalty and vengeance offer an alternative to American justice, which fails people like the undertaker whose daughter's brutal beating by well-connected youths would otherwise go unpunished. Organized crime offers an alternative to the "legitimate" businesses from which immigrants are excluded. Someone like Vito, a poor immigrant at the turn of the century, must carve his empire out of gambling, unions, and other activities shunned by the power elite. It's no accident that the film's first spoken words are "I believe in America."

It is also possible to regard the *Cosa Nostra* (Italian for "our thing") as a metaphor for capitalism, a way of doing business in a world where only the fittest survive. From this perspective, *The Godfather* becomes a shrewd analysis of power politics. Brando saw it as an allegory of corporate America, claiming that "the tactics the Don used aren't much different from those General Motors used against Ralph Nader" (Goodwin and Wise 119). Coppola had a wider historical view, observing that the central story was about a king with three sons; it could be about any dynasty, including the Kennedys (118). Some viewers focused on the patriarchal nature of the Corleone family. They noted that *The Godfather* seems to embrace the title role, endorsing the wisdom and benevolent authority of the head male. Yet the title suggests some ironies. Vito is generous to his friends, but only if they pledge an oath of loyalty. He upholds religion and the family, but he is ready to preserve these values with force if need be. In fact, despite Coppola's expressed desire to minimize the violence, the film revels in blood. Before it is over, some thirty people are killed, not to mention a thoroughbred horse. Many of the deaths are unforgettable. Brasi is garroted (strangled) with a wire while his hand is pinned to a bar counter with a knife. Connie's husband kicks out the car window when he dies. A man on a massage table is shot through the lens of his eyeglasses. Another is gunned down in a revolving door. Sometimes these killings seem like grim jokes. When Paulie is executed, Clemenza says to his fellow henchman, "Leave the gun; take the cannoli" (a line not in the book). Sometimes the deaths seem carefully choreographed, like rituals of the genre. Sonny's killing is a deliberate allusion to the machine-gun death in *Bonnie and Clyde* (1967). This too is what makes *The Godfather* so fascinating and so troubling. For all the carnage, corruption, and greed, the film itself never passes judgment. It's as though Michael's moral blindness—which begins at his wife's death and takes him through acts of calculated vengeance and dispassionate consolidations of wealth and power—has become the consciousness behind the camera.

Yet for all his flaws, Michael remains an appealing character for many viewers. Pacino inhabits his character completely, moving through every step of his transformation with consummate credibility and making his cool detachment seem admirable. As the least Sicilian member of the clan, he becomes our entrée to the Corleone family. We first learn about the Corleones through Michael's commentaries to Kay at Connie's wedding, where he says, "That's my family, Kay. It's not me." Gradually, we are drawn into the messy business of the Mafia as Michael is drawn in: after his trip to Sicily connects him to his roots, after Apollonia's shocking death gives him a motive for vengeance, after Sonny's assassination and Vito's passing leave him with the responsibility of family chief. Gradually, too, we watch the same courage that won medals in the war and the same precise intelligence that won honors at Dartmouth being placed in the service of revenge, greed, and power. Michael becomes the new Don, but with a difference. He eventually embraces the drug trade that his father opposed. And he pays only lip service to Vito's values of family and religion, a hypocrisy brilliantly demonstrated in the movie's final sequence when we see him accept the role of Godfather at the baptism of Connie's child at the same time that his bloody master plan of retribution is being carried out. In the movie's final shot, he closes the door on Kay—and perhaps on us.

The other great performance belongs, of course, to Marlon Brando. Brando's Vito Corleone has become such a legend that it is hard to imagine he almost didn't get the part. For his screen test, he is said to have stuffed a wad of toilet tissue in his gums to extend his jowls and give his voice that fuzzy hoarseness that contrasts so memorably with Vito's clarity of mind. Ruddy's objections vanished when he saw the test results, and makeup expert Dick Smith was hired to fine-tune that harried look with synthetic wrinkles, discolored teeth, and special dentures. Smith averaged an hour and a half to make forty-seven-year-old Brando look like the aging Don. Brando wore earplugs to authenticate Vito's hearing loss and weights on his feet to simulate a limp. But he struggled with a real memory problem. To cover this, he reportedly hid his lines on props and wrote them on his hands and even on his shirtsleeves.

Brando and Pacino are supported by a uniformly strong cast. James Caan's Sonny is appropriately rough-hewn, quick-tempered, and visceral. Robert Duvall's Hagen is sensitive and smart, the family's Irish consigliere whose loyalty never wavers. John Marley plays Jack Woltz, the Hollywood studio boss, as a self-important big shot who thinks himself untouchable until he deals with the Don. Diane Keaton plays Kay Adams as the naive girl from New Hampshire who can't see into the man she is marrying.

Along with directors such as Spielberg, Lucas, and Scorsese, Francis Ford Coppola is part of the film school generation, men who studied film-making in college and went on to make movies that incorporated elements from the works they loved to watch while growing up. Coppola was born in Detroit in 1939, though most of his childhood was spent in Queens, New York. The son of a composer (Carmine) and an actress (Italia), the grandson of a theater owner, Francis grew up in an artistic environment. He loved gadgets. When he contracted polio at the age of ten, his grandfather presented him with an 8mm camera, a creative outlet for his intense, brooding imagination. He studied theater at Hofstra University before entering UCLA's film school, where he took up the craft of moviemaking, a craft he refined while working on low-budget Roger Corman productions. Recruited by Hollywood, he directed *Finian's Rainbow* (1968), a big budget musical, before attempting a more personal picture, *The Rain People* (1969). Both films were box office disappointments. More successful were his scriptwriting ventures. His adaptation of Carson McCullers's novel *Reflections in a Golden Eye,* though uncredited, gave him excellent experience. His screenplay for *Patton* won an Academy Award in 1970. Meanwhile, he gained a reputation as an independent-minded director, a dreamer, energetic and erratic, "a fiercely driven Hollywood outsider," "a brilliant, nervous impresario" (Jones 30).

Coppola went on to make many films after *The Godfather.* Two of these—*The Conversation* (1974) and *Apocalypse Now* (1979)—were critically acclaimed. Others—such as *The Cotton Club* (1984), *Peggy Sue Got Married* (1986), and *Tucker: The Man and His Dream* (1988)—were met with varying degrees of appreciation and disparagement. The real foundation of his career continues to be *The Godfather* and its sequels. *The Godfather: Part II* (1974), which contrasts young Vito's climb to power with his son Michael's ascendance thirty years later, won even more Oscars than Part I. *The Godfather: Part III* (1990) continues the story through Michael's efforts to achieve legitimacy before his death. Together, the *Godfather* trilogy lifts the Corleone family and its struggles to the status of an American myth.

Suggested Films and Readings

More Films by Francis Ford Coppola

Finian's Rainbow (1968)

The Rain People (1969)

The Conversation (1974)

The Godfather: Part II (1974)

Apocalypse Now (1979)

One from the Heart (1982)

The Outsiders (1983)

Rumble Fish (1983)

The Cotton Club (1984)

Peggy Sue Got Married (1986)

Gardens of Stone (1987)

Tucker: The Man and His Dream (1988)

New York Stories (1989)

The Godfather: Part III (1990)

Bram Stoker's Dracula (1992)

More Gangster Films

Little Caesar (1930; dir. Mervyn LeRoy)

The Public Enemy (1931; dir. William A. Wellman)

Dead End (1937; dir. William Wyler)

Angels with Dirty Faces (1938; dir. Michael Curtiz)

Key Largo (1948; dir. John Huston)

The Big Heat (1953; dir. Fritz Lang)

The Killers (1964; dir. Don Siegel)

Bonnie and Clyde (1967; dir. Arthur Penn)

The Brotherhood (1968; dir. Martin Ritt)

Goodfellas (1990; dir. Martin Scorsese)

Books and Articles

Cowie, Peter. *Coppola: A Biography.* Updtd. ed. New York: Da Capo Press, 1994.

Goodwin, Michael, and Naomi Wise. *On the Edge: The Life and Times of Francis Coppola.* New York: Morrow, 1989.

Jones, Kent. "Mythmaker Francis Ford Coppola." *Film Comment* (March 2002): 30–36.

Kawin, Bruce F. *How Movies Work.* New York: Macmillan, 1987.

Lebo, Harlan. *The Godfather Legacy.* New York: Simon & Schuster, 1997.

Messenger, Chris. *The Godfather and American Culture: How the Corleones Became "Our Gang."* Albany: State U of New York P, 2002.

Rosow, Eugene. *Born to Lose: The Gangster Film in America.* New York: Oxford UP, 1978.

Questions for Reflection and Discussion

1. Before screening the film: What do you know about organized crime in the United States? What do terms such as *Cosa Nostra* and the *Mafia* bring to mind? Where do these images come from?

2. After more than thirty years, two sequels, and many spin-offs, *The Godfather* continues to be a popular film. How do you account for its popularity with both the critics and the moviegoing public?

3. Italian rituals play a big part in the film, which highlights the wedding, baptism, and funeral scenes. How are these rituals related to the family "business" of crime? What role do family and religion have in the film?

4. When *The Godfather* was being made, Italian American groups tried to stop production, saying that it misrepresented them. Do you think the final film gives a slanted view of Italians, Sicilians, New Yorkers, or other groups?

5. Coppola said he wanted to minimize the story's violence, but his producer wanted more. How is violence handled in the film? What is your opinion of the level and nature of *The Godfather*'s violent scenes?

6. In the opening wedding scene, Michael tells Kay about his father's strong-arm tactics and says, "That's my family, Kay. It's not me." What sets him apart from the other Corleones? How do you explain his transformation in the course of the film? In what ways does he become like his father? In what ways does he differ from the old Don?

7. Compare the women in the film. What kind of people are Connie, Vito's wife, Kay, and Apollonia? What roles do they play in the world of the film?

8. The first words of the movie, "I believe in America," are uttered by Amerigo Bonasera, who has not been well served by American justice. What alternatives to the American establishment are offered by the Don? To what extent do Vito Corleone and his organization diverge from corporate America or operate along parallel lines?

9. *The Godfather* has been called a masterpiece of filmmaking. Which production values—acting, lighting, color, music, editing, sets, costume design—contribute most to its artistic success? Where in the film are these values most apparent?

10. Compare the novel and the film. What aspects of the story are emphasized in each version? What does the film change, leave out, or add? Ultimately, which is a more satisfying experience for you, the original book or the movie adaptation? Why?

Topics for Further Study

1. Make a list of who's who in gangland. Include the Corleones and the "five New York families" as well as the major characters in Las Vegas and the West Coast. Organize your list to reflect the crime wars in *The Godfather*. Who sides with the Don? Who are the traitors?

2. Create character wheels for Vito, Sonny, Michael, and Tom Hagen. Assess their personal qualities and allot portions of each wheel to these qualities. What portion of Vito's character, for example, would you assign to qualities such as fairness, loyalty, friendship, family feeling, shrewdness, wisdom, or brutality? Be prepared to give examples from the film.

3. Research the topic of organized crime in the United States. Read the biographies (and obituaries) of famous crime figures such as Russell Bufalino, Carlo Gambino, Joe Bonanno, and John Gotti. How closely do their real lives and deaths resemble the characters in Coppola's film?

4. The story of *The Godfather* is filled with Sicilian terms like *omerta*, *pezzanovante*, *consigliere*, *caporegime*, and *lupara*. Find these terms in the novel or the movie and define them. What do these terms tell you about the subculture of the Mafia?

5. Watch one of the documentaries on the making of *The Godfather*, available on the laserdisc and DVD versions of the movie. Then watch the film again. What did you notice during your second screening of the feature film? Did your new knowledge of the film's production contribute to or detract from your appreciation of the film?

6. The Corleones have been likened to a feudal dynasty within contemporary America. Their efforts to gain power, extend their economic reach, wage war and peace, protect their people, reward loyalty, and punish treachery might be compared to the politics of early rulers. Explore this analogy. Why do you think Coppola called *The Godfather* "the story of a king and three sons" and why Puzzo called it "a tragedy"?

7. Compare *The Godfather* to other crime films you are familiar with. Or take this opportunity to watch some early examples of the genre, such as *The Public Enemy* (1931), *Scarface* (1932), *Key Largo* (1948), or *Bonnie and Clyde* (1967). Investigate the tradition of gangster movies in the United States. To what extent does Coppola's film belong to this tradition, and what makes it stand out from the others?

Scenes to Analyze

1. **"I believe in America . . ."** [0:45] The opening words of the film are spoken by Amerigo Bonasera, a man with an Italian accent who has given up on the American legal system and come to Don Vito Corleone for "justice." We see him from the Don's perspective, in a single long take, within Vito's darkened chambers. Notice how each detail—the sepia tones, the venetian blinds, the old-world décor, the Don's distorted face and muffled voice, his conservative tuxedo with the rosebud lapel—contributes to the mood. How would you describe this mood and what it implies about the Don? Why does the camera keep shifting back and forth between this inner sanctum and the noisy wedding party just outside?

2. **Khartoum.** [32:07] The film's first violent act is the killing of a horse, but we never see the act itself. What makes this scene so effective? Most of it is a single long take that gradually reveals the grisly deed. How does Coppola use music, color, texture, voice, and editing to both prepare and shock us?

3. **Meeting with Sollozzo.** [35:38] In one of the film's many "business meetings," Sollozzo tries to convince the Don to help him enter the drug trade. Tom Hagen prepares Vito (and us) with a two-minute briefing about Sollozzo [beginning at 33:50], interspersed with shots of the men arriving for the meeting. How do you know who has the power in this scene? Pay attention to the actors' positioning, their dress and body language, what they say, how they say it, and what they don't say. Analyze the scene from the perspective of a social historian, an economist, a communications expert, or a military tactician.

4. **Luca Brasi Sleeps with the Fishes.** [40:13] Watch how Coppola prepares us for Luca Brasi's death. Begin as Brasi, framed in his bedroom doorway, puts on his bulletproof vest and checks his gun. Follow him through the gleaming hotel corridor to the bar. Notice the fish etched on the glass and the brown tones of the room. Watch the men's hands and faces as they speak in Sicilian. Compare Brasi's strangulation to the other death scenes in the film: Paulie's ("Leave the gun; take the cannolis"), Sonny's (at the tollbooth), Carlo's (who kicks out the windshield), and the multiple murders at the end.

5. **Michael at the Hospital.** [1:01:23] We begin to see a new side of Michael when he takes steps to save his father at the hospital. What personal qualities does he demonstrate in this scene? How does Coppola create suspense and suggest Michael's silent thoughts? Pay close attention to

the sound track, lighting, editing, and other elements of film. Contrast Michael's reflective methods with Sonny's outgoing style in the scenes that follow.

6. **"How's the Italian food in this restaurant?"** [1:21.00] The scene in which Michael shoots Sollozzo and McCluskey at dinner is one of the film's most chilling moments. Which parts of the scene do you find most compelling? Why? Who has the power in this scene? Does the power shift at any point? Do you expect something to go wrong? Does your attitude toward Michael change by the final shot? Explain your expectations and responses in terms of what happens in the scene and how it is filmed.

7. **The Thunderbolt.** [1:39:00] The Sicilian interlude is an important part of the book. Why do you think Coppola chose to include it in the movie? What does it contribute to the story and to our understanding of Michael? Contrast the music, color, and other cinematic qualities of these scenes to those that take place in New York and Las Vegas.

8. **The Don Dies.** [2:29:56] Vito dies in his garden while playing with his grandson. Did you expect him to die when you first saw this scene? What guided your expectations or surprised you? Some of the details (the insecticide gun, the orange) were not in the book. Why do you think they were added to the film? Much of the interaction between Brando and the child was improvised. Does this scene seem different from the rest of the movie?

9. **Baptism and Murder.** [2:36:20] The crosscutting between the church baptism and the revenge killings is the film's grand finale and one of the most celebrated examples of editing in movie history. Why do you think the editors chose to splice together shots from different locations (something that was not in the book)? Notice their use of matching action (like walking up stairs), the priest's voice, music, color, and other film elements to link shots. What thematic connections are suggested here? What does the crosscutting tell us about Michael? How do you judge him at this point in his life?

15 One Flew over the Cuckoo's Nest

Directed by Milos Forman; based on the novel by Ken Kesey; screenplay by Bo Goldman and Lawrence Hauben; produced by Michael Douglas and Saul Zaentz; cinematography by Bill Butler and Haskell Wexler; edited by Richard Chew, Sheldon Kahn, and Lynzee Klingman; art direction by Edwin O'Donovan; production design by Paul Sylbert; music by Jack Nitzsche; costume design by Aggie Guerard Rodgers; released by United Artists in 1975. [133 minutes]

Randle Patrick McMurphy	*Jack Nicholson*
Nurse Mildred Ratched	*Louise Fletcher*
Dale Harding	*William Redfield*
Ellis	*Michael Berryman*
Miller	*Alonzo Brown*
Orderly Turkle	*Scatman Crothers*
Attendant Warren	*Mwako Cumbuka*
Martini	*Danny DeVito*
Jim Sefelt	*William Duell*
Bancini	*Josip Elic*
Attendant Washington	*Nathan George*
Beans Garfield	*Ken Kenny*
Charlie Cheswick	*Sydney Lassick*
Taber	*Christopher Lloyd*
Ellsworth	*Dwight Marfield*
Hap Arlich	*Ted Markland*
Rose	*Louisa Moritz*
Woolsey	*Philip Roth*
Chief Bromden	*Will Sampson*
Frederickson	*Vincent Schiavelli*
Candy	*Mews Small*
Scanlon	*Delos V. Smith Jr.*
Billy Bibbit	*Brad Dourif*

When Ken Kesey's novel first appeared in 1962, it found an instant, enthusiastic audience. Critics praised its literary merits. Young people embraced it as an envoy of their generation, a book that challenged the authority and conformity of their times. By 1975, when the movie version hit the screens, Kesey had become one of the most popular voices of the American counterculture, prescribing large doses of freedom, nature, love, and mind-altering drugs as antidotes to the institutionalized repression widely asso-

ciated with urban riots, Watergate, and Vietnam. Set in a state mental hospital, *One Flew over the Cuckoo's Nest* questioned the sanity of institutions that stripped individuals of their dignity, suppressed their natural inclinations, and treated them like machines. It asked, who is crazier, the patients or the staff?

The story pits Randle Patrick McMurphy, a new arrival at the institution, against Nurse Ratched, the reigning power on the ward. In the novel, McMurphy is a burly, redheaded Irishman with a crude gash stitched across his nose and cheek. Charming and crude, wily and energetic, McMurphy pretends to be crazy so he can trade a six-month sentence of hard labor for an easier stint in the sanatorium. Ratched is a fifty-year-old veteran of the psychiatric staff who is used to controlling every movement on the floor with icy self-assurance. As the conflict builds between these two headstrong personalities, McMurphy's motives widen beyond his instincts of self-preservation. He finds himself leading the other inmates in a revolt against a cunningly repressive regime.

Little by little, scheme by scheme, McMurphy takes ground in the guerilla war against the establishment. He does this through the force of his outrageous personality, boundless vitality, powerful laughter, and shrewd wit. He institutes a regular card game in the unused tub room, rallies the other men behind him in a vote to watch the World Series on TV, organizes a madcap fishing trip, and even sneaks two prostitutes into the ward for a late-night party. Big Nurse counters every move, first with her saccharine smile and sly insinuations, then with rules and regulations, and finally with threats of shock treatment and lobotomy. She relies on institutional weapons and McMurphy's egotism, calculating that his desire for easy winnings and self-preservation will override any true concern for the other men. But her calculations go awry. In the end, despite the efforts to neutralize his body, his irrepressible spirit triumphs in the men who find new freedom, dignity, and power in his example.

While McMurphy is the novel's leading character, its central consciousness is Chief Bromden, a giant Native American who tells the story from his delusional point of view. Pretending to be deaf and dumb, Bromden is given menial jobs by the hospital's African American attendants, who belittle him as "Chief Broom" and talk openly in his presence. Bromden's hallucinatory thoughts give us much of the book's most striking imagery. He believes that the hospital is run by a secret organization called the Combine, which operates the world like a well-oiled machine. He imagines Big Nurse "in the center of a web of wires like a watchful robot," controlling the machinery (Kesey, *One Flew* 26). When his vision of things blurs, he believes that a fog machine has clouded the view. These delusions can be traced to Bromden's personal history and fears (the army trained him in electronics and he saw artificial fog used for concealment during combat), but they also provide universal metaphors for the Establishment and its devious ways. The hospital could be any government or bureaucracy that intimidates its citizens, turning individuals into mindless cogs in a wheel lubricated with hypocrisy.

Randle P. McMurphy, whose initials hint at his frenetic personality, threatens the Combine. Bluntly honest, bursting with sexual vitality and raucous laughter, he appears sometimes more like a cartoon figure than a man: "the logger, . . . the swaggering gambler, the big redheaded brawling Irishman, the cowboy out of the TV set walking down the middle of the street to meet a dare" (Kesey, *One Flew* 189). Bromden sees him as "a giant come out of the sky to save us from the Combine" (225). Kesey plays with the symbolism of his hero self-consciously. He gives McMurphy underwear printed with large white whales, a gift from a "Literary major" girlfriend. Later, when McMurphy lies on the table for shock treatment, he stretches out his arms and asks the technicians, "Do I get a crown of thorns?" (270). Yet, for all the allusions to Western cowboys, literary sea captains, and Christ, McMurphy is also presented as a human being with all-too-human flaws. Harding calls him a "good old red, white, and blue hundred-percent American con man" (254). Nurse Ratched debunks the medical team's various assessments of him as a psychotic version of Napoleon or "reverse Oedipal," saying he is "simply a man and no more" (149). Perhaps nobody sees more deeply into McMurphy's complex character than Bromden, who observes his hero's face reflected in the windshield during an unguarded moment when they pass McMurphy's hometown, "tired and strained and *frantic*, like there wasn't enough time left for something he had to do" (245). Somewhere in the middle of the story, the conflict shifts from a simple clash between McMurphy and Big Nurse to something more complex. McMurphy the gambler sees that there is something beyond keeping up his end of the deal. The rugged individualist looks beyond his own self-interests and puts himself at risk for the community.

According to Tom Wolfe's account in *The Electric Kool-Aid Acid Test*, the inspiration for *Cuckoo's Nest* came to Kesey in a vision. While enrolled in the graduate writing program at Stanford, Kesey was working part time as an orderly on the psychiatric ward of the Veterans Hospital in Menlo Park. It was here that he volunteered to take part in a research study of hallucinatory drugs. In one drug-induced vision, he imagined a huge American Indian sweeping the hospital floors. This was the inspiration for Chief Bromden. Kesey wrote the novel during the summer and spring of 1961, publishing it in 1962.

It was Kirk Douglas, the star of *Spartacus* (1960) and *Paths of Glory* (1957), who bought the rights, imagining himself in the virile role of R. P. McMurphy. Douglas commissioned Dale Wasserman to adapt the novel for the stage and starred in the play's first Broadway production in 1963. It closed after three weeks. Harold Clurman panned the play as "a gruesome soap opera," calling it "a trite canon of hand-me-down psychoanalysis" (qtd. in Kesey, *One Flew* 442). A revised version was more successful, running for six years in San Francisco and later in New York, but with other actors in the leading role. By 1974, Kirk Douglas was too old for the part, so he offered the rights to his son Michael, who decided to produce a movie version with Saul Zaentz. Their first inspired choice was to select Milos Forman as director. Forman was one of the leaders of the Czech new wave, which flourished in the brief period of creative expression before the Soviets crushed all artistic freedom in 1968. Under the communist regime, Forman had experienced tyranny, confinement, and bureaucracy firsthand. He had also honed a fine sense of irony that expressed itself in powerful imagery.

Another smart decision was to cast Jack Nicholson as McMurphy. Nicholson lacked some of the physical qualities of Kesey's hero, but his roles in *Easy Rider* (1969) and *Five Easy Pieces* (1970) had prepared him for the part. Nicholson's wisecracking humor and raw energy made him a model of the sixties rebel. For the role of Nurse Ratched, Douglas and Zaentz ran the gamut of actresses. Anne Bancroft, Colleen Dewhurst, Geraldine Page, Ellen Burstyn, and Angela Lansbury all reportedly turned down the part before it was given to Louise Fletcher only one week before shooting began. Fletcher projects a very different image from Kesey's Big Nurse, with her immense breasts and tiny, doll-like mouth. Fletcher is more human than caricature, at times almost sympathetic. For the patients, Forman cast unknown actors to make their neuroses more believable. Brad Dourif plays Billy Bibbit, the shy, thirty-something boy who stutters incessantly and harbors a deathly fear of his mother. William Redfield plays Dale Harding, the ineffectual intellectual. Some of the actors have since become well known: Danny DeVito (Martini), Sydney Lassick (Charlie Cheswick), and Christopher Lloyd (Taber). Other characters are played by nonprofessional actors who never appeared in another film. The role of Chief Bromden is performed by Will Sampson, a Cree Indian painter who once rode in rodeos. Tom McCall, the former governor of Oregon, has a minor part as a news commentator. The role of Dr. Spivey is played by Dr. Dean Brooks, the actual superintendent of the Oregon State Mental Hospital in Eugene where the movie was filmed. Brooks asked that his patients be hired to work with the crew. According to Forman, they handled the work extremely well and developed self-esteem in the process. One inmate even overcame a life-long problem with stuttering (Forman and Novak 208).

Readers familiar with Ken Kesey see something of the author in the figure of McMurphy. Born in 1935 and raised on farms in Colorado and Oregon, Kesey developed his physical prowess, social skills, and love of nature early in life. He learned to hunt, fish, box, and wrestle and was voted "most likely to succeed" when he graduated from high school in 1953. At the University of Oregon, he was active in sports and theater and grew interested in writing. He applied to the graduate writing program at Stanford, moving to Perry Lane, the bohemian section of Palo Alto, California, where he wrote *One Flew over the Cuckoo's Nest.* In 1964 he made his famous cross-country trip with friends in an old bus, brightly painted and wired for sound, calling the group The Merry Pranksters. The voyage was a kind of promotional tour for his second novel, *Sometime a Great Notion,* and succeeded in captivating the attention of a generation. It also caught the interest of the police, who arrested him after a six-month pursuit and put him in prison for drug possession. This was Kesey's public image, the freewheeling hero of Tom Wolfe's *The Electric Kool-Aid Acid Test* (1968). Kesey's private life was more conventional. He settled down on his father's farm in Pleasant Hill, Oregon, with Faye, his wife and high school sweetheart. He became a family man, a father of four children, with ties to the local community. Although he continued to write, none of his other works was as successful as *One Flew over the Cuckoo's Nest.* He died in 2001 at the age of sixty-six.

Kesey had little to do with the film production. After completing the first script, he argued with the producers, disapproved of the changes they wanted, and ultimately refused the see the movie. Nevertheless, the film enjoyed great success. Budgeted at $4 million, well below the average movie cost, it earned $112 million at the box office by the end of its run and more than $320 million worldwide, making it the seventh-largest grossing film up to that date. At the Academy Awards, it won five Oscars, more than any film since 1934: for Best Picture, Best Actor (Jack Nicholson), Best Actress (Louise Fletcher), Best Screen Adaptation (Lawrence Hauben and Bo Goldman), and Best Director.

Director Milos Forman was born in Cáslav, a small town near Prague, in 1932. During World War II, both of his parents were arrested as partisans by the Nazis and died in concentration camps. Admitted to a special school for victims of the war, he befriended Ivan Passer and Václav Havel, who later became leading figures in the Czech new wave. Forman made his first feature film, *Black Peter,* at the Prague School of Cinema in 1963, becoming part of the wave. This was followed by *The Loves of a Blonde* (1966) and *The Fireman's Ball* (1967), which established his international reputation for witty satires aimed at Czech bureaucracy. After the Soviet crackdown in 1968, he fled to the United States, where he made a successful transition to English-language films, including *Taking Off* (1971), *Hair* (1979), *Ragtime* (1981), *Amadeus* (1984), *The People vs. Larry Flynt* (1996), and *Man on the Moon* (1999). Although *Amadeus* won more Oscars, *One Flew over the Cuckoo's Nest* is widely regarded as Forman's masterpiece.

One reason may be Forman's felt connection to Kesey's story. Interviewed in *Completely Cuckoo*, Charles Kiselyak's documentary about the filming of *Cuckoo's Nest*, Forman explained, "This is a movie about Czech society, about everything I know." In *Turnaround*, his autobiography written with Jan Novak, Forman gives a full account of how he came to make the film, describing his excitement on first reading the novel, which he had not heard of until the producers mailed it to him in New York. He tells how he prepared an outline for the script and took it to Los Angeles, and then worked on it further with Hauben and Goldman while getting to know the hospital in Oregon. He describes how he cast Louise Fletcher deliberately against type and worked with three different cinematographers on the set (Haskell Wexler left partway through production and was replaced by Bill Butler and, later, Bill Fraker, who shot the fishing trip). He explains his editing methods and how cutting seven minutes from the beginning made the film seem longer because audiences felt less engaged without an introduction to the hospital setting and the minor characters. He recalls how composer Jack Nitzsche dismissed the orchestra and created most of the sound track himself with a suitcase full of water glasses.

Forman also clarifies his process of translating a story from page to screen: "The scope of a film is clearly much closer to a short story than to a novel," he says, "so to adopt a book means to pare down and focus its theme." A scriptwriter must be willing "to let go of the precise words of the original to preserve its tone and feeling" (Forman and Novak 206). One of his first decisions was to eliminate Kesey's narrator, shifting the novel's focus on Bromden's inner life to a more objective, realistic perspective. This meant downplaying the book's symbolism and psychedelic hallucinations, replacing allusive caricature and mythic figures with more believable roles. It's easier to identify with the film's characters than with the novel's. The film deletes some characters, like "rub-a-dub" George Sorensen, and adds others (Taber, who is only a memory in the book, becomes a lively presence in the film). It reorganizes certain scenes and modifies the ending. As a motion picture, the film also plays up the visual aspects of certain scenes—like the basketball game and the fishing expedition—in ways that no book or play can do.

Since the film was made more than a decade after the novel, it may also reflect changes in attitudes. More than one critic has commented on Kesey's view of women. Nearly all the patients seem to be victims of female domination. Bromden's father is made small by his white wife, Bibbit is infantalized by his mother, Harding intimidated by his wife's sexuality, and everyone subjugated by Big Nurse, the castrating matriarch. The film softens this theme and minimizes Bromden's racist remarks about the black attendants. And as Forman told film critic Molly Haskell, it eliminates "that whole psychedelic '60s drug free-association thing" ("Film Notes").

Still, the film cannot and does not bring us Kesey's inventive language, sometimes acutely descriptive, sometimes expansively lyrical. Here is Bromden's description of the hand that McMurphy puts out to shake when they first meet:

> I remember real clear the way that hand looked: there was carbon under the fingernails where he'd worked once in a garage; there was an anchor tattooed back from the knuckles; there was a dirty Band-Aid on the middle knuckle, peeling up at the edge. All the rest of the knuckles were covered with scars and cuts, old and new. I remember the palm was smooth and hard as bone from hefting the wooden handles of axes and lines, not the hand you'd think could deal cards. The palm was callused, and the calluses were cracked, and dirt was worked into the cracks. A road map of his travels up and down the West. (Kesey, *One Flew* 23)

And here is how he characterizes McMurphy's laughter as the fishing trip ends:

> It started slow and pumped itself full, swelling the men bigger and bigger. I watched, part of them, laughing with them—and somehow not with them. I was off the boat, blown up off the water, and skating the wind with those black birds, high above myself, and I could look down and see myself and the rest of the guys, see the boat rocking there in the middle of those diving birds, see McMurphy surrounded by his dozen people, and watch them, us, swinging a laughter that rang out on the water in ever-widening circles, farther and farther, until it crashed up on beaches all over the coast, on beaches all over all coast, in wave after wave after wave. (238)

Such passages remind us that a well-written novel can produce a first-rate movie—with Oscar-winning performances, camera work, and sound track—in the mind of any imaginative reader.

Suggested Films and Readings

More Films by Milos Forman

Black Peter (1963)*

The Loves of a Blonde (1966)*

The Fireman's Ball (1967)*

Taking Off (1971)

Visions of Eight (1973)

Hair (1979)

Ragtime (1981)

Amadeus (1984)

Valmont (1989)

The People vs. Larry Flynt (1996)

Man on the Moon (1999)

Related Films

Completely Cuckoo. Dir. Charles Kiselyak. Pioneer Entertainment, 1997/1975.

Sometimes a Great Notion. Dir. Paul Newman. MCA/Universal, 1995/1971.

Books and Article

Ferrell, William K. *Literature and Film as Modern Mythology.* Westport, CT: Praeger, 2000.

"Film Notes." New York State Writers Institute, State University of New York. Last accessed 18 June 2004 <www.albany.edu/writers-inst.fns01n11.html>.

Forman, Milos, and Jan Novak. *Turnaround: A Memoir.* New York: Villard Books, 1994.

Kesey, Ken. *Kesey's Garage Sale.* New York: Viking, 1973.

———. *One Flew over the Cuckoo's Nest.* Ed. John Clark Pratt, Viking Critical Library ed. New York: Viking, 1973.

———. *Sometimes a Great Notion.* New York: Viking, 1964.

Leeds, Barry H. "One Flew, Two Followed: Stage and Screen Adaptations of Cuckoo's Nest." *Take Two: Adapting the Contemporary American Novel to Film.* Ed. Barbara Tepa Lupack. Bowling Green, OH: Bowling Green State U Popular P, 1994. 36–50.

---

*In Czech with English subtitles.

Wasserman, Dale. One Flew over the Cuckoo's Nest: *A Play in Two Acts*. New York: Samuel French, 1970.

Wolfe, Tom. *The Electric Kool-Aid Acid Test*. New York: Farrar, Straus and Giroux, 1968.

Questions for Reflection and Discussion:

1. Before the film: What do you visualize when you think of a psychiatric hospital? Where do these images come from?

2. Does the movie have a clear point of view? To which characters do you feel closest? What helps you identify with them? In the novel, the story is told by Bromden, the silent American Indian. What difference would it make if the film were narrated by him?

3. What do you consider the main conflict in the story? Who are the main opponents and what are they struggling for? Who wins in the end? What is won and what is lost?

4. How does Forman set the scene of the film? Compare the indoor and outdoor scenes. When does the hospital seem to take on symbolic meanings?

5. In some reviews of the film, McMurphy is compared to Christ. How well does he fit this role? Do you see him as a savior, Western hero, con artist, psychopath, or ordinary man? To what other literary figures, legends, or myths can he be compared?

6. What is the role of women in the movie? Consider Nurse Ratched, the other nurses, McMurphy's two "aunts," Billy's mother, and Harding's wife. Are such roles consistent with your view of women in the 1960s? How do you regard these roles today?

7. Audiences in the sixties saw the film as an indictment of the Establishment, which suppressed individual freedom through a web of institutions, regulations, and bureaucratic machinery. Would you agree that this is the film's main theme? What other messages do you notice? Point to specific scenes in which these messages are most strongly conveyed.

8. Children still sing these words when they play tag: "One flew east, one flew west, one flew over the cuckoo's nest . . . O-U-T spells out." Why do you think Ken Kesey used this child's game for the title of his story?

Topics for Further Study

1. Create a character wheel for McMurphy. Divide it like a pie chart into the main features of his character, such as vitality, empathy, humor,

shrewdness, and physical strength. What percentage would you assign to each trait? Based on your judgments, would you consider him to be a hero, a manipulator, a madman, an ordinary human being, or something else?

2. Select two characters—a major figure like McMurphy or Big Nurse and a minor figure like Billy Bibbit or Bromden—and compare their treatment in the novel and the film. Do they look and act the same? How much do you know about their looks, thoughts, and mannerisms? Which scenes reveal the most about them?

3. The psychiatric ward in *Cuckoo's Nest* makes use of shock therapy, lobotomies, and antipsychotic drugs. Look up these forms of treatment. Are they still used today? How would the patients in the movie be treated in a modern psychiatric hospital?

4. Find out more about the counterculture movement of the 1960s. Start by looking up these terms: *beatniks, hippies, psychedelic, The Merry Pranksters, Captain Marvel, Haight-Ashbury, acid rock.*

5. Ken Kesey's novel is written from the perspective of Chief Bromden, a delusional patient on the mental ward. Read part or all of the book to get the flavor of Bromden's narrative. (You may want to compare this to other first-person narratives you have read, such as Melville's *Moby Dick*, Twain's *Huckleberry Finn*, Fitzgerald's *The Great Gatsby*, or Faulkner's *The Sound and the Fury*.) If you were to rewrite the screenplay from Bromden's point of view, what changes would you make to the film?

Scenes to Analyze

1. **Medication Time.** [3:15] When the staff nurse announces "medication time," the patients on Ward 23 line up to take their daily dosage. Notice how this scene establishes the tone of life on the ward. What does the camera focus on? What else is in the frame? What do the music and color scheme contribute to the scene? Why does it end with a shot of Chief Bromden?

2. **McMurphy Arrives.** [4:25] Our first view of McMurphy is from the window as his car pulls up to the hospital. Notice how he's dressed and how he acts. At times, he is an observer checking out the scene; at other times, he gives a crazy laugh or steps into the action. When he enters the ward, the first person he meets is Bromden. Watch their body language and the reactions of the four inmates playing cards. How does he size them up and begin manipulating them?

3. **Basketball Lesson.** [21:21] McMurphy tries to teach Chief Bromden how to play basketball, "an old Indian game." The camera keeps changing its position in this scene. Can you give a reason for each shift? In the novel, we never leave the ward until the fishing trip. Why do you think the film director chose to create this scene and shoot it outdoors?

4. **Group Therapy.** [31:38] When McMurphy asks to see the World Series on television at a group session, Nurse Ratched calls for a vote. The conflict here is low-key. How do we know who has the upper hand? Watch the body language closely: the nurse's subtle smile, McMurphy's astonishment, and the various reaction shots of the other patients.

5. **World Series.** [47:35] The conflict takes a new turn in this celebrated scene when McMurphy pretends to see the game on a blank television screen. Notice the use of sound and windows here. McMurphy's enthusiastic voice triumphs over the insipid music being piped over the loudspeaker. Big Nurse watches helplessly behind her station window while the television screen reflects the gleeful figures of the men.

6. **Fishing Trip.** [55:12] The fishing expedition offers comic relief and a chance to take the camera outdoors. Taking a group of mental patients on an open boat could be disastrous or therapeutic. How does the scene play these two possibilities against each other?

7. **Shock Treatment.** [1:25:10] How would you shoot the scene in which McMurphy gets shock therapy? Who would be in the frame? Where would you place the camera? What would we hear on the sound track? How would it be lit? Compare your vision to the film. How effective were the decisions made by Forman and his technical crew?

8. **"You're coming with me."** [2:04:26] Compare the ending of the film to the book's final chapter. How does Forman use the camera to re-create the force of Kesey's words? Notice how the scene is shot in close-ups and darkly lit. Much of the meaning is carried by the sound track: muffled cries, strange music made by rubbing glasses filled with water, the sound of drum beats—or heartbeats—giving way to a mournful melody as Bromden strains to lift the machine and makes his escape. Taber rises, rousing the others with his manic laugh, and then snaps into a mad stare while a tiny figure heads toward a cloud-filled horizon. Do you find this ending hopeful, ominous, ironic?

16 Glory

Directed by Edward Zwick; screenplay by Kevin Jarre; based on the books
Lay This Laurel *by Richard Benson and Lincoln Kirstein and* One Gallant Rush *by Peter Burchard and the letters of Robert Gould Shaw; produced by Freddie Fields; cinematography by Freddie Francis; edited by
Steven Rosenblum; art direction by Dan Webster; production design by
Norman Garwood; set decoration by Garrett Lewis; music by James Horner;
released by Columbia TriStar in 1989. [122 minutes]*

Col. Robert Gould Shaw	Matthew Broderick
Pvt. Trip	Denzel Washington
Maj. Cabot Forbes	Cary Elwes
Sgt. Maj. John Rawlins	Morgan Freeman
Pvt. Jupiter Sharts	Jihmi Kennedy
Cpl. Thomas Searles	Andre Braugher
Sgt. Maj. Mulcahy	John Finn

Before *Glory* was released in 1989, few people knew that African American soldiers fought in the American Civil War. The director himself, Edward Zwick, often passed a war monument in Boston Commons while he was a student at Harvard, paying little heed to the bronze figure of a white officer on horseback among black soldiers. This is the Robert Gould Shaw Memorial, built in 1897 in honor of the 54th Massachusetts Regiment, the first all-black regiment of regular soldiers recruited in the North to fight for the Union. The white officer was Colonel Shaw, who led the regiment in a courageous attack on Fort Wagner in 1863, a fierce battle in which nearly half his men were killed and he himself died, at the age of twenty-five.

When Zwick finally noticed, he became fascinated by the history of the 54th. He read the two historical accounts on which the screenplay is based: *One Gallant Rush* by Peter Burchard and *Lay This Laurel* by Richard Benson and Lincoln Kirstein. He spent hours in Harvard's Houghton Library reading Shaw's correspondence and the letters written by his men to loved ones and newspapers back home. The bronze figures began to come to life for Zwick as individuals engaged in an important struggle: human beings with feelings, passionate beliefs, and a stirring story to tell.

The historical facts are a matter of record (Benson and Kirstein; Burchard; Duncan). On September 22 1862, President Lincoln signed the Emancipation Proclamation, formally freeing the slaves in the confederacy of Southern states that had rebelled against the Union. But up to that point in the war, African Americans were still victims of widespread discrimina-

tion in the North, where institutional prejudice in the military had prevented black soldiers from taking up arms. The Battle of Antietam, however, had taken a staggering toll on Union forces. On just one day of the battle, September 17, 1862, the North suffered 12,410 casualties. Faced with such losses and a scarcity of white volunteers, the government authorized black soldiers to enlist in the Union army. Although some freed slaves had already been organized as irregulars in occupied Southern territories, the 54th Regiment of Massachusetts became the first all-black Union regiment founded in the North. Black leaders such as Frederick Douglass and Lewis Hayden roused African Americans throughout the Northern states to serve with the regiment. Douglass sent two of his own sons to join. When it was fully constituted, the 54th represented twenty-four states, the District of Columbia, the West Indies, and Africa. More than half the men were literate; most had worked as common laborers; a quarter had been slaves.

Training began at Camp Meigs in Massachusetts on February 21, 1863. Colonel Shaw was appointed commanding officer, with George P. Hallowell as his lieutenant. Shaw was the son of prominent Boston abolitionists and had attended Harvard. He was deeply dedicated to the Union cause. Mustered into service on May 13, 1863, the 54th was ordered to Hilton Head, South Carolina, where it was to join forces against Charleston, "the cradle of succession." Before leaving, the regiment paraded past the Massachusetts State House before an enthusiastic crowd waving Union flags. Once in the South, however, the men were treated more like common laborers than soldiers. The situation grew worse when Col. James Montgomery ordered them to raid the town of Darien, Georgia, on June 11. Reports of burned buildings and looted homes only confirmed stereotypes of black soldiers as marauding beasts. Shaw objected to the raid and petitioned for a combat role. On July 16, the 54th distinguished itself in a skirmish on James Island when Shaw's men bravely stood their ground against Confederate cavalry and infantry, saving a white unit. But the big battle was set for July 18, an assault on Fort Wagner, which controlled the Charleston Harbor from Morris Island. Fort Wagner was a strategic site, heavily armed and surrounded by marshes and moats. The 54th arrived exhausted from two days of marching and reduced to about 600 men by the recent skirmish. This did not prevent it from leading the attack in front of ten white regiments. Under withering, relentless fire, Shaw led his men through the marshland up to the parapets and into the fort. But the attack failed, leaving 1,535 Union soldiers dead or wounded and 181 Confederate casualties. The 54th Regiment suffered the greatest loss. Nearly half of its 600 men lay wounded or dead, including Shaw himself. Some of the survivors were taken prisoner, facing almost certain execution. Yet their bravery became legend. One man,

Sergeant William H. Carney, rescued the Union flag and carried it back to the lines despite multiple wounds, uttering the famous words, "The old girl never touched the ground." Carney became the first African American to receive the Congressional Medal of Honor.

Even after Fort Wagner, the 54th continued to fight for equality. Under the law, black men were paid as laborers instead of soldiers, receiving about half the salary of their white counterparts. This economic inequality wasn't rectified until September 1864, after eighteen months of pay refusals by black soldiers. Ultimately, the valiant struggles of the 54th Regiment inspired many others, white and black. More than 180,000 African Americans enlisted under the Union flag between 1863 and 1865, constituting a tenth of the total Union forces. But their triumph was incomplete. At the end of the war, despite their sacrifices (664 casualties out of 1,354 men who served the regiment), the 54th Regiment of Massachusetts was not invited to the victory parade in Washington, D.C. Eighty years later, during World War II, black combatants were still restricted to segregated regiments. It was not until the end of that war that some black and white soldiers fought together as a unit.

Kevin Jarre's screenplay for the movie follows much of this record, from the founding of the 54th to the battle for Fort Wagner. It makes Col. Shaw a focus of the drama, showing his personal growth from an inexperienced officer to a strong-willed leader of men. His respect for the African Americans in his unit and his deepening relationship with them culminate in the moment when contemptuous Confederates throw his body in a mass grave with his fallen comrades. (This too is a scene from history. When the government offered to restore Shaw's body to his parents back in Boston, they said it should remain among the men he served.) What the screenplay adds are four fictitious characters, played by Denzel Washington, Morgan Freeman, Jihmi Kennedy, and (in his first screen appearance) Andre Braugher: four black actors who epitomize the rank and file while they quarrel, joke, and bond with one another.

Zwick has been criticized for casting Matthew Broderick as Col. Shaw. Some reviewers see Broderick as the cocky teenager in *Ferris Bueller's Day Off* (1986), too young and lightweight to make a convincing Civil War commander. Others defend Zwick's choice, pointing out that Broderick's youth and gentle nature are consistent with the qualities that made Shaw himself struggle so hard for authority in the eyes of his men. All reviewers agree, however, on the contributions of the film's four principal black performers. Freeman's Sergeant Rawlins is a study in dignity and quiet strength. Rawlins, a former gravedigger, is the eldest and wisest of the group. His early cynicism gradually gives way to a personal appreciation of Shaw and a belief in the courage of his comrades. Denzel Washington delivers an outstanding performance as the runaway slave Trip, an angry young man who uses mocking humor to inflict his pain on others. One object of his wisecracks is Thomas Searles, an educated free man played by Andre Braugher. Thomas joins the regiment with passionate conviction only to find that he is shamefully unfit to be a soldier. He spends much of his time struggling to overcome his fear and prove himself equal to the other men. The foursome is rounded out by Sharts (played by Jihmi Kennedy), a simple country boy whose naiveté is balanced by the fact that he's the best shot in the unit.

Zwick begins the film with the battle at Antietam. His original plan was to start with some background scenes to introduce Robert Gould Shaw, but the battle scene makes a strong, immediate impression. It also shows Shaw cowering in the midst of furious fighting, an experience that motivates his later efforts to demonstrate courage and prepares us for the final assault on Fort Wagner. At one point, when his men receive their first firearms and pretend to shoot at one another, we see their horseplay through the eyes of someone who knows what real combat is like.

As with many combat films, much of *Glory* is about training and preparing for battle. Day by day, the raw recruits are drilled into a disciplined fighting unit. They learn to march, shoot, and reload their rifles three times a minute. What makes this all the more remarkable are the racial biases against them. As black soldiers, they will be summarily executed by the enemy if caught, and their own army treats them as lesser beings, reserving the best salaries and supplies for the white units that get combat duty. Shaw shows whose side he's on in key scenes when he demands shoes for his barefoot men, joins their campaign for full pay, and requests a combat role for them. Meanwhile, the foursome (Rawlins, Trip, Searles, and Sharts) learns to live together in close quarters. Their differences give way to a growing intimacy in a succession of scenes that take place mostly in their tent, which becomes a kind of home, a substitute for family. In one particularly moving moment, before the big assault, the soldiers hold a "shout," singing hymns and giving testimony. When it is Trip's turn to speak, he gets up awkwardly and says, "You're the onliest family I got."

The combat scenes are fierce. They show a form of warfare in which men face one another in battle lines and shoot each other at point-blank range, reloading powder and ball as quickly as possible for the next volley and then closing in with fixed bayonets. In addition to the chaos of Antietam, we see the skirmish on James Island, when the 54th Regiment holds its ground against Confederate cavalry and infantry, and the climactic attack on Fort Wagner, when Shaw leads the charge through mud-filled ditches up the battlements against cannons and a thousand rifles raining fire. The film ends with Shaw's body being tossed into a mass grave with his men.

In a commentary accompanying the DVD version of the movie, Edward Zwick describes the production process. He explains how he deleted long sections of exposition from the screenplay to focus on the drama, tightening the structure, heightening the battle scenes, and refining the personal portraits. The Boston scenes were shot in Savannah, Georgia, where the actors rehearsed for three weeks. As they practiced and improvised their scenes, their characters developed and the relationships solidified, fleshing out roles that were only skeletons in the script. With a relatively modest budget of $19 million, the production crew had to be resourceful. They used painted fronts instead of complete buildings and photographed the same uniformed extras again and again. Many of the soldiers were reenactors—hundreds of businessmen, workers, and teachers—who volunteered to take part in the battle scenes, living in tents, eating camp food, and reenacting events they had researched in great detail. For them, the movie was a chance to participate in history.

When Edward Zwick directed *Glory*, his second feature, he was relatively unknown. A native of Illinois, Zwick had studied literature and theater at Harvard before going abroad to work with innovative theater companies in Europe. Back in the United States, he attended the American Film Institute, where an award-winning short led to television work. Here he gained valuable experience writing, directing, and producing the *Family* series. In the 1980s, he teamed up with Marshall Herskovitz to create the Emmy-winning TV series *thirtysomething* and other shows. His first feature film, *About Last Night . . .* (1986), was an adaptation of a David Mamet play. The critical success of *Glory* was followed by a succession of Hollywood films, including two with Denzel Washington: the Gulf War drama *Courage under Fire* (1996) and *The Siege* (1998), an action drama about Muslim terrorists in Manhattan. Zwick has also written screenplays (*The Siege*) and served as producer for several films, including *Shakespeare in Love* (1998) and *Traffic* (2000).

In his DVD commentary on *Glory*, Zwick refers to the memorial that inspired the film. When sculptor Augustus Saint-Gaudens completed his work on the Robert Gould Shaw Memorial, twenty years after Shaw's death, the event was celebrated with fanfare. Booker T. Washington spoke, and William James gave the main address. Henry James was moved to write in admiration. But over the years, the monument, like so many others, became just another unnoticed statue in a park. Zwick hopes that the film will help people realize that the figures carved in bronze were once real men, that history is "not some dead thing, but the result of passionate lives in collision, about ideas that are still important."

Suggested Films and Readings

More Films about War

All Quiet on the Western Front (1930) World War I

Pork Chop Hill (1959) Korea

Platoon (1986) Vietnam

Gettysburg (1993) Civil War

Saving Private Ryan (1998) World War II

Three Kings (1999) First Gulf War

Black Hawk Down (2001) Somalia

More Films by Edward Zwick

Having It All (1982; TV)

About Last Night . . . (1986)

Leaving Normal (1992)

Legends of the Fall (1994)

Courage under Fire (1996)

The Siege (1998)

Abandon (2002)

The Last Samurai (2003)

Books

Benson, Richard, and Lincoln Kirstein. *Lay This Laurel: An Album on the Saint-Gaudens Memorial on Boston Common.* New York: Eakins, 1973.

Burchard, Peter. *One Gallant Rush: Robert Gould Shaw and His Brave Black Regiment.* New York: St. Martin's, 1965.

Duncan, Russell, ed. *Blue-Eyed Child of Fortune: The Civil War Letters of Colonel Robert Gould Shaw.* Athens: U of Georgia P, 1992.

Questions for Reflection and Discussion

1. Unlike most of the other movies discussed in this book, *Glory* is based largely on historical documents. What did you learn about American history by watching the film? What did you learn about army life during the Civil War?

2. How would you describe race relations in the film? What were the conditions of African Americans during the Civil War? What was their sta-

tus in the army? How were they regarded by Southerners, by the Northern officers and soldiers, and by one another? According to the film, what attitudes toward white people were prevalent among the black soldiers?

3. Create a profile describing each of the four black soldiers: Rawlins, Trip, Sharts, and Searles. Where are they from and what are they like? In what ways do they represent the African Americans of their time? Trace their interactions through the film, marking the turning points in their relationships.

4. Shaw's relationship with his men also undergoes certain changes. As he teaches Sharts how to reload his rifle, punishes Trip for deserting, and deals with issues of pay, looting, and shoes, the soldiers grow to respect and admire their white colonel. How do you account for these changes?

5. Director Edward Zwick went through great trouble to keep the sun from shining in the film. How is this accomplished? What do all the shadows, smoke, rain, and mud contribute to the film's atmosphere?

6. James Horner wrote the music for this film. Where were you most aware of his score? What does the music add to—or detract from—your experience?

7. Some reviewers criticized Zwick for casting Matthew Broderick in the role of Col. Robert Gould Shaw and for telling the story of the 54th Regiment through his eyes. Explain why you agree or disagree with this assessment.

8. Morgan Freeman and Denzel Washington give strong performances as Sergeant Rawlins and Private Trip. Compare their roles in *Glory* to their roles in *The Shawshank Redemption* and *Mississippi Masala*. In what other films have you seen them act? Can you think of any works of literature for which you might cast Freeman or Washington?

Topics for Further Study

1. Make a power map to show the relationships among the characters in the film. Who has the upper hand among the white men at various times (Col. Shaw, his drill sergeant, the quartermaster who controls the shoes, the colonel who orders Darien to be looted, and so on)? Who wields the most power among the black soldiers (Rawlins, Trip, Sharts, Searles)? Use arrows or some other system of notation to indicate who dominates whom in terms of military rank or personal authority. Notice which relationships have changed by the end of the film.

2. Read one of the books on which the film is based, *Lay This Laurel* or *One Gallant Rush*. How closely does *Glory* adhere to the facts? What are your criteria for judging a film adaptation of historical events? How well does *Glory* measure up to your criteria?

3. Compare *Glory* to other war movies you have seen. What similarities can you find in their use of characters, settings, props, structure, and themes? What distinguishes *Glory* from the others? Read about combat movies as a genre and explore what makes them so popular with American audiences.

4. If you live in the vicinity of Boston, visit the Saint-Gaudens memorial in Boston Commons. Take note of its location, condition, and the attention it gets from passersby. Record your impressions in your journal or an essay.

5. Find out more about the 54th Massachusetts Regiment and the role of African Americans in the Civil War. You may want to extend your research to include other American wars. How has the status of black soldiers changed since the Emancipation Proclamation of 1863? What remains the same?

Scenes to Analyze

1. **Antietam Creek.** [0:57] Notice how Zwick sets the scene with a montage of camp life followed by a column of marching soldiers, focusing on young Shaw's face while we hear his voice reading a letter to home. What do the sound track, smoke, and camera work contribute to the atmosphere? Compare this mood to the battle scene, which begins three minutes later.

2. **Issuing Arms.** [29:50] When a box of firearms arrives, the men are thrilled. Searles asks Col. Shaw about a rumor that the 54th is to be used only for manual labor. Without answering, Shaw turns away toward a corner of the yard where his men are playing at war. Smoke begins to infiltrate the scene and the sound track carries the noises of real battle. What is Shaw thinking at this point? Compare this mock battle to the action at Antietam Creek. Describe the situation when Shaw teaches Sharts how to fire three aimed shots in a minute.

3. **In the Tent.** [39:00] This is one of several key moments in which the four main black characters—Trip, Rawlins, Searles, and Sharts—develop their relationships. What distinguishes them from one another? Who seems to dominate the scene? How does the tent create a sense of intimacy among the men? This is a good point to talk about the perfor-

mances of Denzel Washington, Morgan Freeman, Andre Braugher, and Jihmi Kennedy. Compare this scene to the following scene (43:56) of Shaw and his fellow officers at Christmas dinner.

4. **Deserter.** [46:00] When Trip is caught away from the camp without leave, he is flogged as a deserter. What is the significance of the scars on his back? Director Edward Zwick says that he just let the camera roll during this scene and let Washington find his role, creating "one of the most extraordinary moments I've seen on film."

5. **600 Shoes.** [50:43] The scene when Col. Shaw confronts the quartermaster about his men's need for shoes introduces a touch of humor and reveals a new dimension to Shaw's character. Pay close attention to the editing here, the camera angles, movement, inserts, reaction shots, and frequent cuts that trace the confrontation from start to resolution.

6. **Time Marches On.** [1:01:04] Historical dramas are often unwitting hosts to anachronisms. Look for the wristwatch in the lower right corner of the screen as Southern black folk greet the regiment in Beaufort, South Carolina. The watch belonged to a tourist who was watching the shoot.

7. **Darien.** [1:05:00] The looting and burning of Darien gives us a chance to contrast Col. Shaw with another Union officer. Col. James Montgomery has a very different attitude toward the African American soldiers under his command. What does the scene show about Shaw's position in the army hierarchy and his efforts to become a strong leader? Due to budget constraints, the set consisted of only a few walls, but they had to be built in order to be burned.

8. **"James Island, South Carolina, July 16, 1863."** [1:17:52] This was actually a minor skirmish, not a major battle, but it enabled the 54th Regiment to prove itself in combat. It also gives us a chance to witness the horrific tactics used during the Civil War. Two columns fire at each other at point-blank range, making every volley count. Zwick used several cameras to shoot the scene from both sides. The horses were trained to fall on command.

9. **The Shout.** [1:32:00] The scene before the big battle when the men prepare their souls was inspired by the director's visit to a Pentecostal church. Much of the acting was improvised, based on churchgoing experiences. The song came from something the extras had been singing. Washington, a minister's son, invented his lines extempore when he said, "You're the onliest family I got. Don't much matter what happen tomorrow, cause we men, ain't we?"

10. **Finale.** [1:43:00] Zwick rebuilt Fort Wagner on Jekyll Island, a few miles from the original location. More than seven hundred extras participated in the scene before the battle when the 54th Regiment marches through a throng of cheering white soldiers toward its destiny (1:37:00). The beauty of the beach contrasts with the carnage that we know lies ahead. Shaw releases his horse (1:40:30), which gallops through the surf, and he is suddenly in the midst of his troops. "If this man should fall, " he says, "who will lift up the flag and carry on?" (1:41:40), and Searles steps forward. Shaw turns toward the fort and his great moment of glory (1:43:00). In a series of reverse-angle shots, we move with the camera into the fort as the cannonade begins. Watch how the camera work and editing capture the heat and chaos of battle. Night falls and Shaw's men hunker down under bursting flares. Under cover of darkness, illuminated by cannon fire, the final charge begins, with Shaw in the lead (1:46:50). When he falls (1:49:39), a chorus rises on the sound track above the din of battle, continuing afterward when his body is dropped in a mass grave among his fallen comrades (1:54:00).

17 Mississippi Masala

Directed by Mira Nair; screenplay by Sooni Taraporevala; produced by Mira Nair and Michael Nozik; cinematography by Edward Lachman; edited by Roberto Silvi; art direction by Jefferson Sage; production design by Mitch Epstein; set decoration by Jeanette Scott; music by L. Subramaniam; costumes by Ellen Lutter, Susan Lyall, and Kinnari Panikar; released by Samuel Goldwyn in 1992. [58 minutes]

Demetrius	*Denzel Washington*
Mina	*Sarita Choudhury*
Jay	*Roshan Seth*
Kinnu	*Sharmila Tagore*
Anil	*Ranjit Chowdhry*
Pontiac	*Mohan Gokhale*
Kanti Napkin	*Mohan Agashe*
Chanda	*Dipti Suthar*
Harry Patel	*Ashok Lath*
Tyrone	*Charles Dutton*
Dexter	*Tico Wells*
Williben	*Joe Seneca*
Aunt Rose	*Yvette Hawkins*
Alicia LeShay	*Natalie Oliver*
Mrs. Morgan	*Karen Pinkston*
Okelo	*Konga Mbandu*
Gossip	*Mira Nair*

A masala is a blend of multicolored spices used in Indian food, an apt metaphor for this film about Asian Indians from Africa tossed together with African Americans in contemporary Mississippi. The Indians in the movie have come from Uganda, where they once lived comfortably on two lush acres of their own land until forced to leave East Africa by the anti-Asian policies of Idi Amin. Eighteen years later they occupy two rooms of a shabby roadside motel in Greenwood, Mississippi. Jay, the father, once a prominent lawyer in Uganda, now manages the motel while his wife, Kinnu, runs a liquor store. Although we learn much about the couple's past and future aspirations, most of the film centers on their daughter Mina (played by Sarita Choudhury), who has grown into a twenty-four-year old beauty. One day she meets an attractive young man named Demetrius (Denzel Washington), and a troubled romance begins.

In some ways, the story may remind viewers of *Romeo and Juliet* (1968) or *Guess Who's Coming to Dinner?* (1967). Demetrius belongs to the African American community, which has an uneasy relationship with its

Asian neighbors. Demetrius is responsible, hardworking, and poor, which makes it harder to accept the fact that after many generations of living in the United States, his family is working for recent immigrants. He has built up a carpet cleaning business that depends heavily on contracts with the area's Indian-run motels. We learn that he has given up a college scholarship in order to support his aging, widowed father in this way. So the film's romantic plot is complicated by issues of race and class.

Unlike most American films that deal with racial issues, *Mississippi Masala* does not present a simple conflict between black and white. Mina's family is not part of the established white culture but a group of newcomers struggling to maintain its ethnic identity. Jay and Kinnu want their daughter to stay within the Indian community. Mina resists their pressure to marry another Indian, such as the eligible Harry Patel. Nor is her mother's preference for Harry just a matter of cultural pride. She subscribes to a hierarchy of color in which light skin tones are more valued than dark tones. At one point, a pair of Indian women (one of whom is played by director Mira Nair) summarizes the system: "You can be dark and have money, or you can be fair and no money. But you can't be both poor and dark." Mina is both poor and dark. Her mother warns her that the liaison with Demetrius is destroying their social and financial status. "You call this love," Kinnu asks Mina, "when all you've done is bring down such shame on our heads?" Mina replies, "This is America. Nobody cares."

Nair represents the Indian and African American communities in some depth through multidimensional contrasts in attitudes and personalities. At Anil's wedding, for example, the gathering is a mélange of old and new. Among the traditional saris, *bindi* marks, and sitars, children are playing cowboys and Indians. Anil's uncle, a practical businessman with an eye for profit, owns a motel and has bought an expensive red car for his nephew. Mira's father, on the other hand, has little interest in buying into the American way of life; his thoughts are preoccupied with his lost Ugandan homeland. Anil himself, obsessed with his new car, has agreed to an arranged marriage with Chanda. It is clear that this couple has none of the passion or intimacy that Demetrius comes to share with Mina.

When Harry takes Mina to the Leopard Lounge, she feels more alive there among the black dancers than at the wedding. The nightclub vibrates with lively soul music, and she ends up dancing with Demetrius. Later, when he invites her home to a barbecue, his family welcomes her with open arms—in contrast to her family's response to him later on. The barbecue gives us a chance to assess Demetrius's personal qualities, which stand out in relief against the members of his family. Williben, his elderly father, is a dignified patriarch at home but humbly deferential to Mrs. Morgan, the white owner of the restaurant where he works as a waiter. The Old South has taught him his place and made him skeptical of crossing boundaries. Demetrius is hardworking, like his father, but unlike his younger brother Dexter, who hangs out with the wrong crowd and makes excuses for not having a job, Demetrius is responsible, sensitive, and well informed. He knows about Idi Amin and tactfully steers the conversation away from Africa when Dexter asks Mina why she left. In contrast to his business partner, Tyrone, who makes sly references to Mina's figure, Demetrius appreciates her as a person.

Denzel Washington gives a skillful, nuanced performance as Demetrius. He can be playful when relaxed and angry when provoked. Sarita Choudhury is convincingly sensuous and strong-willed as Mina. Perhaps her inexperience with acting (she was modeling in England when Nair discovered her) works to her advantage in this role. Since *Mississippi Masala*, Choudhury has found roles in films such as *The House of Spirits* (1993), *Fresh Kill* (1994), and *Kama Sutra* (1996). Washington has appeared in more than a dozen feature films, including *Philadelphia* (1993), *Devil in a Blue Dress* (1995), *Courage under Fire* (1996), *The Siege* (1998), and *Training Day* (2001), for which he received the Academy Award for Best Actor. The role of Mina's father is played by Roshan Seth, whose suffering seems permanently etched in his face. Sharmila Tagore, a veteran actor who has appeared in three films by the renowned Indian director Satyajit Ray, plays Mina's mother.

Although Greenwood is the story's central setting, the film is framed by two long scenes set in Uganda. It opens in 1972, the year that Idi Amin seized power and confiscated the property of Indian settlers who had lived there for three generations. Jay narrowly escapes with his family and his life, leaving behind his beloved homeland and his childhood friend, a black African named Okelo. The film closes with Jay's return in 1990, unprepared for what he will find when he arrives. While some viewers have criticized the Ugandan scenes as distracting from the romantic plot, these scenes add a historical layer of irony to the themes of racism and color consciousness. It was colonialism that brought Jay's ancestors to Africa as cheap labor for the railroad. It was colonialism that brought Demetrius's people to the New World as plantation slaves. It was racism that forced Jay's family out of Africa. Yet, once in the United States, the Indian Africans perpetuate their own form of prejudice against African Americans. There is further irony in the fact that Mina's family has never been to India and Demetrius's family has never seen Africa.

Mira Nair was born in 1957 in Bhubanenswar, a small city in Orissa, in eastern India. As the daughter of a high-ranking government official, she had a comfortable childhood, though her father was emotionally remote and her two brothers received most of the attention. Unhappy at the mediocre local school, she managed to get transferred to an exclusive boarding school, where she developed a lively interest in theater. She went on to study drama briefly at Delhi University and became involved in radical street theater in Calcutta. At age eighteen, she left India on a scholarship to Harvard. She was a good student but found the Harvard theater program too conventional. After taking roles in plays by Shakespeare, Chekhov, Sophocles, and contemporary playwrights, she decided to become a filmmaker, the person in control who tells the story, rather than an actor, who is confined to one role. She had discovered that "creative freedom is imperative for me" (qtd. in Anbarasan and Otchet 43).

Nair's first films were documentaries, all about people on the edge of society. *So Far from India* (1982) follows a New York City immigrant whose family remained home in India. *Children of a Desired Sex* (1987) investigates the thoughts of pregnant Indian women contemplating the abortion of their female fetuses. *India Cabaret* (1985) is about strippers in a Bombay nightclub. These films illustrate Nair's commitment to neglected subjects. They also reflect the visual influence of Mitch Epstein, a young teacher of still photography with whom she studied at Harvard and later married in 1981. Gradually, Nair shifted to feature films. "I was tired of waiting for things to happen," she says, referring to the reliance of documentary films on chance. "I wanted to make them happen" (Simpson). Her first major film was *Salaam Bombay!* (1988), which dramatized the stories of homeless city children. Made on a $900,000 budget, it became a commercial success and was nominated for an Academy Award.

The idea for *Mississippi Masala* came when Nair read about an Indian family forced to leave Uganda during dictator Idi Amin's regime. She enlisted Sooni Taraporevala (the screenwriter for *Salaam Bombay!*) to write a script about one such family after spending several months in Mississippi, where she learned that many motels were run by Indian immigrants. Nair and Taraporevala moved from hotel to hotel, interviewing the families who owned them. They also spent time in the black community, visiting churches, barbecues, and barbershops, where Nair was welcomed "as one of them" (Lahr). When Nair was doing research in Uganda, she met Mahmood Mamdani, a professor of political science who had been expelled by Amin. Like Nair, Mamdani was originally from a small Indian town and had studied at Harvard. They fell in love and married, eventually settling in the house that appears in the film. Epstein agreed to a divorce and stayed on as director of production design. To fund her project, Nair put together a $7 million package from financiers in Europe, India, and Japan, preferring the independence afforded by a small international budget to the strings of a large Hollywood studio.

Since the release of *Mississippi Masala*, Nair's films have continued to reflect her personal values. "I am attracted to ideals that will provoke people and make them look at the world a little differently" (qtd. in Lahr). In *The Perez Family* (1995), she looked at the cultural dislocations of Cuban Americans. In *Kama Sutra: A Tale of Love* (1996), a story of medieval court life, she explored the divine sources of love and sexuality. The film became a cause célèbre in India when she insisted that it be shown to women-only audiences in order to avoid intimidation by men. With *Monsoon Wedding* (2001), set among the upper middle class of Delhi, Nair achieved her most popular success. She called it a "love song to my home city" (Chawda).

In 1996, Nair moved to South Africa with Mamdani, who became head of the African Studies program at the University of Cape Town. Later they moved to New York, where both joined the faculty of Columbia University. Nair has always kept her international perspective, continuing to spotlight issues of nationality, ethnicity, gender, and race in her films, often with a documentary attention to cultural details, always striving to honor the complexities of human life. If "tyranny is the absence of complexity," as she likes to say, paraphrasing André Gide, her life's work is an ongoing call for freedom.

Suggested Films and Readings

More Films by Mira Nair

Features

Salaam Bombay! (1988)

The Perez Family (1995)

Kama Sutra: A Tale of Love (1996)

Monsoon Wedding (2001)

Hysterical Blindness (2002)

Documentaries

Jama Masjid Street Journal (1979)

So Far from India (1982)

India Cabaret (1985)

Children of a Desired Sex (1987)

The Laughing Club of India (1999)

More Films about the Indian Disapora

My Beautiful Laundrette (1985; dir. Stephen Frears)

Bhaji on the Beach (1993; dir. Gurinder Chadha)

East Is East (1999; dir. Damien O'Donnell)

Bend It Like Beckham (2002; dir. Gurinder Chadha)

More Films about Interracial Dating

West Side Story (1961; dir. Robert Wise)

Guess Who's Coming to Dinner? (1967; dir. Stanley Kramer)

Jungle Fever (1991; dir. Spike Lee)

Books and Articles

Anbarasan, Ethirajan, and Amy Otchet. "Talking to . . . Mira Nair: An eye for paradox." *The Unesco Courier* [Paris] 51.11 (November 1998): 46–49.

Andersen, Erika Surat. "Mississippi Masala." *Film Quarterly* 46.4 (Summer 1993): 23–26.

Anwar, Farrah. "Reviews—*Mississippi Masala* Directed by Mira Nair." *Sight and Sound* [London] 1.9 (Jan. 1992): 50.

Canby, Vincent. "Mississippi Masala." *New York Times* 5 Feb. 1992, natl. ed.: B1.

Chawda, Aniruddh. "Something about Mira." *India Currents* 15.12 (Mar. 2002): 21. 13 Feb. 2003. Available at www.Indiacurrents.com.

Freedman, Samuel G. "One People in Two Worlds." *New York Times* 2 Feb. 1992, natl. ed.: H13.

Lahr, John. "PROFILES: Whirlwind: Mira Nair's Cinematic World View." *The New Yorker* 9 Dec. 2002: 100+.

Mehta, Binita. "Emigrants Twice Displaced: Race, Color, and Identity in Mira Nair's *Mississippi Masala.*" *Between the Lines: South Asians and Postcoloniality.* Ed. Deepika Bahri and Mary Vasudeva. Philadelphia: Temple University Press, 1996. 185–203.

Simpson, Janice C. "Focusing on the Margins." *Time* 2 Mar. 1992: 67.

Stuart, Andrea. "Mississippi Masala." *Sight and Sound* [London] 1.7 (Nov. 1991): 6–9.

Wartenberg, Thomas E. "*Mississippi Masala:* Love in a Postcolonial World." *Unlikely Couples: Movie Romance as Social Criticism.* Boulder, CO: Westview, 1999. 153–72.

Questions for Reflection and Discussion

1. Mina and Demetrius meet when their vehicles collide. What other collisions (cultural, political, social) occur in the film? What forces are at work in each of these conflicts?

2. The film has been criticized for having too many subplots. Do you agree or disagree? Trace the different story lines through the film. How are these subplots related to one another?

3. Mina's family belongs to a subculture of Asian Indians living in the United States. What motivates them to be so insular? What are the pressures on their traditional way of life? How do you explain Mina's attraction to Demetrius? What makes her different from the rest of her people?

4. Examine the arguments made by Mina and her parents for and against assimilation. What position would you take on assimilation in your community today?

5. Mira Nair has said, "I wanted to explore the idea of a hierarchy of color being brown within the context of black and white" (qtd. in Chawda). What might she have meant by this? Where in the film do you see this idea being explored?

6. The white community of Greenwood is seen at a further remove and in considerably less depth than the communities to which Mina and Demetrius belong. Among the film's seventy-nine speaking parts, the only white roles are given to characters like the indifferent banker who turns down Demetrius's loan, the police officers who arrest him, and the condescending restaurant owner who hires his father. Is the film guilty of stereotyping white people? If so, what purpose might this serve?

7. Before making feature films, Nair was a documentary filmmaker. Where do you find evidence of this background in the photography or themes of *Mississippi Masala*?

8. At the end of the film, Jay, Kinnu, and Mina are apart. What do you imagine will happen in the next few months?

Topics for Further Study

1. Research the history of Asians in East Africa. Find out more about British colonialism, the independence movement in Uganda, General Idi Amin, and the expulsion of 50,000 Indians and Pakistanis in 1972.

2. *Mississippi Masala* and *To Kill a Mockingbird* are both set in the South but at different times. Compare the portraits of southern towns in these two films. What changes in appearance and attitudes do you see? What seems to be the same?

3. Imagine you are an ethnographer studying the subcultures of Greenwood, Mississippi. Where would you go for evidence of people's be-

haviors, attitudes, and systems of belief? Make a list of the cultural artifacts (e.g., Anil's car, the motel sign, Dexter's pendant) and practices (e.g., eating rituals, forms of entertainment, family structure) that you might find there. What conclusions can you draw from these artifacts and practices?

4. Cinematographer Ed Lachman paid close attention to color in this film. In addition to the color scheme of each setting (Uganda, the wedding, the Leopard Lounge, Biloxi beach), the different shades of skin tone are important. Watch the film again, focusing exclusively on the role of color.

5. Mira Nair is outspoken on the topics of colonialism, prejudices, and women's roles. Find out more about her views by reading interviews and watching her films. Where do these views emerge in *Mississippi Masala*? Do you think they enrich or detract from the story?

Scenes to Analyze

1. **Uganda.** [00:27] The scenes in Uganda that open and close the film almost seem to belong to another movie. Why do you think they were included? What do they explain about Mina's family? Do you think they detract from or contribute to the main story?

2. **Collision.** [17:24] When Mina's car crashes into Demetrius's van, the van is pushed into the vehicle of a white man in front of him. What part does skin color play in the reactions that ensue? How much of this behavior is stereotypical? How much is realistic?

3. **Anil's Wedding.** [27:15] Compare Mina's family as it is represented at the wedding to Demetrius's family at the barbecue. What values and beliefs are expressed in these two scenes? Do these values seem mostly a matter of cultural, national, or individual identity?

4. **After the Wedding.** [38:35] The men sit inside discussing money and prejudice after a few drinks. Mina and her mother are outside by the pool. Notice the use of color, music, camera work, and lighting in these scenes. What moods are created by these film techniques? What do they say about the men and the women being filmed?

5. **United We Stand.** [42:49] Anil's uncle brings tea to Demetrius and Tyrone while they are cleaning his motel carpets. "Black, brown, yellow, Mexican, Puerto Rican—all the same. As long as you're not white, it means you're colored," he tells them. "All of us people of color must stick together." What is his motive? What is his reaction later on when he learns that Demetrius has slept with Mina?

6. **Masala Montage.** [1:20:48] As the news spreads about the arrest of Mina and Demetrius, we see a montage of reactions by a variety of people, including the Indian gossips, Anil, a white man, Tyrone, Mrs. Morgan, Alicia, the Chamber of Commerce, and Demetrius himself. What does the montage reveal about the black, brown, and white communities in Greenwood and their attitudes about color?

18 Schindler's List

Directed by Steven Spielberg; screenplay by Steven Zaillian; based on the book by Thomas Keneally; produced by Branko Lustig, Gerald R. Molen, and Steven Spielberg; cinematography by Janusz Kaminski; edited by Michael Kahn; art direction by Ewa Skoczkowska and Maciej Walczak; production design by Allan Starski; set decoration by Ewa Braun; music by John Williams; released by Universal Pictures in 1993. [197 minutes]

Oskar Schindler . . . . Liam Neeson
Itzhak Stern . . . . Ben Kingsley
Amon Goeth . . . . Ralph Fiennes
Emilie Schindler . . . . Caroline Goodall
Poldek Pfefferberg . . . . Jonathan Sagall
Helen Hirsch . . . . Embeth Davidtz
Malgoscha Gebel . . . . Victoria Klonowska
Shmulik Levy . . . . Wilek Chilowicz
Mark Ivanir . . . . Marcel Goldberg
Béatrice Macola . . . . Ingrid

By any standards, *Schindler's List* is a landmark movie. It has probably had a greater impact on the general public than any other film or book about the Holocaust. Because of its accessibility and emotive power, it is likely to continue to shape the way many young Americans read one of the most troubling chapters in world history.

Spielberg's film tells the story of Oskar Schindler, the German industrialist who employed over a thousand Jewish factory workers during World War II, exploiting their status under Nazi persecution while at the same time saving their lives. Schindler was a cunning businessman, a suave womanizer who drank heavily, socialized with the Nazis, and profited handsomely from the war. Yet, as the war rolled on, he grew more dissatisfied with Nazi policy and more protective of his workers, to the point of risking his own life to sabotage the German war effort and protect the *Schindlerjuden*, the Schindler Jews. Spielberg offers no definitive analysis of Schindler's motives. He leaves the moral judgments to us. Nor does he try to document the horrific magnitude of Hitler's Final Solution with interviews, historical footage, or ingenious fictions, as other filmmakers have done. Instead, he tells Schindler's true story, largely from the German's point of view, letting a few selected Jewish characters and many Jewish names and faces represent the six million who perished in the Holocaust and the hundreds of thousands who survived.

For all the film's awards (it won seven Oscars), critical acclaim (most of the professional film reviewers praised it), and popular success (it grossed over $300 million in its first few years), *Schindler's List* continues to be a topic of vigorous debate. Some critics fault Spielberg for turning a self-serving war profiteer into a heroic figure. Others attack him for turning the unfathomable enormity of the Shoah into a Hollywood media event. Still, it is an important film to study: for its glimpses into history, for the questions it raises about moral choices, and for the resourcefulness of a master filmmaker when confronting "the limits of imagining the unimaginable" (Louvish 75).

Schindler's List is a stunning departure from Steven Spielberg's popular adventure films, which include four of the top ten grossing films in movie history: *Jurassic Park* (1993), *E.T. the Extra-Terrestrial* (1982), *Raiders of the Lost Ark* (1981), and *Jaws* (1975). Although he had attempted serious films before, including *The Color Purple* (1985) and *Empire of the Sun* (1987), they were about other people's ancestries. In fact, Spielberg grew up trying to hide his Jewish identity. Born in 1946 in Cincinnati, he moved with his family to Arizona, where he was ashamed of belonging to the only Jewish family in the neighborhood. His fear of being considered an outsider continued during his high school years in California. Young Spielberg knew that being different could have grave consequences. While his parents never spoke of the Holocaust by name, their talk was full of references to the events of World War II, and he remembers seeing his first concentration camp tattoo at the age of five at the home of his grandmother, who taught English to Holocaust survivors. Spielberg's film career is widely known. He gained valuable experience with home movies, scripting his first amateur film and directing actors by age twelve. Within years he was winning contests. Like other directors of the film school generation, he studied filmmaking in college before landing a job with a major studio, Universal. After ten major Hollywood films, he began his masterpiece on the Holocaust in 1993, at the age of forty-seven.

Spielberg first read *Schindler's List* in 1982. Thomas Keneally, the Australian writer, had published the book earlier that year under the title *Schindler's Ark* in Britain, where it won the coveted Booker Prize. In his preface, Keneally describes how he learned about Oskar Schindler in 1980 in a luggage store in Beverly Hills, California. Leopold Pfefferberg, the storeowner, was a Schindler survivor, one of more than 1,100 Jewish men, women, and children who had been saved through Schindler's efforts. Keneally was fascinated by Pfefferberg's story of the handsome German bon vivant, a savior but no saint, who traded on the black market, kept mistresses, and drank freely with Nazi officers while running a factory with Jewish laborers. How and why would such a man put himself at peril to keep those Jews alive during the war? Keneally traveled to seventeen nations to interview some fifty *Schindlerjuden,* pored through Schindler's personal papers (the man himself had died in 1974), and studied other documentary evidence for his research. As a novelist, his aim was "to use the texture and devices of a novel to tell a true story" while attempting "to avoid all fiction, since fiction would debase the record" (Keneally 10).

Schindler's known historical record is briefly summarized. Born in 1908 in the industrial city of Zwittau, then part of the Austrian Empire, he grew up in the *Sudetendeutsch* community, a German-speaking minority that found itself in the newly formed republic of Czechoslovakia after World War I. His family was Catholic and comfortably middle class. One of his close neighbors was Rabbi Kantor, whose sons played with Oskar and went to the same German-speaking school. The Kantors left Zwittau in the 1930s, but Oskar would remember them. Meanwhile, he seemed less interested in racial politics than in motorcycles. He raced a red Moto-Guzzi while in high school and nearly won a major competition. In time he developed into a polished businessman and married Emilie, a local gentleman farmer's daughter, to whom he was steadily unfaithful. Just before the blitzkrieg of Poland, Schindler joined the Nazi party and served briefly as a German spy, which gave him lucrative connections once the war began. Keneally describes him as a convivial charmer, an impressive figure with the ladies and hard-drinking men, who had more talent for shady business deals than for straightforward industry. This view is borne out by Schindler's career after the war. In 1949 he made his way to Argentina with his wife, mistress, and several *Schindlerjuden* to start a rodent farm. He returned alone in 1958, unable to succeed in the fur business or any other enterprise. Schindler eked out a living with financial support from the Jews whose lives he had saved. He divided his remaining days between Germany, where he was finally given a government pension, and Israel, where he was welcomed as a "righteous gentile."

Even before Keneally's book appeared there were plans to film the Schindler story. As early as the 1960s, Pfefferberg had tried to sell it to MGM, which hired Howard Koch (one of the scriptwriters for *Casablanca*), but the project was dropped. Roman Polanski, Sydney Pollack, and Martin Scorsese had each considered directing *Schindler's List* for Universal before Spielberg took it on. Spielberg planned to make the film in the mideighties but had trouble with the script, passing it from one scriptwriter to another. Keneally himself worked on it for a while, producing a sprawling 250-page docudrama, but eventually Steven Zaillian (the writer for *Awakenings,* 1990) got the job. Zaillian's screenplay, based on Keneally's book and interviews with survivors, was completed in March of 1992. In retrospect, Spielberg was grateful for the delay. In ten years, he had matured and grown more connected to his Jewish roots. The times had changed as well. Grim news of "ethnic cleansing" in Bosnia and Kurdish Iraq was appearing daily in the media. The United States Holocaust Memorial Museum was scheduled to open in 1993. The public was primed for such a film.

Casting began with the character of Itzhak Stern, a composite of several Jews who actually ran the factory while Schindler wined women and Nazi officials. For the part of this "unsung hero," Spielberg chose Ben Kinglsey, who had just won an Oscar for the title role in *Gandhi*. Ralph Fiennes was cast as Amon Goeth, the sadistic prison commandant. Spielberg had seen Fiennes's performance as Heathcliff in *Wuthering Heights* (1992) and had him gain twenty-five pounds for the role. For the part of Helen Hirsch, Goeth's eleven-year-old Jewish maid, he chose the South African actress Embeth Davidtz. Finally, he asked Liam Neeson to play Schindler after seeing his Broadway performance in *Anna Christie*. Spielberg cast Israelis in key Jewish roles—many of them children of survivors—using Catholic Poles in nonspeaking parts. Their etched faces leave indelible impressions of silent suffering and loss.

To make the film as authentic as possible, Spielberg did most of the shooting on location in Poland. In seventy-two days during the winter of 1992, he set up his cameras in the streets of Kraków, in the original SS headquarters, and in Schindler's actual factory and apartment, which were still standing. Since he was not allowed to film within the camp at Auschwitz, he created a replica just outside the gates, setting the train backwards so that it entered the set from the camp. Spielberg was completing postproduction on *Jurassic Park* at the same time, so he felt pulled in two directions. But his methods for these films were completely different. *Jurassic Park* was a blockbuster fantasy filmed in Hollywood with the latest high technology. For *Schindler's List*, he worked quickly, on a low budget, and without storyboards, dollies, or special lights. To avoid beautifying events, he chose black-and-white film stock, the kind that would have been used in the 1940s. Forty percent of the film was shot with handheld cameras, giving it a spontaneous, documentary feel. It was an exercise in simple storytelling, Spielberg explained. "I had to let the facts tell the story" (Guthmann 55).

The final film runs three hours and fourteen minutes, cut from four hours. It has 146 settings in Poland alone, 126 speaking parts, and 30,000 extras, and cost $23 million to make. Spielberg gave all the money he earned to Jewish charities. For the last scene, 128 Schindler Jews from around the world were flown to Israel to place ceremonial stones on Schindler's grave. In retrospect, this film was not just another Steven Spielberg movie. Being there, in Poland, where the actual events had taken place some fifty years earlier had a profound effect on the director. His biographer called it "the transforming experience of Spielberg's lifetime" (McBride 414).

The film opens in glowing color. A match is struck, a candle lit, then another. We hear a male voice intone a Hebrew prayer. A family is celebrating the Jewish Sabbath in an old-world dining room. As the credits begin to roll, the votive candles burn down in slow dissolves until extinguished. The camera follows the smoke upward and we hear the faint sound of a train. Cut to the train in black and white. It's September 1939. The film titles inform us that German forces have defeated the Polish Army in two weeks. Jews have been ordered to register and relocate to major cities. More than 10,000 arrive in Kraków daily. Now we see folding tables set with paper, stamps, and ink. The film's first word in English is a question: "Name?" As a handheld camera pans the crowd of anxious Jews, they speak their names one by one, which are neatly typed: Hudes Isak, Feber, Bauman, Klein. The sequence is factual, straightforward, chilling. We sense that we are witnessing the beginning of an episode in history that these people cannot yet imagine. Later, the smoke will be rising from mass crematoriums. Most of these names, and others like them, will be assigned to the death camps. A smaller number will be on Schindler's list.

Schindler himself is introduced in the next scene, though not directly. First we see a bottle of liquor being poured. A man is selecting his evening dress from an array of expensive suits, silk ties, and cufflinks. We watch as he arranges each article and pulls a wad of bills from a drawer, then a watch, and last, a Nazi pin. The entire scene is shot in close-ups without revealing Schindler's face. Not until well into the next scene, in which he joins a party of Nazi officers, do we get to see his strong, handsome features sculpted in the nightclub's artificial light. We watch him watching the other Germans, like a hunter stalking prey, before he introduces himself and becomes the center of the party.

From this point on, most of the film centers on Schindler. Except for Itzhak Stern, Helen Hirsch, Poldek Pfefferberg, and a few others, the Jews appear generally as names and faces in the background. For the first third of the story, Schindler builds his factory from scratch. Arriving with nothing but confidence and his Aryan good looks, he takes advantage of the situation with cunning and style. Although he knows little about manufacturing, he buys a small factory and turns it into the *Deutsche Emailwaren Fabrik* (German Enamelware Factory), also known as Emalia, turning out military cookware and munitions to ensure its essential status in the war effort. Now that Jews no longer have rights, their possessions and services are at his disposal. He hires Stern, a first-rate accountant, to finance the factory, promising a secure job to the Jewish donors in return. He uses

Pfefferberg's contacts on the black market to get luxury items for bribing the officials. Meanwhile, Jews are summarily evicted from their homes, forced to wear the yellow armband, and pelted by angry Poles as they are funneled into a sixteen-block square of tenements called the ghetto. Only Schindler's Jews seem to be immune. Their blue stamp, or *Blauschein,* marks them as essential workers in a war-protected industry.

But not entirely. When the SS commandeers his workers to shovel snow or shoots one or loads another into a boxcar, Schindler must muster all his skill to intercede. The challenge grows greater after the liquidation of the ghetto, when the Schindler Jews are sent to a forced labor camp in Plaszow. Here enters Amon Goeth, the film's other major character. Goeth is the commandant of Plaszow, a brutal man who is capable of killing Jews for sport. At first the two men seem cut from the same cloth. They are both Aryans; large, impressive figures; sensualists who enjoy wine, women, and power. Both benefit from the war. This comparison is reinforced cinematically. At one point, we watch them as they shave, in different locations, smug in their self-assurance. At another point, the two men are separated by a thin line in the center of the screen, a line that thickens in later scenes. Gradually, they are distinguished from each other. As Goeth gains power, he becomes crueler. He executes a Jewish engineer who offers ideas to improve construction in his camp. Goeth shoots her and then tells his guards to build the barracks her way. In his world, a stolen chicken or a bathtub ring is sufficient cause for a bullet in the head. He grows fat sitting on his balcony with a rifle, randomly aiming at the prisoners in his yard. Meanwhile, Schindler changes in a different way. At first the Jewish workers are an expedient to his career. He has no room for pity. When a one-armed man thanks him for saving his life, Schindler reproaches Stern for keeping such a useless worker in the factory. By the end of the film, however, Schindler is obsessed with saving lives. He barters his entire personal fortune to add a few more names to his list. Perhaps the contrast between Schindler and Goeth is sharpest in their treatment of Helen Hirsch, Goeth's young Jewish maid. Both men take a liking to her and have private moments with her in the cellar. But while Schindler asks about her tormented life, giving her a compassionate kiss on the forehead that lands him in prison, Goeth, torn between sexual attraction and repulsion, ends up beating her. Goeth is Schindler's shadow self, a reminder that our choices determine who we become.

Throughout the film, titles link the story to a historical time line. In 1939 all Jews were forced to relocate to cities like Kraków, where a special Jewish Council (the *Judenrat*) was set up to carry out the German orders. March 20, 1941, was the deadline for entering the ghetto, which was liquidated on March 13, 1943. The Plaszow camp was closed in April 1944, and thousands of murdered Jews were incinerated to hide the evidence. Schindler's new factory in Zwittau-Brinnlitz, Czechoslovakia, operated for seven months, until liberated by the Soviets. Schindler was declared a "righteous gentile" by the council of the Yad Vashem in Jerusalem in 1958.

Spielberg's great achievement in *Schindler's List* is to translate history into motion pictures, scenes that move. He does this in the first few minutes of the film, cutting from a peaceful Shabbat to the mass roundup of evicted Jews and from Schindler's dressing room to a noisy Nazi nightclub. Some scenes are almost unbearable to watch, such as the liquidation of the ghetto or the shower scene in Auschwitz. Occasionally, Spielberg gives us brief moments of comic relief, as when Schindler auditions for a secretary, but the overriding tone is somber and respectful. The film's turning point is arguably the long scene in which Goeth's storm troops invade the ghetto, a scene that unrolls as a series of vignettes. In one room, a frightened family is swallowing jewels rolled in bread, as in some lopsided version of communion. In the hospital, a doctor prepares a toxic dose of medicine for his bedridden patients. A woman hiding in a sunken floor compartment reluctantly agrees to accommodate another woman's child but not the mother. Meanwhile, on the street, a soldier steadies a boy's head with his boot and pulls the trigger. Another soldier fires through a line of prisoners, killing five with one shot. All this is witnessed by Schindler and his mistress, mounted on horseback on a hill above the ghetto. They watch, horrified, as a single child in a red coat makes her way through the carnage, aimless and alone.

Spielberg colorizes the red sweater, singling out this child as a living individual against the black-and-white of history. He uses color elsewhere—in the faint blue tint of the *Blauschein* stamps, for instance, or in the scene at Schindler's grave that ends the film—but the girl in her red coat is truly unforgettable. These effects were created by Janusz Kaminski, Spielberg's Polish cinematographer, who won an Oscar for his work. His lighting and crisp black-and-white tones hark back to German expressionism and Italian neorealism. Michael Kahn was awarded an Oscar for editing. His ingenuity is evident in scenes such as the nightclub, the liquidation, and the barracks wedding, where he cuts back and forth between the wedding in Plaszow, a floor show in Kraków, and Goeth's near seduction of Helen in the basement of his villa. Ewa Skoczkowska and Maciej Walczak won an Oscar for their art direction, which is sometimes more expressive than the actors. Think of the warehouse filled with neatly separated piles of shoes, watches, eyeglasses—and the bag of human teeth that have been saved for their gold fillings. The other Academy Awards went to Spielberg for directing (his first), to Steven Zaillian for his script, to John Williams for his powerfully subtle music, and to the film itself for Best Picture.

Spielberg was criticized for focusing on Schindler: a German, a flawed human being, an individual who could never represent the millions of Jews who suffered and perished. Claude Lanzmann, whose *Shoah* (1985) is widely regarded as one of the best documentary films on the subject, faulted *Schindler's List* for presenting the Holocaust "not as a crime against humanity, but a crime of humanity" (qtd. in McBride 434). Lanzmann believes that the enormity of the event "erects a ring of fire around itself," that "fiction is a transgression, . . . that there are things that cannot and should not be represented" (qtd. in Hartman 63). Geoffrey Hartman criticized the film on two accounts: first, that it is not realistic enough ("a compromise with Hollywood") and, second, that it gives too much attention to the cinematic aspects of history, neglecting things that can't be filmed (63). Other critics offered high praise. David Ansen agreed that Spielberg's talents may have been wasted on inconsequential stories in other films, "but this time the abundant virtuosity is in the service of a harrowing authenticity" (57). Omar Bartov exclaimed that "Spielberg has filmed some of the most haunting moments in any cinematic representation of the Holocaust" (44). David Thomson called *Schindler's List* simply "the most moving film I have ever seen" (90).

Spielberg himself was interested in Schindler precisely because of his flaws. He was fascinated by this rather ordinary man who achieved uncommon results in extraordinary times. The fact that Schindler never had much success in business before or after the war supports this view. His specialty was "presentation," not substance, and his greatest skill was in deception. A more virtuous man probably could not have done as much under the circumstances. Like Goeth and other Germans, he had choices, but the choices he ultimately made were for human life. If he was a hero, his story raises tough questions about heroism. For answers, we might begin by looking at the Talmudic epigraph inscribed within the ring given to Schindler by the people he had saved: "Whoever saves one life saves the world entire."

Suggested Films and Readings

More Films by Steven Spielberg

Jaws (1975)

Close Encounters of the Third Kind (1977)

1941 (1979)

Raiders of the Lost Ark (1981)

E.T. the Extra-Terrestrial (1982)

Indiana Jones and the Temple of Doom (1984)

The Color Purple (1985)

Empire of the Sun (1987)

Indiana Jones and the Last Crusade (1989)

Always (1989)

Hook (1991)

Jurassic Park (1993)

The Lost World: Jurassic Park (1997)

Amistad (1997)

Saving Private Ryan (1998)

A.I.: Artificial Intelligence (2001)

More Films on the Holocaust

Documentaries

Night and Fog (1955; dir. Alain Resnais) In French with English subtitles

The Sorrow and the Pity (1969; dir. Marcel Ophuls) In French with English subtitles

Schindler: The Documentary (1982; dir. Jon Blair)

Shoah (1985; dir. Claude Lanzmann) In German, Polish, French, and English

The Architecture of Doom (1989; dir. Peter Cohen) In German with English subtitles

Dramatizations

The Diary of Anne Frank (1959; dir. George Stevens)

Judgment at Nuremberg (1961; dir. Stanley Kramer)

The Pawnbroker (1965; dir. Sidney Lumet)

The Shop on Mainstreet (1965; dir. Ján Kadár and Elmar Klos) In Czech with English subtitles

Holocaust (1978; dir. Marvin Chomsky) TV docudrama

Sophie's Choice (1982; dir. Alan J. Pakula)

Europa Europa (1991; dir. Agnieska Holland) In German and Russian with English subtitles

Books

Ansen, David. "Spielberg's Obsession." *Oskar Schindler and His List: The Man, the Book, the Film, the Holocaust and Its Survivors*. Ed. Thomas Fensch. Forest Dale, VT: Paul S. Eriksson, 1995. 56–64.

Bartov, Omer. "Spielberg's Oskar." *Spielberg's Holocaust: Critical Perspectives on Schindler's List*. Ed. Yosefa Loshitzky. Bloomington: Indiana UP, 1997. 41–60.

Cole, Tim. *Selling the Holocaust: From Auschwitz to Schindler: How History Is Bought, Packaged, and Sold*. New York: Routledge, 1999.

Doneson, Judith E. *The Holocaust in American Film*. Philadelphia: Jewish Publication Society, 1987.

Fensch, Thomas, ed. *Oskar Schindler and His List: The Man, the Book, the Film, the Holocaust and Its Survivors*. Forest Dale, VT: Paul S. Eriksson, 1995.

Friedman, Lester D. *Hollywood's Image of the Jew*. New York: Ungar, 1982.

Guthmann, Edward. "Spielberg's List." *Oskar Schindler and His List: The Man, the Book, the Film, the Holocaust and Its Survivors*. Ed. Thomas Fensch. Forest Dale, VT: Paul S. Eriksson, 1995. 50–55.

Hartman, Geoffrey. "The Cinema Animal." *Spielberg's Holocaust: Critical Perspectives on* Schindler's List. Ed. Yosefa Loshitzky. Bloomington: Indiana UP, 1997. 61–76.

Keneally, Thomas. *Schindler's List*. New York: Simon & Schuster, 1982.

Loshitzky, Yosefa, ed. *Spielberg's Holocaust: Critical Perspectives on* Schindler's List. Bloomington: Indiana UP, 1997.

Louvish, Simon. "Witness." *Oskar Schindler and His List: The Man, the Book, the Film, the Holocaust and Its Survivors*. Ed. Thomas Fensch. Forest Dale, VT: Paul S. Eriksson, 1995. 75–82.

McBride, Joseph. *Steven Spielberg: A Biography*. New York: Simon & Schuster, 1997.

Taylor, Philip M. *Steven Spielberg: The Man, His Movies, and Their Meaning*. New York: Continuum, 1992.

Thomson, David. "Presenting Enamelware." *Oskar Schindler and His List: The Man, the Book, the Film, and Its Survivors*. Ed. Thomas Fensch. Forest Dale, VT: Paul S. Eriksson, 1995. 90–98.

Questions for Reflection and Discussion

1. What did you already know about the Holocaust before watching *Schindler's List*? Where did your knowledge and impressions come from? What did you learn about the Holocaust from the film?

2. Which scenes are most disturbing to you? Describe what makes them so troubling: what particular images, what sounds, or what things people in the movie do or say.

3. Some viewers see Oskar Schindler as a con man who used Jews to profit from the war. Others see him as a kind of hero. How do you size up the man? On what words and deeds do you base your judgment? Did your opinion of Schindler change? If so, at what point in the film did you notice a change? If not, how does his behavior at the end of the film confirm your initial impressions?

4. Compare Schindler and Goeth. In what respects are they similar? In what respects are they different? Imagine if they had traded places. What kind of commandant would Schindler have been? How would Goeth have run the Emalia factory?

5. How are the Jewish people depicted in the film? Which Jews are given individual identities? How are the millions of other Jews represented?

6. Why do you think Schindler risked his life to save the Jews?

7. In one of the Plaszow scenes, Goeth stands on the balcony of his villa with a rifle in his hands. At first we see him from the yard, the way a prisoner might see him. Then the camera shifts to his perspective. We see what he sees as the barrel of his rifle shifts from one prisoner to another. He selects a slow-moving woman in the distance and fires. In the bedroom behind him, his half-naked girlfriend groans, "Oh, Amon," burying her head in a pillow. Where else in the film does the camera alternate like this among different points of view? What purpose is served by such shifts in perspective?

8. How realistic does the film seem to you? Since Spielberg did not use historical footage, he had to rely on actors, sets, camera work, and the other tools of fiction film to re-create events of the 1930s and 1940s. How well did Spielberg and his crew succeed in making history come alive?

9. What roles does Itzhak Stern play in the story? What is his position in the factory? What influence does he have on Schindler and the Jews?

10. *Schindler's List* shows Jews being mistreated in appalling ways. Where do you see this mistreatment most strikingly? Does the film give an explanation for Nazi anti-Semitism? What reasons can you give?

11. Few people who see the film forget the little girl in the red coat. What makes her so memorable? What does she symbolize to you?

12. History is a record of the choices people have made and the consequences of those choices. What other choices were available to Schindler, Goeth, the Jews themselves, and others in the film? How might their lives—and our history—be different if they had made different decisions? Where do you see similar choices being made in our lives today?

Topics for Further Study

1. Investigate the facts behind *Schindler's List*. Why were Jews persecuted by the Nazis? What happened to them elsewhere in Europe? What forms of resistance to Hitler were mounted by Germans, Jews, and others? Create a time line and place events of the film in their historical context. Explain new terms that you come across, such as *the Final Solution, Aktion, ghetto, concentration camps, SS, Resistance, Zionism, Yad Vashem.*

2. Find out about the real Oskar Schindler. What was he like before the war? What happened to him afterward?

3. Read Thomas Keneally's book and compare it to the film. You may be interested to read about the card game between Schindler and Goeth for Helen Hirsch (it begins on page 277), a scene that was filmed but cut from the final release print. What else does Spielberg leave out of the movie? What changes does he make in the structure of the story, the portraits of people, or the emphasis on certain events?

4. Watch another film about this period in history, perhaps a documentary like *Shoah*, a television docudrama like *Holocaust*, or a feature film like *The Diary of Anne Frank*.

5. Turn off the sound for part of the film. Notice how this changes your awareness of the camera work, the characters' movements, the editing, and other cinematic elements. Then restore the sound. What do the dialogue, music, and sound effects add to your experience of the scene?

6. Analyze the composition of a selected scene. Observe how the actors are positioned within the frame. Notice the way lines (vertical, diagonal, horizontal) and masses (large, small, dark, light) contribute to the overall effect. Where is the lighting coming from, and what does it emphasize? How else might the scene have been framed?

7. At the end of the film, we see real survivors among the actors at Schindler's grave. Find out what happened to them after the war. There are many Web sites on the Holocaust with references to helpful documentaries and readings.

Scenes to Analyze

1. **Schindler's Entrance.** [3:25] Note how we are introduced to Schindler in the dressing room scene. What do the close-ups tell us about the man? When do we first see his face? What does his conduct at the nightclub reveal about his character and intentions? Why does the camera keep changing position? How do the lighting and music comment on the action?

2. **The One-Armed Worker.** [39:35] Schindler is in his office when Stern introduces Mr. Lowenstein, an old man with one arm who is grateful for being allowed to work. Notice the acting here. How does Schindler (Liam Neeson) show his attitude toward Lowenstein and Stern (Ben Kingsley)? Compare this to his attitude in the next scene, when Lowenstein is killed [43:00].

3. **Liquidation of the Ghetto.** [57:00] In a fifteen-minute tour de force, Spielberg plunges us into the terror and horror of the Nazi *Aktion*. Storm troopers burst into homes and shove people onto the street. One family tries to hide beneath the floorboards; another swallows jewels encased in bread. A solider chucks a child on the cheek affectionately while a second soldier shoots a boy in the head. Meanwhile, Schindler and his girlfriend watch silently on horseback from a hilltop. As they look on, a little girl in a red coat walks through the chaos of the night. Examine the scene several times, focusing on a different element of filmmaking each time. Look only at the lighting: the fear and safety of shadows, searchlights scanning frightened faces, flashes of gunfire in the windows. Listen for the sounds: people screaming, dogs barking, gunfire, and a piano playing classical music in the middle of it all. Watch how the camera keeps shifting its position and our point of view. What makes this scene so powerful?

4. **Hinges.** [1:26] When Goeth questions a man making hinges in the factory, Spielberg captures the tension in a masterpiece of editing. Watch how he shows the process—and power play—in a series of close-ups, shifting angles, and quick cuts. Pay particular attention to the camera's positioning in the railroad yard, where Goeth takes the man for execution.

5. **Parallel Scenes.** [1:38:39] When Goeth expresses his feelings for Helen Hirsch in his wine cellar, the scene is intercut with a Jewish wedding in the barracks and a floorshow for the Germans. Why does Spielberg cut back and forth between these scenes? What connections is he making? Compare Goeth's advances to Helen with Schindler's approach to her earlier in the same location. What do the two cellar scenes reveal about the characters of these two men?

6. **The Showers.** [2:18:00] The women arrive at Auschwitz in a cattle car at night. Searchlights illuminate their frightened faces in the falling snow. They are stripped, shorn, and ushered into a large chamber marked "showers," where they huddle naked waiting for a long time. The lights go out, we hear screams, and finally a spray of water falls from one nozzle, then another. The screams turn to cries of relief. But as the Schindler women file out to the sound of a plaintive violin, another line is coming in, and the camera tilts up to show smoke rising from the chimney. What was falling was not all snow. Compare Spielberg's visual treatment of the scene to Keneally's description on pages 305–11 of the book.

19 The Shawshank Redemption

Directed by Frank Darabont; screenplay by Frank Darabont; based on a story by Stephen King; produced by Niki Marvin; cinematography by Roger Deakins; edited by Richard Francis-Bruce; art direction by Peter Landsdown Smith; production design by Terence Marsh; set decoration by Michael Seirton; music by Thomas Newman; costume design by Elizabeth McBride; released by Castle Rock Entertainment in 1994. [142 minutes]

Andy Dufresne	*Tim Robbins*
Ellis Boyd "Red" Redding	*Morgan Freeman*
Warden Norton	*Bob Gunton*
Heywood	*William Sadler*
Captain Hadley	*Clancy Brown*
Tommy	*Gil Bellows*
Bogs Diamond	*Mark Rolston*
Brooks Hatlen	*James Whitmore*
District attorney (1946)	*Jeffrey DeMunn*
Judge (1946)	*John Horton*
Parole hearings man (1947)	*Gordon Greene*
Fresh fish con	*Alfonso Freeman*
Fat Ass	*Frank Medrano*
Elmo Blatch	*Bill Bolender*

Steven King is widely known as the master of modern horror fiction. His bestselling stories of the morbid and macabre have thrilled millions of readers and, adapted for the screen, have reached millions more. *The Shawshank Redemption* marks a notable divergence in the King canon. Based on his novella *Rita Hayworth and Shawshank Redemption,* it tells a starkly realistic tale of men condemned to life imprisonment. If the story contains horror and suspense, they are the daily ingredients of life in a maximum-security prison.

The story begins in 1947, the year Andy Dufresne gets two consecutive life sentences for the murders of his wife and her lover. Sent to Maine's state prison, Shawshank Penitentiary, Andy is a misfit among the hardened criminals serving time. A wealthy banker with small hands and a quiet disposition, Andy (played by Tim Robbins) tries to keep to himself. His prison mates call him a cold fish, the guards dislike the upright way he walks, and he is raped repeatedly by a gang of sadistic thugs known as "the sisters." But Andy has something missing in the lives around him. He has hope.

A central focus of the story is the friendship that develops between Andy and a cynical lifer named Red (Morgan Freeman). Red is the prison supplier, "the man who can get it for you." He smuggles in a rock hammer for Andy, who used to collect rocks as a hobby. Andy uses the hammer to craft a chess set out of stones from the prison yard. Later Red fills other requests, including a poster of the 1940s movie star Rita Hayworth. As time wears on, Red gradually comes to respect Andy for his intelligence, his courage, and his persistence in the face of overwhelming odds, like the steady drip of water on concrete. Geology, Red learns, is a matter of pressure and time. One of Andy's projects is the prison library. Denied funds by the warden, he petitions the State for money, writing a letter every day for years until he gets a check to shut him up. He buys books with the check and goes on writing letters, building the best prison library in the East and transforming hopeless cons into appreciative readers. Another time he locks himself in the warden's office and broadcasts a Mozart aria over the prison loudspeaker to a yard full of rapt listeners—before a guard smashes through the door and drags him to solitary confinement.

But this is not a bloodless story about a do-gooder who loves opera and books, although it sends strong messages about the humanizing powers of music and literacy. Much of the film illustrates the brutalizing forces of imprisonment. When Andy is admitted, he and the other newcomers must walk a gauntlet of hostile guards and taunting inmates. They are stripped, hosed down, plastered with delousing powder, and marched naked to their cells, where the other cons make bets on which of them will crack first. The worst elements among the inmates are the sexual predators, led by Bogs Diamond. When Red points them out, Andy says, "I don't suppose it would help any if I explained to them I'm not homosexual." Red replies, "Neither are they. You have to be human first." The prison guards turn their backs on the brutality with which inmates treat one another, including gang rape. They indulge in their own vicious games. Captain Hadley, the cruelest of the "screws," takes pleasure in beating inmates with his billy club. When he hears a heavyset new prisoner crying in his cell, he clubs and kicks the man senseless. Worst of all is the chief himself, Warden Norton, who barely conceals his malice with a cloak of biblical piety. "Put your trust in the Lord," he tells the prisoners. "Your ass belongs to me." Norton knows the Bible by heart and quotes it often to cover his malevolence. The wall safe in his office is covered by a piece of needlepoint made by his wife, with the inscription: "HIS JUDGMENT COMETH AND THAT RIGHT SOON," words that prove ironically prophetic.

At times the story seems to be an indictment of the prison itself and the system it represents. "These walls are funny," Red explains. "First you hate them, then you get used to them; then you start to depend on them." The dehumanizing effects of institutionalization are made clear in the case of Brooks Hatlen, the kindly old librarian who keeps a pet raven. When Brooks is released on parole after fifty years inside the walls of Shawshank, he is beside himself with anxiety. We see him step outside the gate, a tiny figure in an ill-fitting suit. We watch him stumbling through the traffic, floundering at his job of bagging groceries, and carving his name on the rafter of his cheerless room at the halfway house before hitching a noose to the beam.

This grim spectacle of rehabilitation might suggest a bleak film experience, but the movie has its lighter moments and a few scenes of uplifting triumph. The scene in which Andy wins a round of beer for his fellow inmates is one of these. The film's finale is another. But what keeps the story flowing with the voice of humanity is Morgan Freeman's easygoing narration, which weaves through the action and lends a colloquial grace to the harshest scenes. Like the novella, the film is presented from Red's point of view. We are in the company of an insider, one who knows the language and the facts of prison life.

> The first night's the toughest, no doubt about it. They march you in naked as the day you were born, fresh from a Bible reading, skin burning and half blind from that delousing shit they throw on you, and when they put you in that cell, when those bars slam home, that's when you know it's for real. Old life blown away in the blink of an eye. . . . [N]othing left but all the time in the world to think about it. Most new fish come close to madness the first night. Somebody always breaks down crying. Happens every time. The only question is, who's it gonna be? It's as good a thing to bet on as any, I guess. I had my money on Andy Dufresne. I remember my first night. Seems like a *long* time ago. (Darabont 13–14)

Red is also an outsider, though, with respect to Andy. His first judgment of Andy proves to be wrong. He loses the bet. Only gradually does Red come to understand (as we do) this private, complex individual and to appreciate his remarkable strength of character. Faced with a life sentence and little prospect of parole, Red, a good man who has done a bad thing, has grown layers of protective cynicism. What he learns from Andy is a lifelong lesson about hope.

King introduced his ninety-one-page novella with the part title "Hope Springs Eternal." It appeared along with three other stories in a collection titled *Different Seasons,* each story linked to a different season. The book was well received when it was published in 1982. The *Los Angeles Times*

Book Review compared King to Mark Twain and Edgar Allan Poe, "with a generous dash of Philip Roth and Will Rogers thrown in" (Atchity). A review in *English Journal* likened King to Richard Wright and Feodor Dostoyevsky, for whom "beauty and violence are inextricably intertwined in the drama of human events" (McGill). In his book on literature and film, William Ferrell found traces of classical myths in the story, including Pandora (the prison is a box full of evils: murder, sadism, greed, jealousy, and hypocrisy) and the journey to the underworld (Andy goes through hell before attaining Paradise).

The Shawshank Redemption was directed by Frank Darabont in 1994. In contrast to the art film auteurs graduated by prestigious film schools, Darabont came to the director's chair by climbing the industry ladder. Born in France in 1959 to Hungarian refugees, he moved to Chicago with his parents. At age five, when they divorced, he moved to California with his father. He showed an early interest in horror movies, but he also liked books. He developed a special taste for David Lean, John Ford, Stanley Kubrick, and bad monster movies. By high school graduation, Darabont knew he wanted to be a screenwriter. His break came in 1981, when he found himself on the set of *Hell Night,* a low-budget film produced by Chuck Russell. Russell hired him as a production assistant, and they became creative partners. Darabont moved to the art department, where he spent six years learning the craft on set after set, "the best film school there is" (Kobak). Within nine years of graduation, he was writing scripts. His screenwriting credits include *Tales from the Crypt* (1989), *Mary Shelley's Frankenstein* (1994), and various sequels like *A Nightmare on Elm Street III* (1987). More recently, he wrote, directed, and produced *The Green Mile* (1999), another prison film based on Stephen King's writing.

The Shawshank Redemption was Darabont's directorial debut. He wrote the script in eight weeks, trying to capture the folksy feel of King's first-person narration in a voice-over technique that he considered central to the story. "I couldn't imagine the movie without that voice," he has explained (qtd. in Kobak). Darabont's commentary on the shooting script (published by Newmarket Press) gives a fascinating account of the differences between the book, the script, and the final film. Some things in the book were changed for the movie. In King's story, for example, Red is a redheaded Irishman. The film gives this fact a comic twist when Tim Robbins asks about Morgan Freeman's nickname and Freeman replies, "Maybe it's because I'm Irish." In the book, Brooks's pet bird, Jake, dies and is given a funeral; in the film, Brooks sets him free. Probably the biggest change is the finale. In the book, Warden Norton ends his days consumed by regret; in the movie, he shoots himself in his own office. The book ends with Red out on parole hoping to find Andy. The film ends with a shot of Red and Andy hugging on the beach of Zihuatanejo. Darabont was uncertain about this new ending, but audiences loved it at the previews and it stayed. There were also changes between the shooting script and the actual shooting. In the book, Red summarizes Andy's trial in seven pages, stressing the district attorney's political motives in getting a conviction (King 18–25). The original screenplay added a crude sex scene followed by a lengthy trial. Darabont found this treatment "somewhat protracted and boring" on film (135), so, working with his editor, he combined them into a single title sequence, focusing on the trial with brief flashbacks to the murder. Another change is what the convicts watch during their monthly picture show. The book and script called for *The Lost Weekend* (1945), a sobering film about alcoholism with Ray Milland. The rights for that film proved too expensive for Darabont's budget, so he cast around for something cheaper—and came up with *Gilda* (1946), which has the benefit of Rita Hayworth in the title role. Darabont cites this as an example of "turning disadvantages into strengths" (144).

The completed film was nominated for seven Academy Awards, including Best Picture and Best Actor (for Morgan Freeman). Although it won no Oscars, *The Shawshank Redemption* has continued to win praise from critics and audiences alike. As a Stephen King adaptation, it goes beyond the usual chills and thrills of horror films and investigates the horrors of incarceration and institutionalized inhumanity. As a prison film, it dispenses with the usual melodrama and violent riots in favor of a gritty realism and an unhurried pace to tell a story about friendship, patience, hope, and redemption. There is a lesson, too, about salvation. What Andy has always known, Red comes to understand, and Warden Norton learns too late is that "salvation lies within."

Suggested Films and Readings

More Films Adapted from Stephen King Stories

Carrie (1976)

The Shining (1980)

Cujo (1983)

Children of the Corn (1984)

Stand By Me (1986)

Misery (1990)

The Green Mile (1999)

Hearts in Atlantis (2001)

More Films about Prison

The Big House (1930)

I Am a Fugitive from a Chain Gang (1932)

The Defiant Ones (1958)

Birdman of Alcatraz (1962)

Cool Hand Luke (1967)

Dead Man Walking (1995)

The Green Mile (1999)

Monster's Ball (2001)

Books and Articles

Atchity, Kenneth. Review of *Different Seasons. Los Angeles Times Book Review* 27 Aug. 1982.

Darabont, Frank. The Shawshank Redemption: *The Shooting Script.* New York: Newmarket, 1996.

Ferrell, William K. "Hope Springs Eternal." *Literature and Film as Modern Mythology.* Westport, CT: Praeger, 2000. 65–73.

King, Stephen. *Rita Hayworth and Shawshank Redemption. Different Seasons.* New York: Signet, 1982. 15–106.

Kobak, Stu. "Redeeming the Writer: A Conversation with Frank Darabont." *Films on Disc.* Last accessed 8 June 2004 < www.vzavenue.net/ ~speedtech/interview.htm>.

McGill, Steven T. "Not Your Average Pop Fiction." *English Journal* 87.2 (1998): 108.

Questions for Reflection and Discussion

1. Red narrates the story. What kind of person does he seem to be? What are the advantages of hearing about Andy from Red's point of view? What are the disadvantages?

2. Andy replaces the poster of Rita Hayworth with posters of Marilyn Monroe, Raquel Welch, and (in the book) Linda Ronstadt. What do these posters represent to Red? What do you think they represent for Andy?

3. When you were watching the film for the first time, did you anticipate the ending? Watch the film again and note down any clues, like the rock hammer or the prisoner who finds a book about a prison escape (which he calls "*The Count of Monte Crisco* by Alexandre Dumbass").

4. How well structured is the movie's plot? What were the high points in

interest and suspense? (The book, which has a different ending, devotes two pages to the facts of Andy's escape and ten pages [90–100] to Red's speculations: an exercise in imagination and a suspenseful story-within-a-story of what might have gone wrong with Andy's plan.)

5. How does institutionalization affect the prisoners at Shawshank? Consider the effects of long-term imprisonment on Brooks, Tommy, and Bogs as well as on Red and Andy. Compare Shawshank to the mental institution in *One Flew over the Cuckoo's Nest*.

6. When Andy plays the opera aria over the prison loudspeaker, Red says, "For a few brief moments, every last man in Shawshank felt free." What does Red mean? Andy is sent to solitary confinement for this act, but he later says that Mozart kept him company. What enables Andy to say this? What does Andy know that Red has yet to learn?

7. Andy devotes years to building up the prison library. What does his approach to this project reveal about his character? What does the library mean for the other inmates and for him?

8. What kind of man is Warden Norton? What role does the Bible play in his life? Notice the needlepoint covering his wall safe, which reads, "HIS JUDGMENT COMETH AND THAT RIGHT SOON." Why is this biblical phrase ironic?

9. At one point, Andy confides to Red, "The funny thing is, on the outside, I was an honest man, straight as an arrow. I had to come to prison to be a crook." What are the problems with the penal system as it is represented in the film? What case can be made for prison reform?

10. Despite the years of brutality and hypocrisy it depicts, *The Shawshank Redemption* has a hopeful ending. Do you think this ending is warranted? What makes the ending seem right or wrong to you?

Topics for Further Study

1. In his introduction to Darabont's shooting script, Stephen King says, "I have never written with the movies in mind, but I have *always* written with them in my *eye*. . . . My books are the movies I see in my head" (Darabont ix). Read King's original story and describe what makes it cinematic. Do you think it was a particularly good candidate for a film adaptation?

2. *The Shawshank Redemption* presents an interesting opportunity to trace the progress of an adaptation from the original story to a screenplay and a movie. Select one scene from Stephen King's novella, such as

Andy's trial, his arrival at Shawshank, Brooks's parole, or the ending. Compare this to the way the scene is treated in the shooting script and the way it finally appears on film. What changes do you notice? What reasons can you give for these changes? What is gained or lost in the movement from page to screen?

3. Prison has been a favorite topic for movies since the beginning of Hollywood. Read about the history of the genre and watch two or three prison films that look interesting to you. How would you describe the purpose of each film? How have prisons or our perception of prisons through the movies changed over time?

4. Make a list of special prison terms that Red uses, such as *screw, fish, sisters,* and *tossin' cells.* What do these terms mean? What does this language tell you about the subculture of convicts in the film? What does it reveal about the prisoners' attitudes?

5. One of the joys of movies lies in knowing the trivial details of their production. Where did the director get those early mug shots of Red? What did the crew use to simulate snow? Who was Allen Greene (to whom the film is dedicated)? Are there any anachronisms in the background? Do a little research and create a *Shawshank Redemption* trivia contest for your classmates.

6. What are prisons really like? Investigate the nature of maximum-security prisons and prison life today. Are the conditions in Shawshank an accurate reflection of reality? What purposes do you think our prisons really serve? What proposals have been offered for prison reform? What do you think should be done about the state of our prisons and our prisoners?

Scenes to Analyze

1. **Trial and Murder.** [0:00] The credit sequence establishes the setting, mood, and basic facts of the story. We see Andy sitting in his car with a gun. We hear The Inkspots singing, "If I didn't care" on the radio. We watch flashbacks to the murder while the district attorney hammers down his case against Andy. The judge calls Andy "cold and remorseless," giving him two life sentences back to back. Does Andy's behavior in this sequence seem to justify the sentence?

2. **New Arrivals.** [8:40] Follow the bus as it brings a load of "fresh fish" to the prison. An aerial shot takes us over the walls and towers, showing us a yard full of men looking like ants. (This shot was not in the original

shooting script. It was an on-the-spot idea of production designer Terence Marsh.) What does the shot convey to us? How are the new inmates treated by the guards, the warden, and their fellow convicts?

3. **First Day in Prison.** [12:34] On their first day, the new prisoners are stripped, hosed down, deloused, and humiliated. An inmate who asks, "When do we eat" gets a billy club in his belly. The warden says, "Put your trust in the Lord; your ass belongs to me." How else are the newcomers initiated into prison life? How is this process comparable to (or different from) fraternity hazing or induction into any new group?

4. **Andy Meets Red.** [24:28] The two men have their first exchange in the prison yard while Red is playing catch. Contrast their dress and body language. Notice when they face each other and when they don't. What seems to be the basis of their relationship at this point? Do you see any hints of the friendship to come?

5. **Tarring the Roof.** [33:40] Camera placement is important in this scene, in which Andy cuts through a taboo with a pointed question to Guard Hadley: "Do you trust your wife?" Watch how the division between guards and inmates is established by the framing of each shot as well as the dialogue. Why is the moment a triumph for Andy?

6. **Brooks's Parole Montage.** [1:00:47] The sequence of shots following Brooks's release from prison after fifty years shows the effects of institutionalization. "These walls is funny," says Red. "You get to depend on 'em." How does each successive shot of Brooks show that he has been made incapable of coping with the outside world?

7. **The Italian Ladies.** [1:07:00] One of the film's great moments occurs when Andy plays the gramophone through the prison loudspeakers. The scene uses cutaways (to the guard on the toilet, prisoners in the yard, doctors in the infirmary) to show various reactions to the music. It also uses long shots, close-ups, tracking shots, and dissolves to create a sense of continuity. Red says, "I have no idea what those two Italian ladies were singing about, but their voices soared. . . . And for the briefest of moments, every last man at Shawshank felt free."

8. **Escape.** [1:57:00] Andy leaves Shawshank on a dark and stormy night. In fact, the prison walls are only sets and the sewage is really chocolate sauce, so what makes this scene so convincing and suspenseful? The shot of Andy looking skyward with outstretched arms is one of the film's most celebrated images. Why is this image so significant?

20 Run Lola Run

Written and directed by Tom Tykwer; produced by Stefan Arndt; cinematography by Frank Griebe; edited by Mathilde Bonnefoy; art direction by Attila Saygel; production design by Alexander Manasse; set decoration by Irene Otterpohl; music by Tom Tykwer, Johnny Klimek, and Reinhold Heil; released in the United States by Sony Pictures Classics in 1998; German title: Lola rennt; *in German with English subtitles.* [81 minutes]

Lola	*Franka Potente*
Manni	*Moritz Bleibtreu*
Lola's father	*Herbert Knaup*
Jutta Hansen	*Nina Petri*
Mr. Schuster	*Armin Rohde*
Norbert von Au	*Joachim Król*
Mr. Meier	*Ludger Pistor*
Miss Jäger	*Suzanne von Borsody*
Mike	*Sebastian Schipper*
Doris	*Julia Lindig*
Kassierer Kruse	*Lars Rudolph*
Croupier	*Klaus Müller*
Lola's mother	*Ute Lubosch*
Ronnie	*Heino Ferch*
Ambulance driver	*Volkhard Buff*
Bank security guard	*Marc Bischoff*
Supermarket guard	*Peter Pauli*
Blind woman	*Monika Bleibtreu*

Run Lola Run is a hip, postmodern movie, the hyperactive offspring of interactive video and MTV. Lurching wildly between entertainment and philosophy, flaunting the new technologies with verve and playful ingenuity, it seemed to presage a new digital age of movies when it appeared at the dawn of the millennium. As a product of recent independent filmmaking in Europe, it also offers lively evidence that multimedia innovation has become an international phenomenon.

The movie's premise is simple, almost classical. Lola has twenty minutes to get across town with 100,000 deutsche marks or her boyfriend Manni will die. Manni, a small-time criminal-in-training, lost the money in the subway and is nervously awaiting Lola or the gangster who will kill him, whoever arrives first. By the time Lola takes her first steps down the staircase of her apartment, we know this will be no ordinary thriller. The opening quotation from T. S. Eliot's *Four Quartets*, the dizzy crane shot of the crowd that spells out the movie's title, and the cartoon version of Lola on her mother's television set all tell us to get ready for a mental roller coaster ride.

Like all postmodern stories, this one is a pastiche of genres, styles, and themes. Although the movie's "running time" is barely more than eighty minutes, it has enough forward momentum and suspense for several full-length action films. Director Tom Tykwer adds a few familiar characters from gangster movies; diverse ingredients from romance films, including a few bedroom scenes; the episodic structure of a road movie; some sight gags from slapstick comedy; and the forking pathways of a choose-your-own adventure game, in which we identify with the hero moving through a hostile world without knowing precisely who we are or where we've been.

This game can be played more than once. Tykwer gives us three what-if scenarios, each with a slightly different starting point and a vastly different ending. As Lola races through the streets of Berlin, she encounters a boy on a bike, a nasty lady with a baby carriage, a flock of nuns, and workmen carrying a plate of glass, to name a few. These encounters change the course of action, both for her and for those she meets, and each run-through alters the nature of those meetings in some way. Tykwer shows us the long-term consequences in a comic series of flash forwards. We may be reminded of an anecdote from chaos theory, which holds that a butterfly flapping its wings in Australia can cause a stock market crash on Wall Street.

The movie's strongest influence, however, may be MTV. The pulsating beat isn't the only cinematic element that drives the story forward. There are also the kinetic rhythms of its editing style, a style that reflects a younger generation's fascination with technology and its impatience with old forms. Music television videos have created a new visual vocabulary to express this sense of fragmentation, impermanence, and acceleration, much of which is evident in Tykwer's film. Look for examples of ramping, where the camera changes speed within a shot, so that our attention alternately dwells on and dismisses an object or person in motion, isolating moments in time. Look for uses of the swing or shift lens, which blurs part of the visual field, redirecting our gaze to a portion of the screen or commenting on the relationships between characters. Notice how the film uses different film stocks—the fuzzy look of video, the crisp clarity of 35mm, the sharp contrasts of black-and-white photography—to signal shifts in time, emotion, or gradations of reality. The overall effect can be disorienting for viewers used to the classical Hollywood style, which subordinates technique to narrative, offering strong characters in an engaging story seamlessly told. Here we're shown the seams.

And maybe that's the point. If the fabric of this film keeps unraveling, if this world seems to be all surface and no depth, perhaps the message is the medium. Lola's world is populated by characters who collide rather than connect, or miss one another completely. Her mother's time is split between the television and the telephone. She seems more interested in talking long distance about astrology than in communicating in the here and now. Lola's father, a rich, high-powered businessman, is more attentive to his work and mistress than to his daughter and what is happening at home. Manni himself, the object of Lola's intense energy, appears to be a bumbling sort, at least at first. None of these characters seems to have much depth, nor needs to. The movie's fast-paced action leaves little time for acting. As in the goal-driven world of video games, people are objects to be used or obstacles to be avoided in the pursuit of a single-minded target. And Lola, lean and muscular, with flaming orange hair that stands out in a crowd, is a modern woman with a mission. Yet behind the mission and just beneath the skin is Eliot's reminder about space, time, and knowledge— "that the end of all our exploring will be to arrive where we started and know the place for the first time."

Tykwer says that all his films start with an image. He explains the process in various printed interviews and in a running commentary accompanying the DVD version of the film. "I get an image in my head and I start wanting to get it moving, to build a story around it, and then make a film out of it. In *Run Lola Run* it was a woman running" (Director's Statement). Around this bare image of motion and emotion he built a story. He came up with a title, wrote a three-page synopsis, and then worked out the structure for a script. The production itself took seven weeks, from June to August of 1997, filmed entirely in Berlin. Because timing was so crucial, driven by the need to match three parallel narratives, Tykwer and his crew carefully storyboarded each scene, getting all the clocks in sync, matching the action, actors, backgrounds, and even the weather to create the illusion of continuity. This called for precise planning and creative editing. Some shots had to be expanded, others compressed. All the phone booth scenes were shot in a single location on a single day and later spliced into the rough cut. A broad swath of the city, difficult to cover in a matter of hours, was condensed into a twenty-minute run. The opening crowd scene was filmed in a deserted airport. Since the budget allowed for only three hundred extras, Tykwer made them look like more by using them all for each letter singly, later rearranging the letters on a digital workstation. To capture Lola running from a variety of angles, the crew positioned the camera on a Steadicam and special dolly mounts, shot from windows, erected fences in the foreground, and took overhead shots from a helicopter. According to Tykwer in the director's commentary on the DVD, the final shooting ratio was 20:1.

Tykwer's biggest challenge in the editing room was to present three versions of the same story without boring or confusing his audience. He needed to reveal something new in each retelling in order to maintain suspense. At the same time, he did not want the flashbacks or leaps forward in time to break the forward momentum. "The time-space continuum gets taken right off its hinges without anyone really noticing," he explained, while the film keeps its "breathless, driving edge" (Director's Statement). Tykwer composes music for all his films, a process that for him is linked to editing. "I think, write, and cut in a very musical way," he says. Johnny Klimek and Reinhold Heil worked with him on the sound track, creating individual musical identities, building sample sound banks, honing in on the rhythms for each scene while discovering their visual tempos. You can hear this in the lyrics (usually sung by Franka Potente) and the changing beat while you see it in the frequent shifts from rapid cutting to slow motion, from close-up to long shot, from bright lighting to somber reds and blacks (Director's Statement).

Shot for less than two million dollars, *Run Lola Run* became the highest-grossing German film in the United States since *Das Boot* (1981), catapulting Tykwer to instant prominence. This was gratifying news for someone who had always wanted to make movies but had failed to gain admission to a film school. Born in Wuppertal, Germany, in 1965, Tykwer loved sci-fi and action films as a child. He also enjoyed playing video games, setting a world record for the first Star Wars game. At the age of eleven, he taught himself filmmaking with a Super-8 camera and made several short films, though, as he later admitted, most of these were more imitative than creative. He worked as a projectionist and ticket taker and then, at age twenty, moved to Berlin, where he studied philosophy and became a film theater programmer. Gradually he worked his way up through scriptwriting and television work to directing. His first feature, *Deadly Maria* (1993), is an expressionist thriller about a woman trying to pull free of the oppressive men in her life. *Wintersleepers* (1997), his second film, is about six people whose lives become interconnected in the Alps. One character is a projectionist who makes movies of his life to compensate for short-term memory loss. Soon after the completion of *Run Lola Run*, Tykwer and Potente became a couple. She starred in his next film, *The Princess and the Warrior* (2000), a love story that plays with the themes of fate and choice. Potente is a nurse in a psychiatric hospital who almost dies when she is hit by a speeding truck and is saved by a stranger who abruptly disappears. Did chance or fate place him there at that precise moment? She tries to make her own destiny by seeking him out.

Franka Potente (Lola) has been acting in films since 1995. A student of the Otto Falkenberg Schule in Munich and the Lee Strasberg Theatre Institute in New York, she has appeared in more than two dozen films, including *Anatomy* (2000), *Blow* (2001), and *The Bourne Identity* (2002). Moritz Bleibtreu (Manni) has studied acting in Paris, Rome, and New York. He now has credits in several films and stage productions, including Shakespeare. Nearly all of the other actors, even those with minor roles, are well known in Germany. The fact that small roles are played by leading actors works thematically. Each could be the center of a movie, with Lola and Manni playing bit parts in the background.

The complex crisscrossing of our lives is one of many themes running through the film. Each person Lola meets in her race across Berlin is somehow altered by her passing. The woman with the baby plays out three divergent scenarios, shown in rapid snapshots of her future. Presumably, a few seconds more or less in her encounter with Lola makes a difference in whether she loses her child to a social agency, wins the lottery, or becomes a religious soul. The fate of Lola's father also depends on timing, as do the fortunes of the moped thief, the gangsters, Mr. Meier, the bicyclist, the vagrant, a bank guard, and a large plate of glass. This is a film in which time itself becomes a question, a variable rather than a constant, one more cipher in a complex equation of destiny and choice. But Tykwer did not set out simply to illustrate an abstract philosophical concept. *Run Lola Run* has too much feeling and action for that. "I wanted to do a film about the energy of my generation," he has said, "an energy which all too often is bottled up inside" (qtd. in Winters). Lola's crystal-shattering screams reverberate with this released frustration, the cry of someone powerless to change things but who is learning to repossess her feelings and make a difference for someone she cares about. Seen in this light, the image of Lola sprinting through the streets of Berlin with flaming hair represents a vigorous new force, the life-affirming power of love.

Suggested Films and Readings

More Films by Tom Tykwer

Deadly Maria (1993)

Wintersleepers (1997)

The Princess and the Warrior (2000)

Heaven (2002)

More Films with Alternate Narratives

Last Year at Marienbad (1961; dir. Alain Resnais) France

Blind Chance (1987; dir. Krzysztof Kieslowski) Poland

Sliding Doors (1998; dir. Peter Howitt) England

Articles and Web Sites

Berardinelli, James. *ReelViews.* Review of *Run Lola Run,* 1999. Site inaugurated 26 Jan. 1996. Last accessed 10 Jan. 2003 <http://movie-reviews.colossus.net/>.

Moller, Olaf. "Film Critic Olar Moller Reflects on Current State of German Cinema in the Wake of *Run Lola Run.*" *Film Comment* 37.3 (May 2001): 11+.

Rotten Tomatoes. Reviews of *Run Lola Run.* Site inaugurated 1998. Last accessed 10 Jan. 2003 <www.rottentomatoes.com/m/RunLolaRun-1087932/>.

Tykwer, Tom. Director's Statement. Official *Run Lola Run* Web site, Sony Pictures Classics. No date <www.sonypictures.com/classics/runlolarun/>.

Winters, Laura. "A Rebel with Red Hair Rumples Stuffed Shirts." *New York Times* 13 June 1999, late ed.: sec. 2, 17.

Questions for Reflection and Discussion

1. At which point in the film, if ever, do you start identifying with Lola? Do you share her sense of urgency, the shock of her father's revelation, her moments of intimacy with Manni, her fears, doubts, exhaustion, or relief? What accounts for your identification with her or lack of it?

2. There are times when we'd all like to hit the rewind button of our lives and redo a moment differently. Describe such a moment, tell what went wrong, and explain what other choices you might have made. What might be the consequences of these choices?

3. Early in the film, Manni tells Lola, "You once said that love can do any-thing." Does the film support her claim? Consider the pillow talk be-tween Manni and Lola, the scenes with Lola's father and his mistress, and the looks exchanged by Lola and the bank guard. To what extent is this a love story or an antiromance?

4. The film is filled with recurring images or motifs: clocks, spirals, games, the colors red and green, glass, and running, to name a few. Trace sev-eral of these motifs through the movie. Where do you find them, and what is their significance in the larger story?

5. What kind of environment does Berlin seem to be? Describe the buildings, the people, the mixture of old and new. Could this film take place anywhere at any time, or does Lola's run through the streets of Berlin represent something specific about Germany today?

6. Check out Lola's appearance: her green pants, blue tank top, tattoos, Doc Martens, and red hair. What do they tell you about her? How typical is she of her generation or yours?

7. Tykwer includes moments of action (Lola's energetic running, the supermarket holdup), drama (her father and his mistress), and romance (Manni and Lola in bed). Examine these scenes and explain what makes them different from one another. What cinematic resources (e.g., lighting, editing, acting, décor, film stock, camera movement, camera speed) contribute to the mood of these scenes?

8. Does *Run Lola Run* remind you of other movies, film genres, television shows, or video games? What do its story structure, plot, and themes have in common with these other works? If imitation is a hallmark of poststructuralist art, where is the originality?

9. Each successive version of the story seems to build on Lola's knowledge of previous events. What does Lola learn from her first two runs that helps her make the third attempt more successful? To what extent is her final happy ending due to chance or to choice?

Topics for Further Study

1. The film's opening quotation was taken from T. S. Eliot's "Little Gidding," one of the poems in his *Four Quartets:* "We shall not cease from exploration, / And the end of all our exploring / Will be to arrive where we started / And know the place for the first time." Read Eliot's poem and any others you can think of that deal with the issues of time you find in *Run Lola Run.*

2. Most scenes in the film were meticulously planned with storyboards to work out the precise details of action, location, and camera work. Examine ten frames from the casino scene or another tightly constructed sequence and create your own storyboard to show the following: action (what happens in the shot), transition (cut, fade, dissolve), framing (close-up, long shot, medium shot), camera angle (high, low, eye level), camera movement (tracking, panning, tilting, boom), lighting (high key, low key, eye lighting, backlighting), sound (dialogue, sound effects, music, voice-over).

3. Some critics see the principle of determinism or chaos theory at work in the film. Look up these concepts and find out more about them. Do you agree with the critics?

4. Get a map of Berlin and trace Lola's route. Use street names and buildings as clues. Why do you think Tykwer selected these locations for his film? How long do you think it would take someone to run this distance in real time?

5. The DVD version of *Run Lola Run* contains a running commentary by Tom Tykwer and Franka Potente. Take this opportunity to watch the film while listening to what went on behind the camera scene by scene.

6. Listen to the movie's sound track and lyrics. The songs include "Believe" and "What a Difference a Day Makes." How would you describe or classify this music? Some of these sounds have been used in commercials (for *Survivor* and tampons), television shows (an episode of *Roswell*), and various movie trailers (*Any Given Sunday, Highlander,* and *The Bourne Identity*). Where else have you heard them?

7. Foreign films with subtitles call for special viewing skills. What is your experience with such films? How do you meet the need to read while you watch? Some foreign language films are dubbed, with the dialogue spoken in English by unseen actors. Do you prefer subtitles or dubbing?

Scenes to Analyze

1. **Title Sequence.** [1:10] Watch how Tykwer introduces the film's themes (time, speed, life's mysteries), visual motifs (clock, spiral), and minor characters (find them in the crowd) in this startling opening.

2. **"Where were you?"** [4:56] There is little time to set up the story and tie us to the major characters, but Tykwer does both in this brief dialogue between Lola and Manni on the telephone. Where are they? What problem do they face? What options do they have? How are we given the background information that we need to understand what happens next? How are we made to care about Lola and Manni?

3. **Decision.** [11:00] "Every day, every second, you're faced with a decision that can change your life." Confronted with the urgent need to bring 100,000 marks to her boyfriend in twenty minutes, Lola faces her options. As a spiral of dominoes starts tumbling on a television screen, the camera swirls around Lola while she considers all the people she might turn to, whispering their names, and making a final choice. Follow the camera work as it explores Lola's decision-making process.

4. **"Open your eyes!"** [13:15] Each time Lola passes the lady with a baby, we see the woman's life flash forward in a sequence of still photographs. Find each of these scenes [36:31; 56:01] and compare the different futures that lie ahead for her. What might account for these forking paths?

5. **Poppa I.** [18:51] The pace of Lola's running, and of the film, slows down for a moment of drama in the bank, where Lola's father has been talking with his mistress, Jutta Hansen. What do we learn about Lola's life in this scene? What new emotions come into play?

6. **Supermarket.** [26:00] Examine the robbery scene, a study in bad timing. Notice how Tykwer uses a split screen to show two locations at the same time and build suspense. Manni's approach differs from Lola's, revealing major distinctions in their characters. How would you describe their competence and attitudes? At one point, the action slows down while they speak to each other through the plate glass window (one of several such scenes in which glass proves no barrier to communication). How does Tykwer's camera work and editing prepare you for what happens next?

7. **In the Bedroom.** [31:56] We get a new view of Manni and Lola as they lie in bed. How are they framed and positioned in this scene? What mood is created by the lighting? Compare this moment to the other bedroom scene [52:50], when the roles are reversed.

8. **In Pursuit.** [1:02:04] In the third version of the story, an extraordinary sequence of events enables Manni to catch the bum who took his moneybag. Who are the links in this chain of cause and effect? When Manni does catch the bum, he takes the bag and gives the man his gun. What do you think he'll do with that gun?

9. **"Everything's O.K."** [1:13:22] The final version has a happy ending. Manni has no idea what Lola's done for him. Do you think she'll ever tell him? Should she? Which of the three versions do you prefer?

21 The Matrix

Written and directed by Andy and Larry Wachowski; produced by Joel Silver; cinematography by Bill Pope; edited by Zach Staenberg; art direction by Hugh Bateup and Michelle McGahey; production design by Owen Paterson; set decoration by Lisa Brennan, Tim Ferrier, and Marta McElroy; music by Don Davis; costume design by Kym Barrett; fight choreography by Yuen Wo Ping; visual effects by John Gaeta; released by Warner Brothers in 1999. [115 minutes]

Neo/Thomas A. Anderson	*Keanu Reeves*
Morpheus	*Laurence Fishburne*
Trinity	*Carrie-Anne Moss*
Agent Smith	*Hugo Weaving*
Cypher/Reagan	*Joe Pantoliano*
Oracle	*Gloria Foster*
Tank	*Marcus Chong*
Apoc	*Julian Arahanga*
Mouse	*Matt Doran*
Switch	*Belinda McClory*
Dozer	*Anthony Ray Parker*

Almost immediately after its release in 1999, *The Matrix* became a cult classic. Word spread quickly that something rich and strange had brought a sea change to the movies. Science fiction fans flocked to the theaters along with action film aficionados. The film especially appealed to a younger generation raised on comics, computer games, and digital effects, although it also drew more widely from mythology, legend, popular literature, and, of course, other movies. Viewers found themselves in an imaginary world controlled by intelligent machines, a dystopia in which human beings are trapped in a computer program called the Matrix. It seems like an ordinary world in most respects, but for those who understand its secrets it is possible to defy the prison of a programmed existence—to leap across rooftops like a superhero, deliver lightning blows like a kung fu master, and join an underground resistance movement pledged to free humanity.

The Matrix had its detractors too. Janet Maslin of the *New York Times* criticized the script for its "pretentious plotting" and belittled the film itself as a hodgepodge of borrowed concepts and techniques. Roger Ebert thought it was "visually dazzling [and] . . . full of kinetic excitement," but he was disappointed by its final retreat to a formulaic showdown between good and evil. Dennis Lim of the *Village Voice* saw it as "a tunnel-visioned crowd pleaser . . . composed mostly of mile-a-minute gobbledygook and mystic hogwash" and wished "it was more than simply a neat way of introducing really cool effects."

Judging by its overall reception, though, *The Matrix* was a huge success. It grossed more than $171 million in the United States alone (over half a billion dollars worldwide) and won three Academy Awards (for film editing, sound, and visual effects). It was also the first film to sell a million copies on DVD, making it available for repeated viewings and analysis. Young audiences everywhere have memorized the words of Neo, Morpheus, and Trinity the way other generations have learned the lines from *Casablanca* or *Gone with the Wind*. Some reread the movie to better understand its underlying philosophy or details of the plot. Others enjoy watching its extraordinary action scenes and special effects again and again. Many appreciate the interplay of action and ideas, the spectacle of thought in action on the screen. If the movie borrows from earlier films, it also has a unique identity: a concept and style that have influenced succeeding movies, commercials, fashion trends, and everyday speech.

First-time viewers often find the plot difficult to follow because it zigzags through time and space. The action takes place in two different eras and locations simultaneously. In the real world, set in the distant future, humanity has lost the war against machines. Stripped of their power and individual freedom, people are being farmed like livestock by computers for the purpose of supplying energy. Millions of human beings are plugged from birth into a vast electronic network that simulates the universe as they once knew it. They believe they are living ordinary lives (the events in the film cover a period of nineteen months, from February 18, 1998, to September 18, 1999), but they are really serving as batteries for the Matrix.

The film's protagonist has a double identity. By day he works for a large software company as Thomas A. Anderson; by night he perpetrates clever computer crimes as a hacker going by the name of Neo. Neo is uneasy with his regular existence. He does not like being a cog in a large, impersonal corporation, and he senses that something is not quite right with the world. For some time, he has been using his home computer to look for a mysterious figure known as Morpheus who holds the answer to a haunting question: "What is the Matrix?" But while Neo has been searching for Morpheus, Morpheus has been seeking him. The contact is made through his computer and a knock on the door. Neo follows a trail of cryptic clues and his own instincts to Trinity, a smart, agile woman in a sleek, black vinyl outfit. Neo knows her reputation as a hacker. "I thought you were a guy," he tells her. "Most guys do," she replies.

Neo's first encounter with Trinity is brief and disorienting, like a dream, and what happens next seems a bewildering mixture of hallucina-

tion and reality. Neo finds himself pursued by a trio of men in suits led by
Agent Smith. The three agents wear geeky dark glasses and narrow ties,
and they appear to defy the laws of physics. They chase Neo through his
office and implant an electronic "bug" in his navel. Trinity arrives to de-
bug him and leads him to Morpheus, who offers him two pills. The blue
pill will leave him as he is; the red pill will lead him down the rabbit hole
to knowledge of the Matrix. Neo learns that what he has taken for reality is
a kind of electronic theme park, a computer-generated dream world built
to keep him—and others—in mental captivity while intelligent machines
sap his energy for their own use. Stunned to the point of nausea, Neo can
hardly accept this startling news. Morpheus introduces Neo to the crew of
his ship, the *Nebuchadnezzar.* He meets Switch, Cypher, Tank, and the other
men and women who have pledged to fight the machines. They accept Neo
as one of their own and train him for the struggle ahead. Morpheus explains
that they have been waiting for him; they believe him to be The One (an
anagram for Neo) long prophesied to lead the battle to freedom.

As in most films of this genre, the roles call for more action than act-
ing. Keanu Reeves requires little subtlety for the part of Neo. He plays the
protagonist with a straight face and earnest physical effort. Carrie-Anne
Moss gives a more supple performance as Trinity in the supporting role.
She is already a nimble fighter, and she knows a few things about loyalty
and love. The part with most depth belongs to Laurence Fishburne, whose
Morpheus carries the authority and moral weight of a Zen master.
Morpheus is a compassionate patriarch, calm and centered even when he's
under attack. Some of the minor characters are the most fun. Hugo Weav-
ing manages to give Agent Smith an amusing blend of menace and mo-
notony. He sounds and looks a little like Richard Nixon. Joe Pantoliano plays
the part of Cypher, a Judas figure, with ruthless cynicism. Gloria Foster gives
a delightful performance as the Oracle, who turns out to be a grandmoth-
erly type who bakes cookies in a homey kitchen.

Little has been written about the film's directors, Larry and Andy
Wachowski, who rarely give interviews, preferring to stay behind the curtains like the Wizard of Oz. The brothers were born in Chicago—Larry in
1965, Andy in 1967—to a businessman father and a mother who was a
painter and a nurse. Both Larry and Andy dropped out of college (Bard
and Emerson respectively) to pursue their creative dreams. They ran a car-
pentry business (their enthusiasm for constructing things is evident in their
film work), found employment with Marvel Comics (writing dialogue for
Clive Barker's *Hellraiser*), and carried on endless philosophical debates with
each other. Inspired by a book about filmmaker Roger Corman, they wrote
a script for a movie that became *Assassins* (1995). When the film met with a

disappointing reception, they wrote and directed their own movie, *Bound* (1996), which has been variously described as a dark romantic heist thriller and a lesbian neo-noir.

The success of *Bound* gave them leverage to pitch another script to Warner Bros., one they had been working on for years. With the help of artists Geof Darrow, Tani Kunitake, and Steve Skroce, they developed an elaborate comic-style storyboard (Lamm), which they brought to Joel Silver, known for producing hit movies about alternate realities, like *Predator* (1987) and *Demolition Man* (1993). Silver liked the script immediately. The Wachowskis were hired to direct their dream movie, *The Matrix*. Principal photography took twenty-five weeks, with much time and technical attention devoted to the intricate action scenes. The opening three minutes alone required four days to shoot. Since the directors wanted no stunt doubles for the combat scenes, Reeves, Moss, and Fishburne underwent five months of rigorous physical training, each supervised by a personal kung fu master. The fighting scenes were designed by Yuen Wo Ping, the legendary actor, director, and martial arts coach for Jackie Chan and other Hong Kong action stars.

Most of the location shoots were in Sydney, Australia. Some of the sets from *Dark City* (1998) were recycled for the rooftop scenes, but much of the visual design was new. The set designers used only a few miniatures (the helicopter), matte shots (the future city skyline), and scale models (the elevator shaft and a quarter-size building that was blown up late in the movie). For the most part, they relied on digital effects. As the film's conceptual artist, Goef Darrow prepared elaborate blueprint drawings for the main deck of the *Nebuchadnezzar,* the infirmary, and the fetus stalk (where human embryos are wired to the Matrix) as well as the eerily biomechanical bug and sentinels. These designs were then rendered by computers as animated images and combined with live action on a blue or green screen. The final effect on screen was the result of countless hours of meticulous work and many talented hands, all of it generated from the inventive minds of the Wachowski brothers.

Viewers were impressed by the film's distinctive look. Colors are used thematically, like leitmotifs. Green tints dominate scenes of the Matrix; blue predominates in the real world. Most organic hues are leached out to remove all traces of vitality, leaving the impression of a cold, synthetic world. Many scenes have their own visual texture. Trinity and Switch meet Neo in a heavy, claustrophobic rain. Morpheus encounters him in a white room without floor or ceiling, as if their rendezvous takes place in a void. The power plant scene is awash in fleshy, embryonic goo. The whole movie has a dark, nocturnal tone, with little sunlight to dispel the mystery and gloom. The filmmakers give close attention to visual transitions. Frequently, the camera enters a computer or a television screen and comes out a window, as if glass were the interface between two worlds. The number of reflective surfaces—looking glasses—is significant too. Morpheus's dark spectacles reflect the options he offers Neo, a pill reflected in each lens. When Neo swallows the red pill, his body morphs into a shiny metallic object. Later he sees his inverted image in a doorknob and a spoon. Sometimes subtle messages are conveyed by changes in camera speed. When Neo is driven through the rainy city streets, the view outside the car window is projected at a different frame rate than the action inside, a hint that something is amiss. Elsewhere, shifts in tone and pacing are suggested by slow motion or a series of quick cuts. These visual effects are all part of the filmmakers' broad palette, ingeniously selected and combined to tell the story.

Under John Gaeta's direction, *The Matrix* employed 412 special effects shots. Neo's sealed mouth and the bug that penetrates his navel were digital creations. Since the sentinels and other mechanical life-forms are supposed to be creatures of computer evolution, Gaeta wanted them to move in predictable patterns, as if motivated by algorithms. His biggest achievement, though, was the development of "bullet time," an effect created by one hundred synchronized cameras arranged around the subject in a ring. When the film from all these cameras is stitched together into a continuous sequence, we seem to be encircling a moment frozen in time. Trinity is caught spread-eagle in a midair karate move. Neo and Agent Smith defy gravity as they square off gun to gun. Neo dodges bullets that float before his eyes. These memorable images, each a meditation on time and perspective, have become hallmarks of the film.

In addition to John Gaeta's digital wizardry, Bill Pope's cinematography, Owen Paterson's production design, and Kym Barrett's costumes contribute to the movie's visual style. Barrett drew her sartorial inspiration from fairly tales, Tibetan monk robes, samurai movies, Westerns, and mod fashion trends. Most of the costumes are urban camouflage. Trinity's glistening graphite suit is meant to look mercurial, impossible to catch. Neo's black leather trench coat flares aggressively when he enters the lobby filled with police officers, revealing an arsenal stitched into the lining. The agents look like those from *Men in Black* (1997), parodies of parodies made even funnier with their 1950s ties and goofy shades.

Like any self-respecting postmodern movie, *The Matrix* quotes a bewildering variety of sources. The film's combat choreography pays homage to Hong Kong action movies, its morphing effects to *Terminator 2: Judgment Day* (1991), its insectlike robots to *Aliens* (1986). Pop culture historians identify vestiges of comic books, graphic novels, Japanese anime, and video games. Science fiction fans trace features of the plot to the computer simulations of *Dark City* (1998), the virtual reality of *Strange Days* (1995), the cyberpunk of William Gibson novels, and the dystopian fiction of Philip K. Dick. Academics find elements of Gnosticism, Baudrillard, messianic Christianity, and Zen Buddhism. And any schoolchild can recognize the references to *The Wizard of Oz, Alice in Wonderland,* and Wylie Coyote. These citations are deliberate, ubiquitous, part of the fun.

For fans who take the movie's premise seriously, there is a lot to occupy the mind. Much has been written by academics and armchair philosophers about alternate realities, mental freedom, and millennium angst. The film regularly teases us with scenes in which a character quotes Baudrillard ("Welcome to the desert of the real"), a sage child bends a spoon with his thoughts ("It is not the spoon that bends; it is only yourself"), or machines address people as if they belonged to a dying species ("Human beings are a disease . . . and we are the cure"). But what could have been a more heavy-handed treatment of such themes is intermittently lightened by lines such as "Our way or the highway," "Dodge this," "You all look the same to me," "Why didn't I take the blue pill?," and "Whoa!"

The film has generated a large share of trivia. *Matrix* cultists like to point out that Neo's martial arts training is taken from a Jackie Chan movie (*Drunken Master,* 1978); that Mr. Wizard is an allusion to the1960s cartoon *Tooter Turtle;* that the Bow Whisk Orchestra is an anagram for the Wachowski Brothers; that Neo's room number is 101, the number of the torture room in Orwell's *1984* (where victims wrestle with their worst nightmares); and that Cypher's name is Reagan (like the former president, he wants to be someone important, maybe an actor, and "remember nothing"). It has also spawned a swarm of imitators, from car commercials and music videos to musicals and video games. The bullet time effect has been copied or spoofed in *Charlie's Angels: Full Throttle* (2003), *Daredevil* (2003), and *The Simpsons,* to name a few. Meanwhile, *The Matrix* continues to spin off its own sequels in several media, including a video game (*Enter the Matrix*), *The Animatrix* (a set of nine animated shorts that dovetail with the original film), and two follow-up features: *The Matrix Reloaded* and *The Matrix Revolutions,* both released in 2003. The Wachowski brothers continue to be the creative minds and active voices behind these projects. Whatever new films they may direct, they have already left a lasting legacy.

Suggested Films and Readings

More Films by the Wachowski Brothers

Bound (1996)

The Matrix Reloaded (2003)

The Matrix Revolutions (2003)

Other Films about Alternate Realities

Predator (1987)

Demolition Man (1993)

Strange Days (1995)

Dark City (1998)

eXistenZ (1999)

The Thirteenth Floor (1999)

Books and Articles

Ebert, Roger. "*Matrix* Leaves Us Hanging." Rev. of *The Matrix*. *Chicago-Sun Times* 31 Mar. 1999, late ed.: 48.

Gordon, Devin. "Who's Next: The Matrix Makers." *Newsweek* 30 Dec. 2002–6 Jan. 2003: 81+.

Haber, Karen, ed. *Exploring the Matrix: Visions of the Cyber Present*. New York: St. Martin's, 2003.

Irwin, William, ed. The Matrix *and Philosophy: Welcome to the Desert of the Real*. Chicago: Open Court, 2002.

Lamm, Spencer, ed. *The Art of* The Matrix. New York: Newmarket, 2000.

Lim, Dennis. "Grand Allusions." *Village Voice* 7–13 Apr. 1999: 150.

Maslin, Janet. "The Reality Is All Virtual, and Densely Complicated." *New York Times* 31 Mar. 1999, late ed.: E1.

Questions for Reflection and Discussion

1. Describe the protagonist's double life as Neo and Thomas Anderson. What do his two names represent about his dual identity? Why does he sense that "there is something wrong with the world"?

2. When the film begins, Neo has been searching for a man named Morpheus. Who is Morpheus and why is he important to Neo? When Neo and Morpheus meet, what do they learn about each other?

3. One of the film's big questions is "What is the Matrix?" How would you answer this question to a science fiction fan, a child, a computer programmer, or a corporate executive?

4. What is Neo up against? What is the nature of his challenge? Who or what is on his side? What do you consider to be his most important weapon?

5. *The Matrix* deals in big ideas that have occupied philosophers for centuries. What messages does it convey about freedom, reality, loyalty, identity, and love? What does Neo learn to believe in during the course of his adventures?

6. The war between humans and machines is a staple of science fiction. What other books or movies address this conflict? *The Matrix* adds a new twist by making computers the enemy but relying on digital technology to narrate the story. Explore the relationships between humans and machines in the way the film was made and in the story it tells.

7. Viewers have noticed allusions and parallels to *Alice in Wonderland*, the Bible, kung fu movies, comic books, and many other well-known texts of arcane and popular culture. How are these sources used in *The Matrix*? What functions do they serve? How do you answer critics who see the film as "a hodgepodge of borrowed concepts and techniques"?

8. Many people comment on the movie's distinctive visual look. What do Bill Pope's cinematography, Kym Barrett's costumes, Owen Paterson's production design, and John Gaeta's special effects contribute to this look? Specifically, how does their work support the movie's tone and themes?

9. Trace the motif of reflective surfaces throughout the movie. How many kinds of mirrors can you find? Why do you think Andy and Larry Wachowski include them in the story?

10. The Wachowski brothers have discounted the death and violence in their movie by saying that most of the fatalities are only "virtual beings," not flesh and blood. Do you think this makes a difference?

11. A case can be made that Trinity is a more important character than Neo. Trace her roles as woman warrior, Neo's partner, and bearer of love. What is her main purpose in the story? What does she accomplish at the beginning and end of the film?

12. Analyze the movie's secondary characters. Is Agent Smith a machine with human frailties? Why does Cypher betray his human colleagues? What makes Tank tick? Is the Oracle a sage in an apron or a fraud?

13. The makers of *The Matrix* claim to have staged action stunts never before seen on film. Which action scenes do you find most effective or original? What makes them so special?

Topics for Further Study

1. Check out the original reviews for *The Matrix*. Read negative comments (Gordon, Lim, Maslin) as well as positive reviews. Which assessments seem most persuasive to you?

2. Spencer Lamm has edited an impressive volume of artwork related to the film titled *The Art of* The Matrix. The book includes storyboard

sketches by Steve Skroce (who explains how his work expresses the directors' evolving ideas), color drawings by Tani Kunitake (who had worked on action movies such as *Armageddon* and *Batman and Robin* before joining the Wachowski brothers), and Geof Darrow (whose elaborate drawings served as blueprints for the infirmary, the main deck of the *Nebuchadnezzar*, the fetus stalk, and other sets). Compare these drawings to the final film.

3. Learn about bullet time and other special effects used in *The Matrix*. Watch one of the documentaries about the film's production, read about John Gaeta's ingenious techniques, or search through any of the five million Web sites related to the film.

4. Read Karen Haber's anthology of essays, *Exploring the Matrix*, culled chiefly from science fiction authors associated with the cyberpunk movement. Among other things, the essayists explore literary and cinematic influences on *The Matrix*, the nature of cyberpunk heroes, and modern life as a simulation.

5. For a more philosophical approach, consult William Irwin's The Matrix *and Philosophy*. The essays in this volume, most written by professors of philosophy, relate the film to Plato's Cave and Descartes's *Meditations*, metaphysics and neopluralism, Kant and Dostoyevsky, nihilism and Zen.

6. A growing body of movies and novels is based on the concept of alternate realities. What is the concept, and what might account for its popularity in science fiction? Watch some of the other movies listed above to help you formulate your answers.

7. Historians have begun to talk about "millennium angst," the anxiety people felt at the end of the second millennium, when *The Matrix* was released. Research the period. Find out what people were concerned about and how their concerns were expressed. Speculate on how the public's attitudes at the time may have shaped the film and the response of its audience in 1999.

8. Watch the two sequels, *The Matrix Reloaded* and *The Matrix Revolutions*. What do they add to the story? What mysteries do they explain or raise? Do these sequels measure up to the first film? Explain your assessment.

Scenes to Analyze

1. **Opening.** [0:00] The film begins with green digits on a computer screen and the voices of Trinity and Cypher. They're discussing Morpheus

and "The One" when the phone line is compromised and police break in with guns drawn. We're introduced to a cocky police chief ("I think we can handle one little girl") and the three agents ("Lieutenant, your men are already dead"). Notice how all the shots are edited together for suspense. Revisit the opening after completing the film to see how Trinity's conversation with Cypher offers clues to the conclusion.

2. **Trinity in Action.** [3:00] The film's first action scene is of Trinity fighting the police with incredible strength, speed, and acrobatic ingenuity; it also features the movie's first bullet time shot. What makes Trinity in action so engaging to watch? What qualities make her a modern action hero?

3. **Wake-Up Call.** [6:36] Neo awakes surrounded by his stereo and computer, which are still on. The screen blinks a cryptic message: "The Matrix has you. Follow the white rabbit." He's startled by a knock on the door. What does this scene tell you about Neo? Notice the condition of his room and his room number.

4. **Squeegees.** [12:04] All through an otherwise tedious reprimand from his boss, Neo hears the squeak of windows being washed. What does this sound add to the scene? Take note of the colors. Colors will be a clue to location and mood throughout the film.

5. **Bugged.** [20:20] "What good is a phone call if you're unable to speak?" says Agent Smith. His Gestapo tactics with digital effects illustrate how the film mixes humor with tension and suspense. This is a good point to observe the agent's dress code and diction as well as the claustrophobic set design, weird music, color scheme, and camera angles, all of which contribute to the overall effect. How would you describe the scene's dominant tone?

6. **Getting the Bug Out.** [22:37] The scene with Trinity and Switch has a different visual tone created by the rain, thunder, and dark, deserted city streets. Notice how the droplets cascade down the car window like digits on a computer screen.

7. **Morpheus's Proposal.** [25: 09] The setting for Neo's meeting with Morpheus is an old walk-up with faded Victorian décor. Morpheus is standing at the curtained window wearing dark glasses and a long black coat. He speaks slowly, softly, like a gentleman. "Let me tell you why you're here," he says, and offers Neo a choice in the form of two pills. What do these details tell you about Morpheus? What makes Neo choose to follow him?

8. **Down the Rabbit Hole.** [31:40] The consequences of Neo's decision to choose Wonderland are made strikingly clear by the camera work, sets, and sound track for this scene. In what sense is this scene a kind of rebirth? How are we made to identify with Neo? Do any moments remind you of other movies? Speculate on how the special effects were achieved, and test your speculations with some research on the making of the film.

9. **The *Nebuchadnezzar.*** [34:00] The control room of Morpheus's ship was modeled on Jules Verne's classic, *20,000 Leagues under the Sea.* For a detailed blueprint of the set, see *The Art of* The Matrix, edited by Spencer Lamm.

10. **"Welcome to the desert of the real."** [39:33] This is the scene in which Neo learns about the Matrix. Morpheus uses "the construct," a computer program, to explain. How is the world's artificiality represented visually? Try listening to Morpheus's voice with your eyes closed. Does his explanation sound more visionary or more like gibberish?

11. **"I know kung fu."** [49:12] The choreography for Neo's martial arts training has been compared to a 1930s dance movie. Keanu Reeves and Laurence Fishburne underwent five months of preparation under the direction of Yuen Wo Ping, who trained Jackie Chan. The movements involved intricate wirework as well as strenuous physical endurance. Since every move was blocked out ahead of time, the editing was easy. What makes the fighting seem like a video game simulation?

12. **The Oracle.** [1:10:40] Neo's audience with the Oracle holds some surprises, including the waiting room of prodigies and the appearance of the Oracle herself. Notice the color scheme of her kitchen and its homey details. What does Neo learn from the child with the spoon? How does he interpret the Oracle's words?

13. **Déjà Vu.** [1:18] A black cat seen twice indicates a glitch in the Matrix and a trap for the freedom fighters. A police raid sends them scrambling through an elevator shaft: a long, narrow, vertical set with its own peculiar hazards. Watch for the cinematographer's use of lighting and the editor's handling of many simultaneous actions from different points of view.

14. **Heroes Unplugged.** [1:27:00] Cypher talks to the limp bodies of the crew while we see their active doubles stranded in the Matrix, connected through the fragile lifeline of a phone chord. What motivates Cypher's treachery? How well does Joe Pantoliano play the villain?

15. **Lobby Shootout.** [1:46:15] This scene took ten days to shoot. The script called for all live action—no digital work—so Reeves and Moss did nearly all the stunts themselves. Moss reportedly hurt her ankle while performing the cartwheel but kept on. Editing was difficult because the film from multiple cameras had to be coordinated to keep the parallel progress of Trinity and Neo moving forward. How do people you know respond to the scene's high volume of violence?

16. **"Dodge this."** [1:31:30] The battle on the rooftop features Neo dodging bullets in bullet time and a spectacular helicopter rescue. The screen is filled with falling shells, masonry, and other debris while the sound track roars with nonstop gunfire. How else do the filmmakers create excitement in this scene?

17. **Subway Dual.** [1:53:28] While Neo and Trinity wait by a phone booth to be rescued, a homeless man morphs into Agent Smith, and the film's final face-off begins. Trinity escapes, but Neo stays to test his newfound powers. What emboldens him to stand and fight instead of fleeing? When Trinity returns to his inert body, she kisses him, a reversal of the Sleeping Beauty story. What gives her the power to restore him to life?

22 Bend It Like Beckham

Directed by Gurinder Chadha; screenplay by Gurinder Chadha, Guljit Bindra, and Paul Mayeda Berges; produced by Gurinder Chadha and Deepak Nayar; cinematography by Jong Lin; edited by Justin Krish; art direction by Mark Scruton; production design by Nick Ellis; set decoration by Thorwald Kiefel-Kuhls and Sara Neighbour; music by Craig Pruess; released in the United States by Fox Searchlight Pictures in 2003. [112 minutes]

Jess Bhamra	*Parminder Nagra*
Jules Paxton	*Keira Knightley*
Joe	*Jonathan Rhys-Meyers*
Mr. Bhamra	*Anupam Kher*
Pinky Bhamra	*Archie Panjabi*
Mel	*Shaznay Lewis*
Alan Paxton	*Frank Harper*
Paula Paxton	*Juliet Stevenson*
Mrs. Bhamra	*Shaheen Khan*
Tony	*Ameet Chana*

Most of the movies in this section have been hailed by critics as important films, works of artistic innovation or thematic depth. Some movies, though, are meant primarily to please. We watch them more for entertainment than for any messages they might convey. From the beginning, *Bend It Like Beckham* seems to be such a film. Even reviewers who liked the movie— and most reviews were favorable—used terms like *warm-and-fuzzy, genial,* and *feel-good* to describe its many charms. The *New York Times* likened its plot to the neat, schematic shape of a sitcom, adding that it might have been titled *My Big Fat Sikh Wedding* (Scott). In a BBC interview, the director herself admitted that she "introduced an English family and the backdrop of the sister's wedding to make it more commercial" (Crowther). In fact, it was a big fat commercial success, becoming the highest-grossing film ever financed and distributed by Britain, where it was made in 2002. *Bend It Like Beckham,* then, affords an opportunity to dissect a crowd-pleaser, to understand what makes some movies irresistibly popular. At the same time, as a film that respects its characters and touches on some vital themes, it gives us a chance to ask what distinguishes skillful storytelling from mindless formula.

The plot centers on Jess Bhamra, the teenage daughter of middle-class immigrants living in West London. Jess's parents are conventional Punjabi Sikhs who moved to England from Uganda and still cling to their

Indian culture. They expect Jess to follow the lead of her older sister, Pinky, who is planning to marry a nice Indian boy in a traditional Punjabi wedding. Jess respects her family and its heritage, but she has plans of her own. She loves soccer—the British call it football—and displays considerable native talent at pickup games when she plays footie with the boys. One day, Jess meets Jules, a talented athlete who plays for a local women's soccer team. Jules encourages her to try out for the team, a fact that Jess hides from her parents. She impresses the team's coach, a handsome Irish lad named Joe, with more than her athletic gifts. Their mutual attraction threatens Jess's growing friendship with Jules, who has long harbored feelings for Joe. Meanwhile, the girls' mothers express growing disapproval of their soccer activities. Jules's superfeminine mom can't understand why her daughter prefers sports to shopping. Jess's mom wants her to stop playing "childhood games" and learn how to cook *aloo gobi*. Neither parent can appreciate her daughter's dream, even though Jules and Jess are genuinely talented and have a good shot at being recruited by a U.S. college. As Pinky's wedding day approaches and the big game draws near, the conflicts come to a head.

These ingredients—sports, romance, ethnic comedy, intergenerational disputes, and a big wedding—may not be strikingly original, but they are blended and served up with exuberance and considerable skill. A highlight of Gurinder Chadha's directing is her ability to manage stock characters without reducing them all to caricatures. Jess's parents have all the familiar mannerism of stereotypical South Asians, but they also are understandable as human beings. Anupam Kher, a veteran of more than 270 Bollywood films, plays the father as a troubled patriarch. Driven by loyalty to his ancestral beliefs and sensitive to his wife's wishes, he is also moved by a deep love for his daughter. The fact that he was once the victim of prejudice in Uganda, where the English players snubbed him on the cricket field, makes him want to protect Jess from a similar humiliation. Shaheen Khan, who plays the mother, may be comically extreme in her devotion to Indian customs and cuisine, but we can see her struggling to do her job by preparing Jess to be the wife and mother she herself was raised to be. Mrs. Paxton, Jules's flighty mother, has less depth. Juliet Stevenson, the British star comedian, plays the part for laughs. Her efforts to interest Jules in Wonderbras and stylish dresses are frenetically inane. Yet some of the domestic scenes with her husband, when she tries to cope with her suspicion that Jules is a lesbian, can evoke genuine sympathy. The two girls themselves are easy to like. Parminder Nagra (as Jess) and Keira Knightley (as Jules) bring warmth, charm, and energy to their roles. Even the minor characters are likeable. Irish actor Jonathan Rhys-Meyers makes Coach Joe emotionally and physically appealing, engaged in his own struggle against prejudice and his father's expectations. Jess's cousin Tony (Ameet Chana) has his own secrets to bear. Singer-songwriter Shaznay Lewis (of All Saints) gives a spirited performance as Mel, a black member of the women's soccer team. Nearly everyone in this movie is humanized by an internal conflict or full-bodied character development.

Gurinder Chadha was attracted to the movies while she was writing a dissertation on images of women in the media. "I got very, very interested in how powerful the media was in constructing ideas about people like me and my community," she says. "I thought it was very important to get involved." (Dawson). She became a BBC news reporter before directing several award-winning documentaries for British television. Among her early work was *I'm British But . . .* (1990), a thirty-minute exploration of young English Asians who embrace Western pop culture, and *A Nice Arrangement* (1994), a short film about a multicultural wedding. Chadha's first feature, *Bhaji on the Beach* (1993), is about a busload of Anglo-Asian women on holiday. Temporarily separated from their traditional community, they're free to explore new roles while confronting the realities of sexism, racism, and their own stultifying fears. Her second feature, *What's Cooking?* (2000), focuses on four families—Vietnamese, Mexican American, Jewish, and African American—as they celebrate Thanksgiving in the same Los Angeles neighborhood. Like her other films, it explores issues of tradition and assimilation with a light touch, and it won several awards.

The idea for *Beckham* arose during the 1998 World Cup. "I went to my local pub to watch the games and was amazed to see grown men crying on the pavements of Camden High Street when England was out of the cup," she explains. "I had got the football bug and thought, 'wouldn't it be great to take all this energy and put two girls in the middle of it all?'" Chadha set her story in West London and Southall, where she was raised. "Although I do believe it's a very different time now for girls," she says, "in other ways this film is my most autobiographical to date. Not only is the film set . . . where I grew up, but the relationship between Jess and her father is very similar to my relationship with my dad. I made this film as a tribute to him" ("Production Notes").

Chadha co-wrote the script with Guljit Bindra and Paul Mayeda Berges. For Jess's spiritual mentor, they chose David Beckham, at that time star of the Manchester United soccer team, who is also married to one of the Spice Girls. Not only is Beckham a world-class player on the field, but also in his personal life he questions public expectations about masculinity the same way that Jess and Jules question their families' notions of femininity. "In many ways, Beckham is the perfect catch for an Indian mother," says Chadha. "He loves his wife, he has a son, he is also a good father and he's changed the meaning of what we used to consider the traditional macho footballer." Beckham is also a skillful athlete, known for his ability to curve the ball around the goalie into the goal. As Chadha puts it, "we came up with the title because it also works as an excellent metaphor for the film as the girls 'bend' the rules rather than 'break' them so they can get what they want" (Dawson).

Principal photography began on June 18, 2001. Chadha shot for nine weeks in London and Shepperton Studios and then filmed the semifinal scenes over a three-day period in Hamburg, Germany. The film was released in the U.K. on April 12, 2002, and earned more there than any previous film financed and distributed in Britain. It also topped the box office charts in Australia, New Zealand, and South Africa. Its many awards include the Locarno, Sydney, and Toronto film festivals.

It's not difficult to see why the film's themes would have such wide appeal. First, there is the topic of women in sports. "The whole thing is about being a girl and the hoops that you go through to get what you want," says Chadha (Dawson). Today's students may be more accustomed than their parents to successful female athletes in field hockey or soccer (the U.S. women's team tends to fare better than its male counterpart in world soccer), but the hurdles for young women are still higher in some ways than they are for men. In modern life, as in the movies, it is often women like Mrs. Bhamra and Mrs. Paxton who are more resistant than the men. Teenage rebellion is another surefire topic. Jules and Jess have dreams and talents that their mothers don't understand. Jules, at least, has the support of her father, who plays ball with her in their backyard as if she were his son. Jess is up against stronger opposition. Her mother can see no future beyond cooking, marriage, and a well-ordered household. Her father sees no further than the bigotry that kept him from playing cricket. Besides, he believes "it isn't nice" for a lady to play football. Jess's sister is no help; she's a shopaholic with no greater aspirations than her approaching wedding day. The only member of her clan who seems to understand her is Tony, who is also hiding something. Unwilling or unable to rebel openly, Jess responds by following a curved trajectory. She neglects to tell her parents that she is on the team and sneaks out of the house for practice. When the team travels to Hamburg, she lies about her whereabouts. Even at the big wedding, she knows that she will soon exchange her sari for a team jersey and join the big game.

Complicating the intergenerational conflicts is the tension between East and West. Chadha highlights the culture clash in many ways. The portrait of a Sikh patriarch in the Bhamra living room contrasts sharply with the poster of Beckham on Jess's bedroom wall. The wedding scene—with its colorful garb, exotic foods, and Asian music—is crosscut with shots of the Hounslow Harriers performing on the soccer field. And when a sharp ring interrupts the wedding celebration, all the aunts go fumbling for their cell phones. The quarrel between tradition and assimilation has been treated in other movies about South Asian immigrants, particularly in Great Britain. *East Is East* (1999) centers on a Pakistani father and his English wife. *My Beautiful Laundrette* (1985) and *My Son the Fanatic* (1997), both based on plays by Hanif Kureishi, are about a laundry owner and a taxi driver respectively. Mira Nair's last two films, *Mississippi Masala* (1992) and *Monsoon Wedding* (2001), examine cultural differences with considerable depth. By comparing *Bend It Like Beckham* to these more pointedly political films on the one hand and to *My Big Fat Greek Wedding* (2002) on the other, it may be easier to see the dividing line between light entertainment and the kind of comedy that conveys real insights and thematic substance.

Suggested Films and Readings

More Films by Gurinder Chadha

Bhaji on the Beach (1993)

What's Cooking (2000)

Other Films about South Asian Immigrants

My Beautiful Laundrette (1985; dir. Stephen Frears)

Mississippi Masala (1992; dir. Mira Nair)

My Son the Fanatic (1997, dir. Udayan Prasad)

East Is East (1999, dir. Damien O'Donnell)

Books, Articles, and Web Sites

Crowther, Jane. Films: Interview with Gurinder Chadha. *Bend It Like Beckham*. BBC. 20 Mar. 2002. Last accessed 10 June 2004 <www.bbc.co.uk/films/2002/03/20/gurinder_chadha_bend_it_like_beckham_interview.shtml>.

Dawson, Bruce. Interview with Gurinder Chadha. *Korean Herald* 4 Apr. 2002. *Soccerphile*. Archived at <www.soccerphile.com/soccerphile/archives/wc2002/fo/co/gci.html>.

"Production Notes." *Rotten Tomatoes*. Info & Tidbits on *Bend It Like Beckham*. Last accessed 10 June 2004 <www.rottentomatoes.com/m/BendItLikeBeckham-1119809/about.php>.

Scott, A. O. "Her Mom May Kick, but a Girl Plays to Win." *New York Times* 12 Mar. 2003, late ed.: E5.

Questions for Reflection and Discussion

1. Contrast Jess's friends with her sister's friends. How do they dress, talk, and behave? How might these differences be explained?

2. Early in the film, the camera cuts back and forth between the Bhamra sisters and Jules shopping with her mom. How are the two families different and alike?

3. What does Jess's room tell us about her and her dreams? Compare her poster of Beckham to the Sikh spiritual leader's portrait in living room.

4. In what ways does Jess seem to be a typical teenager? In what ways is her life complicated by her Indian heritage and her interest in sports? What choices can she make about her future?

5. *Bend It Like Beckham* has been accused of perpetuating stereotypes. How true is this accusation? Where do you see stereotypes in the film, and how are they used? Where do you see fully developed human beings?

6. Gurinder Chadha has said, "What I try to do is show everyone's point of view, where you can sympathize with the parent's generation, the kid's generation, where the boys are coming from, where the girls are coming from." How many different points of view were you aware of while watching the film? Who do you think is right or wrong? Do you think the director takes sides?

7. How does Chadha keep the movie light and quick? Pay particular attention to her use of music, editing, and humor.

8. Trace the theme of homophobia throughout the film. What differences do you find in the treatment of Mrs. Paxton's open hostility ("Get your lesbian feet out of my shoes.") and Tony's secret?

Topics for Further Study

1. Women have a strong presence in American sports these days, but this was not always the case. Learn more about the history of women in sports. Where have female athletes made the most progress? Which sports are still largely closed to women? What predictions can you make about the future of women in these sports?

2. Find out more about British soccer star David Beckham. Why is he so famous, and why would Chadha choose his name for the title of her film?

3. Create a theme wheel for the movie. Divide a circle into sections representing sports, romance, cultural conflicts, and other themes. What portion of the film is devoted to each of these themes?

4. The *Indian Diaspora* is a term used to describe the migration of people from India to other countries. Millions were displaced from their homeland when imperial Britain imported Indian labor and soldiers to places as far-flung as Guyana, Trinidad, Malaysia, Uganda, and South Africa. Today the dispersal continues, largely voluntarily, as Punjabi, Gujarati, and other groups seek better opportunities throughout the world. Do some research on the Indian Diaspora and find out how Bollywood movies help to keep these groups connected to their traditions and one another.

5. How similar are the teenagers in this movie to those in your neighborhood? Find out more about youth and pop culture in England. What are the fashions like? Who are the stars? Are young people around the world more like one another than they are like their own parents?

6. Check the box office charts for *Bend It Like Beckham*. How do you explain its rating compared to other movies of its kind?

7. Write two alternate endings for the film, one in the spirit of *Mississippi Masala* and one more like *My Big Fat Greek Wedding*. What audiences do you have in mind? Explain your choices as you create your two scripts.

Scenes to Analyze

1. **Pickup Game.** [6:40] As Jules watches from a distance, Jess runs circles around the bare-chested neighborhood boys. Notice what the quick cutting and rapid camera work add to this scene.

2. **Jess's Room.** [7:44] In a few seconds, we get a glimpse of Jess's dreams and obstacles. Her dad, wearing a turban, enters her room and refers to her poster of Beckham as "this bald man."

3. **The Engagement Party.** [8:42] The extended family is gathered in their finest clothes at the Bhamra household. When the phone rings, every middle-aged woman on the couch reaches for her cell phone. Pay close attention to the costumes, set décor, and special props. How would you describe the humor in this scene?

4. **Welcome to the Harriers.** [12:00] This is one of several montage sequences of female camaraderie. Contrast the way these athletes play together to Pinky and her shopping friends.

5. **No More Football.** [21:15] When Mrs. Bhamra sees Jess roughhousing with the local boys, she puts her foot down. "You've played enough," she says. "I don't want shame on my family." "Your mother is right," her dad agrees. Who has the power in this contest? Later, walking with

Tony, Jess protests, "Anyone can cook *aloo gobi,* but who can bend a ball like Beckham?"

6. **Joe's Visit.** [43:24] Notice the cultural differences in this scene and the reaction shots when Jess's coach tries to explain her special talent to her parents.

7. **Clubbing.** [51:26] Joe and Jess come face to face with their feelings on the balcony of the Hamburg dance club. Trace the romantic subplot up to this point and beyond.

8. **The Winning Goal.** [1:28:40] When Jess makes the final goal kick, the defending players look like her aunts, but she bends the ball around them for the winning goal. Watch how the film editor crosscuts between the wedding and the game, contrasting the two lifestyles from which Jess must choose.

9. **Lesbians?** [1:33:26] Mrs. Paxton disrupts the wedding party with an accusation for Jess: "You've been kissing my daughter." How does the film use humor to handle the homophobia theme?

10. **No More Lies.** [1:38:00]. Jess finally stands up for herself after Tony tries to help her with more deception. "I'm not lying any more," she says. Who is in command now? How do you explain the shift in power?

11. **Off to America.** [1:42:14] Jess and Jules say goodbye at the airport. How many of the film's conflicts have been resolved? Which questions are still unanswered?

12. **End Titles.** The last scene shows Joe playing cricket with Mr. Bhamra on the lawn before the family house. What will happen next?

23 Whale Rider
Maori Title: *Te kaieke*

Directed and written by Niki Caro; based on the novel by Witi Ihimaera; produced by Tim Sanders, John Barnett, and Frank Hübner; cinematography by Leon Narbey; edited by David Coulson; art direction by Grace Mok; production design by Grant Major; music by Lisa Gerrard; released in the United States by Newmarket Films in 2002. [105 minutes]

Paikea	Keisha Castle-Hughes
Koro	Rawiri Paratene
Nanny Flowers	Vicky Haughton
Porourangi	Cliff Curtis
Uncle Rawiri	Grant Roa
Hemi	Mana Taumaunu
Shilo	Rachel House
Dog	Tammy Davis
Maka	Mabel Wharekawa
Miro	Rawinia Clarke
Miss Parata	Tahei Simpson
Hemi's dad	Roi Taimana

Whale Rider contains many of the elements of a good children's story: a young protagonist coming of age, magical connections to nature, and a journey on a whale. There is a difference, though, between a children's story and a story about children for adults. This is a film that works on several levels, skillfully layering themes of family disjunction and female empowerment with ancient myths and issues of cultural continuity and change.

At the center of the story are Paikea, an eleven-year-old New Zealand girl, and Koro, her silver-haired grandfather. Koro is the patriarch of a Maori tribe that has lived in the coastal village of Whangara for a thousand years. Koro's hopes for the future of his people are dashed at the beginning of the film when Pai's twin brother dies along with her mother during a difficult childbirth. Maori chiefs have always been firstborn males, and the child's death looks like the end of Koro's bloodline. Although Pai's father, Porourangi, would normally be next in line, he has chosen the life of an artist. He is so distraught by the loss of his wife and son that he takes off for Europe, leaving Pai in the care of his parents.

At first, Koro wants nothing to do with his newborn granddaughter. He resents her, as though she were responsible for this disruption in his family and the lifeline of his tribe. She should have died instead of his grandson, he believes. But Koro's wife, Nanny Flowers, comes to Pai's rescue. She makes Koro hold the helpless infant in his arms. Eleven years later, a special affection has developed between Koro and Pai. He rides her through the village on his bicycle while she looks at him adoringly. Yet he remains adamant about excluding her from tribal activities. When Koro begins the process of choosing a future tribal chief from among the village boys, he chases her away. Pai watches from a distance, secretly memorizing the Maori chants and enlisting her uncle to teach her how to wield the ancient war stick. Pai learns the old traditions quickly, better than the boys, and her determination is a match for Koro's obstinate adherence to the male bias of his culture. Koro fails to understand that Pai is meant to lead, a destiny manifested in her special ability to communicate with whales.

The role of Pai is played by Keisha Castle-Hughes, a twelve-year-old from Auckland who is half Australian and half Maori. She was selected from thousands of young auditioners by casting director Diana Rowan, who also discovered Anna Paquin, the Oscar-winning child actress of *The Piano* (1993). Unlike Paquin, Castle-Hughes had never acted before, not even in school productions. She was so eager for the part that she lied when asked if she could swim. When it was time to shoot the underwater scenes, she finally confessed, and a double had to be found. By then she had won over everyone on the set with her dark, intelligent eyes and her heroic performance. In a BBC interview, she explained why she was suited for the role: "I think we're both strong-willed and independent, and Pai has a great unique quality about her. She's an eleven-year-old girl who's confident about who she is and knows exactly who she is. Not many eleven-year-old girls are like that. She's a great role model for young girls. I think I'm like that too" (Brett).

Rawiri Paratene's Koro is a stern and solemn man: a dignified patriarch, stubborn and inflexible, hard on everyone, including himself. His demanding nature has taken a toll on his relationship with his first son, who wants to be an artist, not a chieftain. When Koro learns that Porourangi has chosen a European wife, he is even more incensed. His whole world seems to be falling apart. The role of Porourangi is performed by Cliff Curtis, a Maori actor whose previous parts have included Cuban, Chechen, and other ethnic characters. Curtis was eager to return to his own cultural roots. *Whale Rider* gave him a chance to play someone of his own ethnicity in a film linked to the Maori tradition of oral storytelling.

The film was shot among the Ngati Kanoahi tribe of Whangara, descendents of the whale rider legend. According to tradition, Whangara was founded by Paikea, who was lost at sea when his fishing canoe capsized.

Paikea rode to shore on the back of a whale, and custom decreed that his progeny would lead the tribe in a line of firstborn sons. That was a thousand years ago. The coastline of modern Whangara is strikingly photographed by Leon Narbey, who captures its enchantment by moonlight and in full sunlight. The lush setting is never merely picturesque, however. It is always part of the story, reminding us of the close affinity between the people and the sea.

Niki Caro became involved as the film's director in 1999. Her first feature, *Memory & Desire* (1997), had won the prize for Best Film at the New Zealand Film Awards. It was based on a story by Peter Wells about young Japanese lovers escaping to New Zealand from the repressive customs of their homeland when tragedy strikes. Producer John Barnett of South Pacific Pictures asked Caro to base her next film on Witi Ihimaera's 1987 novel *The Whale Rider*. The project had been in development for nearly ten years, going through several scripts. Caro wrote her own version, producing five drafts and several polishes in eighteen months. Not being Maori herself (she is a *pakeha*, a New Zealander of European descent), Caro consulted Maori elders to authenticate the details, but the broad vision was her own. She wanted to make "a film with a powerful, magical quality that moves effortlessly between the real and the spiritual. A film for people of all ages, that is relevant (in different ways) to both adults and children. A film that honors the original material but brings it into a real, contemporary setting" (*Au-Cinema*). In order to connect with the people of Whangara, she studied their language and addressed them in their own tongue. She took special care to enter their community slowly, through face-to-face meetings, gradually developing trust and mutual respect (Mottesheard). She found it "an enormous privilege to work with these people in this place" (Caro).

Maori culture is part of the story. Much of the action takes place in and around the meetinghouse (*Wharenui*), built on a design dating back to the twelfth century. Structurally, it represents the human body, with a carved head at the front apex of the roof and large sideboards stretched out like arms. Within are intricate carvings and latticework embodying Maori history, myths, and legends (*Maori Treasures*). It is in the meetinghouse that Koro welcomes his son with the traditional male greeting (*Hongi*), whereby men press foreheads and noses together in a gesture of intimacy and peace. Later on, women lead the formal welcome ceremony (*Powhiri*), a special call and response (*Karanga*) in which the hosts (led by Nanny Flowers) welcome the visitors (led by Pai) into the sacred courtyard (*Marae-Atea*). While women have a place in traditional Maori customs, they are also bound by strong taboos. This explains why Pai says nothing when Koro orders her to move from the front bench in the courtyard; she has no speaking rights and should not be sitting with the men. It also explains why he does not allow her to use the fighting stick (*taiaha*) when he gives lessons to the young village boys. When she finally sits beside him in the war canoe (*Waka Taua*), she has earned an honored position previously reserved only for men.

For all these authentic details, though, *Whale Rider* is not an ethnological tract. Nor is it, like *Once Were Warriors* (1994)—another well-known film about Maori life—primarily about culture clash. Its themes are more universal. This is a story about family, identity, abandonment, grief, fear, and love. Koro is motivated by his deeply felt responsibilities as tribal leader; Porourangi seeks to find his own way as an artist; Pai is moved by a child's need for acceptance and a maturing sense of her rightful place in the life of her community. Caro tells the story with a mixture of humor and respect. The Maori women smoke, play cards, and tell crude jokes. Uncle Rawiri appears whenever food is on the table. A cardboard whale farts on stage. Yet Koro's anger is chillingly palpable. Pai's desperation, when she dedicates her school speech to her absent grandfather, is painfully real. And the night scenes of villagers moving among beached whales add an authentically spiritual dimension. These qualities are why Roger Ebert called *Whale Rider* "transcendent," while the *New York Times* review spoke of "the inspiring resonance of found art" (Mitchell). They are probably why adults as well as children will continue to find magic in the film.

Suggested Films and Readings

More Films by Niki Caro

Sure to Rise (1994) Short

Memory & Desire (1997)

Other Films Featuring Maori Culture

The Piano (1993; dir. Jane Campion)

Once Were Warriors (1994; dir. Lee Tamahori)

Books and Articles

Au-Cinema. Whale Rider. Last accessed 10 June 2004 <www.au-cinema.com/ Whale-Rider.htm>.

Brett, Anwar. Films: Interview with Keisha Castle-Hughes. *Whale Rider. BBC.*° Last accessed 16 June 2004 <www.bbc.co.uk/films/2003/07/08/ keisha_castle_hughes_whale_rider_interview.shtml>.

Caro, Niki. Director Commentary. *Whale Rider.* DVD Special Edition. Columbia TriStar, 2003.

Ebert, Roger. "Powerful *Whale Rider* Doesn't Sink to Obvious Clichés." Rev. of *Whale Rider*. *Chicago Sun-Times* 20 June 2003: 32.

Maori Treasures. Te Whanau Paneke Incorporated. Last accessed 10 June 2004 <www.maoritreasures.com/konae_aronui/customs.htm>.

Mitchell, Elvis. "A Girl Born to Lead, Fighting the Odds." *New York Times* 6 June 2003, late ed.: E14.

Mottesheard, Ryan. "Girl Power: New Zealand Writer/Director Niki Caro Talks about *Whale Rider*." *indieWIRE*. Last accessed 10 June 2004 <www.indiewire.com/people/people_030606caro.html>.

Questions for Reflection and Discussion

1. Is *Whale Rider* primarily for children or for adults? What features of the film might appeal to each group? Compare it to other films you know for or about children.

2. Keisha Castle-Hughes, the twelve-year-old actress who plays the part of Pai, says that her character is a good role model for young girls today. Do you agree or disagree? What positive or negative qualities does she possess? Compare her to Jess in *Bend It Like Beckham*.

3. Some viewers consider Koro to be a male chauvinist, stubbornly refusing to allow his granddaughter to be equal to the village boys. Others believe that he is responsibly striving to maintain his heritage, upholding a thousand-year-old tradition. How do you regard his attitude toward Pai? How should he have responded to her pleas for acceptance and equality?

4. Consider the story's other characters, such as Nanny Flowers, Porourangi, Uncle Rawiri, and Hemi. What personal traits do they reveal? What roles do they play in Pai's life?

5. The people of Whangara have followed Maori traditions for more than a millennium. Where do you see signs in the film of their assimilation into European culture? Are these changes basically beneficial or harmful? Why?

6. At one point, Koro says, "You don't mess around with sacred things." What is he referring to? What things are sacred in the story? To what extent do the people of Whangara respect their sacredness?

7. Director Niki Caro tried to give her film a spiritual dimension that she found in the original book. How well has she integrated spirituality and everyday life, realism and the features of myth?

8. There is an ongoing debate about who should tell indigenous stories. Some believe that only Native Americans or Maori filmmakers should

make movies about their own people. Explain why you agree or disagree. Does it matter to you that Niki Caro is not a native Maori but a New Zealander of European descent?

Topics for Further Study

1. Read Witi Ihimaera's 1987 novel on which the film is based. What difference does it make that Uncle Rawiri narrates the story? What other changes do you notice? How closely do the characters in the book resemble those in the movie? How well does the movie capture the style and spirit of the original?

2. Find out more about Maori culture. What traditions do these native inhabitants of New Zealand still follow? How accurately does *Whale Rider* represent their customs, stories, and beliefs?

3. In 1994, Lee Tamahori directed *Once Were Warriors,* which is based on a novel about an urbanized Maori family. Watch the film and compare its characters to the village community of Whangara. How does modern life affect the people in Tamahori's film? Where do you find similar effects in *Whale Rider*?

4. Listen to Niki Caro's commentary on the DVD version of *Whale Rider.* Take note of what you learn about her intentions and the production of the film.

Scenes to Analyze

1. **Opening.** [0:00] The beginning of the film is narrated by Pai: "When I was born, my twin brother died and took our mother with him." Notice how extreme close-ups, odd angles, mournful music, and other film techniques are used to capture the sadness and confusion of the moment. Caro explained that the Maori lament for the dead, heard on the sound track, is not translated out of respect for the lyricism of the Maori language. Should she have used subtitles?

2. **"Take her away."** [6:14] When Koro rejects his newborn granddaughter, Nanny Flowers makes him hold the child in his arms. At one point, we see Flowers and Pai in the center foreground speaking to Porourangi on the right while Koro is isolated in the background in the left panel. How else is the wide screen used to represent relationships?

3. **Porourangi's Art.** [13:37] In the great hall of the meetinghouse, Koro looks on while his son touches the sculpted figures of his ancestors.

Later, after an intimate exchange of greetings, Porourangi reveals a secret during a slide show of his artwork [20:10]. Contrast the words and body language of father and son in these two scenes.

4. **Knotty Lesson.** [17:25] While fixing the outboard motor, Koro teaches Pai how to splice rope to make it stronger. When she applies the lesson and makes the motor run, she receives his anger instead of praise. What emotional dynamics are working here, and how are they conveyed?

5. **War Dance.** [47:57] Koro teaches the village boys a traditional war dance (*haka*), which involves bulging eyes, protruding tongues, and sharp slaps to the chest. Hemi's father arrives with his mates in an American car. Later, when Koro discovers that Pai has been practicing in secret with the *taiaha*, or fighting stick, he shouts at her in anger, "What have you done?" [53:00]. Contrast the assimilated adults in this scene with Koro's efforts to uphold ancient customs.

6. **Pai's Speech.** [1:09:15] The scene in which Pai dedicates her school speech to Koro is one of the film's most moving moments. It was originally shot with two cameras, but the second camera ran out of film during shooting. Can you tell? In addition to Pai's performance, what cinematic choices (music, camera work, editing, costumes, makeup, set design) contribute to the emotional impact of this scene?

7. **Beached Whales.** [1:16:24] Caro could not afford sophisticated electronic whales for this important scene. The synthetic creatures had men inside, and only two whales were capable of movement. Many of the people tending to the beached whales were nonactors from the Whangara community, actual descendents of the whale rider story. They worked in bitter cold under an overcast sky. How realistic is the final effect?

Appendix 1
More Great Films

There are many ways to organize a film unit or course. Film adaptations can be matched with the literature on which they're based. Films can also be grouped thematically, like literature. They can be studied by director, genre, period, or nationality. What follows are a few suggested titles arranged to illustrate some popular options.

Film and Literature

Many English teachers feel most comfortable teaching a course such as Fiction into Film, Film as Literature, or some variation. Typically, these courses stress continuities between movies and written fiction. They often compare film versions of short stories and novels with the original texts, noting differences and similarities as well as investigating the process of adaptation. They may also treat film as a form of literature in its own right, tracing traditions of storytelling from oral cultures to our own technical-minded times. Chapter 1 offers some ideas for studying adaptations.

Such a course might include these course objectives:

1. To read and understand film as a form of literature, recognizing the traditional elements of fiction—plot, character, setting, point of view, symbol, theme—in one of our culture's most recent and influential forms of storytelling

2. To contrast written, oral, and visual modes of storytelling in order to appreciate the major differences between film and earlier forms of narrative

3. To develop film literacy through a working knowledge of the basic technical and critical vocabulary of motion pictures

4. To analyze film as a cultural phenomenon: how it reflects and shapes the changing nature of our heroes, values, and beliefs

5. To question our roles as passive spectators and to increase the ability to watch films actively and critically

6. To develop guidelines for judging films in personal, aesthetic, historical, and ideological terms

Selected Movie Adaptations

Wuthering Heights (1939) William Wyler

Pride and Prejudice (1940) Robert Z. Leonard

Oliver Twist (1948) David Lean

The Old Man and the Sea (1958) John Sturges

The Innocents (1961) Jack Clayton (an adaptation of *The Turn of the Screw*)

To Kill a Mockingbird (1962) Robert Mulligan

Billy Budd (1962) Peter Ustinov

The Swimmer (1968) Frank Perry

The Godfather (1972) Francis Ford Coppola

One Flew over the Cuckoo's Nest (1975) Milos Forman

A Passage to India (1984) David Lean

The Silence of the Lambs (1991) Jonathan Demme

Forrest Gump (1994) Robert Zemeckis

The Shawshank Redemption (1994) Frank Darabont

Clueless (1995) Amy Heckerling (a modern adaptation of *Emma*)

Lord of the Rings: The Fellowship of the Ring (2001) Peter Jackson

Harry Potter and the Sorcerer's Stone (2001) Chris Colombus

Adaptation (2002) Spike Jones (an adaptation of *The Orchid Thief*)

Changing Images

Another popular approach to film study is to focus on a specific group, such as women or teenagers, and study how that group is represented in the movies. An images course might be organized chronologically to show how women or teens have appeared on screen during different eras in history. Or it might compare different cultures, attitudes, and points of view. The movies could be mainstream Hollywood films, which both reflect and help shape popular conceptions (and misconceptions), but it is often a good idea to include some alternative views as well from independent filmmakers or films from other cultures. See Chapter 8 for a closer look at issues of representation.

Changing Images of Women in Film
(arranged chronologically)

Mildred Pierce (1945) Michael Curtiz

Fried Green Tomatoes (1991) Jon Avnet

Thelma & Louise (1991) Ridley Scott

Mississippi Masala (1992) Mira Nair

The Joy Luck Club (1993) Wayne Wang

Orlando (1993) Sally Potter

Clueless (1995) Amy Heckerling

Waiting to Exhale (1995) Forest Whitaker

Courage under Fire (1996) Edward Zwick

A Price above Rubies (1998) Boaz Yakin

Girl, Interrupted (1999) James Mangold

Erin Brockovich (2000) Steven Soderbergh
Bend It Like Beckham (2002) Gurinder Chadha

(arranged by country)
An Angel at My Table (1990) Jane Campion [New Zealand]
The Story of Qiu Ju (1992) Zhang Yimou [China]
Antonia's Line (1995) Marleen Gorris [Netherlands]
Run Lola Run (1998) TomTykwer [Germany]
Monsoon Wedding (2001) Mira Nair [India]

Images of Native Americans in Film

Stagecoach (1939) John Ford
The Searchers (1956) John Ford
Cheyenne Autumn (1964) John Ford
Little Big Man (1970) Arthur Penn
Dances with Wolves (1990) Kevin Costner
Smoke Signals (1998) Chris Eyre

Black Images on Film

The Birth of a Nation (1915) D. W. Griffith
Within our Gates (1919/1920) Oscar Micheaux
Gone with the Wind (1939) Victor Fleming
A Raisin in the Sun (1961) Daniel Petrie
The Learning Tree (1969) Gordon Parks
A Soldier's Story (1984) Norman Jewison
Glory (1989) Edward Zwick
Do the Right Thing (1989) Spike Lee
Boyz N the Hood (1991) John Singleton
Waiting to Exhale (1995) Forest Whitaker

Thematic Approaches to Film

Teachers who want to integrate movies into a literature course often do this thematically. If the class is reading several works on the theme of growing up, for example, *Stand by Me* and *The Graduate* might be added to the reading list. Students get to explore the transition from childhood to adulthood in another medium. The following themes and movies are meant to suggest some possibilities.

Growing Up

Oliver Twist (1948) David Lean
Rebel without a Cause (1955) Nicholas Ray
Lord of the Flies (1963) Peter Brook

The Graduate (1967) Mike Nichols

The Last Picture Show (1971) Peter Bogdanovich

The Outsiders (1983) Francis Ford Coppola

Stand by Me (1986) Rob Reiner

Overcoming Disabilities

The Miracle Worker (1962) Arthur Penn

The Elephant Man (1980) David Lynch

Rain Man (1988) Barry Levinson

My Left Foot (1989) Jim Sheridan

Awakenings (1990) Penny Marshall

A Beautiful Mind (2001) Ron Howard

School Days

Blackboard Jungle (1955) Richard Brooks

Rebel without a Cause (1955) Nicholas Ray

Fast Times at Ridgemont High (1982) Amy Heckerling

The Breakfast Club (1985) John Hughes

Stand and Deliver (1987) Ramón Menéndez

School Daze (1988) Spike Lee

Dead Poets Society (1989) Peter Weir

Good Will Hunting (1997) Gus Van Sant

Election (1999) Alexander Payne

Nature versus the Human Race

King Kong (1933) Merian C. Cooper and Ernest B. Schoedsack

Moby Dick (1956) John Huston

The Birds (1963) Alfred Hitchcock

Twister (1996) Jan de Bont

The Perfect Storm (2000) Wolfgang Petersen

The World Looks at War

All Quiet on the Western Front (1930) Lewis Milestone [USA]

Grand Illusion (1937) Jean Renoir [France]

The Best Years of Our Lives (1946) William Wyler [USA]

Ballad of a Soldier (1959) Grigori Chukhraj [USSR]

Yojimbo (1961) Akira Kurosawa [Japan]

Dr. Strangelove (1964) Stanley Kubrick [England]

Das Boot (1981) Wolfgang Petersen [West Germany]

No Man's Land (2001) Danis Tanović [Bosnia-Herzegovina]

Genres

Chapter 7 describes some of the more popular film genres around which a course on film can be created. An entire course on film genres, or a single genre, might explore the features (iconography, typical plots, characters, settings) that characterize the genre, its historical evolution, and its special appeal to audiences. Or films can be integrated into a literature course that deals with the same genres, pairing, for example, *2001: A Space Odyssey* (1968) and *The Matrix* (1999) with stories by Arthur C. Clarke and Philip K. Dick.

Science Fiction

Things to Come (1936) William Cameron Menzies

Forbidden Planet (1956) Fred McLeod Wilcox

Invasion of the Body Snatchers (1956) Don Siegel

Fantastic Voyage (1966) Richard Fleischer

Close Encounters of the Third Kind (1977) Steven Spielberg

The Matrix (1999) Andy Wachowski and Larry Wachowski

Screwball Comedy

It Happened One Night (1934) Frank Capra

My Man Godfrey (1936) Gregory La Cava

Bringing Up Baby (1938) Howard Hawks

Mr. Smith Goes to Washington (1939) Frank Capra

His Girl Friday (1940) Howard Hawks

Mystery

The Maltese Falcon (1941) John Huston

Double Indemnity (1944) Billy Wilder

The Killers (1946) Robert Siodmak

Touch of Evil (1958) Orson Welles

Chinatown (1974) Roman Polanski

The Musical

42nd Street (1933) Lloyd Bacon

Swing Time (1936) George Stevens

Singin' in the Rain (1952) Gene Kelly and Stanley Donen

West Side Story (1961) Robert Wise and Jerome Robbins

Oliver! (1968) Carol Reed

Tommy (1975) Ken Russell

Moulin Rouge! (2001) Baz Lurhmann

Chicago (2002) Rob Marshall

Appendix 2
Student Film Study Projects

The following projects are examples of what students can do to supplement class screenings and discussions. I have used them all in my classes.

1. Group Viewing Profile

Complete the following questionnaire about your movie viewing and then compare your findings with those of several other students. Prepare a group profile that reflects the preferences and habits of your group. What is your group's preferred format for watching films? What genres do you have in common?

  A. How many films do you generally watch a month? Distinguish between films that you see at a theater, on television (broadcast TV, cable, pay-per-view), on the Internet, and on video or DVD.

  B. What are your favorite movies and movie genres (action, comedy, science fiction, romance, and so on)?

  C. What special habits do you notice about the way you watch movies? Do you like to eat while watching them at home? Do you prefer to watch films alone, with a friend, or in a group? Do you watch videos straight through or do you jump around with the remote? How do these habits depend on the kind of movie you are watching or where you're watching it?

2. Oral Presentation

This is an opportunity to study one film in some detail and share what you learn with others in the class. You are encouraged to work in groups of two or three for each presentation. Each group selects a film from the course listing (films we will be screening later in the term) and prepares a brief introduction, handouts, and questions for discussion.

  The introduction will be oral. It may include background information about the film's origins, its creators and cast, its reception, or its main themes. You may also want to point out particular things to look for in the film. Please limit your introductory remarks to ten minutes or less.

  The handouts should include film credits (director, scriptwriter, principal actors, etc.), further readings (books, articles, reviews, Web sites), and study questions. Please bring enough copies for everyone.

  Using your study questions as a guide, lead a class discussion after viewing the film. You may want to focus on the acting, directing, film techniques, or theme. You may explore the class's emotional responses or examine the film's symbolic levels.

Note: You will be graded as a group, so full group cooperation is a must. Be sure to select people you can work with.

3. Behind the Scenes

We often appreciate a movie more when we know how it was made. What went into its creation behind the scenes? How, for example, did the art director design the sets for *Citizen Kane*? How did the photographer achieve those striking camera movements and lighting effects? Where did the ideas for the screenplay come from, and what did each writer contribute to the script?

This assignment is an opportunity to look behind the scenes at a particular aspect of filmmaking that interests you. First, select a film you would like to learn more about. Then, choose one of the following topics and write a report on what you learn.

A. *Script Writing*. Who was responsible for the film script? Where did the main idea originate? If the film is based on literature, consult the original text and compare it to the final film.

B. *Photography*. Who was the film's chief cinematographer? What is he or she most noted for? Are there any technical innovations in camera work or lighting? How were they achieved?

C. *Set Design*. Who was involved in selecting and creating the film's sets? Were any special problems encountered in making the sets? How were they solved? How important are the sets in the final film?

D. *Music*. Does the film use familiar music or an original score? What musical decisions were made by the composer? What effects was the composer striving for? Are different melodies used for different characters or scenes? How do they contribute to the total film experience?

E. *Direction*. Some directors have a stronger hand than others in the making of a film. Directors may be interested in different elements of filmmaking. What role did the director have in producing the film you chose? What are the director's hallmarks in this and other films?

F. *Acting*. Select two or three actors in the film and find out more about them. Why do you think they were chosen for the film? What other roles have they played? Are they versatile or stereotyped? What can you learn about their behavior on or off the set during the film's production?

G. *Reception*. Do some research to find out how the film was received during its first release. What did the critics say? How did the general public respond? How do you account for the reception in its own time and today?

4. Shot-by-Shot Analysis

Good movies, like good stories, poems, and plays, are best read more than once. Under close analysis, a well-made film can reveal qualities and meanings that we miss the first time through. The purpose of this assignment is to take another, careful look at part of a familiar film in order to appreciate how it was made and how it works.

A. Select a film to study from the course list. View the entire film and then choose a scene (from ten to twenty shots in length) to analyze.

B. Do a shot-by-shot analysis of the scene. Your analysis should include the following for each shot:

1. A brief description of the shot (action, setting, characters)
2. Framing (close-up, medium shot, long shot)
3. Camera angles (low angle, high angle, eye level)
4. Camera movement (tilt, crane, zoom, pan, tracking, none)
5. Lighting (high key, low key, back lighting, front lighting, normal)
6. Sound (describe any dialogue, music, voice-over, or sound effects)
7. Transitions (cut, dissolve, wipe, other optical effects)

Note: You may list the elements (1–7) for each shot or describe them in paragraph form, but they should all be accounted for.

C. Answer the following questions about your chosen scene:

1. *Plot.* How does this scene contribute to the ongoing story? Give a brief overview of your chosen film (what is it about?) and explain how the scene fits in.
2. *Point of view.* Does this scene present an objective view of events, or does it represent someone's subjective account? Explain. How is the camera used to emphasize this point of view?
3. *Character.* What does this scene tell you about the major character or characters? Refer as specifically as you can to the actors' movements, words, and dress as revealed by the camera.
4. *Tone.* Describe the overall mood of this scene. Is it mysterious, funny, sad? How do the lighting and camera work help to create this mood?

You are encouraged to complete the shot-by-shot analysis in groups of two. Students have found that collaborative viewing helps them see more clearly (four eyes are better than two) and think more sharply (discussion nourishes ideas) than they would alone. You are expected to answer the questions in part C by yourself.

5. Contemporary Film Review

This assignment is an opportunity to apply what you have learned this term to a contemporary film of your own choice. Select a new film that has just been released or one that has been made available recently for home viewing. Choose a movie that genuinely interests you or puzzles you—a movie that you want to think about and examine more carefully than usual. Since this will be a critical review, you need to go beyond a simple statement of your likes and dislikes. Be prepared to use what you have learned about film technique, theory, and history to illuminate this film. Find out more about the director, the actors, and the issues so you can make an informed evaluation. You might want to consider some of the following topics in your review:

A. *Personal Issues.* What struck the most responsive chords in you? How can you account for such a strong emotional or intellectual response? To what extent do you believe that your response can be generalized to other viewers? Why?

B. *Technique.* Were there any exceptionally good (or bad) uses of music, dialogue, camera work, editing, or special effects? Considering what you now know about the process of producing a film, what are the film's technical strengths and weaknesses?

C. *Acting.* What were the principal roles and how well were they performed? Were the actors typecast or miscast? How credible were their performances?

D. *Plot.* Outline just enough of the story so a reader who has not seen the film can understand your comments. How original, how compelling, did you find the plot?

E. *Themes.* What are the main ideas or issues of the film? Is it a simple love story, or does it make a thought-provoking statement about certain kinds of relationships? Are there any hidden or blatant messages? Are the messages distracting, intrusive, or integrated with the plot?

F. *Genre.* Does this film belong to a class of similar films, such as Westerns, horror films, or musical comedies? If so, what other films does it resemble? What are the common characteristics of these films? Why do you think this genre is popular today?

G. *Representation.* How does the film represent different kinds of people: men and women, rich and poor, various ethnic groups? Why do you think it represents them in this way?

H. *Ideology.* What cultural beliefs (e.g., about sexuality, politics, family) were challenged or confirmed by the film? How was this accomplished?

6. Fiction into Film

Most movies these days seem to be based on books. Literary classics are revived for the modern screen, bestsellers are converted into box office sales, and even obscure stories become major motion pictures. This is your chance to adapt a work of written fiction into film. In the process, you'll learn what goes into the making of a movie, you'll appreciate the differences between two important media, and you'll become a better reader of both fiction and film.

Begin by reading lots of fiction: short stories, novels, and narrative poems that might lend themselves to adaptation. Your job is to find a promising story and explain its cinematic possibilities to the others in your group. This can be done in a written film proposal that outlines the plot, sketches the main characters, suggests locations for the major scenes, and speculates on the technical challenges a camera crew might face.

Re-read the original story closely with the film in mind. Look for details of character to help you cast the principal actors. Pay attention to the setting so you can scout locations and design interior sets. You'll need to be aware of the story's point of view in order to decide on camera setups for each shot. Most important, you'll need to understand the story's tone and theme if your film is going to be faithful to the original.

Once the group has decided on a story, the film proposal can be transformed into a storyboard or shooting script. A storyboard tells the story, shot by shot, in pictures and text. The pictures show what the camera will see. The text provides the dialogue and action; it also gives cues about camera position, lighting, editing, and other production technicalities. A shooting script describes each shot, but without pictures. Like the storyboard, the shooting script is a blueprint for constructing the final film.

In addition to the actors and scriptwriters, your group will need production specialists, including a director to direct the action and overall shooting of each scene; a script supervisor to plan each day of shooting and check the results against the storyboard or shooting script; a cinematographer to set up and operate the camera; a set designer to create the sets or furnish them with props; a lighting crew to illuminate each indoor scene; a sound technician in charge of the sound track (sound effects, music, dialogue); and an editor to splice together the final film, or combine the final video electronically if you use videotape.

A successful film production depends on many things, not the least of which is responsible group participation. Every member of the group has a specific job to do. The group depends on everyone doing her or his job reliably. Only if everybody works together can a work of fiction come alive on film.

7. How Films Are Made

This is a competitive activity. Your group will compete with other groups in the class to identify the steps involved in filmmaking and the specialists who perform each task. In your group, list as many steps—in order—as your group can think of, from the original conception to the final screening. For each step, try to give the professional title of the person or people responsible for that phase of film production. The group that can prepare the most complete, accurate list wins the competititon.

8. Evolution of a Genre

Select several clips from films that illustrate changes in a film genre over time. You might choose, for example, combat films from the time of World War II, the

Korean War, Vietnam, and other recent conflicts. Or you might choose films from a single war (*The Green Berets*, 1968; *Apocalypse Now*, 1979; *Platoon*, 1986). Explore the changes reflected in these clips. How do these films reflect historical attitudes toward combat? How do they show changes in film technique and popular taste? Other genres to consider include science fiction, Westerns, romance, comedy, adventure, and film noir.

9. Compare the Classic and the Remake

Select comparable scenes from two versions of the same story and screen them in succession. You might show scenes from J. Lee Thompson's *Cape Fear* (1962) and Scorsese's 1991 remake in order to explore the evolution of film noir. You might compare the original *King Kong* (1933) with one of its more recent incarnations (1968, 1976, 1986) to trace changes in special effects. Or you might show *The Searchers* (1956) and *Star Wars* (1977) to see how Lucas borrowed from Ford to re-create the sci-fi genre in the image of the Western.

10. Case Study

Do a case study of a movie star. Identify the star's three levels of identity: the real person, the actor's roles (the kinds of characters he or she plays in the movies), and the star's persona (the image projected in the popular media). Cull your information from sources such as movie magazines, advertisements, posters, talk shows, documentaries, the Internet, and the films themselves. Analyze the images you find. What impressions are they intended to convey? How do you account for your own response to these images? How do you explain the star's popularity?

11. Content Analysis

Sociologists do a lot of counting. They count the number of violent acts or instances of "explicit language" in films to study trends in social behavior or censorship. They analyze the roles given to women or minorities in order to follow patterns of representation over time. Do some counting of your own to prepare for a discussion of representation and influence: to what degree do movies reflect reality or help shape reality?

12. Film Segmentation

A film segmentation breaks down the structure of a film into its component parts. It identifies the main elements of the story and shows how these elements are arranged. Sometimes the story is told chronologically, as a straight narrative. Sometimes it is presented as a flashback or a series of jumps in time, as in *Pulp Fiction* (1994) or *Memento* (2001). Use this partial segmentation of *To Kill a Mockingbird* (1962) as a guide:

1. Credit Sequence: Close-ups of objects set nostalgic mood and introduce thematic symbols.

2. Maycomb, Alabama: Daybreak. Sets story in rural South of 1930s. Introduces Scout, Atticus, Jem, and Dill. Atticus is "too old to

play football for the Methodists." Dill learns about the mysterious Boo Radley next door.

3. Finch Yard: Atticus and the children greet the ornery Mrs. Dubose.

4. Scout's Room: She reads aloud to Atticus and asks about her dead mother.

5. Front Porch: Judge Taylor asks Atticus to take the case of Tom Robinson, a Negro accused of raping a white woman, Mayella Ewell.

Select a film you want to study in this way. Identify the major scenes and notice how they are arranged. Write an explanation of your findings, including any patterns of narrative progression, symmetry, zigzagging, or circularity. What is the overall shape of the plot? How does the narrative pattern contribute to the movie's theme?

13. Direct This Scene

Read the following descrption of a scene from Brian De Palma's *Scarface* (1983):

> Miami 1950. The inmates in a Cuban refugee camp have begun to riot. Hundreds of men are burning tents and attacking guards with pipes, sticks, and rocks. In the general mayhem, one man is pulled out of a telephone booth. Blinded by broken glass, he is pushed through the crowd and staggers into a tent where boisterous prisoners are shouting and wrecking everything in sight. Suddenly, he looks up and sees that he is being followed. One of his stalkers peers at him from beyond a bunk bed. Another, closer, holds a knife. The hunted man tries to escape through the crowd, but he is struck two knife blows in the stomach, one by each assailant. He staggers and falls. He is dead.

How would you shoot and edit this scene if you were the director? Use a storyboard to help you visualize it shot by shot. For each shot, draw a rough sketch of the actors (stick figures will do fine) and any significant props. Beneath each sketch, describe the following: (1) action (what happens in the shot); (2) framing (CU, MS, LS, ECU, ELS) and camera angle (low angle, high angle); (3) any camera movement (track, boom, pan, tilt, zoom); (4) lighting (low key, high key, backlighting); and (5) sound (dialogue, sound effects, voice-over, music).

> Example: MS of the stalker from below. Camera zooms in to CU of his brooding face in shadow, then tilts down to show a knife cradled in his hand. The switchblade flashes as it opens. Stalker: "I have something for you, Tony." Music swells.

Appendix 3
Great Film Web Sites

The World Wide Web has become an indispensable tool for learning about film. Without leaving your computer, you can find up-to-date information on recent movies or the classics, research various topics in depth, and locate film programs or distributors across the country. You can download entire movie scripts, sample independent movies in streaming video, or play the movie stock market in an interactive game. Although Web sites come and go, the following movie Web sites have been active for several years.

Individual Movies

BBC films
www.bbc.co.uk/films/

> In addition to the usual plot summaries, reviews, and background information for current movies, the British Broadcasting Corporation presents short interviews with actors and film directors.

The Internet Movie Database
www.imdb.com

> One of the most widely used film archives on the Web, the IMDB features a searchable database of over 260,000 film and television productions made since 1892. Users can also find thousands of articles about the industry, movie stars, and new releases. The site includes themed message boards, trivia games, and an extensive photo gallery. For those who want inside information, there is a section users must pay for with links to business contacts and hundreds of movies in production.

Moviefone
www.moviefone.com/

> Frankly commercial, like its telephone counterpart, Moviefone.com gives showtimes for all movies in theatrical release. You can see what's playing in your neighborhood by theater, title, or genre. The site also offers lots of peppy features about the stars and events of human interest behind the screen. Now that America Online, Inc., owns the site, AOL users have access to additional features.

Movie Review Query Engine
www.mrqe.com

> This is the first place to go for a comprehensive listing of film reviews on the Internet. More than 36,000 titles are available, plus

convenient links to film festivals, recent releases, and the most popular recent movies.

New York Times **Current Movies**
www.nytimes.com/pages/movies/index.html

> Subscribers have free access to the newspaper's impressive archives as well as current film reviews. Each review includes a listing of cast and crew.

Rotten Tomatoes
www.rottentomatoes.com/

> If you're looking to compare reviews, this is the place to come. Search a recent title and the site displays quotations from scores of film reviews with links to full texts. The reviews are culled from regular print and online sources. A tomatometer rating summarizes the film's total score, showing the percentage of reviews that consider it fresh or rotten.

TV Guide
www.tvguide.com/movies

> The Web site for this popular magazine offers reliable thumbnail descriptions of movie personalities and the many films that are shown on television, plus links to full cast and credits. By selecting your cable TV provider, you can tailor a weekly schedule of upcoming films in your area.

Film Research

Drew's Script-O-Rama
www.script-o-rama.com

> Here you'll find links to dozens of famous film scripts and transcripts, many downloadable. For some titles, you can compare early drafts with revisions and the final shooting script. The list includes *The Godfather, The Matrix,* and many of the other movies featured in this book.

The Greatest Films
www.filmsite.org

> If you're looking for more depth, consult this valuable resource by Tim Dirks. Originally conceived as a guide to the "100 Best Films," it has expanded to include hundreds more film titles from classical Hollywood as well as topics such as movie genres, film terms, and star filmographies. Dirks writes with a lively style and thickens his articles with fascinating production information as well as generous selections from movie scripts.

UC Berkeley Media Resources Center
www.lib.berkeley.edu/MRC/FilmBibMenu.html

> The University of California at Berkeley offers one of the most com-

prehensive listings of film studies resources. It includes extensive academic bibliographies and links to books and journals in its collection. UC Berkeley's list of annotated links to online sources is a good place to begin any serious research.

Film Education

Filmmaker.com
www.filmmaker.com/

> This homepage for filmmakers announces funding opportunities, contests, film festivals, and the like. Users can also download a number of production, editing, and writing tools.

Media Literacy Clearinghouse
http://www.med.sc.edu:1081/

> Frank Baker's Web site, designed for K–12 educators who want to learn more about media literacy, provides links to dozens of excellent resources, including the National Telemedia Council, the Center for Media Literacy, and the Alliance for a Media Literate America.

Sample Course Syllabi
www.screensite.org

> This page from the University of Alabama's ScreenSite provides links to film course syllabi from around the world.

Screen/Writing Resources
www.auburn.edu/~rileyjl/screenwriting/home.html

> This is a new site "devoted to gathering and sharing useful resources for educators interested in incorporating film and television in writing instruction." In addition to a list of useful links, it includes a section on class assignments and lesson plans.

UFVA Film School Directory
www.temple.edu/ufva/dirs/text52usa.htm

> The University Film and Video Association lists film schools and departments by state.

Yahoo Film School Directory
http://dir.yahoo.com/Entertainment/Movies_and_Film/Film_Schools/

> Yahoo's listing of film schools is alphabetical.

Education and Entertainment

FilmSound.org
http://filmsound.org/

> Follow the fascinating acoustic world of movies with updated articles on sound effects, film sound history, Foley artistry, sound design for recent movies, and much more.

Hollywood Stock Exchange
www.hsx.com

> Trade paper money and follow the fortunes of new films and rising stars. Besides being lots of fun, this is an excellent interactive tool for learning about the economic risks and rewards of the movie industry.

IFILM
www.ifilm.net

> For those who like to watch their films online, here is a site that offers clips from independent movies in streaming video. A fast modem is required.

The Movie Cliches List
www.moviecliches.com

> This humorous Web site lists well-worn film formulae by topic, from alcohol and aliens to women and war.

The Movie Sounds Page
www.moviesounds.com/

> Download sound bites from well-known films—if you don't mind all the ads along the way.

Film Journals

Film Quarterly
www.ucpress.edu/journals/fq/

> Intended for informed filmgoers beyond the narrow range of academic readers.

Journal of Popular Film and Television
www.findarticles.com/cf_0/m0412/mag.jhtml

> Features articles on the commercial film and television industry, including critical essays, sociopolitical perspectives, and book reviews.

Kinoeye
www.kinoeye.org/

> Specializes in European cinema.

Sight and Sound
www.bfi.org.uk/sightandsound/archive/index.html

> Offers selections from the British Film Institute's premier journal of film.

Studies in French Cinema
www.ncl.ac.uk/crif/sfc/home.htm

> A refereed journal for teachers and students of French film history, genre studies, theory, and technique.

Film Organizations

American Film Institute
www.afi.com/education/

> The AFI is "the preeminent national organization dedicated to advancing and preserving film, television and other forms of the moving image." Founded in 1967, it has a mandate to promote film education through its Conservatory, sponsored screenings, and various publications.

Center for Cognitive Studies of the Moving Image
www.uca.edu/org/ccsmi/

> The CCSMI is "an independent organization of scholars, international in scope, attached to the Department of Mass Communication and Theatre at the University of Central Arkansas." The group operates a clearinghouse for the relatively new field of cognitive film studies.

Society for Cinema & Media Studies
www.cmstudies.org

> Founded in 1959, SCMS is "a professional organization of college and university educators, filmmakers, historians, critics, scholars, and others devoted to the study of the moving image." It sponsors an annual meeting and the publication of *Cinema Journal,* a scholarly journal of film studies.

Film Distributors

Facets Multimedia
www.facets.org/asticat

> One of the largest distributors of classic, foreign, and hard-to-find videos, Facets boasts an inventory of more than 40,000 titles. The company also sells and rents DVDs.

Film Forum
www.filmforum.com/distributor.html

> Provides a list of film distributors.

Kino International
www.kino.com/

> Since 1977, Kino has built a small but solid repertoire of classic and international films based on the Janus Collection and other prestigious film libraries, with many titles now on DVD.

National Asian American Telecommunications Association (NAATA)
www.naatanet.org/

> NAATA's mission is "to present stories that convey the richness and diversity of the Asian Pacific American experience to the broadest audience possible." It funds and distributes films, videos, and other media.

The National Center for Jewish Film
www.brandeis.edu/jewishfilm/

> The world's largest archive of films and videos on Jewish themes is located at Brandeis University. The NCJF distributes film and videocassette versions of selected titles.

New Yorker Films
www.newyorkerfilms.com/

> Founded by Daniel Talbot, who pioneered the U.S. exhibition of international films in the 1960s, New Yorker Films has become a premier source of challenging and often controversial movies from abroad. It distributes films to both schools and professional theaters.

Swank Motion Pictures, Inc.
http://swank.com/college/main.html

> Swank represents many of the largest entertainment feature film production companies, distributing their popular titles to U.S. colleges and universities.

Women Make Movies
www.wmm.com/

> Established in 1972, this "multicultural, multiracial, non-profit media arts organization" distributes independent films by and about women. More than half of the works in its collection were produced by women of diverse cultures.

Zeitgeist Films
www.zeitgeistfilms.com/

> A relatively small independent distributor, Zeitgeist specializes in lesser-known films for academic audiences.

Glossary

Academy ratio: The original standard dimensions of the projected image on a movie screen, fixed by the Academy of Motion Pictures as three units high by four units wide: an aspect ratio of 1.33:1.

adaptation: A movie based on a book, usually a novel.

ambient sound: Local background noises usually recorded before or after the shoot to lend authenticity to the sound track.

animation: An effect created when a drawing or object is changed slightly every time the camera stops. When the film is projected, the objects appear to move of their own accord.

anime: Japanese animated feature films.

aspect ratio: The relationship between the horizontal and vertical dimensions of the screen.

assembly cut: An edited version of the film in which the best shots are trimmed and spliced end to end into a tentative order. Also known as the *editor's cut*.

assistant director: Handles delegated tasks like planning the day's shooting, managing the extras, or keeping interlopers off the set.

auteur theory: Holds that film directors are the authors of their films, just as the writers of novels bear responsibility for the artistic spirit and integrity of their work.

automated dialogue replacement (ADR): The process of synchronizing an actor's voice with the actor's image on the screen during postproduction. This is done when there is too much noise on the set, when a movie filmed in one language is recorded into another, or when the script is altered after shooting.

avant-garde: An artistic movement of experimental films that deliberately violate the conventions of mainstream movies.

backlighting: A strong light from behind separates the subject from the background. Backlighting creates a silhouette effect when the subject is not illuminated from the front.

blaxploitation films: Cheaply made Hollywood movies of the 1970s that exploited the box-office value of black performers for black audiences.

blind bidding: The practice of requiring film exhibitors to bid on and contract for movies without seeing them first.

block booking: The practice of requiring film exhibitors to contract for several movies as a package in order to exhibit any one of them.

blocking: The term for walking the actors through each movement before shooting.

blue screen process: A special effects technique in which an actor is filmed in front of a blue (or sometimes green or red) screen. When the film is processed, the blue area becomes transparent so that a background image can be filmed and inserted, seamlessly matched to the action.

boom shot: A shot in which the camera moves vertically through space, sometimes lifted by a boom or crane. Also known as a *crane shot.*

camera obscura: Literally "dark room" in Italian, the term from which the word *camera* is derived. When light enters a hole in the window shade of a darkened room, it projects an inverted image from outside onto the opposite wall much as light entering a camera's aperture projects an image onto film.

camera operator: Runs the camera under the cinematographer's supervision.

celluloid: Film coated with light-sensitive chemicals. When exposed to light through the aperture of a motion picture camera, a celluloid strip becomes a series of still photographs that can be developed and projected as a movie.

***cinema novo* ("new cinema"):** Film movement of the 1960s led by Brazilian director Gláuber Rocha, characterized by native folklore traditions and a Marxist view of poverty.

CinemaScope: A widescreen process developed in 1952 using an anamorphic lens to squeeze a panoramic view onto standard 35mm film and later project the image onto a screen with an aspect ratio of 2.35:1.

cinematographe: Invention by August and Louis Lumière used to record and project motion pictures for a theater audience in 1895.

cinematographer: Responsible for the camera work and related operations. Also called *director of photography.*

cinéma vérité: The use of handheld cameras, natural lighting, shooting on location, improvised plots, and deliberately disruptive editing techniques, which make films look more like real life than artificial constructs.

cinerama: A widescreen process introduced in 1952 that used three interlocked cameras to produce movies that were projected onto a curved screen with an aspect ratio of 2.77:1.

classical Hollywood style: A distinctively American mode of making movies that favors efficient, plot-driven, character-centered, seamlessly edited stories.

click track: Measures each scene of a film in frames per musical beat, or clicks. Click tracks are usually prepared by the **music editor,** whose main task is to coordinate the visuals with music written by the **composer** or arranger.

close-up (CU): A shot in which the camera is relatively near the subject. A close-up might show, for example, an actor's head or hand.

cognitive science: An interdisciplinary movement concerned with the nature of perception and thought. Cognitive film studies draw on empirical tests and computer simulations to understand how movies work in terms of mental representations and processes.

composer: Creates the musical score to be performed for the sound track of a film.

composite master: The final product of sound mixing is sent to the photographic lab for synchronization with the negative print.

computer-generated imagery (CGI): Visual elements of a movie created on a computer using digital technology.

crane shot: See **boom shot.**

crosscutting: An editing technique that shows two simultaneous actions in alternating shots, the camera shifting from one action to the other. Also known as **parallel montage.**

cuer: A film technician who helps keep track of dialogue during a shoot.

cultural studies: A critical movement concerned with the cultural contexts of films and other forms of popular culture. Critical studies often focus on the ideological messages of films, who creates them, how they are encoded, and how they are perceived by various audiences.

cutaway: A shot of something off screen, like an airplane flying overhead, that is cut into a scene.

daguerreotype: A process for reproducing sharp, permanent images on treated metal plates, developed by the French chemist Louis Daguerre in 1837 and announced in 1839. The forerunner of modern photography.

dailies: The film from a day's shooting, usually printed overnight and viewed the next day by the director and the editor. Also called *rushes.*

das neue Kino **("the new cinema"):** Film movement originating in West Germany during the 1960s.

deconstruction: An approach to cinema opposed to structuralism, holding that any effort to categorize films by genre, history, or any other category is inadequate. Practitioners seek to deconstruct the text by exposing its internal contradictions.

dialogue: Words on the sound track spoken aloud by actors in the film.

dialogue director: Coaches the actors in their lines.

digital compositing: The process of combining digital images on a computer.

digital nonlinear editing: The process of assembling electronic images, stored as computer files, into a sequence. This process allows editors to choose selected scenes or individual frames at will and recombine them automatically.

digital photography: A process for recording images in electronic form that can be manipulated on a computer.

director: Has the responsibility for directing the actors, supervising the technicians, and managing all action on the set.

director's cut: A tighter version of the edited film than the assembly cut. It may include some sound and is often screened for the studio executives.

discourse: The manner of narrating the story (how it is told) in a film as distinct from the story's content (what is told).

dissolve: A visual effect in which one image seems to blend into the next. A dissolve is made by superimposing a fade-out over a fade-in.

Dogme: A Danish movement begun in the 1990s advocating a policy of artistic self-discipline. The Dogme Manifesto outlined this policy as a reaction to a film culture considered to be too unrestrained and superficial.

dolly shot: A shot in which the camera moves horizontally through space with, towards, or away from the subject. Also called a **tracking shot.**

dubbing: A process by which dialogue is recorded after the shooting and synchronized with the lip movement of actors in the scene.

DVD (digital video disc): A DVD is a high-density medium for storing large amounts of data on a compact disc in digital form, especially high-resolution audiovisual material such as a full-length movie.

editing: The process of compiling a film from its constituent parts. Shots filmed separately are spliced together (cut, edited) into a continuous sequence. Also called *cutting.*

editor's cut: See **assembly cut.**

establishing shot: The opening of a movie intended to orient the viewer.

Expressionism: An artistic movement that sought to render subjective emotional and mental states on film, especially popular in Germany during the 1920s.

eyelight: A small spotlight placed near the camera to add sparkle to the subject's eyes.

fade: A visual effect created by darkening or lightening each successive frame. In a fade-out, the image gradually grows black. In a fade-in, the image appears from a black screen.

fast motion: A film technique in which action is speeded up, produced by undercranking the camera.

feminist theory: In film study, feminist theory focuses on the way women are represented in movies and the ideological forces that shape their representation.

Fifth Generation: Name given to Chinese filmmakers who emerged from Beijing's film school after Mao's Cultural Revolution of the 1960s and 1970s.

fill light: Provides a weaker, broader glow than the key light and is used to fill in shadows.

film noir: A genre originating in the 1940s characterized by dark lighting, seedy characters, sudden violence, unsentimental dialogue, intricate plots, disorienting camera angles, and a hard-boiled outlook on life.

film stock: Undeveloped celluloid that may vary in sensitivity to light, fast film stock being more sensitive than slow film stock.

fine cut: The final version of the edited film forwarded to the sound mixers and photographic laboratory for final processing.

first-run theater: A theater that is granted exclusive rights to exhibit a new movie within a prescribed zone during its initial release.

floodlight: A light that washes the scene with a diffuse form of illumination.

focal length: The distance from the plane of the film to the optical center of the lens when the lens is set to infinity. A short focal length produces a wider image, making objects seem farther away. A long focal length produces the opposite effect.

Foley editing: A process by which live sound effects are replaced with synchronized substitutes. The sound of hollow coconut shells being thumped in a studio, for example, might be used to simulate the sound of horses on the screen.

follow focus: When the camera is moved, a camera operator may keep adjusting the lens to keep the subject in focus.

frame: (1) An individual photograph on a strip of flim. (2) The rectangular area in which the image appears on screen.

Freeze-frame: A special effect created by reprinting the same frame many times in succession so that the action seems to stop suddenly.

front lighting: A form of illumination that can soften a face, flattening the features and sometimes hiding facial marks.

gaffer: The chief electrician, responsible for lighting the set as directed by the cinematographer.

genre: A classification of films into categories like Westerns, gangster movies, or romantic comedies.

glass shot: A special effect created with scenery painted on transparent glass. The camera photographs the action through the glass so that the painted portions seem to be continuous with the action.

gofers: Run errands for everybody else, who order them to "go for this" and "go for that."

grips: Take care of equipment, sets, and props.

HDTV: See **high-definition television.**

high-angle shot: A segment of film photographed from above the subject.

high-definition television (HDTV): The use of special cameras and recording equipment to produce high-quality pictures. High-definition digital images have a higher resolution than analog television images (1,080 lines versus 480) and use a wider screen format (16:9 width to height ratio versus 4:3).

high-key lighting: A method of flooding a scene with bright illumination, giving it a cheerful, buoyant tone.

Industrial Light & Magic (ILM): George Lucas founded this company in 1975 to create the special effects for *Star Wars*. Since then, it has refined the art of model building and propelled it into the digital age.

insert: A shot of some detail, like the close-up of a gun in the actor's pocket, inserted into a scene or sequence.

iris: A circular mask surrounding the screen image, sometimes used to draw attention to a detail or to close a scene.

jump cut: Discontinuity created when the action in two consecutive shots does not match up.

key light: The chief light illuminating the subject to be filmed.

Kinetograph: A precursor of the modern camera, William Dickson's Kinetograph used a roll of celluloid film to record sequential photographs that were then viewed through a peephole in his Kinetoscope. Perforations in the film allowed it to be moved behind a shutter frame by frame, creating the illusion of motion pictures. As Dickson's employer, Thomas Edison took legal credit for these inventions.

letterboxing: A method of adapting widescreen movies to the boxy dimensions of a television screen by placing blank bars above and below the full frame so that its original aspect ratio is preserved. Also called **widescreen.**

long shot (LS): A shot in which the camera is relatively far from the subject. A long shot might show the actor's entire figure running through a field.

low-angle shot: A segment of film taken from below the subject.

low-key lighting: A method of lighting in which the illumination is low and soaked with shadows, creating an ominous or melancholy mood.

mag stock: A length of magnetic tape on which sound is recorded before being synchronized with the visual elements of a film.

Marxism: Based on the work of Karl Marx, Marxist film theory is concerned with social class and the economic forces that account for poverty and wealth.

master shot: A continuous long shot covering the entire action. Portions of the action may be filmed again, from different distances and angles. Later, the best shots will be selected and edited for continuity, using the master shot as a general guide.

match cut: An editing technique for achieving continuity when a single action is covered by two shots. The second shot begins precisely when the first shot ends.

matching action: An editing convention that joins two shots so that the action in one shot seems to continue in the following shot.

matte shot: A special effect that uses an opaque screen or matte to obscure certain portions of the frame. The film is exposed twice, first with one matte, and then with a second matte that covers the area obscured by the first. When projected, the two separately filmed sections of the frame appear as a single image.

medium shot (MS): A shot in which the camera is at a medium distance from the subject. A medium shot might show an actor's body from the knees up.

melodrama: A form of storytelling that stresses strong emotional content and often makes sharp distinctions between good and evil.

method acting: A school of performers based on the teachings of Konstantin Stanislavsky. Method actors try to get in character by identifying personally with the role, making emotional connections between their character's plight and events in their own lives, drawing on genuine feeling rather than relying on external acting techniques.

mise-en-scène: Refers to what happens within a movie frame (literally, what is put into the scene), including staging, lighting, camera work, costume, and set design.

mixing: The process of blending separate sound tracks (dialogue, sound effects, music, voice-over narration) into a single channel, or composite master, which is then synchronized with the edited print of the film.

montage: (1) A term for the dynamic editing of film. (2) An editing technique that combines related shots in quick succession, usually to show the passage of time or to illustrate an idea, such as the process of falling in love.

Motion Picture Production Code: The Motion Picture Production Code listed what was or was not permitted in Hollywood films. Created in the 1930s with the approval of the Hayes Office, the code was a way for the industry to avoid outside censorship by regulating itself.

musical conductor: Leads the orchestra during the postproduction phase when the sound track of a film is created.

music editor: Coordinates the visual elements of a film with music during postproduction.

negative: When undeveloped celluloid is exposed to light, the portions of the chemical coating that receive the most light turn darkest, forming a negative image of the visual event. This negative makes it possible to reproduce the image, for when light is directed through the negative onto another piece of film, a positive print is the result.

negative cost: All expenses incurred to produce the first negative of a film, from pre-preproduction to postproduction.

neorealism: An artistic movement originating in Italy after World War II, characterized by the use of nonprofessional actors, location shooting, gritty photography, and a focus on common people struggling with their daily lives.

nickelodeons: Beginning in 1905, the earliest movie theaters in the United States charged customers a nickel a week for a program of vaudeville acts and silent movies, often with a live piano accompaniment.

nouvelle vague ("new wave"): A school of young creative directors who began their careers as critics for *Cahiers du cinéma* and revitalized French filmmaking in the late 1950s.

optical effects: The name for fades, dissolves, superimposition, and other visual tricks, commonly produced by the photographic lab after the film is shot.

optical printer: A machine for filming film. The optical printer can rephotograph any frame and manipulate it visually, creating fades, dissolves, and other optical effects.

pan: A shot taken by a camera while it pivots horizontally left or right.

pan and scan: A method of adapting widescreen movies to the boxy dimensions of a television screen by masking parts of the original image.

paradigm: In semiotics, the choice of signifiers (words, film frames) at any point within a sequence.

parallel montage: See **crosscutting.**

persistence of vision: A feature of human vision that accounts for the illusion of smooth motion in a movie. The retina retains the image for an instant longer than the image is presented, just enough time for a new frame to replace it on the screen.

pixilation: People are animated like objects by moving them slightly every time the camera stops.

playback: A prerecorded sound track used on the set to help synchronize the action to continuous music or sound effects. Many shots of the action may be taken from different angles during filming. Later, the shots will be edited to match the music.

poetic realism: An artistic movement popular in France during the 1930s that derives from literary naturalism and blends lyrical photography with realistic characters.

postmodernism: A trend of self-conscious borrowing that began to influence filmmaking in the latter part of the twentieth century.

producer: Bears the ultimate responsibility for the final film.

production mixer: Decides how to set up the sound equipment for the best sound.

race movies: A term for independent films produced by black directors with black performers for black ghetto audiences during the silent movie period.

reaction shot: Shows a character's reaction to something important.

realism: A belief that film should duplicate the look of objective reality.

rear projection: A special effect created when the action is filmed in front of a screen while another action is projected on the screen from behind.

reception studies: Film study concerned with the roles played by viewers in determining what a movie means.

released print: The final version of a film, produced from the negative print and approved for distribution in theaters.

reverse-angle shot: A shot that reverses the point of view, created when the camera turns 180 degrees in the opposite direction.

runaway productions: Movies that are produced overseas, relying on foreign labor and facilities.

rushes: See **dailies.**

scene: A segment of film usually composed of several shots of the same general action, time, and location.

scoring session: A rehearsal of the studio orchestra during which it plays music specially composed or arranged for a film. The recorded music is then added to the film's sound track.

screenplay: A full version of the film narrative that fleshes out the action, dialogue, and perhaps some directions for the camera.

screwball comedy: A variation of romantic comedy originating in the 1930s and featuring the zany antics of the male and female leads, who usually begin at odds and end up happily married.

scrim: A translucent shade placed between the subject and a light source to soften the illumination.

script supervisor: Keeps track of the script, noting which shots are filmed, ever on the lookout for variant readings and visual discontinuities, such as a change in lighting or the length of a lit cigarette.

segue: A gradual transition between sounds, the auditory equivalent of a dissolve.

semiotics: The study of signs and symbols in language or other sign systems.

sequence: A segment of film often composed of scenes from different times and locations but unified by a common idea or thematic concern.

shooting script: Usually provides a shot-by-shot blueprint of the film.

shot: A single length of film produced by a continuous running of the camera.

shutter: A mechanical device, usually a revolving plate, between the lens and the film that stops the light just long enough so that the image frozen on a single frame of film can be moved out of position and a new frame moved into its place. Without a shutter, a camera would produce an undifferentiated blur on the moving film, and a projector would project a blurred image on the screen.

sidelight: Adds solidity and depth to the subject by accentuating prominent features.

sign/signifier/signified: In semiotics, a **sign** is the relationship between a signifier and what it signifies. The **signifier** is the part of the sign that represents something else (its referent), like the word *cat* or a drawing of a cat, each of which refers to a four-legged, furry animal with whiskers and (usually) a tail. The **signified** is the conception evoked by the signifier, like a reader's mental image of a cat or the ideas that a viewer might associate with cats.

slapstick: A form of comedy based on rowdy physical situations, like a Keystone Kops chase or a pie in the face.

slow motion: When the camera is speeded up, or *overcranked*, the action appears slower during projection.

sound cut: A sharp shift from one sound to another.

sound effects (SFX): Noises on the sound track that emanate from things on the set, such as a roaring brook, the whistling wind, or gunfire. Sound effects may also be made by animals or people if they are not speaking dialogue.

sound mixer: Controls the volume and quality of each separate sound track and combines tracks into a composite track for the final cut of the film.

sound track: A magnetic or optical stripe of recorded sound commonly placed alongside the picture on a strip of film.

spectatorship: How do spectators interpret what they see and hear? What cultural and private filters color their perceptions? What makes them accept a film's illusions as reality or resist its ideological messages? Such questions inform the study of spectatorship.

spotlight: A light that projects a concentrated beam on the subject.

Steadicam: A stabilization device that gives flexibility to the camera operator by combining the fluidity of a dolly with the freedom of handheld filming.

stop-motion photography: A special effect created by interrupting the shooting at intervals. As a result, objects seem to move at a rapid rate. If the scene is rearranged during intervals, objects can appear to move of their own volition.

structuralism: An interpretive method of film study that examines relationships between elements of a film.

studio system: An arrangement for controlling all phases of film production, distribution, and exhibition that flourished in the 1930s and 1940s. A typical film studio contained everything it needed to produce a film from start to finish, organized hierarchically and run like an assembly plant.

subsidiary rights: Marketing options beyond a film's theatrical release in the United States. These rights may include foreign sales, cable and network television, video and DVD, books, television series, clothing, and toys.

superimposition: A double exposure in which one image appears over another.

synopsis: A brief description of the movie's plot.

syntagm: In semiotics, the order of signifiers (in film, the images and sounds) in a sequence.

take: (1) An unedited shot. (2) An attempt to photograph a shot. Each repetition of the same shot is a new take.

Technicolor: A process in which the primary colors of an image are recorded on separate strips of film and recombined in the lab.

technique acting: A traditional method of stage and screen performance. Technique actors try to convey character by imitating visible behavior. Each gesture is a technique, a sign deliberately adopted to represent a given mood.

telephoto lens: Also called a *long-focus lens,* because it's longer, a telephoto lens takes in a narrow field of view.

3-D: A system of film production based on principles of binocular vision that creates an illusion of depth for the viewer.

three-dimensional (3-D) photography: Uses two lenses spaced 2 1/2 inches apart to record a scene as if it were being viewed by a pair of human eyes.

tilt: A shot taken by a camera while it pivots up or down along a vertical axis.

Todd-AO: A wide-film process introduced in 1955 to give viewers a greater sense of presence through a combination of special cameras, 70mm film, and special sound technology.

tracking shot: See **dolly shot**.

transition: A term for the visual effects that join two shots, such as fades, wipes, or dissolves.

treatment: A more complete version of the story than a synopsis. A treatment might contain scenes, character development, and some dialogue, much like a short story, but without detailed descriptions of the set or camera setups.

undercranking: When the camera is slowed down, or undercranked, during shooting, motion appears faster during projection.

VCR (video cassette recorder): An electronic device for recording and playing back video images and sound on a videocassette. The sound and images on a videocassette are stored in analog form on magnetic tape.

vertical integration: A business practice enabling film studios to control the three sectors of production, distribution, and exhibition.

VHS (video home system): The standard video system for home use, which plays 1/2-inch videocassettes on a VCR.

voice-over: Words on a sound track that are not spoken aloud or in sync with the picture, such as the silent thoughts of a character or the narration in a documentary film.

wide-angle lens: Also called a *short-focus lens,* because it's shorter, a wide-angle lens takes in a wider field of view so that objects seem farther away.

widescreen: A movie image with more width than the Academy ratio, introduced in the early 1950s and standardized in Europe as 1.66:1 and in the United States as 1.85:1.

wipe: A visual effect in which one image seems to wipe another off the screen.

zones: Geographical divisions designed by film exhibitors to control marketing. A new film might be distributed first to one theater in each zone at a higher price before being released to other theaters.

zoom lens: A lens that combines the features of normal, long, and wide-angle lenses, enabling the filmmaker to change the focal length during shooting. Results in a **zoom shot.**

zoom shot: May move smoothly from a close-up to a long shot or vice versa.

Works Cited

Amelio, Ralph J. *Film in the Classroom: Why Use It, How to Use It*. Dayton, OH: Pflaum/Standard, 1971.

American Film Institute Desk Reference. Pref. Jean Picker Firstenberg. New York: DK, 2002.

Anderson, Joseph D. *The Reality of Illusion: An Ecological Approach to Cognitive Film Theory*. Carbondale: Southern Illinois UP, 1996.

Andrew, Dudley. "Adaptation." *Film Adaptation*. Ed. James Naremore. New Brunswick, NJ: Rutgers UP, 2000. 28–37.

———. *Concepts in Film Theory*. New York: Oxford UP, 1984.

———. *The Major Film Theories: An Introduction*. New York: Oxford UP, 1976.

———. "An Open Approach to Film Study and the Situation at Iowa." *Film Study in the Undergraduate Curriculum*. Ed. Barry Keith Grant. New York: Modern Language Association, 1983. 39–48.

Arnheim, Rudolf. *Art and Visual Perception: A Psychology of the Creative Eye*. Berkeley: U of California P, 1969.

———. *Film as Art*. Berkeley: U of California P, 1966.

Balázs, Béla. *Theory of the Film: Character and Growth of a New Art*. 1952. Trans. Edith Bone. New York: Dover, 1970.

Basinger, Jeanine. *A Woman's View: How Hollywood Spoke to Women, 1930–1960*. New York: Knopf, 1993.

Bazalgette, Cary, ed. *Primary Media Education: A Curriculum Statement*. London: British Film Institute Education, 1989.

Bazin, André. *What Is Cinema?* Trans. Hugh Gray. Berkeley: U of California P, 1967.

Beach, Christopher. *Class, Language, and American Film Comedy*. Cambridge: Cambridge UP, 2002.

Beach, Richard. "Issues of Censorship and Research on Effects of and Response to Reading." *Dealing with Censorship*. Ed. James E. Davis. Urbana, IL: National Council of Teachers of English, 1979. 131–59.

Beja, Morris. *Film & Literature: An Introduction*. New York: Longman, 1979.

Belton, John. *American Cinema/American Culture*. New York: McGraw-Hill, 1994.

———. "The Work of Art in the Age of Mechanical Reproduction." 1935. *Film Theory and Criticism: Introductory Readings*. Ed. Gerald Mast and Marshall Cohen. 3rd ed. New York: Oxford UP, 1985. 675–94.

Berg, Charles Ramirez. "Stereotyping in Films in General and of the Hispanic in Particular." *Latin Looks: Images of Latinas and Latinos in the U.S. Media*. Ed. Clara E. Rodriguez. Boulder, CO: Westview, 1998. 104–20.

Bielefield, Arlene, and Lawrence Cheeseman. *Technology and Copyright Law: A Guidebook for the Library, Research, and Teaching Professions.* New York: Neal-Schuman, 1997.

Bloom, Benjamin S., ed. *Taxonomy of educational objectives: The classification of educational goals.* New York: Longmans, Green, 1956.

Bluestone, George. *Novels into Film.* Baltimore: Johns Hopkins P, 1957.

Bogle, Donald. *Toms, Coons, Mulattoes, Mammies, and Bucks: An Interpretive History of Blacks in American Films.* New York: Continuum, 1989.

Bohnenkamp, Dennis R., and Sam L. Grogg Jr., eds. *The American Film Institute Guide to College Courses in Film and Television.* Princeton, NJ: Peterson's Guides for the American Film Institute, 1978.

Bordwell, David. *Narration in the Fiction Film.* Madison: U of Wisconsin P, 1985.

Bordwell, David, and Noël Carroll, eds. *Post-Theory: Reconstructing Film Studies.* Madison: U of Wisconsin P, 1996.

Bordwell, David, Janet Staiger, and Kristin Thompson. *The Classical Hollywood Cinema: Film Style & Mode of Production to 1960.* New York: Columbia UP, 1985.

Bordwell, David, and Kristin Thompson. *Film Art: An Introduction.* New York: Knopf, 1986.

Braudy, Leo, and Marshall Cohen, eds. *Film Theory and Criticism: Introductory Readings.* 5th ed. New York: Oxford UP, 1999.

Brunette, Peter, and David Wills. *Screen/Play: Derrida and Film Theory.* Princeton, NJ: Princeton UP, 1989.

Burress, Lee. "A Brief Report of the 1977 NCTE Censorship Survey." *Dealing with Censorship.* Ed. James E. Davis. Urbana, IL: National Council of Teachers of English, 1979. 14–47.

Carringer, Robert L. *The Making of* Citizen Kane. Berkeley: U of California P, 1985.

Carroll, Noël. *Mystifying Movies: Fads & Fallacies in Contemporary Film Theory.* New York: Columbia UP, 1988.

Carson, Diane, Linda Dittmar, and Janice R. Welsch, eds. *Multiple Voices in Feminist Film Criticism.* Minneapolis: U of Minnesota P, 1994.

The Celluloid Closet. Dir. Rob Epstein and Jeffrey Friedman. SONY Pictures, 1996.

Chatman, Seymour. *Story and Discourse: Narrative Structure in Fiction and Film.* Ithaca, NY: Cornell UP, 1978.

Cohan, Steven, and Ina Rae Hark, eds.. *Screening the Male: Exploring Masculinities in Hollywood Cinema.* London: Routledge, 1993.

Cohen, Keith. *Film and Fiction: The Dynamics of Exchange.* New Haven, CT: Yale UP, 1979.

Collins, Jim. "Genericity in the Nineties: Eclectic Irony and the New Sincerity." *Film Theory Goes to the Movies.* Ed. Jim Collins, Hilary Radner, and Ava Preacher. New York: Routledge, 1993. 242–63.

Congress of the United States, Office of Technology Assessment. *Copyright & Home Copying: Technology Challenges the Law.* OTA-CIT-422. Washington, DC: U.S. Government Printing Office, 1989.

Costanzo, William V. "Fiction into Film: Learning Literature with a Movie Camera." *Teaching English in the Two-Year College* 12.1 (1985): 52–56.

———. *Reading the Movies: Twelve Great Films on Video and How to Teach Them.* Urbana, IL: National Council of Teachers of English, 1992.

———, ed. *Report on Film Study in American Schools.* Urbana, IL: National Council of Teachers of English, Committee on Film Study in the English Language Arts, 1987. ERIC Doc. No. ED 287 165.

Cripps, Thomas R. *Making Movies Black: The Hollywood Message Movie from World War II to the Civil Rights Era.* New York: Oxford UP, 1993.

Cunningham, Michael. "For *The Hours,* an Elation Mixed with Doubt." *New York Times* 19 Jan. 2003, sec 2: 1, 22.

Dale, Alan. *Comedy Is a Man in Trouble: Slapstick in American Movies.* Minneapolis: U of Minnesota P, 2000.

Dick, Bernard F. *Anatomy of Film.* New York: St. Martin's, 1978.

Dixon, Wheeler Winston, ed. *Film Genre 2000: New Critical Essays.* Albany: State U of New York P, 2000.

Donelson, Kenneth L. "Censorship in the 1970s: Some Ways to Handle It When It Comes (and It Will)." *Dealing with Censorship.* Ed. James E. Davis. Urbana, IL: National Council of Teachers of English, 1979. 162–67.

———. "Ruminating and Rambling: The Censorship of Non-Print Media Comes to the English Classroom." *English Journal* 62 (1973): 1226–27.

Draigh, David. *Behind the Screen: The American Museum of the Moving Image Guide to Who Does What in Motion Pictures and Television.* New York: Abbeville, 1988.

Durgnat, Raymond. *The Crazy Mirror: Hollywood Comedy and the American Image.* New York: Horizon, 1970.

Eisenstein, Sergei. *Film Form: Essays in Film Theory.* Ed. and trans. Jay Leyda. New York: Harcourt, Brace & World, 1949.

———. *The Film Sense.* Ed. and trans. Jay Leyda. New York: Harcourt, Brace, 1947.

Elsaesser, Thomas. "Tales of Sound and Fury: Observations on the Family Melodrama." *Film Genre Reader II.* Ed. Barry Keith Grant. Austin: U of Texas P, 1995. 350–80.

Fantel, Hans. "Film to Videotape: A Ticklish Transfer." *New York Times* 25 Mar. 1990, sec. 2: 18, 32.

Feuer, Jane. *The Hollywood Musical.* Bloomington: Indiana UP, 1982.

Focillon, Henri. *The Life of Forms in Art.* Trans. Charles Beecher Hogan and George Kubler. New York: New Haven, CT: Yale UP, 1942.

Forsdale, Joan Rosengren, and Louis Forsdale. "Film Literacy." *Teachers College Record* 67 (1966): 608–17.

Friedman, Lester D. *Hollywood's Image of the Jew.* New York: Ungar, 1982.

————. *The Jewish Image in American Film.* Secaucus, NJ: Citadel, 1987.

Gabler, Neal. *An Empire of Their Own: How the Jews Invented Hollywood.* New York: Crown, 1988.

Geuens, Jean-Pierre. *Film Production Theory.* Albany: State U of New York P, 2000.

Giannetti, Louis. *Understanding Movies.* 5th ed. Englewood Cliffs, NJ: Prentice Hall, 1990.

————. *Understanding Movies.* 9th ed. Upper Saddle River, NJ: Prentice Hall, 2002.

Giddings, Robert, and Erica Sheen, eds. *The Classic Novel from Page to Screen.* Manchester, UK: Manchester UP, 2000.

Gledhill, Christine. "Recent Developments in Feminist Criticism." *Film Theory and Criticism: Introductory Readings.* Ed. Gerald Mast and Marshall Cohen. 3rd ed. New York: Oxford UP, 1985.

————, ed. *Film Study in the Undergraduate Curriculum.* New York: Modern Language Association, 1983.

Griffith, James. *Adaptations as Imitations: Films from Novels.* Newark: U of Delaware P, 1997.

Hall, Stuart. *Stuart Hall: Critical Dialogues in Cultural Studies.* Ed. Dave Morley. London: Routledge, 1996.

Harrington, John. *Film and/as Literature.* Englewood Cliffs, NJ: Prentice Hall, 1977.

————. *The Rhetoric of Film.* New York: Holt, Rinehart and Winston, 1973.

Harvey, James. *Romantic Comedy in Hollywood from Lubitsch to Sturges.* New York: Knopf, 1987.

Haskell, Molly. *From Reverence to Rape: The Treatment of Women in the Movies.* New York: Holt, Rinehart and Winston, 1974.

Hawkes, Terence. *Structuralism & Semiotics.* London: Methuen, 1977.

Higashi, Sumiko. "Ethnicity, Class, and Gender in Film: DeMille's *The Cheat.*" *Unspeakable Images: Ethnicity and the American Cinema.* Ed. Lester D. Friedman. Champaign: U of Illinois P, 1991. 112–39.

Hill, John, and Pamela Church Gibson, eds. *The Oxford Guide to Film Studies.* New York: Oxford UP, 1998.

Hobbs, Renee. "Curriculum Design in Media Literacy Education." National Media Education Conference. Baltimore, MD. 29 June 2003.

Hogan, Robert F. "Some Thoughts on Censorship in the Schools." *Dealing with Censorship.* Ed. James E. Davis. Urbana, IL: National Council of Teachers of English, 1979. 86–95.

Hull, Mary E. *Censorship in America: A Reference Handbook.* Santa Barbara, CA: ABC-CLIO, 1999. Italic Studies Institute. "Image Research Project: Italian Culture on Film (1928–2001)." March 2002 <italic.org/imageb1.htm>.

Jeffords, Susan. *Hard Bodies: Hollywood Masculinity in the Reagan Era.* New Brunswick, NJ: Rutgers UP, 1994.

Jenkinson, Edward B. "Dirty Dictionaries, Obscene Nursery Rhymes, and Burned Books." *Dealing with Censorship.* Ed. James E. Davis. Urbana, IL: National Council of Teachers of English, 1979. 2–13.

Johnson, William, ed. *Focus on the Science Fiction Film.* Englewood Cliffs, NJ: Prentice Hall, 1972.

Jojola , Ted. "Absurd Reality II: Hollywood Goes to the Indians." *Hollywood's Indian: The Portrayal of the Native American in Film.* Ed. Peter C. Rollins and John E. O'Connor. Lexington, KY: UP of Kentucky, 1998. 12–26.

Kawin, Bruce F. *Faulkner and Film.* New York: Ungar, 1977.

———. *Faulkner's MGM Screenplays.* Knoxville: U of Tennessee P, 1982.

———. *How Movies Work.* New York: Macmillan, 1987.

Kawin, Bruce, and Gerald Mast. *A Short History of the Movies.* 3rd ed. New York: Longman, 2003.

Kolmar, Wendy, guest ed. "Looking across the Lens: Women's Studies and Film." *Women's Studies Quarterly* 30.1&2 (Spring/Summer 2002).

———. *Theory of Film: The Redemption of Physical Reality.* New York: Oxford UP, 1960.

Lindsay, Vachel. *The Art of the Moving Picture.* New York: Macmillan, 1915.

López, Ana M. "Are All Latins from Manhattan? Hollywood, Ethnography, and Cultural Colonialism." *Unspeakable Images: Ethnicity and the American Cinema.* Ed. Lester D. Friedman. Champaign: U of Illinois P, 1991. 404–24.

Lupack, Barbara Tepa, ed. *Vision/Re-vision: Adapting Contemporary American Fiction by Women to Film.* Bowling Green, OH: Bowling Green State U Popular P, 1996.

Maltin, Leonard, ed. *Leonard Maltin's Movie & Video Guide 2004.* New York: Penguin, 2003.

Mast, Gerald. *The Comic Mind: Comedy and the Movies.* 2nd ed. Chicago: U of Chicago P, 1979.

———. *A Short History of the Movies.* 3rd ed. Indianapolis: Bobbs-Merrill Educational, 1981.

Mast, Gerald, and Marshall Cohen, eds. *Film Theory and Criticism: Introductory Readings.* 3rd ed. New York: Oxford UP, 1985.

Mayne, Judith. *Cinema and Spectatorship.* London: Routledge, 1993.

McBride, Joseph. *Orson Welles, Actor and Director.* New York: Harvest/HBJ, 1977.

McDougal, Stuart Y. *Made into Movies: From Literature to Film.* New York: Holt, Rinehart and Winston, 1985.

McLuhan, Marshall. *Understanding Media: The Extensions of Man.* 1964. Cambridge, MA: MIT, 2004.

Mellen, Joan. *Big Bad Wolves: Masculinity in the American Film.* New York: Pantheon, 1977.

Metz, Christian. *Film Language: A Semiotics of the Cinema.* Trans. Michael Taylor. New York: Oxford UP, 1974.

——. *The Imaginary Signifier: Psychoanalysis and the Cinema.* Trans. Celia Britton et al. Bloomington: Indiana UP, 1982.

Miller, Jerome K. *Applying the New Copyright Law: A Guide for Educators and Librarians.* Chicago: American Library Association, 1979.

Miller, Mark Crispin. "What's Wrong with This Picture?" *The Nation* 7/14 Jan. 2002: 18–36.

Miller, Toby. "Hollywood and the World." *The Oxford Guide to Film Studies.* Ed. John Hill and Pamela Church Gibson. New York: Oxford UP, 1998. 371–81.

Monaco, James. *How to Read a Film: The Art, Technology, Language, History, and Theory of Film and Media.* New York: Oxford UP, 1977.

Mordden, Ethan. *The Hollywood Studios: House Style in the Golden Age of Movies.* New York: Knopf, 1988.

Mulvey, Laura. "Visual Pleasure and Narrative Cinema." *Film Theory and Criticism: Introductory Readings.* Ed. Gerald Mast and Marshall Cohen. 3rd ed. New York: Oxford UP, 1985. 803–16.

Münsterberg, Hugo. *The Film: A Psychological Study: The Silent Photoplay in 1916.* 1916. New York: Dover, 1970.

Naremore, James, ed. *Film Adaptation.* New Brunswick, NJ: Rutgers UP, 2000.

NCTE. "On Media Literacy as High School English Courses." Position statement, 1997 <www.ncte.org/about/over/positions/category/media/107517. htm>.

NCTE Task Force on Guidelines for Dealing with Censorship. "Guidelines for Dealing with Censorship of Nonprint Materials." Position statement last accessed 14 Apr. 2004 <www.ncte.org/about/over/positions/level/gen/ 107611.htm>.

NCTE/IRA. *Standards for the English Language Arts.* Last accessed 21 January 2004 <www.ncte.org/about/over/standards/110846.htm>.

Nichols, Bill. *Ideology and the Image: Social Representation in the Cinema and Other Media.* Bloomington: Indiana UP, 1981.

Nolley, Ken. "The Representation of Conquest: John Ford and the Hollywood Indian (1939–1964)." *Hollywood's Indian: The Portrayal of the Native American in Film.* Ed. Peter C. Rollins and John E. O'Connor. Lexington: UP of Kentucky, 1998. 73–90.

Norris, Christopher. *Deconstruction: Theory and Practice.* London: Methuen, 1982.

Ondaatje, Michael. *The Conversations: Walter Murch and the Art of Editing Film.* New York: Knopf, 2002.

Peacock, Richard Beck. *The Art of Moviemaking: Script to Screen.* Upper Saddle River, NJ: Prentice Hall, 2001.

Peirce, Charles Sanders. *Philosophical Writings of Peirce.* Comp. and ed. Justus Buchler. New York: Dover, 1955.

Pudovkin, V[sevolod] I. *Film Technique* [1926], *and Film Acting* [1935]. Ed. and trans. Ivor Montagu. New York: Grove, 1960.

Quart, Barbara Koenig. *Women Directors: The Emergence of a New Cinema.* New York: Praeger, 1988.

Rogin, Michael. *Blackface, White Noise: Jewish Immigrants in the Hollywood Melting Pot.* Berkeley: U of California P, 1996.

Rowe, Kathleen. *The Unruly Woman: Gender and the Genres of Laughter.* Austin: U of Texas P, 1995.

Russo, Vito. *The Celluloid Closet: Homosexuality in the Movies.* Rev. ed. New York: Harper & Row, 1987.

Said, Edward W. *Orientalism.* New York: Vintage, 1979

Sánchez, Alberto Sandoval. "*West Side Story:* A Puerto Rican Reading of 'America.'" *Latin Looks: Images of Latinas and Latinos in the U.S. Media.* Ed. Clara E. Rodriguez. Boulder, CO: Westview, 1998. 164–79.

Sarris, Andrew. *The American Cinema: Directors and Directions, 1929–1968.* New York: Dutton, 1968.

———. "Oscar Hangover, Third-World Crossover." *Village Voice* 24 April 1984: 49–50.

Schatz, Thomas. *The Genius of the System: Hollywood Filmmaking in the Studio Era.* New York: Pantheon, 1988.

———. *Hollywood Genres: Formulas, Filmmaking, and the Studio System.* Philadelphia: Temple UP, 1981.

———. "The New Hollywood." *Film Theory Goes to the Movies.* Ed. Jim Collins, Hilary Radner, and Ava Preacher Collins. New York: Routledge, 1993. 1–7.

Schillaci, Anthony, and John M. Culkin, eds. *Films Deliver: Teaching Creatively with Film.* New York: Citation, 1970.

Scholes, Robert. *Semiotics and Interpretation.* New Haven: Yale UP, 1982.

ScreenSite. University of Alabama, College of Communication & Information Sciences, Department of Telecommunications and Film. Last accessed 15 April 2004 <www.tcf.ua.edu/ss/>.

Seger, Linda, and Edward Jay Whetmore. *From Script to Screen: The Collaborative Art of Filmmaking.* New York: Henry Holt, 1994.

Shaheen, Jack G. *Arab and Muslim Stereotyping in American Popular Culture.* Washington, DC: Center for Muslim-Christian Understanding, Georgetown University, 1997.

Shim, Doobo, "From Yellow Peril through Minority Model to Renewed Yellow Peril." *Journal of Communication Inquiry* 22.4: (1998): 385–409

Sikov, Ed. *Screwball: Hollywood's Madcap Romantic Comedies.* New York: Crown, 1989.

Sinofsky, Esther R. *Off-Air Videotaping in Education: Copyright Issues, Decision, Implications.* New York: R. R. Bowker, 1984.

Small, Robert C., Jr. "Censorship and English: Some Things We Don't Seem to Think about Very Often (but Should)." *Dealing with Censorship.* Ed. James E. Davis. Urbana, IL: National Council of Teachers of English, 1979. 54–62.

Sobchack, Vivian. "Postmodern Modes of Ethnicity." *Unspeakable Images: Ethnicity and the American Cinema.* Ed. Lester D. Friedman. Champaign: U of Illinois P, 1991. 329–52.

Stam, Robert, and Toby Miller, eds. *Film and Theory: An Anthology.* Malden, MA: Blackwell, 1999.

Thornham, Sue, ed. *Feminist Film Theory: A Reader.* New York: New York UP, 1999.

Troost, Linda, and Sayre Greenfield, eds. *Jane Austen in Hollywood.* Lexington: UP of Kentucky, 1998.

Visions of Light: The Art of Cinematography. Dir. Arnold Glassman, Todd McCarthy, and Stuart Samuels. American Film Institute and NHK Japan Broadcasting Corp. with American Society of Cinematographers, 1992.

Wead, George, and George Lellis. *Film: Form and Function.* Boston: Houghton Mifflin, 1981.

Webster's New World Dictionary of the American Language. 2nd college ed. Ed. in Chief David B. Guralnik. Simon & Schuster, 1982.

Wilson, John Morgan. *Inside Hollywood: A Writer's Guide to Researching the World of Movies and TV.* Cincinnati, OH: Writer's Digest, 1998.

Wollen, Peter. *Signs and Meaning in the Cinema.* Rev. ed. Bloomington: Indiana UP, 1972.

Wood, Michael. *America in the Movies: or, "Santa Maria, It Had Skipped My Mind."* New York: Basic Books, 1975.

Wu, Frank H. *Yellow: Race in America beyond Black and White.* New York: Basic, 2002.

Yoffe, Emily. "Play It Again, Mom." *New York Times* 13 July 2003: AR 9, 16.

Author

William V. Costanzo is professor of English and film at Westchester Community College, New York, where he has taught courses in writing, literature, and cinema for more than thirty years. His publications include *Double Exposure: Composing through Writing and Film* (1984), *The Electronic Text: Learning to Write, Read, and Reason with Computers* (1989), *Reading the Movies: Twelve Great Films on Video and How to Teach Them* (1992), and more than fifty articles and reviews. Since receiving his Ph.D. from Columbia University, he has received state and national awards for teaching and scholarship and for designing educational software. Costanzo lectures widely on film and the educational uses of technology and has led workshops on media and English across the country. Within NCTE he has served as director of the Commission on Media, chair of the Committee on Film Study in the English Language Arts, and chair of the Assembly on Media Arts. Future projects include a textbook for first-year college composition, *The Writer's Eye*, and a book on global cinema.

This book was typeset in Palatino and Helvetica by Electronic Imaging.
Typefaces used on the cover were BinnerD and Frutiger.
The book was printed on 50-lb. Accent Opaque paper by Versa Press, Inc.